JENS JENSEN

CREATING THE NORTH AMERICAN LANDSCAPE

Consulting Editors
   Gregory Conniff
   Bonnie Loyd
   Edward K. Muller
   David Schuyler

Published in cooperation with the Center for
American Places, Harrisonburg, Virginia

Jens Jensen

Maker of Natural Parks and Gardens

Robert E. Grese

THE JOHNS HOPKINS UNIVERSITY PRESS
BALTIMORE AND LONDON

This book has been brought to publication with the generous assistance of the Horace H. Rackham Publication Fund of the University of Michigan.

© 1992 The Johns Hopkins University Press
All rights reserved
Printed in the United States of America on acid-free paper

The Johns Hopkins University Press
701 West 40th Street
Baltimore, Maryland 21211-2190
The Johns Hopkins Press Ltd., London

LIBRARY OF CONGRESS CATALOGING-IN-PUBLICATION DATA

Grese, Robert E., 1955–
    Jens Jensen : maker of natural parks and gardens / Robert E. Grese.
        p.   cm. — (Creating the North American landscape)
    Includes bibliographical references and index.
    ISBN 0-8018-4287-5
    1. Jensen, Jens, 1860–1951.   2. Landscape architects—United States—
Biography.   3. Conservationists—United States—Biography.   4. Native plant
gardening—United States—History.   I. Title.   II. Series.
SB470.J4G74   1992
712'.0973'092—dc20
[B]   91-41190

Frontispiece: Jens Jensen at Lincoln Memorial Garden, Springfield, Illinois.
Photograph courtesy of Lincoln Memorial Garden.

For Mom and Dad

Every plant has fitness and must be placed in its proper surroundings so as to bring out its full beauty. Therein lies the art of landscaping.

—Jens Jensen, *Siftings*

Our native landscape is our home, the little world we live in, where we are born and where we play, where we grow up and finally where we are . . . laid to eternal rest. It speaks of the distant past and carries our life into the tomorrow. To keep this pure and unadulterated is a sacred heritage, a noble task of the highest cultural value.

—Jens Jensen to Camillo Schneider, 15 April 1939

Contents

Preface and Acknowledgments

As I was completing the manuscript for this book, Alfred Caldwell, one of Jensen's associates and close friends, asked me why I had chosen to write about Jensen. After all, he noted, the bulk of Jensen's work had long since deteriorated. Frankly, he said, I was forty or fifty years too late. I thought for a moment, somewhat taken aback. More than eight years into my research on Jensen, I had stopped asking myself why I was working on this book—I knew it had to be written. Through my research, I had begun to see Jensen as something of a mentor, and I felt that his work could provide inspiration for a whole new generation of designers. Through his designs for natural parks and gardens, he sought to awaken people to the beauties around them and to reconnect them to the biological heritage of their region. Perhaps more than any other designer in this century, he demonstrated how a deeply felt land ethic could be translated into physical landscape form and ritual.

As a student of Jensen, I have learned much about the subtleties of the native American landscape and how to accentuate those qualities in design. In the process, I believe I have become a better designer. This book, then, is not so much a biography of Jensen's personal life as it is an analysis of his work and his contributions to America's thinking about its landscape. It is my hope that the reader will share some of the same joys I experienced while learning about Jensen and his career.

Many friends and colleagues provided help and encouragement to me during the writing of this book, and I am deeply grateful to all of them. Darrel Morrison first introduced me to Jensen while I was a graduate student at the University of Wisconsin, Madison, and he, as well as the other members of my thesis committee—Arnold Alanen, Evelyn Howell, and Wayne Tlusty—was always enthusiastic and supportive. An individual fellowship from the National Endowment for the Arts sponsored my initial study of Lincoln Memorial Garden in Springfield, Illinois, and a second fellowship allowed me to extend my study to Jensen's contemporaries. The Edsel and Eleanor Ford House sponsored my study of its gardens, which greatly enriched my understanding of Jensen's relationship with the Ford family. Luther College in Decorah, Iowa, hired my good friend John Harrington and myself to do a historical study and management plan for the campus landscape, which was originally designed by Jensen. Our work there gave me a richer understanding of the challenges of maintaining the spirit of Jensen's work in a place that has changed dramatically over the years.

I have benefited from the work of other Jensen scholars, notably Stephen Christy, Malcolm Collier, and Leonard Eaton. Hudson Wheeler and Bruce Johnson have been more than generous in sharing memories of their grandfather, and Dorothy Waugh has provided enchanting stories about her father, Frank A. Waugh, and his association with Jensen. Christopher Graham and Scott Hedberg have shared information about E. Genevieve Gillette, and Christopher Vernon has been particularly generous with information he has gathered in his own research. Alfred Caldwell has helped me see the Jensen he knew as artist and mentor, and Sybil Shearer and Jim Cunningham have shared many anecdotes about Jensen that have helped me see his humorous side and his strong convictions.

Many others—far more than I can name here—also graciously shared memories and records relating to Jensen and his work. Peggy Kusnerz and Dorothy Shields provided ready access to the Jensen Collections at the Art and Architecture Library at the University of Michigan, Ann Arbor, and Carol Doty at the Morton Arboretum in Lisle, Illinois, was untiring in helping me track down information. I owe particular thanks to my good friend Julia Sniderman at the Chicago Park District and her associates Robert Pleva, Bart Ryckbosch, and Will Tippens, who also lent me considerable time and help. My colleagues and students at the University of Michigan's School of Natural Resources in Ann Arbor have been especially supportive and patient with my work. Dean Jim Crowfoot provided enthusiastic encouragement, and Rachel Kaplan frequently offered sound advice on balancing research efforts and teaching. Several of my students—Lisa Delplace, Beverly Johnson, Scott Lewis, Bruce Moore, and Jack Morris—helped with various aspects of my research on Jensen, and I am grateful for their diligent work.

Finally, several people helped me get this manuscript into shape; Anne Beebe, Carol Doty, Emma Pitcher, and Julia Sniderman deserve special credit for reading through early versions. I am particularly grateful to my editors, David Schuyler and George Thompson, who read through very rough drafts of the manuscript and provided invaluable suggestions for sharpening my scholarship and making the book richer and more readable. Without their help and encouragement, I probably would have given up long ago.

JENS JENSEN

ONE

Jensen's Early Background

Jens Jensen was always a man of contradictions, if not of extremes. His ideas and work have drawn both ardent admirers, who raise him to Olympian heights, and heavy-handed critics, who argue there was little of substance in anything he did. While the work that he loved best was the parks he created for the general public, he is most often remembered as a designer of estates for the very rich. Enjoying both show and controversy, he was not a quiet man; yet his landscape designs display a tranquil, subtle beauty and speak of harmonies with nature. As a pioneer in the field of landscape architecture, he, like Frederick Law Olmsted, Sr., hated the term *landscape architecture* and instead wanted to be known as a maker of natural parks and gardens.[1]

To many he was a dear friend, a mentor, and a sage. With his thick red hair (which turned a striking white in later years), his fine clothes, and his tall stature, he cut a striking figure. He loved children and was full of compassion and patience for those who wanted to learn, and he was eager to share his enjoyment and understanding of the natural world. At the same time, however, he had little tolerance for those who, in his view, lacked moral values and ethics.

Jensen was a powerful speaker and champion of environmental causes who, when he became agitated about a particular issue, was said to "screech like an eagle." Perhaps one of the more eloquent tributes is an account by Alfred Caldwell, one of Jensen's most trusted foremen and an accomplished designer in his own right. At his first meeting with Jensen in 1925, Caldwell was taken by Jensen's broad environmental perspective:

> The man [Jensen] talked about what interested him: about nature, about the parts of the state [Illinois] he wanted preserved against exploitation, about protecting the redwood forests of California, the Appalachian mountains of Virginia, the Everglades of Florida, the remnant wilderness part of Minnesota. The man talked about river valleys, bog lands, and canyons, disposing of these vast sections of the earth's surface with unique and

magnificent grandeur. The man talked about ecology, the relation of living things to each other and to the soil, explaining that the landscape enabled mankind to survive on this planet. So if we destroyed the natural landscape, we would inevitably be destroyed ourselves.[2]

For Caldwell, Jensen was a teacher with a clear vision of the implications of society's wastefulness and destruction of natural habitat:

> "For the first time in the course of human history," said he, "mankind actually possesses power and the might to alter and throw out of harmony the natural order of the earth. We cut down the forests, erode the hills and the gullies. We poison the lakes and the rivers with industrial chemicals, incidentally killing the fish and then drinking the water ourselves. We poison the very air we breathe. What is happening to our once beautiful landscape, beautiful America, is a catastrophe of the first magnitude. The future will curse us." The man at that time was about sixty years of age and had been saying this to deaf ears for at least forty years, besieging state governors and legislatures. He had set himself up as a one man lobby representing nature and ecology in the interest of the citizens of the United States.[3]

This eloquent champion of the American landscape was not born in the United States, but had immigrated to America in his twenties. Although little is known of Jensen's early life in Denmark, it is obvious that these years had a profound effect upon his character and outlook on the world around him. Memories of landscape experiences from his youth dominated much of his later writings, and an understanding of these experiences is necessary to appreciate fully his thinking about landscape design and conservation.

Jensen was born on 13 September 1860 near Dybbøl, in Slesvig, Denmark, into a prosperous family. Growing up on his family's ancestral farm, the young Jensen learned an early appreciation for the world of nature and the great sense of history that is associated with it. During long winter evenings, the family would gather to tell stories of recent wars and human hardships with nature. These tales made a lasting impression on Jensen: "This understanding of the immediate environment, this knowledge of the mysteries of the sea and of the land across the fjord, and those stories of the Vikings of an earlier period who dared the sea and the unknown for adventure stimulated the imagination and left their unmistakable mark on the growing mind."[4]

In a country with long, gray winters, the young Jensen developed an appreciation for the changing seasons. In his book *Siftings*, he fondly describes trips with his father to search out the spring wildflowers along the ocean bluffs and notes "hours of much romance and child adventure"

Labels on map: Sweden, JUTLAND, Vinding, Copenhagen, Tune, Northern boundary of Slesvig before 1864, Northern boundary of Slesvig 1864-1920, Southern boundary of Denmark since 1920, Dybbøl, FUNEN, SEELAND, SLESVIG, HOLSTEIN, Germany, LAUENBURG

0 25 50 KM

Figure 1. Map of Denmark showing Slesvig and its boundaries as they changed during Jensen's time. Adapted from Rørdam 1980, 32b; Danstrup 1948, 4; and Oakley 1972, 172.

along the lanes and fence rows of the family farm. Annual festivals marked the changing seasons and helped establish a sense of continuity with the history of the land: "This great love for the out-of-doors, for its history and its beauty and its spiritual message, was so woven into the lives of my people that it resulted in many festivals during the year: Spring festivals, sunrise festivals, summer concerts in the forest, camp fires dating back to this land's pagan days, and many public meetings were held in the out-of-doors." Later in his career Jensen would place particular emphasis on designing places for precisely such celebrations.[5]

During the mid-1800s, the Slesvig, Holstein, and Lauenburg duchies of Denmark were the scene of a bitter struggle between German and Danish nationalists. When Jensen was just four years old, the German army stormed the Dybbøl Peninsula, where his family's farm was located

(Figure 1). Some of Jensen's most vivid early memories were of his family's farm buildings burning in the wake of that attack. The charged political atmosphere that followed the German invasion dominated Jensen's youth and left deep impressions on his later thinking.[6]

The Slesvig-Holstein question centered on whether these two provinces should remain united with Denmark or become part of the German confederation. Whereas the people of Slesvig maintained strong language and cultural ties to the rest of Denmark, Holstein became increasingly dominated by the German language and German customs. By the 1830s, a strong sense of Danish nationalism was seen as crucial to holding together these outlying provinces.

In partial response to these concerns, Bishop Nikolai Frederik Severin Grundtvig established what came to be known as the Danish folk schools. These schools were intended to foster strong Danish patriotic sentiments combined with a liberal Christian outlook on life in general. Grundtvig saw the youth of Denmark as the hope and future of the country, and he sought to develop an educational program that would tap their energy and encourage their creative spirit. The emphasis was on "education for life," and teachers combined direct study of nature with traditional subjects of science and history. Teachers were masters of storytelling, and history was taught as a living narrative. Folk songs, ballads, and Norse sagas helped develop a strong sense of pride in Denmark's heritage. In the Peace of Vienna, which ended the war with Germany in 1864, Denmark lost control of the Slesvig, Holstein, and Lauenburg provinces, and the role that the provinces' folk schools had in building a sense of national pride took on added significance. The Danish adopted the motto "We must win inwardly all that we have lost outwardly."[7]

In the occupied province of Slesvig, many parents sent their children to the Danish folk schools to ensure that they grew up appreciating their Danish heritage. Jensen's parents were no exception, and at the age of nineteen, after working for several years on the family farm, Jensen was sent to Vinding Folk School. Normally, Danish country boys completed elementary school when they were fourteen or fifteen years old, and worked for several years before attending the folk high schools. The program at Vinding stressed a strong liberal arts education that included music, arts, and history. Classes were frequently held "out-of-doors, in the woods, on a hill, or around a blazing fire," with numerous festivals and much singing, storytelling, and other group activities. The usual folk high school session was a five-month period during the winter for young men and a three-month period during the summer for women. Like many other farmers' sons, Jensen followed his time at the folk high school with courses at an agricultural school. Jensen attended Tune Agricultural School out-

Figure 2. Jens Jensen, date unknown. Courtesy of Jensen Collection, Morton Arboretum, Lisle, Illinois.

side Copenhagen (København), where technical training in botany, chemistry, soil analysis, and related farm subjects was emphasized. Both schools stressed the individual's relationship to, and understanding of, the locality and region and, more important, emphasized "the soil itself as the source of all life." This philosophy became the foundation for Jensen's intense response to nature and regional landscapes and his desire to arouse a similar response in those around him.[8]

With Slesvig under Prussian rule, Jensen, like other young men, was expected to serve in the German army. Jensen's service took him to Berlin, where he was a member of the Imperial Guard. Although he resented being forced to serve in the German army, his period in Berlin exposed him to the landscape parks by Baron Georges Eugène Haussmann being built at that time in the then-fashionable French and English styles. These urban parks had a lasting impact on Jensen. In *Siftings* he compared his impressions of "French Garden" parks with "English Garden" parks; he likened the contrast to that of a pompous monarchy with democracy and its freedoms. In Jensen's mind the straight lines and ornamentation of the French gardens represented a style of design associated with "a time when

Figure 3. "View in Union Park," from Andreas 1886. This engraving depicts Union Park as it appeared during Jensen's early years with Chicago's West Parks.

the ruling forces spent public money so lavishly that it continually brought into poverty the people who had to pay the upkeep." In contrast, the English garden "had a certain sense of freedom," which was "more in keeping with the life of the people." For Jensen, this experience was "never entirely forgotten."[9]

In 1884, shortly after Jensen completed his term of military duty, he decided to leave Denmark and come to the United States (Figure 2). He did not emigrate for political or economic reasons. Rather, his chief reason seems to have been that his family disapproved of his marriage to Anne Marie Hansen. As large landholders, Jensen's family was reluctant to sanction his marrying a woman from the "Cottager class." As the eldest son, apparently, Jensen was also expected to carry on the family farm. Jensen had little desire for settling down to such a life and chose instead to seek his fortune across the sea with the woman he loved.[10]

After coming to the United States in 1884 (at the age of twenty-four), Jensen worked for a short time in Florida and Iowa before settling into a street-sweeping job for the Chicago West Parks District in 1886. At the time, Chicago had growing populations of immigrants throughout the city, and the Jensens moved into the close Scandinavian community around Humboldt Park. With a young family and his meager salary as a laborer in the parks, Jensen had to search for other work during the off-season periods. During the winters, he found nursery work with Swain Nelson. A Swedish landscape gardener, Nelson had been responsible for many of the improvements made in Lincoln Park and some in Union Park as well (Figure 3). Through Nelson and his work at the nursery, Jensen was able to further his horticultural skills and sharpen his knowledge of the plants that grew well around the Chicago region.[11]

During the next years, Jensen began taking weekend trips with his family into the prairie countryside. Traveling on the rail lines to their outermost limits, Jensen came to know the remaining wild places of northern Illinois and northwestern Indiana and started what was to be a lifelong study of the landscape and plants of the Chicago region. He took comfort in American plants similar to ones that he remembered from Denmark: the blackberries, hawthorns, and wild roses of thickets and hedgerows, century-old oaks, and the sweet flag that dotted wetland borders. He also found similarities in physiography, for here were sand hills (dunes) and vast plains. And, in the prairie, Jensen saw great similarities to the sea that had fascinated him as a young boy. Like the sea, the prairies had "the distinct power of drawing one out, of arousing one's curiosity to investigate what is beyond the horizon." Yet Jensen noted that "the prairies give a far more secure feeling than the sea. The prairies are inhabited; they are human." With these resources as a base, he felt certain that the midwestern prairie region had the potential to become the great cultural center of the country.[12]

Gradually, Jensen's attraction toward the native plant communities of the region began to influence his work with the parks. Up to this time, he had undoubtedly been involved with the manicured flower beds and other formal plantings typical of the early park designs in Chicago's West Parks. In 1888, however, Jensen claims to have created what he called "the American Garden" in a corner of Union Park (Figure 4). The only documentation of this garden is from an undated plan signed by "James" Jensen. Exactly how Jensen moved from street sweeper to garden designer is unclear from existing park records. It is likely that he gradually assumed more responsibility for plantings and was allowed to tinker with this corner of Union Park. Up until 1885, when the animal house in Lincoln Park was opened, the seventeen-acre Union Park had held the zoological garden and was one of the city's major attractions. After the bears, eagles, and monkeys were moved, the popularity of Union Park dwindled. Jensen's creation of the American Garden may have been an effort to spark a new interest in the park.[13]

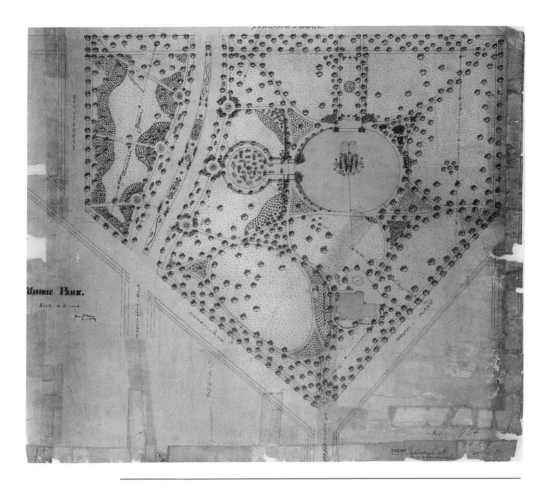

Figure 4. Jensen's plan for Union Park, likely delineated between 1888 and 1894. Courtesy of Special Collections, Chicago Park District.

The garden, which was a collection of native perennials set against a background of native trees and shrubs, marked the first of Jensen's major public landscape designs. "As I remember," he later wrote,

> I had a great collection of perennial wild flowers. We couldn't get the stock from nurserymen, as there had never been any requests for it, and we went out into the woods with a team and wagon, and carted it in ourselves. Each plant was given room to grow as it wanted to. People enjoyed seeing the garden. They exclaimed excitedly when they saw flowers they recognized; they welcomed them as they would a friend from home. This was the first natural garden in Chicago, and as far as I know, the first natural garden in any large park in the country. To my delight the transplantings flourished and after a while I did away with formal beds.[14]

Jensen's insistence that this was the first garden of its kind was pre-sumptuous. Frederick Law Olmsted, Sr., H. W. S. Cleveland, and other designers in the Chicago area were also employing "naturalistic" forms in their work, but in general they did not give the same attention to local plant associations. In the early 1880s, O. C. Simonds had begun trans-forming Graceland Cemetery using wild plants typically found along the wayside, and he established a design practice that would parallel Jensen's in many respects. Jensen was undoubtedly familiar with the efforts of each of these landscape architects and, in seeing their success, was likely encouraged to experiment on his own.[15]

The West Park commissioners apparently also took a broader interest in promoting native plantings in the parks. During the same year that Jensen began the American Garden in Union Park, the commissioners ordered that the northern part of Garfield Park be "planted with every variety of tree grown wild in this latitude, including Oak, Elm, Maple, Basswood, Wild Cherry, and especially all nut-bearing trees, which shall be labeled with scientific names placed on the same, and that the same be so arranged as to familiarize the public with the names of trees, shrubs, and vines growing wild in this climate." It is not clear whether Jensen had anything to do with this decision, but the fact that the commissioners promoted the use of native trees indicates support for his general ideas. Seven years later, the commissioners named Jensen superintendent of Union Park.[16]

The American Garden set the tone for Jensen's career of designing what he liked to call "natural parks and gardens." In the following years, he continued to experiment with native plantings in parks, along highways, on private estates, and on the grounds of hospitals, schools, and libraries. Through the careful manipulation of colors, textures, sunlight, and space, Jensen's designs recalled the spirit of the natural landscape and brought to people who resided in the city a sense of the cycles of nature around them.

TWO

A Cultural Context
for Jensen's Work

A full appreciation of Jensen's career depends upon an understanding of the professional, social, and artistic background of his work. During the nineteenth and early twentieth centuries, the field of landscape gardening and park design was growing and developing as its practitioners experimented with new forms and styles, all the while defining and expanding the boundaries of the emerging profession of landscape architecture. Initially, ideas came primarily from Europe; later, Americans looked increasingly to their own landscape for inspiration for garden design and sent ideas back across the Atlantic. A study of the relationship of Jensen's work to the traditions established in the early history of the profession of landscape architecture indicates that Jensen was much less of an isolated "maverick" than historians of landscape architecture or Jensen's ardent followers suggest. There are direct lines of landscape design tradition and philosophy that extend from Brown, Repton, and Pückler in Europe and Downing, Olmsted, Vaux, and Cleveland in America to Jensen and some of his contemporaries. These traditions primarily involve structural techniques for handling space and organizing a landscape in increasingly naturalistic forms and an emphasis on preserving the local character of a place. In the Midwest, and particularly in Chicago, the nineteenth and early twentieth centuries were marked by rapid growth, social reform, and a regional cultural renaissance that Jensen both observed and helped lead.[1]

While there were contradictory movements within the landscape design profession during Jensen's career, there were also designers and teachers such as O. C. Simonds and Frank A. Waugh who, like Jensen, strove to develop close ties between the native landscape and their designs. As the field of ecology grew, notions of plant communities and their dynamics also became important to these landscape architects, who sought through their designs to further people's understanding and appreciation of nature. These landscape architects were no longer content with harmonies of form, line, color, and texture in the abstract sense, but chose instead to work with harmonies learned from nature's own arrangements of species within a given region.

The European Roots of American "Native" Landscape Design

Developments in early nineteenth century American landscape architecture were heavily influenced by traditions born in Europe, particularly in England. The eighteenth century saw the flowering of what came to be known as the English style of landscape gardening. This movement, an outgrowth of widespread changes in English society during the eighteenth century, continued into the nineteenth. Sweeping shifts in land-tenure patterns and technological changes in English agriculture allowed the landed gentry in England to create large country estates separate from their working farms. A growing dissatisfaction with the topiary and geometry of earlier French gardens combined with a new-found fascination with nature to create a revolution in landscape design. Writers such as Alexander Pope and Horace Walpole called for a marriage of poetry, painting, and gardening. Landscape gardeners such as Stephen Switzer, Charles Bridgeman, and William Kent responded in the early 1700s, banishing much of the earlier formalism and carefully creating picturesque landscapes.[2]

During the late eighteenth century, Lancelot "Capability" Brown further revised English landscape design. He eliminated picturesque ruins, terraces, and other vestiges of formalism and emphasized gently rolling landforms, placid water surfaces, clumps of trees, and wooded groves around a property's border to create a pastoral landscape which, in his mind, mimicked uncultivated nature. He was criticized for destroying much past garden heritage and substituting scenes that "differed little from common fields."[3]

With Brown's death in 1783, the controversy over his design ideas intensified. Proponents of an evolving theory of picturesque principles pushed for landscape design that emphasized a series of scenes similar to those made popular by painters such as Claude Le Lorraine, Nicolas Poussin, and Salvator Rosa. The Reverend William Gilpin expounded on these thoughts in *Remarks on Forest Scenery and Other Woodland Views*, published in 1791. Gilpin argued for preserving the forest brush and twisted trees that Brown and his followers cleared to reveal topographic forms. He violently objected to the indiscriminate damming of scenic forest streams to provide reflective ponds as part of landscape improvements. Gilpin noted that the scenery of each region had its own beauties that should be preserved and enhanced rather than reduced to the formula landscapes he accused Brown of producing. In 1794, Uvedale Price elaborated on Gilpin's ideas in *An Essay on the Picturesque*. Price was particularly interested in developing a consistent theory of picturesque principles (then common in landscape painting) which could be effectively applied to architecture and landscape gardening.[4]

While writings by Gilpin and Price provided a foundation for much of the aesthetic theory of the late eighteenth and the nineteenth century, their ideas did not in themselves produce a picturesque school of landscaping. Instead, the traditions set by Brown were continued by Humphry Repton, who built a wide and lasting influence through such books as *Sketches and Hints on Landscape Gardening* (1795) and *Observations on the Theory and Practice of Landscape Gardening* (1803). Repton broke with Brown's practice of bringing an unbroken lawn up to the house and chose instead to use terraces, courts, and balustrades to provide an architectural setting for the structure and to place high priority on the comfort of the owner. Repton stressed the use of nature rather than works of art as a model for landscape gardening and emphasized a series of practical principles for achieving convenience as well as beauty. His books contained detailed suggestions for working with grades, bodies of water, and vegetation. According to Repton, the objective of shaping the earth should be to create grades that appeared "as if art had never interfered." He tried to dispel old rules, such as the magic attributed to using odd numbers in groups, and emphasized subtler qualities of design, such as the treatment of a wood's edge and the manipulation of sunlight and shadow.[5]

In the United States, the gardens of George Washington at Mount Vernon and Thomas Jefferson at Monticello provided models of how to adapt principles of the English gardening traditions to the young American republic. Both Jefferson and Washington attempted to create models of the *ferme ornèe,* or ornamental farms; gardens of the young republic had to be functional as well as ornamental. Jefferson, in particular, struggled with the problems of adapting a style of gardening based on undulating lawn surfaces and borders of untrimmed vegetation to a country that was largely forested and still wild. He suggested that Virginians could improve their gardens in the English style by simply thinning the understory of native woods, thereby creating a shaded "Elysium" that would be protected from "the beaming, constant and almost vertical sun of Virginia." At Monticello, Jefferson aptly chose a mountaintop setting, where he selectively cleared the forest and created garden rambles and walks from which to enjoy the panoramic scenery.[6]

This emphasis on native scenery and its enhancement continued to be a concern of early nineteenth century American landscape gardeners. An-

A CULTURAL CONTEXT FOR JENSEN'S WORK

drew Jackson Downing, the famous nurseryman and landscape gardener from Newburgh, New York, was easily the most effective at capturing the imagination of American society. Through his popular *Treatise on the Theory and Practice of Landscape Gardening, Adapted to North America,* which was first published in 1841, and his essays in the *Horticulturist* in the mid-1840s, Downing encouraged people to take an interest in their environs, particularly around their homes. Influenced by the Romantic thinking of the early 1800s, Downing was convinced that human behavior was greatly affected by the environment. He equated improving one's home with morality and patriotism, and promoted the horticultural arts as a way of "elevating the character of our whole rural population." The ideal home, according to Downing, was what he termed a "suburban villa"—essentially a small-scale rural landscape where one could enjoy many of the healthful aspects of country living near the convenience and culture of city life. Downing also felt that the center of a successful community should be a large public park, which would provide the natural amenities so essential to healthful living.[7]

Downing relied heavily upon English landscape traditions and stressed two basic approaches to landscape design: "the picturesque" and "the graceful" (which was later called "the beautiful"). The picturesque borrowed directly from Gilpin's characterization of scenery, emphasizing the irregular, contorted outlines of old trees, the uneven ground surfaces of rock outcrops, rough grass, and shrub thickets. Trails were laid out in sharp turns leading to surprising views or objects. The graceful repeated the "simple and flowing forms" advocated by Brown and Repton. Trees of rounded character were to be established across open lawns with broadly curving walks circumscribing the entire area. Downing provided few clear directives for implementing his design ideas, and the diagrams included in his *Treatise* suggest more of a random scattering of trees or shrubs across a lawn surface than any conscious design. Nonetheless, Downing helped promote a democratic interest in the horticultural arts and urged Americans to take a genuine pride in improving the overall environment of their homes and towns.[8]

Downing noted that foreign traditions in landscape gardening were not necessarily adaptable to the Americas because of differences in soil, climate, society, and political traditions. He lamented the American fascination with foreign plants, pointing to "epidemic" plantings of Lombardy poplar, tree-of-heaven, and paper mulberry. Instead, he pleaded for more attention to "the finest indigenous, ornamental trees in the world growing in our native forests." He suggested that many native plants could be improved by cultivation. In the garden, the landscape gardener could "bring about a higher beauty of development and a more perfect expression than nature itself offers." His advice to "the rising generation of planters" was to "study landscape in nature more, and the garden and their catalogues less."9

While Downing was promoting his adaptation of English landscape design principles in the United States, another important landscape critic and designer, Prince Herman Ludwig Heinrich von Pückler-Muskau, was developing his version of the English landscape garden in Germany. The son of a German count, Prince Pückler traveled extensively on the European continent as well as in Africa, Asia, and America from 1816 to 1822. He was particularly impressed with the work of Brown and Repton on his visits to England. In the early 1830s, he published his letters to his wife as *Briefe eines verstorbenen,* or *Tour in England, Ireland, and France in the Years 1828, 1929.* These letters contained what John Nolen would later describe as "discriminating criticism of landscape art" and helped establish Prince Pückler's reputation as a leading authority on landscape gardening.10

On his family's landholdings along the river Neisse in Germany, Prince Pückler experimented with his landscape design ideas. He carefully re-shaped the village of Muskau and the surrounding landscape, preserving the best characteristics of the original scenery and siting any new features to complement the old. Prince Pückler was also concerned with the social implications of his work. He intended "to elevate and enrich" the lives of the two hundred plus villagers who worked in his factories and on his landholdings, and he was careful not to violate their local heritage. Later, Charles Eliot would call for an American philanthropist to finance the same sort of improvements and enhancements in the United States:

> When shall a rich man or a club of citizens, an enlightened town or a pleasure resort, do for some quiet lake-shore of New England, some long valley of the Alleghenies, some forest-bordered prairie of Louisiana, what Pückler did for his valley of the Neisse? He destroyed neither his farm nor his mill, nor yet his alum works; for he understood that these industries, together with all the human history of the valley contributed to the general effect a characteristic element only second in importance to the quality of the natural scene itself.11

Like Downing, Prince Pückler considered "untrammeled Nature" the basic inspiration for landscape art. At Muskau, Prince Pückler arranged a network of interconnected open fields and meadows backed by forest plantings. Drives bordered and intersected these spaces and were laid out in broad curves that followed the contours of the ground. Prince Pückler insisted that there had to be apparent reasons for curves to exist: "In places obstacles must be set up where they do not naturally occur in order to make the graceful line appear natural." Groups of trees or small hills on the inner side of a curve could easily serve this purpose, and Pückler noted that these plantings also created a sense of mystery and enticed the traveler to follow the path just around the bend as if led "by an invisible hand." Pückler recognized the importance of the subtler "nuances" of design, which he felt could be learned only through "years of practice and experience." Of particular interest are his comments on the effects of using "the contrast of dark shade with bright sunlight"; this approach would later become distinctive in Jensen's work. Pückler also promoted the use of plants appropriate to the local region. He stated: "In the park I avail myself, as a rule, of native or thoroughly acclimated trees and shrubs, and avoid all foreign ornamental plants, for idealized Nature must still be true to the character of the country and climate to which it belongs so as to appear of spontaneous growth and not betray the artifice which may have been used."[12]

In 1834, Prince Pückler published an account of his work at Muskau and his thoughts on landscape gardening in *Anderungen*. While it was not until much later that *Anderungen* was published in English, Pückler's advice and ideas were much respected in Europe and known in the United States through his earlier letters. Many of the practicing landscape gardeners of the late nineteenth and early twentieth centuries traveled extensively in Europe and made the park at Muskau an important part of their itinerary. John Nolen called Prince Pückler "one of the best interpreters of landscape art of his time" and "a prophet of city-planning." Charles Eliot described the park at Muskau as "the most remarkable and lovable park I have seen on the Continent." In 1917, Prince Pückler's *Anderungen* was published in the United States as *Hints on Landscape Gardening*, the second in a series of authoritative books on landscape architecture sponsored by the American Society of Landscape Architects. The first book in the series was Humphry Repton's *Art of Landscape Gardening*.[13]

Frederick Law Olmsted and the "Natural" Style

After 1858, Frederick Law Olmsted, Sr., became the leading spokesperson for the emerging profession of landscape architecture in the United States. Together with Calvert Vaux, who had been an assistant to Downing, Olmsted applied and refined Downing's principles of landscape design to large urban parks such as Central Park in New York City and Prospect Park in Brooklyn.

The idea for Central Park and for urban parks in general became an urgent plea of social reformers in the mid-1800s as they looked around American cities and saw rampant pestilence and disease. Outbreaks of cholera convinced them of the need for better sanitary conditions. Many of these reformers believed that open space and trees would help clear the air of the miasmas that were thought to transmit disease in crowded cities. There also was a growing notion that solitude and personal communion with nature had restorative effects on the human mind and soul. The writings of the eighteenth-century physician Johann Georg von Zimmerman served as support for much of this thinking. In nature, Zimmerman found deep solace for the pains and melancholy of life, and he advised his readers to do the same. In the United States, nineteenth-century American thinkers such as Ralph Waldo Emerson and Henry David Thoreau found similar values in the beauty of nature and were dismayed by the dehumanizing aspects of city life. In 1844, William Cullen Bryant, American poet and editor of the *New York Evening Post,* called for the development of a public park in New York City, and the idea was quickly picked up by others. When Olmsted and Vaux submitted their winning entry in the competition for the design of Central Park (1858), the vision of nature as a healthful antidote to the city was foremost in their minds. Zimmerman's writings were eagerly read by Olmsted and served as a cornerstone for his understanding of the importance of parks. With his taxing work schedule, Olmsted himself occasionally suffered bouts of nervous and physical exhaustion and spent recuperative periods in pleasant scenery.[14]

The argument for parks as a way of counteracting public health problems in urban areas continued through the late 1800s as well. In a paper read before the American Social Science Association in 1870, Olmsted proudly noted that New York physicians were prescribing time in Central Park as routine treatment for their patients. He also reported that the park provided relief during the heat of the summer, when thousands were accustomed to escaping to the country. This was especially important for the urban poor, who had no means of getting away. Later, in 1897, the American Park and Outdoor Art Association, with landscape architect Warren H. Manning as secretary, surveyed physicians to learn if they had noted any relationship between the presence of urban parks and the general health of the population. Twenty-one physicians responded. Although most noted that no objective study had been done on the subject, they generally agreed that quiet parks and gardens serve as an antidote to many nervous disorders and may have positive influences on healing in general. In Chicago, T. T. Johnson compared the death rate with population densities in various parts of the city and found a high correlation between scarlet fever, diphtheria, and various intestinal diseases and crowded areas in which people had limited access to open air and parks. He concluded that for the health of the people, parks should be more evenly distributed throughout the city. In 1904, Chicago's Special Park Commission, of which Jensen was a member, used reasons of health as one of its strong arguments for expanding the park system.[15]

For Olmsted, parks also became a great civilizing force in cities, providing a democratic setting in which both the poor and the wealthy could gather. He categorized the types of gatherings that seemed to take place in parks as "gregarious" and "neighborly." Gregarious gatherings were those in which large groups of people came together for the simple pleasure of being together "in pure air and under the light of heaven." Olmsted remarked: "I have studiously watched the latter [these large gatherings] for several years. I have several times seen fifty thousand people participating in them; and the more I have seen of them, the more highly I have been led to estimate their value as means of counteracting the evils of town life." Olmsted observed that such gatherings seemed to be "a distinct requirement of all human beings," and suggested that all towns ought to provide grounds for such gatherings.[16]

Neighborly recreation included outings by couples who were courting, families, groups of families, and neighborhood and church organizations. Olmsted noted that Prospect Park was designed to handle "several thousand little family and neighborly parties to bivouac at frequent intervals through the summer, without discommoding one another, or interfering with any other purpose." To accommodate these activities, Olmsted suggested that a park should provide "the greatest possible contrast" with the city proper:

> We want a ground to which people may easily go after their day's work is done, and where they may stroll for an hour, seeing, hearing, and feeling nothing of the bustle and jar of the city put far away from them. . . . Practically, what we most want is a simple, broad, open space of clean greensward, with sufficient play of surface and a sufficient number of trees about it to supply a variety of light and shade. This we want as a central feature. We want a depth of wood enough about it not only for comfort in hot weather, but to completely shut out the city from our landscapes.

The provision of such places could only encourage virtues of courtesy, self-control, and temperance among "the most unfortunate and lawless classes of the city."[17]

Olmsted's ideas about aesthetics and landscape design were heavily influenced by Uvedale Price's *Essay on the Picturesque* (1794), William Gilpin's *Remarks on Forest Scenery and Other Woodland Views* (1791), and the writings of Humphry Repton. Having worked as a farmer on Staten Island, New York, prior to embarking upon a career in landscape design, Olmsted was also familiar with Downing's essays in the *Hor-*

ticulturist and Journal of Rural Art and Rural Taste and Downing's *Treatise on the Theory and Practice of Landscape Gardening, Adapted to North America.*

Unlike the gardenesque approach to design and the often spotty collections of plants that dominated Victorian gardens, Olmsted held fast to Repton's emphasis on subtle massings and unity. He suggested that the creation of scenery such as he was attempting in his park designs was entirely different from the decorative nature of most garden traditions. Olmsted also relied upon observations made while visiting the landscape parks of England and continental Europe. He was deeply impressed by the English parks and had spent much time analyzing their designs. In *Walks and Talks of an American Farmer in England*, Olmsted recounted his impressions of Birkenhead Park, near Liverpool:

> Five minutes of admiration and a few more spent in studying the manner in which art had been employed to obtain from nature so much beauty, and I was ready to admit that in democratic America there was nothing to be thought of as comparable with this People's Garden. Indeed, gardening had here reached a perfection that I had never before dreamed of. I cannot undertake to describe the effect of so much taste and skill as had evidently been employed; I will only tell you, that we passed by winding paths, over acres and acres, with a constant varying surface, where on all sides were growing every variety of shrubs and flowers, with more than natural grace, all set in borders of greenest, closest turf, and all kept with most consummate neatness.

Birkenhead Park's central meadow spaces and network of roads and looped pathways at the perimeter provided a clear example of how "rural scenery" could be adapted to a park in an otherwise urban context.[18] In their designs for Central Park (1858–63, 1865–78) and in subsequent designs for Prospect Park in Brooklyn (1865–73), the South Parks in Chicago (1871), and Franklin Park (1884–85) and the Muddy River Parkway (1878) in Boston, Olmsted and Vaux established traditions of American park design that persist today. A rural or pastoral quality reminiscent of Downing's "the beautiful" dominated the parks, which were characterized wherever possible by large open lawns and meadows bounded by thick tree and shrub plantings at the borders. Olmsted noted that this quality of openness was crucial in providing sufficient contrast to the city: "It should be the beauty of the fields, the meadow, the prairie, of green pastures, and the still waters. What we want to gain is tranquility and rest to the mind." In Central Park, creating such "prairie-like simplicity" came at great costs. Whereas the upper part of the Central Park site was readily adapted to such pastoral scenery, the lower part of the park

Figure 5. Meadow in Washington Park, South Park District, Chicago, Illinois, designed by Frederick Law Olmsted, Sr., and Calvert Vaux. Courtesy of Special Collections, Chicago Park District.

contained uneven terrain with scattered rock outcroppings and wetlands. Creating level areas required considerable blasting and grading as well as the construction of more than sixty miles of underground drainage pipes. Some 4,825,000 cubic yards of soil and stone were moved in the construction of Central Park, enough to cover the entire park's surface to a depth of four feet. In contrast, the flat terrain of south Chicago was easily transformed into pastoral landscapes by adding "an irregular border formed by massive bodies of foliage" to provide the variation that moderate hills brought to other settings (Figure 5).[19]

Where other landscape types existed, Olmsted wisely chose to accentuate the qualities inherent to the site. He noted: "The type of scenery to be preserved or created ought to be that which is developed naturally from the local circumstances of each case. Rocky or steep slopes suggest tangled thickets or forests. Smooth hollows of good soil hint at open or 'parklike' scenery. Swamps and an abundant water supply suggest ponds, pools, or lagoons." At Mount Royal in Montreal, therefore, Olmsted urged the owners to consider the intrinsic value of the mountain scenery rather than attempt to modify or deface it in the process of creating a public park. Likewise, where abrupt topography existed in Central Park, Olmsted and Vaux highlighted rocky crags with dense shrub plantings, creating scenes reminiscent of Downing's "picturesque" style. Olmsted warned against the tendency to include "the highly exotic and artificial" gardenesque plantings then becoming popular in French and English parks. In his view, such plantings negated the worth of the park as a work of art, treating it instead as merely a surface for decoration or as a collection of art oddities.[20]

Paths and roads were "to be regarded simply as instruments by which the scenery is made accessible and enjoyable." In Central Park this meant establishing a distinct hierarchy of roads and paths to provide separate routes for walking, riding horses, or traveling in carriages. Olmsted insisted that care be taken when laying out roads to avoid "shattering" the unity of unbroken meadows or other bits of scenery. This restriction usually resulted in gently curving circuit roads and paths at the forested borders of central meadow spaces. Dense borders of trees and shrubs effectively screened the park pathways from "all ugly or town-like surroundings."[21]

Formal design was generally limited to areas around buildings or to special gathering areas or promenades such as the Mall and Bethesda Terrace in Central Park. Olmsted and Vaux were frequently challenged to defend this exclusion of the city's straight lines and formal geometry. Perhaps one of the most serious challenges took place in 1864, when the Central Park commissioners adopted architect Richard Morris Hunt's plans for monumental gateways at the southern entrances to the park. According to Hunt's vision, the park would become an extension of the city, with monuments, statues, conservatories, museums, and restaurants scattered throughout. Olmsted and Vaux found such proposals completely contradictory to their view of the park as a refuge from the city characterized by the simplicity of nature.[22]

Although Downing and other American designers had promoted "the natural style," Olmsted more clearly advocated an appreciation of nature as encountered on a site. In his design for Central Park, Olmsted tried wherever possible to use existing native trees and shrubs, supplementing them as necessary with plants from both American and European nurseries. On the east side of Central Park, Olmsted and Vaux planned a forty-acre arboretum of American trees and shrubs to acquaint the general public with the plants native to the northern and middle sections of the United States. The arboretum was arranged to "present all the most beautiful features of lawn and wood-land landscape, and at the same time preserve the natural order of families." Trees were to be planted on open lawns and in groupings, and shrubs were to be planted in thickets, "as may best accord with their natural habits and be most agreeable to the eye."[23]

In the area of the Ramble, Olmsted developed what Europeans were then calling an "American Garden." This was a garden composed of native ericaceous plants such as rhododendron, azalea, and mountain laurel. Olmsted noted that the area already had many interesting features and could be improved with selective clearing and planting. Here, as

A CULTURAL CONTEXT FOR JENSEN'S WORK

elsewhere, Olmsted advocated the adage "plant thick and thin quick," fully intending that a planting would be thinned as it matured. In general, he emphasized the "beauty and effectiveness of groups, passages, and masses of foliage" over the form of individual trees.[24]

In the selection of plants, Olmsted distinguished little between native plants and plants from abroad that could be easily naturalized. Like many nineteenth-century gardeners, he was quite willing to experiment with exotic plant species that were still untested in the climates of the United States. Some of these have become persistent pests, such as Japanese knotweed (*Polygonum cuspidatum*), which Olmsted is credited with introducing. In his descriptions of Central Park, Olmsted generally called for "American trees of the stateliest character" and a liberal use of native shrubs. An examination of the lists he compiled for the commissioners, however, demonstrates a willingness to use whatever plant he thought would achieve a particular effect rather than plants suited to particular soil conditions or found together in natural associations. For instance, Olmsted was particularly taken with tropical scenery on his trip across the Isthmus of Panama in 1863 and wanted to create the same effect in Central Park regardless of whether such scenery was appropriate to a temperate climate. His instructions to the chief landscape gardener were to employ whatever plants would grow in the New York climate to achieve the tropical lushness he desired. Occasionally, Olmsted was challenged to defend his willingness to interchange native or foreign plants. In an article entitled "Foreign Plants and American Scenery" in *Garden and Forest,* Olmsted responded to those who would restrict their plantings to native species: "Does the white willow flourish better or grow older or larger in any of the meadows of its native land than in ours? . . . But on this point of the adaptability of many foreign trees to flourish in American climes, only think of Peaches, Pears, and Apples." Nonetheless, despite the apparent inconsistency of Olmsted's theory and practice in using native plants, the emphasis on the native flora was strong enough in his writings to be associated with his name and to be adopted to varying degrees by his followers.[25]

Olmsted and Vaux were often credited with reproducing "nature" in their designs, yet their parks often bore scant resemblance to the existing landforms and plant communities indigenous to a site, nor was that their intention. They argued, as Jensen did later, that their work was "art" and provided a "suggestion" rather than an imitation of natural scenery. Following the techniques used by their predecessors in the tradition of English landscape parks, the "nature" Olmsted and Vaux sought to replicate was not really wilderness at all but rather the human-made "meadow and woods" to be found in the landscape of the rural countryside and in the

Connecticut River valley of Olmsted's youth. Still, politicians and other artists often equated these pastoral landscapes with any other vacant lands waiting to be embellished or otherwise developed. Foreshadowing the problems Jensen would encounter with the park commissioners in Chicago were Olmsted's constant fights to defend parks as works of art.[26]

In the latter half of the nineteenth century, the majority of the emerging leaders in the new profession of landscape architecture had direct ties to Olmsted's office. Olmsted was quite proud of his role in creating "an American school" of landscape architecture and of the fact that apprentices in his office were trained for a career in "the art of design." Early influential landscape architects who apprenticed in this way included John C. Olmsted (Frederick Law Olmsted Sr.'s nephew and stepson), Henry Sargent Codman, Charles Eliot, Frederick Law Olmsted, Jr., and Warren H. Manning. Others, such as Ossian Cole Simonds and Jensen, made no secret of their deep respect for Olmsted's philosophy and considered him an exemplar for the profession. Elbert Peets, an early critic of the profession who graduated from the landscape architecture program at Harvard in 1915, believed that the adoration of Olmsted actually hindered the advancement of the profession. He suggested that Olmsted's followers constituted a "landscape priesthood" of sorts which dominated the profession and was perpetuated by the landscape architecture schools.[27]

Formalism and the Search for an American Style

Following in Olmsted's footsteps, the profession of landscape architecture during these early years seemed to embrace broad areas of social welfare and to concern itself with the general improvement of urban conditions. Near the end of the century, however, many professionals shifted their emphasis away from the design of parks and open spaces toward opportunities to work on private estates. While the principles of park design advocated by Olmsted were widely imitated by professionals in the design of large romantic parks, the younger generation of landscape architects felt that these principles were not as appropriate to residential design, which was fast becoming the mainstay of their work.[28]

With the rapid growth and industrialization that followed the Civil War and proceeded into the early 1900s, relatively large numbers of Americans suddenly found themselves extremely wealthy. Cities expanded rapidly, and large country estates became a popular status symbol for those who could afford them. As architectural historian Montgomery Schuyler noted, the country cottage and bourgeois mansions of earlier periods now became palaces. With the new demand for these places in the country, many architects responded by using eclectic approaches, often borrowing their models from French and Italian Renaissance buildings. Architect Richard Morris Hunt, who had studied at the École des Beaux-Arts in Paris, became a leading advocate of Renaissance architecture. Schuyler praised Hunt's Ochre Court, his design for Ogden Goelet in Newport, Rhode Island (1885–89), as a "château" by its architecture and a "villa" by its surrounding gardens, which also were designed by Hunt. Increasingly, many architects and landscape designers began to feel that the looseness of the "Romantic school" of gardening, as advocated by Downing, was inappropriate to the new, imposing architecture of such country homes. They began to search for a more formal style of design that would carry the architectonic lines of the building into the landscape. Hunt and Olmsted's design for the Biltmore, North Carolina, estate of George Washington Vanderbilt (1890–95), later described as the largest private house in the United States, was cited as "an excellent example of a general balance in composition" combining "wild natural surroundings" and "more strict and formal geometry" near the house.[29]

In 1892, the well-known landscape painter Charles A. Platt published the first of two articles on "Formal Gardening in Italy" in *Harper's New Monthly Magazine*. Then, in 1894, Platt published a small book, *Italian Gardens*, illustrating nineteen of "the more important gardens of Italy" in a series of watercolor plates and photographs. Despite complaints about its lack of notes and thorough scholarship, the book helped fuel a renewed interest in the use of formal geometry in landscape design. Platt advocated the adaptation of organizational principles used in Renaissance Italian villas as a means of unifying house and garden. His designs consisted of simple, rectilinear spaces bordered by strict vertical planes and linked by long axes and sight lines. With interests in sculpture, painting, and architecture, Platt believed that the "naturalized" approach to landscape design as promoted by Olmsted neglected the architectural aspects of outdoor design. He proposed instead a revival of the formal garden, basing the design of both house and landscape on adaptations of the Italian villa (Figure 6).[30]

By the beginning of the twentieth century, American landscape designers were avidly engaged in a dispute over the appropriateness of the irregular, or "natural," designs espoused by Olmsted and his followers and the formal geometries championed by Charles Platt and other painters, sculptors, and architects with "classical predilections" who also engaged in landscape design. In his entry on "Landscape Architecture" in *A Dictionary of Architecture and Building* (1901), Russell Sturgis agreed that many of these formal gardens were "very beautiful in design," but he argued that "the question will be for the future to decide whether the greater pleasure and recreation is to be got from these or from the more

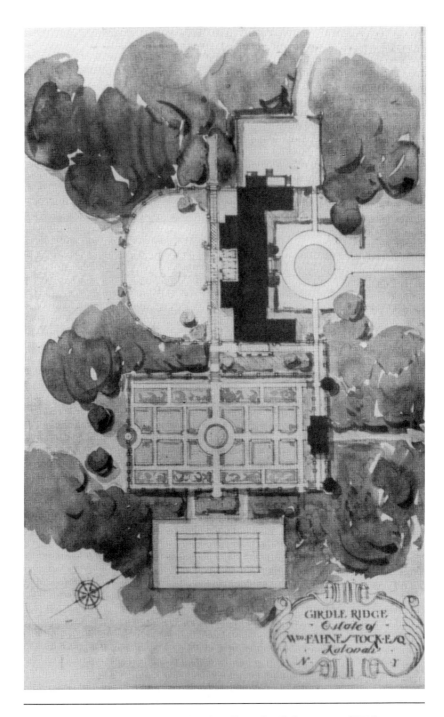

Figure 6. Charles Platt's design for "Girdle Ridge," the estate of William Fahnestock, Esq., in Katonah, New York. Plan was published in Elwood 1924.

A CULTURAL CONTEXT FOR JENSEN'S WORK

naturalistic treatment of the ground." In 1903, the publication of Edith Wharton's popular *Italian Villas and Their Gardens* further advanced the use of Italian gardens as a model.[31]

Formalists argued that they saw far too little of what they considered "art" in naturalistic designs. They suggested that the natural style completely ignored the heritage of formal gardens. In a June 1902 article in *Architectural Record*, the New York landscape architect George F. Pentecost argued that "the principles of the natural style have no value so far as artistic expression is concerned and [no] relevancy in connection with artistic or artificial surroundings." He further suggested that the imposition of the natural style on small city parks was an "artistic crime." The Olmsted Brothers firm, which began work on the design of several small parks and playgrounds for the South Park Commission in Chicago in 1903, agreed wholeheartedly that formal landscape design was preferable for small parks. Frederick Law Olmsted, Jr., noted that the firm's inspiration for designs for playgrounds came from "the beautiful tree-framed grassless plazas of the south of France and Italy and Spanish countries."[32]

In the December 1902 issue of *Architectural Record*, a response to Pentecost's article affirmed many of his arguments in favor of the formal garden. The author of the article suggested that in the eighteenth and nineteenth centuries, landscape gardening had been "violently divorced" from architectural design, and that the current revival of the formal garden had renewed interest in and lent validity to landscape architecture as an art. The author further noted that the bulk of influential landscape design work in the United States was going "to architects who are at the same time landscape architects." Perhaps, the author suggested, this trend was preferable since it was desirable for "the whole design" to be "imagined and worked out by the same designer." Ralph Rodney Root (1921a, 1921b) suggested that the best examples of designed gardens were from sixteenth-century Europe, and had been laid out by architects and planted by landscape gardeners. In these places, house and garden became one.[33]

Picture books of landscape architecture published during this period illustrated just how pervasive the architectonic approach had become. *American Gardens* (edited by Guy Lowell, published in 1901) and *American Landscape Architecture* (edited by P. H. Elwood, Jr., published in 1924), were dominated by formalist works. The vast majority of the gardens displayed in Lowell's book had been designed by architectural firms rather than by landscape architects. The gardens described in Elwood's book did include three examples of "natural design"—Jensen's work for the Alexander and Simms families at Spring Station, Kentucky, and O. C. Simonds' work at Graceland Cemetery in Chicago—but the rest displayed an eclectic collection of colonnades, statuary, clipped shrubs, and formal allées. Similarly, *Illustrations of Work of Members*, published annually by the American Society of Landscape Architects from 1931 to 1934, continued to focus on formal gardens from nearly every region of the country.[34]

Supporters of a more formal approach to design particularly objected to the naturalistic treatment of grounds immediately around a building. While such treatment would be acceptable "beyond the garden wall," it certainly had no place near "the dominating influence of the house itself." Root suggested that a formal garden around the house would act as a frame of the world beyond, be it natural scenery or the city. Furthermore, he stated, "we should not here try to imitate the unnatural effect of wild nature, but should frankly show that we are in the house plan itself. We do not want our guests to believe that they are walking in the forest, but that they are in a part of the grounds to be used as the house itself." Other "formalists" charged that any attempt by the "natural" gardener to screen the boundaries of a property and suggest a limitless expanse of nature was deliberately deceptive.[35]

During this same period, many writers championed the search for an American style of landscape architecture. As Downing had argued earlier, Lowell, in his introduction to *American Gardens*, suggested that Americans "borrow . . . details from Italy, France, and England," but "adapt" them "to our needs" and give them "the setting which they require." He went on to suggest that "our gardens need not, when adapted to this country, follow any recognized style." Root cautioned against forgetting "the traditions and great designs of the past" in attempting to develop a new style:

> To steep oneself in tradition and then to set to work to invent new forms which shall be guided by the principles and contain within themselves the boundaries of the old, is the right method in designing landscapes, and is the only way to design successfully. This makes for a continuity of tradition and leads one away from a too exclusive study of nature and an attempt at imitating natural scenery with unsuitable materials where conditions are not suitable for such imitation.[36]

For some landscape architects, the mere geometry and order of these new American formal landscapes was less disturbing than the values they seemed to represent. In his book *Formal Design in Landscape Architecture* (1927), Frank Waugh noted that the earliest pioneer gardens assumed a formal geometry as a measure of the "constant struggle with nature" (Figure 7). These new gardens, however, represented more of a "spirit of social display" and ostentatious wealth. The design traditions being copied by American designers on formal country estates were rooted more

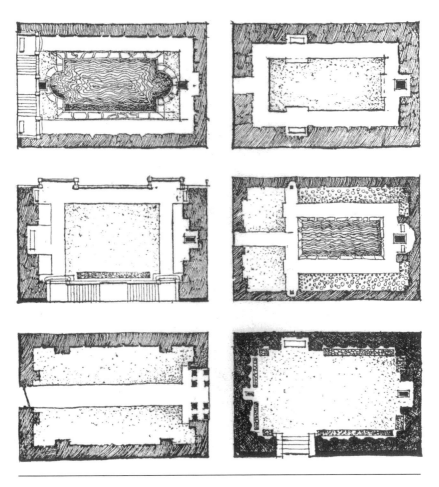

Figure 7. Drawings of rectangular gardens. From Waugh 1921, 24.

in European imperialism than in American democracy. Like Italian villas or French châteaus, these estates served the sole purpose of amusing the owner by displaying personal wealth. Unlike the English country homes, however, the majority of the American estates had no farm operation. As home places, these elaborate formal gardens were particularly trouble-some. Sturgis noted that it was not a matter of creating landscapes of beauty, but of creating landscapes that would have personal meaning for those who lived there:

> The unquestioned possibility of producing designs of extraordinary beauty in the formal garden is to be urged on one side; the desire of the citizen or hardworked man, even of a country town, to have as much as possible of free nature, or of a semblance of free nature, around him is to be weighed on the other side.[37]

Jens Jensen clearly worried about the effects of such "show" gardens on American society. In an opening talk at the Twenty-seventh Annual Meeting of the American Society of Landscape Architects (ASLA) in Chicago in 1926, Jensen called for the use of native plants and the development of "native styles" to be used in home gardens throughout the country. He argued that the home landscape influences "the soul of a people," and he cautioned that imported "formal" gardens were "inappropriate to the manner of life of our people." He suggested that landscape architects ought to work to cultivate "the simple native tastes of this country." At the close of Jensen's talk, the well-respected estate designer and then ASLA president, James L. Greenleaf, thanked Jensen for his views but remarked that he doubted if all members of the ASLA would concur. In a short discussion following Jensen's talk, the relative merits of formal versus informal design and of native versus non-native plants were debated, but a consensus was not reached.[38]

The Chicago Landscape

As landscape architecture developed into a profession during the late nineteenth century, the Midwest came into its own as a major force in American culture and economic life. The city of Chicago, with its expanding rail network and its location on Lake Michigan, was aptly positioned to dominate midwestern business markets. By the time Jensen arrived in Chicago in 1886, the city was well on its way to becoming the major cultural center of the region as well. Chicago, still on the rebound from the disastrous fire of 1871 and the effects of the economic panic of 1873, reflected a cocky optimism, and as the small village on the lake grew into a dominant metropolis, Chicagoans seemed particularly determined to make their mark with indigenous forms of architecture and landscape design.[39]

The first notable advances in landscape architecture in Chicago took place in the design of the city's parks. When the city was founded in 1837, the city fathers adopted the motto *urbs in horto,* or "the city set in a garden." Jensen and other conservationists would later claim that Chicago's original gardens were the native prairies that abounded on its perimeter, but it is likely that the city fathers were here referring to horticultural gardens and organized parks. Early Chicago settlers brought with them a tradition of private horticulture and public promenading. In 1841, John S. Wright proposed a chain of parks and parkways along the lakeshore and throughout the city. Few, however, were implemented, and by the mid-1850s Chicago had only a handful of public squares and small

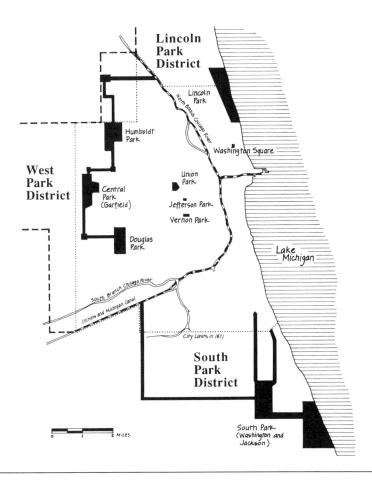

Figure 8. Chicago Parks and Park Districts in 1872. Adapted from Chicago Park Districts Map, R. L. Dobson (1 December 1928), courtesy of Special Collections, Chicago Park District; and from "Parks and Railroads in 1871," in Mayer and Wade 1969.

parks, none more than twenty acres in size or involving landscape improvements of any significance.[40]

In 1869, the state legislature passed into law a plan for developing a parks and boulevard system in Chicago and established three independent district commissions: South, West, and Lincoln (Figure 8). For each district, the governor would appoint the commissioners, who were to be owners of real estate in the city but not in a position to gain from land sales or other business transactions associated with the parks. There was a general feeling that the proposed parks and parkways—a "green belt" throughout the city—would help boost Chicago's cosmopolitan character. Despite the lack of picturesque scenery, planners were intent on providing Chicagoans with something they could point to with great pride:

> The courageous planners of the park system saw no discouragement in the monotonous swampy barrenness of the only available sites for the proposed recreation grounds. Lacking the natural features of eminences, ledges, rippling streams, lakelets, and stately forest growths, Chicago none the less was bent upon having public parks and parkways that should not be surpassed by those of any city in the world.[41]

Soon after the establishment of the park districts in 1869, Frederick Law Olmsted and Calvert Vaux were hired to develop designs for the tracts that were collectively known as the South Park. Olmsted found little to appreciate in the existing natural conditions of the lands he was to develop. Instead of picturesque scenery, he faced a "forbidding place" of marshes, ponds, and sand ridges, relieved only by an occasional stunted oak tree. Nonetheless, he encouraged the South Park commissioners to develop three elements of scenery that in his view were essential to any park: turf, foliage, and still water. These could easily be created on each site. He proposed that the marshes of the lakefront property (later known as Jackson Park) be deepened into lagoons and inlets cut to Lake Michigan. For the inland tract (later known as Washington Park), he suggested that the prairie be developed into a broad sheep meadow with the existing grove of oak trees as a backdrop.[42]

Chicago's great fire in May 1871 destroyed the park commissions' tax records, and in the strained economic times following the fire, all work on the parks was halted. As a practical solution to the mess of trying to levy taxes and to begin implementing a cheaper version of Olmsted and Vaux's improvements, the city appointed H. W. S. Cleveland "Landscape Architect of the South Park and Connecting Boulevards."[43]

Cleveland had moved to Chicago from Salem, Massachusetts, in 1869 and set up practice as a landscape architect. His background was in civil engineering, but in Massachusetts he had trained himself in the horticultural arts. In the mid-1850s he and Robert Morris Copeland had set up a "Landscape and Ornamental Gardening" practice near Boston to provide plans for cemeteries, public squares, pleasure grounds, farms, and gardens. The firm had submitted a plan in the competition for the design of Central Park, and although it did not win, Cleveland had thereafter formed a lasting friendship with Olmsted and Vaux.[44]

Cleveland was dismayed by the public's general perception of landscape architecture as merely a decorative art and in 1871 published his *Landscape Architecture as Applied to the Wants of the West*. He saw Chicago—and the West in general—as an opportunity to provide the preliminary planning and design necessary before "ornamentation" was added. Olmsted may also have suggested that Cleveland move to Chicago so that he could take advantage of the new park opportunities developing there. Soon after arriving, Cleveland published a pamphlet entitled *The Public Grounds of Chicago: How to Give Them Character and Expression* (1869), which was likely intended to promote his services as a designer. He warned Chicagoans against developing parks merely as a means for display and argued that parks should be thought of in connection "with the future welfare of the city." In addition, he suggested that parks should not necessarily imitate those that had been developed in the East, but should maximize the advantages of their own local settings:

> Every city has a character of its own, resulting from the nature of its situation, and the topography of its surroundings as well as from its history and growth—and in the creation of its parks, or whatever other description of public grounds may be desirable for its adornment, and the health and recreation of its inhabitants—the aim should always be, if possible, to give them a character of individuality which shall harmonize with that of the city itself.

He severely criticized the designers of Chicago's then existing lakefront parks (presumably Lincoln Park, established in 1860 as Lake Park) for creating their parks around small, human-made lagoons when mighty Lake Michigan was just next door. He lamented that the best views of the lake were not from any of these parks, but from warehouses and loading docks.[45]

Accustomed to the landscapes of the Northeast, Cleveland thought that the prairies around Chicago lacked character and that scenery would have to be created in them. He noted that "Nature has not even offered a suggestion for art to develop." In a letter to Olmsted in 1893, Cleveland described the original landscape of Washington Park in Chicago as the "dismal monotony of the original prairie and swamp" compared to the improved landscape advocated by Olmsted in his park designs.[46]

Giving new emphasis to John Wright's earlier proposal for a system of parkways, Cleveland argued for a grand boulevard three hundred feet wide and fourteen miles long to connect the properties of the three park commissions. Along the boulevard, the land would be sculpted to simple and graceful forms, and an arboretum of trees would be planted for botanical study as well as for the general enjoyment of the public as "avenues of light and fresh air." Although the city did not follow Cleveland's advice completely, by 1872 twenty-six miles of boulevards had been developed. Commercial traffic was excluded from these boulevards, and the Lincoln, South, and West Park commissioners were to have jurisdiction over them.

Cleveland's early attention to establishing a network of park spaces along boulevards would later be repeated in Daniel H. Burnham and Edward H. Bennett's *Plan of Chicago* (1909) and in Jensen's *Greater West Park System* (1920).[47]

Cleveland's work on South Park was never fully implemented, and it ended with litigation for the payment of his fees in 1873. In 1883, Cleveland prepared a plan for a system of parks and parkways for Minneapolis, and in 1885 he outlined a complementary plan for St. Paul. His forward-looking plans provided for a network of open spaces throughout the Twin Cities that helped guide the development of that metropolitan area until the mid-twentieth century.[48]

In spite of Olmsted's and Cleveland's pleas for an emphasis on "natural scenery" in the parks, the South Park Commissioners insisted that curious plant sculptures and other gardenesque features be used in Washington Park. These included a "succession of surprises in the shape of the most remarkable animals formed of plants, models of the earth twenty feet in diameter, the 'gates ajar,' a sun-dial of echeverias, or a calendar, changed daily, of house leeks." Other subjects of these floral gardens included President Grant, Uncle Sam, and two men riding in a canoe (a reference to early settlers of the region). In addition, in 1872 the commissioners formed a Board of Botanical Directors to seek seeds and bulbs for mass flower plantings from all over the United States, Europe, India, and Australia. Despite these "incongruous floral toys" around the perimeter of Washington Park, its central feature remained Olmsted's "100 acres of flat, smooth turf, a bit of real prairie" (Figure 5). Jensen deeply admired Olmsted's prairie in Washington Park and later shaped similar "prairie meadows" in the West Parks.[49]

With its expansive lakefrontage, Lincoln Park, on the north side of the city, had perhaps the most beautiful views of any of Chicago's public lands. Lincoln Park quickly became popular with the general public as a recreation ground. Originally, however, the land itself was considered a "barren, sandy waste," and the shoreline dunes were constantly battered and eroded by Lake Michigan's wave action. Olaf Benson, the park's first superintendent, and Swain Nelson, the Swedish landscape gardener, shaped the original park, carefully preserving existing sandy ridges and reinforcing the shoreline with an elaborate system of brush matting and stonework. They also created several small lakes, added picturesque plantings of trees and shrubs throughout the park, and built separate carriage and pedestrian paths. Other improvements included a small zoo, with bear pits and paddocks for keeping deer and elk; ornamental fountains and honorary sculpture; and general floral displays. Between 1903 and 1921, O. C. Simonds served intermittently as consulting landscape gardener for Lincoln Park and planned the extension of the park from Diversey Parkway to Devon on the north side and made revisions to the older parts of the park.[50]

The properties available for the West Parks were perhaps the most challenging for any of Chicago's park designers. Whereas South Park and Lincoln Park adjoined Lake Michigan, with its summer breezes and expansive views, the properties of the West Parks were landlocked. Alexander Wolcott and Edward A. Fox, surveyors of the West Parks, described the lands as "flat, treeless, uninviting prairie." In an article published in *Harper's Weekly* in 1891, Clarence Pullen described a photograph of one of the West Parks properties as "an unbounded expanse of bleak plain, destitute of vegetation, except low prairie herbage and a distant line of spindly young trees, hardly more sylvan in appearance than telegraph poles. In the foreground are stagnant pools of water and an unfenced, ungraded prairie trail. The scene is as barren, lone and desolate as could well be conceived." In addition, unlike the wealthier neighborhoods that surrounded the parks on the north and south sides of the city, the West Parks bounded growing industrial districts and moderate-to-low-income neighborhoods.[51]

William Le Baron Jenney came to the West Parks in 1870 as chief engineer, having trained at the École Centrale des Arts et Manufactures in Paris. There he had been deeply impressed with the work of Baron Georges Eugène Haussmann and Jean-Charles Adolphe Alphand in improving the parks and boulevards of Paris. Jenney was particularly taken by their work at the Bois de Boulogne, where Haussmann and Alphand had literally transformed the seventeenth-century park, with its allées and ronds characteristic of the French Garden tradition, to a park in the English fashion.[52]

At this time the West Parks consisted of three large tracts for South Park (later renamed Douglas), Middle Park (later renamed Central and then Garfield), and North Park (later renamed Humboldt); the existing Union, Vernon, and Jefferson parks were transferred to the West Park Commission in 1885. Jenney called for a system of tree-lined boulevards connecting the parks with a series of parklike squares, in keeping with the existing grid of the city's streets. Formal plantings and statues or monuments were to mark the intersections of the boulevards.[53]

Each of the park properties presented different problems, and Jenney responded with individual solutions for each park. The drainage problems caused by the relatively flat topography and heavy soil of the region were solved by creating large ornamental lakes. In some places, large irregular rock formations were placed along the shores of these human-made lakes in an effort to make up for the general lack of picturesque scenery (Figure

Figure 9. "View in Douglas Park," from Andreas 1886. This clearly shows the picturesque rockwork that Jensen modified from Jenney's and Dubuis's designs in the West Parks.

9). Formal plazas with flower beds marked the major entrances to each park, and roads were organized around circles and ellipses characteristic of French parks. Double rows of trees marked the borders of the parks, and a dense planting of shrubbery was intended to help screen the interior of each park from the surrounding city. Rustic chalets, kiosks, refectories, bridges, and shelters dotted the parks, and Jenney proposed a large museum and conservatory for Central Park.[54]

Jenney's major designs for the West Parks were drawn prior to 1871, when the great Chicago fire brought most municipal park work to a halt. The subsequent economic panic of 1873 further slowed park improvements, and apparently only limited portions of Jenney's designs were ever implemented. Still, in 1879 the West Park commissioners confirmed his drawings as the official plans for the parks. Over the next two decades, Jenney was consulted intermittently about specific park projects, but routine improvements became the responsibility of the board's engineer, Oscar F. Dubuis. Dubuis, who began work for the board as draftsman, was elected engineer in 1880 and also served as general superintendent from 1884 to 1888.[55]

During his tenure as engineer, Dubuis seemingly contributed many of his own ideas to the development of the West Parks in addition to following Jenney's plans. The parks Jensen experienced in the 1880s and 1890s likely had as much to do with Dubuis as with Jenney. In Humboldt Park, for instance, Dubuis reshaped the lagoons to the configurations that Jensen inherited and kept intact. Dubuis also introduced elements that Jensen would later develop as his own trademarks. In his 1889 plan for Humboldt Park, Dubuis surrounded an artesian spring with rustic rockwork and created a quiet stream to feed the lagoon. Jensen would reemphasize that feature in Humboldt Park and create a similar setting in Columbus Park as well as in other designs.[56]

Concurrent with these park developments, in the 1860s three large private cemeteries were established just beyond Chicago's city limits: Graceland, Oakwood, and Rosehill. These were developed in the "rural" or "parklike" cemetery style that had become popular throughout the country. Most celebrated of the three was Graceland Cemetery, originally designed by William Saunders and later extended and extensively transformed by O. C. Simonds (Figure 10).[57]

O. C. Simonds, who would be named with Jensen as a developer of the "prairie style" of landscape design, was born in 1855 in Grand Rapids, Michigan. Growing up on his father's farm, he acquired a special appreciation for native forests and fields. He studied civil engineering at the University of Michigan at a time when Jenney was a commuting professor there and, after graduation, went to work in Jenney's Chicago office. As a young civil engineer, Simonds was sent in 1878 to do surveying work for a lagoon in Graceland Cemetery. Through that job, he developed a close friendship with Bryan Lathrop, who at the time was president of the Graceland Cemetery Association and a devoted admirer of landscape gardening traditions. When the cemetery association acquired additional land for expansion of the cemetery, Simonds was hired as engineer, and in 1881 he became superintendent of Graceland. Simonds used thickets of native shrubs and trees with gently sculpted landforms and bodies of water in his attempt to make Graceland a quiet, restful image of the midwestern landscape (Figure 11). His work at Graceland brought him renown as "dean" of American cemetery design and led to work designing parks and estates throughout the Midwest and the rest of the nation.[58]

Other major landscape designs of the Chicago region in the late 1800s included the development of several planned suburbs. In line with Downing's thoughts on "country villages" and suburban estates, real estate developers promoted these suburbs as providing good access to the city as well as all the advantages of living close to nature. The extension of railroad lines north and south of Chicago led to the development of completely new residential enclaves. Lake Forest, which was laid out in

Figure 10. Ossian Cole Simonds near the entrance to Graceland Cemetery. Simonds' office was in the railway depot building at Graceland on Buena Avenue. Courtesy of Landscape Architecture Program, School of Natural Resources, University of Michigan, Ann Arbor.

Figure 11. View of Lake Hazelmere in Graceland Cemetery, designed by O. C. Simonds. Courtesy of Landscape Architecture Program, School of Natural Resources, University of Michigan, Ann Arbor.

A CULTURAL CONTEXT FOR JENSEN'S WORK

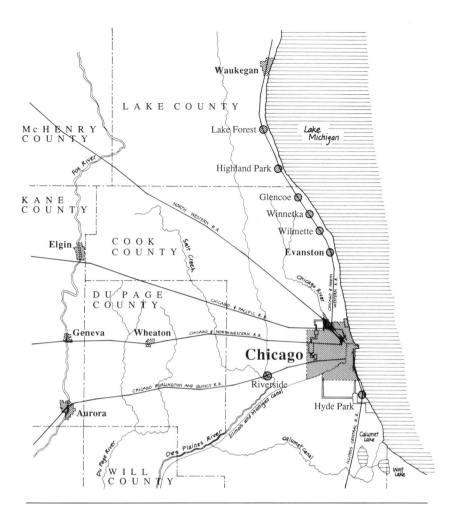

Figure 12. Chicago's suburbs in the early 1870s. Adapted from Rand, McNally and Company's map of Chicago as printed in Mayer and Wade 1969.

1856 by Almerin Hotchkiss of St. Louis, was the first such development and ultimately remained the most exclusive. Highland Park and Winnetka, also located along the North Shore of Lake Michigan, were designed just prior to the 1871 Chicago fire by the team of H. W. S. Cleveland and W. M. R. French, a Chicago civil engineer who would later become director of the Art Institute of Chicago. Their sensitive plan for the 1,200-acre site of the Highland Park Building Company, which preserved much of the natural charm of the ravines and lakeshore, would serve as groundwork for Jensen's later residential design work in Highland Park. The suburbs of Glencoe and Wilmette were established at about the same time (Figure 12).[59]

On the west side of Chicago, the suburban community of Riverside was being developed along the Des Plaines River. The Riverside Improvement Company was organized in 1868, and Olmsted and Vaux were hired as designers and superintendents. Olmsted and Vaux proposed an essentially rural village, with ample setbacks and winding streets to provide an open character and an extensive system of parks and open spaces along the river. They noted that suburbs ought to provide the conveniences of a city, such as good walks and roads, with "the conditions which are the peculiar advantage of the country," including "purity of air," parks and drives with "pleasant openings and outlooks," and "distance from the jar, noise, confusion, and bustle of commercial thoroughfares." Later, Jensen would emphasize these same qualities in the private homes he designed on the North Shore. Like Olmsted and Vaux, he noted the need for a quiet and restful atmosphere around a home to offset the tensions of urban life.[60]

Riverside instituted several important innovations, including building setbacks, tree-planting requirements, a network of community parklands, minimum house prices, and a ban on fences, all of which were written into deeds. Connected to Chicago by rail line, the suburb boasted a small business district. Its railroad station and first commercial building were designed by Olmsted and Vaux's former partner, Frederick C. Withers. A hotel and an imposing water tower were designed in the Swiss style by William Le Baron Jenney. Almost immediately after it was begun, Riverside hit upon hard times in the aftermath of the 1871 Chicago fire and the economic panic of 1873, but it eventually developed into the type of quiet residential community Olmsted and Vaux had envisioned. In the early 1900s, Jensen would design two residences in Riverside: the Henry Babson House (designed in collaboration with Louis Sullivan) and the Avery Coonley House (designed with Frank Lloyd Wright).[61]

Chicago's advances in the arts and urban reform during the late 1800s and early 1900s were not limited to parks and romantic suburbs. There was as well a general upwelling in the arts and sciences and in education and industry as Chicagoans tried to win national and international prominence for their city. The Columbian Exposition of 1893 was at least partly intended to affirm Chicago's push to be considered the capital of the Midwest. The designers of the fair attempted to create a dazzling ideal city that would remove the fair-goer from the "world of toil, of injustice, of cruelty and of oppression outside its gates." The fair was a wonder of sanitary reform, and it demonstrated what collaboration among landscape architects, architects, and engineers could produce. Olmsted's Wooded Island at the center of the fair site provided an idyllic setting as a park prototype. The lagoon around the Wooded Island was intended "to look like a natural bayou" with "a thick, luxuriant growth of herbaceous aquatic vegetation along the shores." While Olmsted used primarily the plants "indigenous to the river banks and swamps of northern Illinois," he added others to provide greater "intricacy and richness" of foliage and "a gay and festive aspect through a profusion of flowers." Winding paths and masses of naturalized trees and shrubs provided both relief from the crowded walks and a vantage point from which to view the monumental buildings of the fair. It was Olmsted's hope that the "apparently natural scenery" of the Wooded Island would provide a "quieting influence . . . counteractive to the effect of the artificial grandeur, and the crowds, pomp, splendor, and bustle of the rest of the Exposition." The "natural" park thus became an integral part of the ideal city.[62]

With its plazas, wide boulevards, and neoclassical architecture, the fair helped establish standards for civic design which persisted for decades afterward. It validated an East Coast trend toward Beaux-Arts motifs as the appropriate style for civic places. Although an economic downturn in 1893 dampened any immediate push for civic improvements, memories of the fair guided the committee charged with developing the 1901 McMillan Plan for Washington, D.C. Shortly thereafter, in 1906, Burnham and Bennett presented their *Plan of Chicago*, which was published in 1909. With its expressed debt to Haussmann's plan for Paris, the 1909 document called for the development of a grand civic center on the lakefront and sought to solve circulation problems and organize the city as the center of industry and commerce.[63]

Burnham and Bennett's Chicago Plan, with its Beaux-Arts emphasis, did not sit well with many Chicagoans, however. Louis Sullivan was adamant in his resistance, describing the postfair emphasis on classical and Renaissance architectural traditions as a virus that "slowly spread westward, contaminating all that it touched both at its source and outward." He predicted that the neoclassical architecture of the fair would set back the development of American architecture by fifty years. Jensen noted that the plan emphasized glamorous "civic centers and magnificent boulevards" while overlooking the "filth and squalor" that permeated the remainder of the city. He declared that the "formal show city" proposed by Burnham and Bennett was "distinctly imperialistic" and ultimately "destructive to the morals of its people." He questioned the emphasis on commercial aspects of the city, arguing instead that the city should emphasize its homelike qualities. "The American home," said Jensen, "is the foundation upon which the world's greatest democracy rests. It is the unit, of which the city is made up, and in it should center the whole force of city planning, in order to foster the highest ideals in its people, and to be an expression of the best in mankind."[64]

Jensen supported parts of the Chicago Plan wholeheartedly, however.

The plan incorporated ideas for the greenbelts and playgrounds that Jensen and other members of the Special Park Commission had promoted in their 1904 report, and it reminded citizens that Chicago's motto was *urbs in horto* ("a city set in a garden"). Burnham and Bennett urged the city to establish a wide system of parks and forest preserves focused on an extensive lakefront park. With its credo as a "big plan" that was "high in hope," and with its ability to "stir men's blood," the Chicago Plan had great patriotic appeal.[65]

As chairman of the City Planning Committee of the Chicago City Club, Jensen was critical of the naive enthusiasm for City Beautiful schemes that had "taken our cities by storm." In his 1911 article entitled "Regulating City Building," Jensen cautioned that "it is too much to assume that our cities can be transformed as quickly as the paper receives the ink of the enthusiastic designer, nor is it to be expected that the lines so cleverly laid down by the rule can as readily cut through the physical complexities of a great city." Instead, Jensen proposed a system of "proper regulation guided by high ideals and common sense" to shape the con- tinued growth and expansion of the city. A "department of civics" would oversee this regulation to help the city "improve step by step, day by day, in a sane and natural manner, rather than in the spasmodic spurts which result from business booms." The department would be made up of "an engineer, an architect, a good business man, a sculptor, [and] a landscape architect" who would "guide, advise, adjust, and pass" on all city develop- ment and growth. Jensen believed that a city could be made more home- like by integrating homes, schools, and factories around human-scale centers. The school, Jensen thought, was underutilized as the center it could be in stimulating a lifetime of learning, appreciation of culture, and promotion of family life. Like the folk schools he had experienced in Denmark, he suggested that Chicago's schools be made centers of culture and healthful recreation throughout a person's life, as well as "a pleasant spot to which [one] may return when old." Around each neighborhood school should be clustered "churches, settlements, and club halls" as "centers of enlightenment."[66]

Jensen was most likely influenced by the ideas of English planner Raymond Unwin, who had given a talk earlier in 1911 at Chicago's City Club. Speaking on "Garden Cities in England" and featuring his own work at Letchworth, Unwin argued that "the art of city planning, like all other art, is primarily a form of expression and . . . is only healthy and sound when it is a natural, straightforward, and honest expression of the needs of the community." Unwin continued, "We must begin to realize that city planning must be a combination of the art of man and the beauty of nature and that one of the first things to be remembered in the planning of cities is that any site, which is to be covered with buildings, should be approached with reasonable respect for the beauty already upon it and that as much of that beauty as possible should be preserved."[67]

Jensen later acknowledged Unwin's comments in his introduction of Thomas Mawson, who spoke at the City Club in November of that same year on town planning in England. Calling Mawson "the greatest landscape architect in the present time in Britain," Jensen echoed many of the points made by Unwin. Noting his appreciation of Europe's preindustrial towns built during the Middle Ages, Jensen suggested that the town builders had taken "inspiration from the landscape by which they were surrounded" and regarded those cities as home environments. Instead of emphasizing commerce and efficient transportation, which were hallmarks of the Chicago Plan, Jensen argued for planning that aspires to "harmony with the laws of nature." As he noted, an "artificial" type of plan (probably referring to the Chicago Plan),

> while it permits a man to arrive at his business in so much shorter time and allows him to run from one thing to another with less expenditure of effort and money, [it] makes no provision for the cultivation of his soul. A little inconvenience for the sake of a better environment is well worth the cost. To shut out nature from man's whole life is to shut out the inspiration of noble and humanitarian things. The artificial state has come to be the producer of insanity, crime, and immorality.

Referring to the housing conditions of the poor on the west side of Chicago, Jensen further noted: "You cannot have a good and beautiful city with ideal conditions on its fringe and rotten conditions in its interior."[68]

Jensen's ideas on city planning were consistent with many of the goals espoused by the Regional Planning Association of America in the 1920s. Organized in 1923 and lasting for approximately ten years, the association sought to develop communities that balanced human biological and social needs. Noting that the historical development of cities often resulted in their haphazard growth and the despoliation of the countryside, the association pursued a regional approach to planning that would create an organic balance between wilderness, urban, and rural habitats. As defined by Lewis Mumford, the aims of regional planning were to encourage "development that will eliminate our enormous economic wastes, give a new life to stable agriculture, set down fresh communities planned on a human scale, and above all, restore a little happiness and freedom in places where things have been pretty much wrung out."[69]

Jensen's sense of social conscience must be seen against the background of reform movements already under way in Chicago in the late 1800s. The University of Chicago, which served as a catalyst for much of this reform and progressive thinking, was officially organized in 1891. With substantial endowments by John D. Rockefeller and Marshall Field, it rapidly established itself as a major academic institution. Unlike most American universities in the 1890s, the University of Chicago saw itself as an intrinsic part of the city both in its physical placement and in its moral emphases. In the work of sociologists such as Thorstein Veblen, the city itself and urban values became topics for study. Early ecological studies by John Coulter and Henry C. Cowles centered on natural environs and their relationship to both human and natural forces of change.[70]

The social reform ideas of Jane Addams and the various meetings held at Hull-House in the 1890s and early 1900s helped solidify Jensen's thinking about urban recreation, the arts, and democracy in general. Jane Addams essentially "urbanized the village tradition of neighborliness" in her attempts to humanize the commercial city. Hull-House served as a refuge for the urban poor—immigrants as well as natives, women as well as men. It was also an important center for the arts and crafts, public education, and a general exchange of ideas. As a result of his own education in the Danish folk schools, Jensen placed a high value on direct involvement in the arts, and Jane Addams may well have reinforced his thinking about pageantry, theater, and drama. She saw drama not only as an "agent of recreation and education, but also as a vehicle of self-expression." Given the diversity of the immigrants who gathered at Hull-House, the theater provided an important cross-cultural language for teaching democratic ideals and easing the transition from the immigrants' homeland. In *Twenty Years at Hull-House*, Addams recounted how Greek immigrants presented classical Greek plays in their ancient texts and were thus able to maintain "their history and classic background," which was so often "completely ignored by Americans." Other ethnic groups also presented plays in their native language and used the plays as a way of sharing their fears and frustrations as immigrants in a new land. The dramas at Hull-House provided "a sense of companionship" to people who often felt extremely isolated. Jensen later used drama and pageantry to bring people together in parks and as a way of teaching people about each other and their relationship to the world around them. Places for outdoor drama and pageants were prominent in his landscape designs, and plays became an important tool for teaching the public about conservation. Like Addams, Jensen recognized the powerful appeal of the primitive emotions used in drama and the usefulness of live theater in strengthening a democratic society.[71]

The earliest public playgrounds in Chicago were established on the grounds of Hull-House and other settlement houses by Northwestern University and the University of Chicago. Addams noted that the play of city children in the streets was constantly interrupted by traffic and had little of the continuity, rich imagery, and companionship with nature that she had enjoyed in her rural Illinois childhood. On the Hull-House playground, she hoped to provide an alternative to the "rude horse-play" and "passive 'standing 'round' " that filled so many urban children's free time. Addams saw play as an "instrument for bringing about a purer democracy and a higher morality to the life of American cities." Play activities taught the rules upon which democracy was based. She especially sought out the folk dances and traditional games of immigrant groups as a way of providing common cultural bases for play and other forms of social interaction.[72]

In 1898, Jacob Riis gave a talk at Hull-House before the Municipal Science Club, of which Jensen was an active member. Riis vividly described the need for play areas for children trapped in city slums, and he urged that greater emphasis be placed on public playgrounds. In 1899, the Chicago City Council adopted a resolution calling for the formation of the Special Park Commission, which was to be charged with a systematic study of parks and recreation grounds and with developing a consistent plan for the metropolitan area. The commission was to include nine members appointed by the mayor, three members appointed by the park commissions (one from each), and up to six members elected by the commission itself. Of the nine to be appointed by the mayor, three were to be selected from each of the park commissions; six of the nine were to hold no other official position; and four of those six were to be of "recognized ability" in the professions of law, civil engineering, landscape gardening or architecture, and medicine or sanitary engineering. Early members included architect Dwight Perkins, Graham Taylor (representing the Chicago Commons Settlement House), O. C. Simonds, and Professor of Sociology Charles Zueblin (from the University of Chicago). Although not a member of the original Special Park Commission, Jensen had become a member by 1904, when it issued a report making sweeping recommendations for the comprehensive development of Chicago's parks and other recreation areas, including a network of small parks and playgrounds. In 1905, the commission reemphasized the need for playgrounds with their report *A Plea for Playgrounds*. In 1906, the Playground Association of America was formed at the national level, and in Chicago the local chapter became known as the Chicago Playground Association, of which Jensen was an active member.[73]

The wealthier South Park Commission had taken the lead in establishing numerous playgrounds and small parks, including indoor and outdoor gymnasiums, running and jumping tracks, wading pools, sand pits, play yards for young children, and community centers. In contrast, the poorer west side was seen as woefully deficient in providing play-places for children. Jensen responded with designs for the West Park District and for playgrounds to be implemented by the Special Park Commission. His early designs followed the tight, formal organization that the Olmsted Brothers had introduced in the playgrounds of the South Park District. Although he used a strict geometry to fit all of these activities on the small park sites, he introduced plants to provide "a touch of the home idea":

> For ornamentation, arbors will be constructed over the entrance, a few flowers will decorate the entrance to the field house, and trees and shrubbery will soften the hard lines of the formal layout, unavoidable in this class of parks. The purpose of arbors and flowers is to convey to the mind of the visitor the feeling of a park or garden, and to add that refinement which is so necessary in the communities where our park centers are located.

With his design for Franklin Park in 1916, Jensen realized that he could utilize more organic forms in these small parks. He began to provide not only places for children to get physical exercise but also settings for storytelling, music, and dancing—all activities important in his Danish folk school days.[74]

The Prairie as a Regional Style

In the period following the Columbian Exposition, while architects and landscape architects around the country expressed fascination with neoclassical design, a group of Chicago designers experimented with various ways of fitting their designs to the broad, flat, or gently rolling landscapes of the Midwest. In architecture, John Wellborn Root and Louis Sullivan had promoted an honest expression of structure and materials and exhibited sensitivity to the way a building hugged the earth and met the sky. In landscape architecture, Cleveland, Olmsted, and Vaux had demonstrated that quiet beauty could be developed without creating an artificially picturesque setting. In the period after the Columbian Exposition and in the early 1900s, the followers of these designers continued to refine such notions of integration in architecture and landscape architecture. Eventually, their work became known as the "prairie style."

The work of Root and Sullivan was confined largely to public and commercial structures, but domestic commissions formed much of the work of the prairie architects who followed them. These included George Elmslie, Hugh M. G. Garden, Walter Burley Griffin, George W. Maher, Dwight H. Perkins, William Purcell, Richard E. Schmidt, Robert Spencer, Frank Lloyd Wright, and John S. Van Bergen. Some, like Wright and Griffin, often blurred the distinction between architecture and landscape architecture, designing both buildings and grounds. The majority were members of the Cliff Dwellers, a downtown club of prominent Chicago men founded in 1907, and many shared offices in Steinway Hall.[75]

Steinway Hall was located at 64 East Van Buren Street in Chicago, just east of the Loop. Perkins, who had designed the building, rented the loft and part of the top floor and offered space to other architects shortly after its completion in 1896. Early members of the group at Steinway Hall included Myron Hunt, Perkins, Spencer, and Wright. Others came and went at various times over the years. All shared the same secretary and collaborated on projects informally and occasionally in formal associations.[76]

The leading prairie landscape architects were Ossian Cole Simonds and Jens Jensen. Like the prairie architects, both were members of the Cliff Dwellers. Simonds' office was at Graceland Cemetery, while Jensen maintained an office in Steinway Hall. As Cleveland and Olmsted had advocated before them, Simonds and Jensen insisted that design forms and materials should relate directly to the surrounding region. Despite frequent descriptions of the prairie landscape around Chicago as "dismal" and "featureless," Jensen and Simonds became ardent champions of the flora and subtle landforms of the prairie region. Like the prairie architects, they celebrated the flatness and openness of this part of the Midwest by emphasizing and accentuating the broad horizontal lines of the prairie landscape. Even in the North Shore region of Chicago, where one found steep ravines and forests, they created small openings edged with hawthorn and other low trees with spreading branches to emphasize the horizontal and to give the impression of much larger spaces. Both Jensen and Simonds insisted that their designs were idealizations rather than literal re-creations of nature; they emphasized the "spirit" of the regional landscape rather than its precise physical forms.[77]

The prairie movement in landscape gardening was described by Wilhelm Miller in *The Prairie Spirit in Landscape Gardening* (1915) (Figure 13). Miller recognized Simonds and Jensen as the leaders of the movement and did much to advertise and promote their design principles. Miller was perhaps the first to recognize the work of Jensen and Simonds as a distinctive American style of landscape architecture, and he wrote widely about their projects in a series of articles in *Country Life in America*, *Architectural Record*, and elsewhere. Miller suggested that the prairie style consisted of three basic principles of design: conservation (or preservation), restoration, and repetition. He wrote:

> I called this manner of doing things the "prairie style" of landscape gardening, defining it as an American mode of design based upon the practical needs of the middlewestern people and characterized by preservation of

I—The Prairie Style of Landscape Gardening

A New Mode of Designing and Planting, Which Aims to Fit the Peculiar Scenery, Climate, Soil, Labor, and Other Conditions of the Prairies, Instead of Copying Literally the Manners and Materials of Other Regions

THE Middle West is just beginning to evolve a new style of architecture, interior decoration, and landscape gardening, in an effort to create the perfect home amid the prairie states. This movement is founded on the fact that one of the greatest assets which any country or natural part of it can have, is a strong national or regional character, especially in the homes of the common people. Its westernism grows out of the most striking peculiarity of middle-western scenery, which is the prairie, i. e., flat or gently rolling land that was treeless when the white man came to Illinois. Some of the progress that has been made toward a prairie style of architecture is incidentally illustrated in these pages. (See front cover, and Figs. 1, 5, 17, and 76.)

The progress in landscape gardening is typified by the following statement from one member of the new "middle-western school of artists: "When I was landscape gardener for the West Side parks in Chicago I directed the expenditure of nearly $4,000,000 on projects inspired by the prairie. Some of the money went for salaries and maintenance, but there was a bond issue of $3,000,000 for new construction. This was chiefly spent on such designs as the Prairie River in Humboldt Park (Fig. 2), the Prairie Rose-garden (Fig. 8), and the Conservatories in Garfield Park (Figs. 25-34). Of course, the primary motive was to give recreation and pleasure to the people, but the secondary motive was to inspire them with the vanishing beauty of the prairie. Therefore, I used many symbols of the prairie, i. e., plants with strongly horizontal branches or flower clusters that repeat in obvious or subtle ways the horizontal line of land and sky which is the most impressive phenomenon on the boundless plains. Also, I aimed to re-create the atmosphere of the prairie by restoring as high a proportion as possible of the trees, shrubs, and flowers native to Illinois."

The principles of design on which the "prairie men" lay most stress are conservation, restoration, and repetition, as illustrated on the contents page and by Figs. 2 and 3.

A great field for applying these principles is offered by our parks. Of course, literal restoration of prairie scenery is impractical in places that are visited by thousands of people daily. But the spirit of truth can be restored to every large city park in the Middle West, witness the Prairie River and its adjacent meadow (Fig. 2). Each city can produce a different picture by restoring its local color, or characteristic vegetation. There are three ways of doing this, for the prairie spirit can be idealized, conventionalized, or symbolized. For example, it is idealized in the Conservatories (Figs. 25-34) by suggesting the appearance of Illinois in geological periods before the coming of man. It is conventionalized in the Rose-garden (Fig. 8) so much so that there are no prairie flowers in it, and in Humboldt boulevard (Fig. 59). It is symbolized in the playground at Douglas Park (Figs. 55-56) by means of plants with horizontal branches and flower clusters.

The same principles and methods have been used on many private estates, which offer a larger canvas for pure restorations than the average farmstead or city lot. However, every home can express the new idea in proportion to its means. The farmer may idealize his farm view by fram-

1. The Prairie Style of Landscape Gardening Married to the Prairie Style of Architecture

"The environment is woodland," says the landscape architect, "but the newly planted crab apples are designed to frame the view of the house and give an invitation to the prairie which is not far away." (Home of Henry Babson, River Forest; Louis H. Sullivan, architect.)

Figure 13. First page of Wilhelm Miller's extension publication, *The Prairie Spirit in Landscape Gardening* (1915), which characterized the work of O. C. Simonds and Jens Jensen as a uniquely midwestern style.

typical western scenery, by restoration of local color, and by repetition of the horizontal line of land or sky, which is the strongest feature of prairie scenery.[78]

Perhaps the most important characteristic described by Miller was that of repetition; the level horizon of the prairie landscape was repeated in many different forms throughout the design. Miller emphasized the use of what he termed "stratified" materials—for example, rockwork made up of

flat limestone layers, or plants characterized by distinctive horizontal branching or flower clusters. Both of these elements were common in Simonds' and Jensen's work. Prairie architects also used stratified materials and forms in the buildings they designed. Low-hung walls and roof overhangs made houses seem to merge with the surrounding landscape. Wright and Griffin further extended the lines of houses into gardens, using terraces, pools, walls, and planting boxes; in their work, plants became important tools for linking houses to nature. By contrast, in Simonds' and Jensen's work, gardens most often maintained a separate identity from buildings.[79]

Working in the same area and sharing common concerns about regional design, Jensen, Simonds, and the leading Chicago architects most likely collaborated with one another on many projects. After leaving Jenney's office, Simonds had formed a short-lived partnership with architect William Holabird, and he later collaborated with the firm of Holabird and Roche on several projects. Records of relatively few of O. C. Simonds' residential jobs survive, and it is especially difficult to determine much about his collaborations with various architects. Certainly, most would have been aware of his work in Graceland Cemetery, where Sullivan's celebrated designs for the Ryerson Tomb (1887) and the Getty Tomb (1890) were located.[80]

Jensen collaborated with prairie school architects on several important projects: the Henry Babson place in Riverside, Illinois, with Louis Sullivan; the Harry Rubens place in Glencoe, Illinois, with George W. Maher; the A. C. Magnus place in Winnetka, Illinois, with Robert Spencer; the I. B. Grommes place in Lake Geneva, Wisconsin, with Richard Schmidt; and the Manitowoc High School in Wisconsin, with Dwight Perkins. In addition to the projects listed here and those mentioned in the appendix, others may have been handled on an informal basis. Occasionally the Steinway Hall architects exhibited their work, and Jensen showed his work alongside theirs. In their 1907 exhibit, Jensen featured photographs of Humboldt Park and the Rubens and Magnus estates. Through the Chicago City Club, Jensen also participated in various design competitions with local architects. He helped jury the "City Residential Land Development" competition and produced a noncompetitive entry for the "Design for a Neighborhood Center" competition.[81]

Jensen collaborated on several design projects with Wright, including the Avery Coonley House in Riverside, Illinois, the Avery Coonley School and Kindergarten in Downers Grove, Illinois, the Sherman M. Booth place in Glencoe, Illinois, and the Abby Beecher Roberts place in Marquette, Michigan. On some of these projects, such as the Avery Coonley place, it is unclear how much of the work was done by Jensen. Wright and

Jensen respected each other's work, but their personalities and differing views on design made working together difficult. Their collaboration on the Roberts place turned into a constant battle over "the grade for the house, the screening of the house from the road, the vistas, etc." Jensen insisted that "when it is finished it will be trees with a cottage, not a cottage with trees," and to Wright's dismay, Mrs. Roberts listened.[82]

As for Wright's architecture, Jensen questioned what he perceived to be an increasingly Oriental influence and a turning away from vernacular forms more appropriate to the Midwest. In particular, he would object to the flattened rooflines of Wright's later buildings. Jensen urged a building style that was more closely linked to local climatic conditions. As examples, he pointed to the Sioux, with their tall tepees on the Great Plains, and the Amerindians of the arid Southwest, with their solid, flat-roofed structures. He suggested that American architects learn from their Amerindian forebears:

> I do see that the same environmental power that formed the Indians' love of color and simple design will also some day influence us, especially those of the great Mid-American plains. The varied climatic conditions of our Country makes one type of architecture for all of our people both inconsistent and disturbing to our rich landscape.

In a letter to Michael Mappes in Berlin, Germany, Jensen noted that the steeply pitched roofs common in Germanic vernacular buildings in Wisconsin were much more appropriate to the landscape there than the flatter-roofed structures Wright was developing.[83]

Simonds and Jensen were more careful in selecting indigenous species than Wright or Griffin were in their ventures into landscape architectural design. As his style matured, Jensen increasingly relied upon native plant communities when making selections for plant combinations. He knew, as Miller suggests, that it was the unique combination of plants and their repetition which gave the Midwest its regional identity:

> Any botanist can demonstrate that the Middle West contains few plants of the first importance that are not also native to the East. Nevertheless, nature has emphasized certain things in the Middle West—bur oak, stratified haws and crabs, prairie rose and low rose, American bluebells, wild blue phlox, phlox divaricata, sunflowers, purple coneflowers, gaillardia, compass plant and others. The result is a landscape very different from one dominated by pine or palm. It is the frequent combination of a few species that makes "local color."[84]

In their designs, both Simonds and Jensen delighted in taking the "common" plants of the countryside and elevating them to a new respect.

As Simonds suggested, "Sumacs, elderberries, hazel bushes, goldenrods and asters, once considered so common as to command little more respect than weeds, are found to be really valuable in landscape making." While they realized it was possible to preserve only relatively small portions of "idealized nature" in their work, Simonds and Jensen used their designs to try to teach the general public about the natural heritage of midwestern landscapes. In describing the prairie flowers that he included in his design for Lincoln Memorial Garden, Jensen wrote: "Here we have them in a limited way, but still sufficient in their grandeur to reflect some of the beauty which was Illinois and teach coming generations a love for this beauty that has changed into fields."[85]

This attitude was fundamental to the practitioners of the prairie style of landscape architecture. Miller used a patriotic pitch to challenge people to plant in the "Illinois Way" in his many agricultural extension publications. For example, in *The Prairie Spirit in Landscape Gardening* (1915), he included what he called a " 'Short Ballot' for Illinois Citizens" whereby readers would promise to make some ornamental plantings around their homes in the upcoming year. He also adapted the famous Athenian Oath as "The Illinois Citizen's Oath," and suggested that each town create its own version for its local citizenry. Perhaps the strongest summary of Miller's ideals is the manifesto he called "The Prairie Spirit":

I believe that one of the greatest races of men in the world will be developed in the region of the prairies.

I will help to prove that the vast plains need not level down humanity to a dead monotony in appearance, conduct, and ideals.

I feel the uplifting influence of the rich rolling prairie and will bring its spirit into my daily life. If my home surroundings are monotonous and ugly, I will make them varied and beautiful. I will emulate the independence and progressiveness of the pioneer.

I will do what I can to promote the prosperity, happiness, and beauty of all prairie states and communities.

I will try to open the eyes of those who can see no beauty in the common "brush" and wild flowers beside the country roads. If any souls have been deadened by sordid materialism I will stand with these people on the highest spot that overlooks a sea of rolling land where they can drink in the spirit of the prairies.

I will fight to the last the greed that would destroy all native beauty. I will help my state establish and maintain a prairie park, which will restore for the delight of future generations some fragment of wild prairie—the source of our wealth and civilization.

I will plant against the foundations of my house some bushes that will

remind me of the prairie and be to my townsfolk a living symbol of the indomitable prairie spirit.[86]

Simonds also felt that landscape gardening could influence people to appreciate their general surroundings. Like Andrew Jackson Downing, he viewed the landscape gardener as a crusader and hoped to influence the tastes of the general populace: "A landscape designer is in many ways a missionary: that is, he might consider himself having a mission to investigate, study, and acquire knowledge regarding the beauty of Nature and to impart this knowledge to those with whom he comes in contact." Noting that landscape gardening was a young profession, he suggested that as the art developed, it would bring about an increased appreciation of nature:

> It will open the eyes of the farmers and their families to the beauty that is always around them in the sky and in their fields, and, if they possess them, in their wood-lots, their orchards, springs, streams, and hedgerows, and in the birds that delight in the bushes and trees. . . . It will teach the city dweller, who, to a certain extent, is fond of nature, that it is not the [better] part of wisdom to create beautiful drives or parkways and then border them with bill-boards. It will teach him to respect the wooded bluffs and hillsides, the springs, streams, river banks and lake shores within the city boundaries, and preserve them with loving care.[87]

Stylistically, the work of Simonds and Jensen was quite similar. Simonds, with his design work at Graceland Cemetery starting in 1878, began practicing landscape architecture prior to Jensen. As Miller noted, Simonds had "drunk deep of the spirit of Downing and the elder Olmsted who taught that the preservation of the natural landscape is usually more beautiful and less costly than levelling every hill and filling every ravine." Jensen shared this same spirit as he began his design career with the design of the American Garden at Union Park in 1888. While the degree of influence these two men had on each other is impossible to document, it is clear they shared a mutual respect and many of the same basic principles of design.[88]

Consistent with the Olmstedian tradition, flowing outdoor spaces became the core of a Simonds or Jensen design. In 1914, in his article "A Series of Outdoor Salons," Miller noted Simonds' development of small, roomlike spaces. Space flowed from one of these outdoor "living rooms" to the next, thereby creating a dynamic experience of the landscape in much the same way as Wright and other prairie architects used space in their designs for buildings. As Miller wrote, "Each room contracts at either end, so as to make a sort of natural door, through which you get alluring vistas of the rooms beyond." Jensen used similar sequential effects in the trail gardens at the Henry Ford estate in Dearborn, Michigan, and later at

Lincoln Memorial Garden in Springfield, Illinois. Describing Simonds' Hibbard estate in Winnetka, Illinois, Miller wrote: "In the Hibbard garden we have grouping, composition, design, unity, a series of dissolving pictures, all arranged in orderly sequences and revealing new beauties every few steps."[89]

As was also true of Jensen, Simonds created a series of irregular bays at the edges of major open spaces and suggested using masses of shrubs as transitions from the larger forest trees behind. In his book, *Landscape Gardening* (1920), Simonds wrote: "[Shrubs] are employed to grade down the higher outlines of trees to the surrounding surface of a lawn or other low area. . . . They will be used to separate bays so that one part of the lawn or lake will be hidden from another." Simonds also suggested that "the broader growing trees and shrubs should be planted at the projections forming the boundaries of bays of foliage, [with] relatively narrow specimens in the deeper portions so that the bays will not be filled up with years of growth and thus lose their significance." This same technique was used by Jensen when he placed hawthorn and other small trees on peninsulas of vegetation along the edges of openings or at turning points along trails.[90]

Respect for nature was prevalent in the work of the prairie landscape architects, but it is also clear that they considered their work as "art" rather than as an imitation of nature. Simonds frequently referred to nature as "the great teacher," but admitted that nature sometimes needs "help" in creating compositions to be enjoyed by people. In *Landscape Gardening*, he observed:

> While nature is the best teacher and does some things incomparably well, she does not always produce the most artistic effect, at least from man's point of view. She will close the edges of a wood so tight with foliage that the eye cannot penetrate beyond the outer covering. . . . In such cases the judicious use of the axe will greatly aid in nature's own arrangement.

Likewise, Simonds suggested that landscape designers should abide by the old adage "plant thick and thin quick," which had been advocated by Olmsted.[91]

Simonds apparently had reservations about the label "prairie landscape architect." He preferred to think of himself as a landscape gardener who responded to local conditions. In fact, Simonds' practice was hardly limited to the prairie states. By the time of his death, he was said to have worked in every state of the union. Jensen, in contrast, was attracted to Wilhelm Miller's description of a prairie style, and while he, like Simonds, accepted commissions throughout the country, he felt most comfortable in the landscapes of the Midwest, which he had grown to love.[92]

The Emphasis on Native Plants in Design

The use of native plant materials in design was not limited to Jensen, Simonds, or the Midwest region. Jensen was probably more celebrated and more vocal in his advocacy of native plants, but other landscape architects also supported the use of native materials.

From Olmsted on, many landscape architects included native plant materials in their designs, but usually not to the exclusion of other materials. William Robinson's *The Wild Garden*, published in 1870, provided a model for a wilder aesthetic. The showier native shrubs and trees had long been accepted as standard landscaping tools, but the idea of using masses of the more common native shrubs and trees—as one might find them in ecological association—was rather new. The notion of plant "communities" and the science of ecology were just beginning to develop at this time. In 1899 the botanist Henry C. Cowles of the University of Chicago published "The Ecological Relations of the Vegetation on the Sand Dunes of Lake Michigan," which became a classic in its focus on plants as living communities. Jensen struck up a friendship with Cowles. Together they rambled through the sand dunes of Illinois and Indiana along the shores of Lake Michigan, and hiked in the prairie, woodland, and wetland areas of the Chicago region. Their study of plant "sociology" (or "plant ecology," as it was later called) influenced Jensen's thinking about the use of native plants. He noted how plants "fit" together aesthetically and functionally into communities of "friends." Jensen's photographs of plants and their wild habitats illustrate his thinking. He took not only closeups, showing the detail and special features of an individual plant (Figure 14), but also more general shots, showing the plant's character and associated habitat (Figure 15). Jensen was also attracted to the spatial qualities and light contrasts that are found in prairie remnants and their forested borders, and he took special note of the transitional zones between the two plant communities.[93]

In the late 1800s and early 1900s, numerous guidebooks to the native flora of different parts of the country were published and helped intensify an already growing interest in America's natural heritage. These included Thomas Meehan's *Native Flowers and Ferns of the United States in their Botanical, Horticultural, and Popular Aspects* (1878), Mrs. William Starr Dana's *How to Know the Wildflowers* (1893), Anton Kerner and F. W. Oliver's *Natural History of Plants* (1895), Neltje Blanchan's *Nature's Garden* (1899), Willard N. Clute's *Our Ferns in Their Haunts* (1901), Nathaniel Lord Britton and the Honorable Addison Brown's *Manual of the Flora of the Northern States and Canada* (1901), Charles Sprague Sargent's *Manual of the Trees of North America* (1905), and Ferdinand

Figure 14. Photograph of starry false Solomon's seal (*Smilacina stellata*) taken by Jensen at Dune Park, Indiana, 10 May 1913. Courtesy of Jensen Collection, Art and Architecture Library, University of Michigan, Ann Arbor.

Figure 15. Photograph labeled by Jensen as "Flowering Dogwood Habit," taken at Bailytown, Indiana, 17 May 1913. Courtesy of Jensen Collection, Art and Architecture Library, University of Michigan, Ann Arbor.

Schuyler Matthews' *Field Book of American Wildflowers* (1912).

During the 1890s, in articles for *Garden and Forest*, Charles Sprague Sargent eloquently pleaded for the protection of native plants and for the preservation of natural scenery. Each issue of the journal carried articles on little-known native plants and provided helpful information in regular columns entitled "Notes on Wildflowers" and "Notes on Some North American Trees." Sargent lamented that too often "nature's handiwork is altogether swept away before the gardener is asked to begin his work." The artistic gardener, he suggested, "carefully preserves nature's preliminary provisions when he begins his work, accepts them as the nucleus of his design, and adds nothing which is inharmonious." He noted that many "naturalistic" American gardens were similar, despite extreme variations in climate, geology, and flora:

> No two natural landscapes are alike, and within a very few miles we always find many which are surprisingly unlike in radical character and general effect as well as in details. Therefore, an art which is based upon the study of Nature cannot be going right when its products all bear a close family likeness to each other, and this not only as regards a single stretch of country-side, but as regards regions that lie far apart and are wholly different in climate, geological conformation and native vegetation.[94]

Warren H. Manning was another important advocate of native plantings. Although he is best known as a promoter of large-scale planning, his early work in his father's nursery in Reading, Massachusetts, instilled in him a lasting love for working with plants. He spent eight years with the Olmsted office in New York City and Boston, assisting with the site work at the Vanderbilt estate in Biltmore, North Carolina, and at the Columbian Exposition in Chicago in 1893. He also orchestrated the botanical inventory of the Blue Hills, Middlesex Fells, Stony Brook, and Beaver Brook reservations for Boston's Metropolitan Park Commission in 1896. In 1899, he published *A Handbook for Planning and Planting Small Home Grounds* for the Stout Manual Training School in Menomonie, Wisconsin, in which he advised careful attention to the "native tangle of plants" found on a property as well as sensitive management and observation before structuring a garden. The handbook's extensive list of plants represented in the school's collections included varieties that had been introduced, but Manning also encouraged the use of native varieties and provided descriptions and information about their cultivation.[95]

Several of Manning's projects were among the earliest "native" gardens to be publicized nationally. In 1899, his design for Dolobran, the home of Clement A. Griscom outside Philadelphia, was featured in an article in *Outlook* entitled "An American Garden." The estate contained several old quarries which Manning aptly reclaimed as gardens featuring native woodland and wetland species. In 1908, Manning described his own "bog garden" in Massachusetts in an article in *Country Life in America*.[96]

Like Simonds and Jensen, Manning was also involved in work in the immediate Chicago area. He had designed the Cyrus McCormick estate in Lake Forest, Illinois, which involved an attempt to reforest and stabilize the bluffs on Lake Michigan. In the November 1915 issue of his journal, *Billerica: The North Shore Illinois Edition*, Manning argued for setting aside wildflower preserves in the suburbs north of Chicago. In the same issue, Georgia Douglas Clarke described the "Wildflowers of the North Shore," and Everett L. Millard proposed "A Municipal Wild Flower Preserve" for Highland Park, Illinois. Manning was obviously familiar with Jensen's work, and he admired Jensen's artistry and conservation efforts. While on a tour sponsored by the American Civic Association in 1929, Manning lauded the "good work" being done by Jensen's Friends of Our Native Landscape "to save all places of beauty and interest that will tie the present and future generations of America to the past, and serve as playgrounds for the people and sanctuaries for wild plant and animal life." The Friends of Our Native Landscape was a conservation group organized by Jensen to preserve and celebrate the native landscape. The activities of the group are discussed in more detail in Chapter 3.[97]

Another important preservation effort called for the saving of native plants and natural areas as models for design. Victor Shelford's *Naturalist's Guide to the Americas* (1926) included an essay by Stanley White entitled "The Value of Natural Preserves to the Landscape Architect." In his arguments for preserving areas of unspoiled nature, White, who was then a professor of landscape architecture at the University of Illinois, stressed the necessity of including in the education of landscape architects the study of natural areas: "The training of the landscape architect begins not only with pictorial composition and practical design, but also with the study of plants, of soils, of bodies of water and of all the great natural forces and influences that have shaped and given character to the physiognomy of the land and its vegetation." He further noted:

> From these great sources of natural beauty comes all our inspiration; from them comes the unlimited store of fine examples teaching us the arrangement of our materials; from them comes the lessons of growth, development and natural strife that shows the way to a permanent landscape; and finally, from them comes the suggestion to the layman of the value of beauty and the desire for it in the surroundings of human habitations.

This guide also asserted the value of natural areas in other fields such as art and literature, forestry, fisheries, geography, biology, and agriculture, and provided a state by state guide and inventory of many of the natural areas still existing at that time.[98]

Other books advocating the use of native plants in design included *Taming the Wild Things*, by Herbert Durand, and *American Plants for American Gardens*, by plant ecologist Edith Roberts and landscape architect Elsa Rehmann. Durand argued that "the trees and shrubs used in the composition of landscape pictures should be confined almost exclusively to kinds that grow naturally in the vicinity." This was essential, he asserted, in creating "harmony with the surrounding scenery." Roberts and Rehmann advanced the idea of using plant ecology as a basis for landscape design. They noted that in plant ecology, "observations are made as to what plants grow together and how they compose the groups known as associations." Such observations, they suggested, should guide the landscape architect and gardener in designing the landscape. In selecting plants, attention should "be focused upon those that really belong to the particular scene and compositions made of them may be true reproductions or sympathetic interpretations of the landscape."[99]

Roberts and Rehmann described eleven different plant communities commonly found in the northeastern United States and states as far south as Georgia: (1) the open field, (2) the juniper hillside, (3) the gray birches, (4) the pines, (5) the oak woods, (6) the beech-maple-hemlock woods, (7) the hemlock ravine, (8) the streamside, (9) the pond, (10) the bog, and (11) the seaside. For each community, they discussed design characteristics and provided lists of appropriate species. Formerly a student of Henry Cowles, Roberts had established an "ecological garden" for the study of plant communities on the Vassar College campus in Poughkeepsie, New York. A study of the flora of New York's Dutchess County done by Roberts and Margaret F. Shaw served as the basis for *American Plants for American Gardens*. Roberts and Rehmann hoped that companion studies would be done for other regions of the country.[100]

As Roberts and Rehmann observed, the use of native plants in home gardens had become increasingly popular. Garden magazines, as well as landscape architectural publications, carried articles on the use of native plants. In "New Uses for Native Plants" (1925), Mary Cunningham suggested that "perhaps the most distinctive thing in the history of planting during the last ten years is our use of native plants." She noted the great popularity of a wild plant show in Boston in which "plants were shown in appropriate habitats and combinations."[101]

Landscape Architecture, the quarterly magazine of the American Society of Landscape Architects, published a wide range of articles devoted to the subject of native plants in design, many of which provided technical information or species lists such as "Increasing Native Perennial Flowers" or "A Reference Table of the Native Ferns." Charles Downing Lay's "What the Nurseries Should Grow" lamented the extreme difficulty in finding many native plants, despite the growth in the number of nurseries dealing exclusively with natives. Jensen constantly battled this problem on his large projects, and resorted to plants collected in the wild to supplement those propagated by the nurseries. At Lincoln Memorial Garden in Springfield, Illinois, the Illinois chapters of the Garden Club of America organized a massive plant-rescue network to provide many of the plants for the memorial.[102]

In 1901, the Society for the Protection of Native Plants had developed out of the New England Botanical Club and the Massachusetts Horticultural Society with the goal of preventing the local extermination of wildflowers and encouraging their propagation. In 1912, Henry Cowles helped organize the Wild Flower Preservation Society, and in 1921, Vermont became the first state to enact a law to protect wild plants. A 1924 article by Jensen's friend Paul B. Riis pointed to the seriousness of the problem:

> The plans of landscape architects often call for thousands of ferns, columbines, violets, or other wildings for great masses of naturalistic plantings. Perhaps there is some justification for collecting these plants from little visited places and placing them in extensive home grounds or parks where they will be enjoyed throughout their life. But this can never be justified if such collection of plants for transplanting threatens extinction of species from any locality.

Riis argued that only plants sufficient for propagation should be taken from the wild and urged a combination of laws and public education programs to protect wild plants and animals.[103]

One of the most intriguing articles in *Landscape Architecture* during this period was Harold A. Caparn's "Thoughts on Planting Composition" (1929). Like Jensen and Simonds before him, Caparn recommended that landscape architects study the patterns and arrangements found in nature for inspiration and guidance in their landscape designs. Although "a careless glance at the plantings of nature might give the impression that, as far as anything that artists would term 'design' goes, they are purposeless and confused," Caparn suggested that "more deliberate observation will show in them certain characteristics of a work of art." He further noted that nature's plantings "have unity and repose, by which is meant that their constituent parts produce an impression of being the right thing in the right place."[104]

Caparn believed that the landscape architect should study the sizes and forms of groups of plants in fields and forests, their massings and voids, and the patterns and repetitions they created. He noted that there is a great deal of unity in the natural environment, not only among plants, but also among the elements of sky, land, water, and vegetation. As he described it, "Anyone who will take the trouble to block out the lights and shadows, the foliage or flower masses with spaces between them, the solids and voids of one of them will find the same kind of subtle relation of form and proportion that appears in forest meadow or drift of clouds." Caparn also argued that tremendous order is found in nature and that nature offers economies which the landscape architect should study as a model for landscape design; an understanding of the processes and functions found in nature was as necessary as mere observation of its physical forms. He suggested that natural areas

> demonstrate an economic system of entire perfection, a product adapted
> exactly to soil, climate, water and food supply and total environment, and
> [that] one of their innumerable results was to provide scenes made up of
> forms, colors, textures and arrangements which poets have so often sung,
> and to which painters and the rest of us desiring suggestion and inspiration
> must always finally resort in the hope of catching the spirit of their form and
> relationship.[105]

Another prominent advocate of the use of native plants in design was Frank A. Waugh, a professor of landscape architecture at Massachusetts Agricultural College in Amherst (later known as the University of Massachusetts) (Figure 16). Waugh wrote widely as a landscape historian and critic of landscape design instruction. Three books generally describe Waugh's evolving philosophy of design: *The Landscape Beautiful* (a series of essays on landscape issues and American landscape architecture), *The Natural Style in Landscape Gardening*, and *Textbook of Landscape Gardening*. Many of the ideas expressed in *The Natural Style in Landscape Gardening* were notably close to those later recorded by Jensen in *Siftings*. Sometime after 1900, Jensen and Waugh became good friends and remained so until Waugh's death in 1943. Waugh admired Jensen's work immensely and frequently used pictures of Jensen's designs to illustrate principles in his books.[106]

Waugh was one of the few academics Jensen admired. In 1938, Jensen invited him to serve as an instructor at The Clearing, Jensen's school in Ellison Bay, Wisconsin, but Waugh was too ill at the time to make the trip. Like Jensen, Waugh promoted a naturalistic approach to design. He believed that the ideas, motives, and methods of a landscape architect must come directly from nature. In addition, he felt that the designer needed to go beyond a purely objective understanding of the landscape and develop an emotional attachment to nature: "It would seem certain

Figure 16. Frank Waugh playing the flute. Waugh frequently entertained his students with music. Courtesy of Collection of the Department of Landscape Architecture and Regional Planning, University of Massachusetts, Amherst.

that any landscape architect of any school must know and love the land-scape. Such knowledge and sympathy would be fundamentally and abso-lutely necessary."[107]

This attitude of sacred reverence toward the landscape is common throughout much of Waugh's writings, as it was in Jensen's and Simonds' work. Waugh wrote:

> Of course the student will visit the landscape—no, he will live with it—with an open mind and heart. He will be trying to see what the landscape has to offer, trying to hear what it has to tell. He will look long, quietly, silently, intently at the horizon, or at the distant valley, or at the mountains. And most of all he will consciously seek their spiritual message.

Waugh used a variety of inventive approaches to teach his students these values and pique their interest. Students would create designs in response to classical music and take field trips at night or during rain or snow storms to learn to appreciate the landscape in its varied modes of dress.[108]

During the late 1920s, Waugh involved his students in a series of landscape studies, some of which he published in *Landscape Architecture* and *American Landscape Architecture*. The studies were grouped around ecological, physiographic, and interpretive themes; he fully intended to publish them together as "Guide to the Landscape: A Textbook for Motorists, Boy Scouts, and for all Lovers of the Native Landscape, Especially for Painters and Landscape Architects," but never found a publisher. Each study encouraged careful observation of a natural plant community or landform as a model for similar situations in design. Topics included the pine woods, the juniper landscape, pond and lakeshore, the forest margin, roadside ecology, natural plant groups, and sand dunes.[109]

Waugh shared Jensen's commitment to conserving both cultural and natural features of the American landscape, and pioneered conscious planning efforts for the National Forest Service and National Park Service. He pressured the agencies to recognize officially the recreational uses of wildlands and sought to plan carefully for their impacts. During the summer of 1917, Waugh visited national forests across the United States and provided a critical assessment of the nation's current planning in *Recreation Uses on the National Forests: A Study of Their Extent and Character, with a Discussion of Public Policies and Recommendations as to Methods of Development and Administration*. During a period when city planning was coming to the fore, Waugh argued that similar attention ought to be directed toward training landscape architects in the management and interpretation of wildlands. He regarded the ability to "read" the landscape as an essential skill for landscape architects: "The landscape architect ought to become the great interpreter of the native landscape to a generation hungry for the solemnity of the mountains, the quiet of the woodlands, the music of running waters, the freshness of the wind across the prairies, and the inspiration of the clean blue sky overhead." Perhaps the best surviving example of Waugh's interpretive work is the public drive in Mount Hood National Forest in Oregon. Later, during the 1930s, Waugh developed a "Check List of Descriptive Data on the Landscape of a Region" as part of a recreational resources study for the Civilian Conservation Corps. It was an attempt at systematizing the analysis of the ecological and aesthetic resources of a region for the planning and design of large regional landscapes.[110]

Like Jensen, Waugh was concerned about the general failure of politicians and the profession of landscape architecture to respond in a meaningful way to issues of conservation and natural beauty. In a 1936 letter to Jensen, he suggested that in the post-Depression years, the profession would have to develop a new role for itself:

Just what the future of our profession is going to be, nobody knows at the present time. However, we can be certain that it will not look like anything in the past and certainly not like the kind of practice which has been preached for years by the American Society of Landscape Architects and the rest of the Brahmins. At any rate, we are going ahead hoping that our boys at least will be able to come down to earth and do some useful work for the common people.

Waugh and Jensen agreed that the profession was heading in the wrong direction. Waugh argued that the landscaper should be "a dirt gardener and not a white collar high priest." Jensen noted the "strong tendency by the American Landscaper to get away from gardening, as if that word smelled of cabbage. He has a fear of being classed with the craftsman instead of the professional, and today the art is practically killed, because of his efforts to make a profession of it."[111]

By the late 1930s, the market for designing large estates had dried up, and fewer large municipal parks were being designed. Yet there was still a need to respond to the increasing pressures being placed on the native landscape. In 1938, Waugh again wrote to Jensen: "This problem of preserving and improving the native landscape is the greatest one before the profession of landscape architecture and one of the greatest questions anywhere in the nation. Unfortunately the American Society of Landscape Architects has heard nothing about it, and of course will do nothing about it." Still, Waugh held out hope for the future: "Of one thing we may be sure, however, [and] that is that the general public generally is becoming more conscious of the value of the native landscape. Eventually we will be able to capitalize [on] this public interest and thereby to curb some of the vicious practices and spoiled politics and unintelligent industrialism."[112]

Jensen devoted his career to "this problem of preserving and improving the native landscape." Through his natural parks and gardens, he hoped to awaken others to the beauty of wild nature. For Jensen, this was not merely a profession; it was his religion. To him, the garden was a sermon, speaking of harmony with God's out-of-doors. Perhaps more successfully—certainly more fervently—than his contemporaries, he merged his work as artist, conservationist, ecologist, and teacher.[113]

THREE

Jensen's Design Career

Jensen's design career was marked by incredible energy and diversity, especially for someone who began designing relatively late in life (the bulk of Jensen's work was done between the ages of forty-five and seventy-five). From his design for the American Garden in Chicago's Union Park in 1888 to his shaping of The Clearing in Ellison Bay, Wisconsin, Jensen honed his skills of working with the land to create landscapes in harmony with their regional setting. As his reputation grew, his commissions spread throughout the Midwest and into the Northeast, the South, and the Great Plains. He even designed two parks in Pasadena, California.

In order to trace Jensen's design career in a logical order, it makes sense to group his work into several distinct categories: the West Park District in Chicago, where he spent much of the first half of his career; his residential design work, which was spread throughout his career and intermixed with the park work; public and institutional work; his conservation efforts, which were logical outgrowths of his design activities throughout his life; and his school, The Clearing, in Ellison Bay, Wisconsin. In all his works, Jensen emphasized simplicity of design and accentuated an emotional response to landscape.

Chicago's West Park District

During his early years with the West Parks, Jensen impressed his superiors with his unusual inventiveness in solving park problems and generally improving the parks. His American Garden in Union Park was the first in a string of designs and innovations in management that he proposed. For example, Jensen developed an apparatus for raking the weeds that choked the lakes during the summer months and interfered with boating. The commissioners were impressed enough to recognize his work in their *Annual Report* in 1894.[1]

Jensen made good use of his background in agriculture in the West

Parks, honing his skills in planting trees and other horticultural practices. In 1899, Jensen, who at this time used "James" as his first name, published an article entitled "Transplanting Trees during Mid-Winter," in which he outlined step-by-step instructions for transplanting large trees. Although he specifically recommended transplanting large elms, he noted: "I have transplanted almost everything that is grown in these parts." In addition to his growing knowledge as a plants specialist, Jensen also developed expertise in other technical aspects of design, especially road work and concrete construction.[2]

Perhaps because of his technical competence and innovative ideas for the parks, in 1895 Jensen was made superintendent of Union Park. Prior to this time, Union Park, which was the site of the park headquarters for the West Park District, had no superintendent. Jensen renovated Jenney's earlier layout for the park, adding many of his own ideas. It was a period of experimentation; Jensen later admitted that at this time he designed without a conscious sense of where it would lead. In 1896, he was promoted to superintendent at Humboldt Park, which was then scheduled for expansion. Despite his inventive ideas and hard work, Jensen had continuous battles with the political appointees running the parks, and in 1900 these came to a head. He refused to participate in the political graft that was rampant throughout the system, and as a result he was dismissed from his West Parks position.[3]

Jensen did not go quietly, however. Instead, he became a leading spokesperson for park reform. At the Sixth Annual Meeting of the American Park and Outdoor Art Association, Jensen lectured the park commissioners' section on "Parks and Politics." He suggested that the practice of treating park trustee appointments as political favors was wreaking havoc on the system. Such appointees, said Jensen, furthered the selfish interests of their political bosses "to the continual detriment of the parks and its supporters." With colorful language, he outlined the results of such practices:

> Statuary of questionable art is accepted, or through an over-zealous attempt to procure images of every one's idol, the quiet sylvan scenery of the park has been turned into an ancestral show-place, suggestive of certain of our cemeteries. Buildings of ugly and ill-fitting architecture obtrude upon pastoral meadows or are placed in spots inappropriate for any building. There are innovations of all kinds, including midways where the "real thing" kneels down and loads or unloads its merry crew of sightseers. Visionary tiger hunts are indulged in from the safe back of a serviceable elephant, whose sudden appearance to the timid and unwary park visitor may cause hysterical convulsions. There are ice carnivals and dances—all for the good of the party. The advertisements of some merchant who is

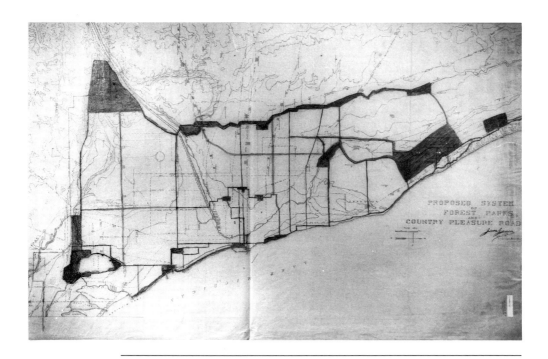

Figure 17. Jensen's hand-drawn map of "Proposed System of Forest Parks and Country Pleasure Road[s]" (1903). The map is drawn over a geologic map showing ancient beach ridges in the Chicago area. Courtesy of Jensen Collection, Art and Architecture Library, University of Michigan, Ann Arbor.

termed a "good fellow" are thrown upon the canvas at public concerts running riot with the sacred melodies of Wagner. Floral designs of the most ridiculous and fantastic kinds find themselves perfectly at home in this great aggregation of show fixtures. The products of the conservatories are placed at the disposal of political friends, and free boating and fishing permits are scattered broadcast as bait for the unscrupulous voter. These are undeniable facts, misleading the uneducated as to what a park should be—a place of natural scenery and sylvan beauty brought to his very doorsteps and in which his weary body and overworked nerves can find needed rest and comfort.[4]

Although Jensen was not professionally affiliated with the West Parks during this time, he continued his official involvement with Chicago's parks as a member of the Special Park Commission. This commission had been organized in 1899 to develop plans for a metropolitan park system similar to that which Charles Eliot and Sylvester Baxter had established in Boston. The report of the Special Park Commission was made in early 1904, and although compiled by Dwight Perkins, it undeniably bears the mark of Jensen. Jensen was responsible for much of the inventory work

Figure 18. Illustration of land recommended for acquisition in the *Report of the Special Park Commission to the City Council of Chicago on the Subject of a Metropolitan Park System* (Perkins 1904, 53). This photograph is labeled "Opening in the forest close to the Desplaines River—Young seedling trees in the foreground."

that went into this report as an outgrowth of his long-term interest in the soils and vegetation of the region.[5]

Through numerous weekend outings into the wilds around Chicago and his close friendship with Dr. Henry C. Cowles, Jensen was well aware of the patterns of the regional flora. He was interested not only in the visual and spatial character of the native vegetation but also in understanding the ecological niche of each species. In 1903, Jensen demonstrated his understanding of the natural areas of the region with a map showing a "Proposed System of Forest Parks and Country Pleasure Road[s]" (Figure 17). Then, in early 1904, he published a two-part article entitled "Soil Conditions and Tree Growth around Lake Michigan," in which he discussed the distribution of species such as tulip poplar (*Liriodendron tulipifera*), red cedar (*Juniperus virginiana*), and American beech (*Fagus grandifolia*) around the Great Lakes in general and particularly in the Chicago area.[6]

Part 6 of the *Report of the Special Park Commission*, entitled "Report of the Landscape Architect," was written by Jensen. In it he described the

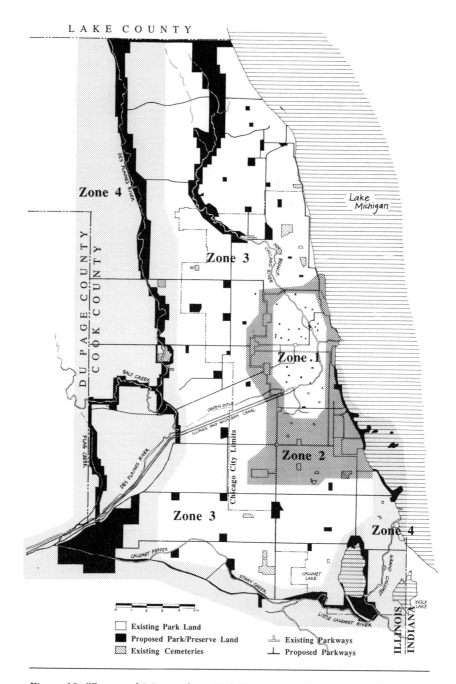

Figure 19. "Proposed Metropolitan Park System for Chicago, 1904." Redrawn from the original by Dwight Perkins as included in Perkins 1904.

physiographic and vegetative character of the Chicago region and made suggestions for preserving, enhancing, and restoring the natural beauty of the area. Jensen also included in his report his photographs of the interesting landscape features of the region, keying them to maps of areas he suggested for preservation. Slides of these photographs were used to build support for the commission's recommendations at several of its public meetings (Figure 18).

The plan divided the metropolitan area into four zones (Figure 19). Zone 1 included densely populated parts of the city, for which the commission recommended the creation of small parks and playgrounds. No one, the commission asserted, should live more than one-half mile from a park or playground. Zone 2 included the current system of parks and boulevards, and the commission basically affirmed work that was already under way. Zone 3 began at the northern boundary of the park system near Glencoe, and the commission recommended acquisition of 1,000 acres of small parks and an area of 8,300 acres known as Skokie Park. Zone 4 included a wide belt of preserves proposed by the commission as a greenway encircling the city. These preserves began with Lake Michigan and the county line on the north side of the city, extended along the Des Plaines River and the drainage canal to the west and south, and ended at Calumet Lake on the south side. At the southwest corner of this zone, the commission recommended preserving a large, hilly area of the Sag and Des Plaines valleys as a 7,000-acre natural park. This area contained the highest land of the Chicago region and provided contrast to the generally level prairie landscape. The commission noted that the Chicago region was growing at a rapid rate and that efforts should be made to secure these lands before property values rose or the intrinsic beauty of the lands was destroyed through development. Although the report was not implemented in its entirety, it did lay the groundwork for many park improvements and for the establishment of the forest preserve system which was to follow.[7]

Meanwhile, reform efforts were under way in Chicago politics, and serious efforts were being made to rid the parks of the corruption that had brought about Jensen's ouster in 1900. While the South Park Commission had been relatively free from political corruption, the Lincoln Park Commission, like that for the West Parks, had had its problems with politically tainted park appointments. Even when the Lincoln Park Commissioners were committed to reforming the park, they found that the general public regarded park positions as political rewards rather than as jobs awarded on the basis of personal qualifications for park work. Bryan Lathrop recounted the commissioners' search for a new superintendent for Lincoln Park:

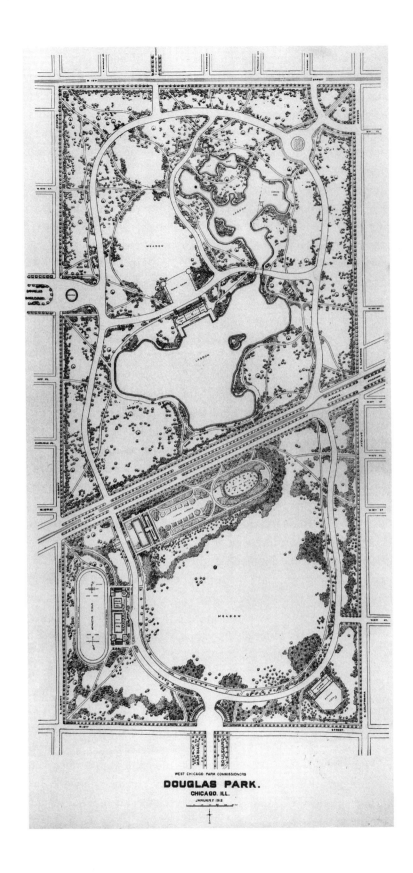

WEST CHICAGO PARK COMMISSIONERS

DOUGLAS PARK.

CHICAGO. ILL.

JANUARY 1912

We were deluged with letters recommending for Superintendent a very estimable gentleman, a retired quarter-master of the United States army, who had every qualification for the office except one: he knew nothing of the making and care of parks. . . . The letters of recommendation came from presidents of railways and of banks, and leading men of affairs and of the learned professions; and in all these letters there was not one word about landscape gardening, or a suggestion that any knowledge of it is a requisite in the management of parks. It was this that surprised and shocked me.[8]

In July 1905, Bernard Eckhart, a well-respected banker and business-man, was appointed commissioner of the West Parks as part of reform efforts there. Eckhart immediately dropped numerous political job holders from the parks payroll and undertook a thorough investigation into the condition of the parks. Within weeks, Eckhart rehired Jensen as "Super-intendent and Landscape Architect" of all the West Parks. During the years of Jensen's absence (1900–1905), the condition of the parks had deteriorated from neglect, and Jensen faced serious problems:

Greenhouses were falling to pieces, their girders and supporters having crumbled into rust. Band stands were toppling on shaky foundations while walks and driveways were filled with ruts and mud holes. Lagoons were eating their way into the banks, and acres of land were without trees or shrubbery. Fountains were out of repair, bridges had rotted until they were dangerous to cross, and the whole system bore evidences of rack and ruin.[9]

In November 1905, voters approved $2 million in bonds for refurbish-ing and extending the parks. Jensen seized this opportunity to experiment further with his own ideas and ideals about park design. Douglas, Gar-field, and Humboldt parks became laboratories for Jensen as he modified the design schemes that Jenney and Dubuis had proposed but that had been only partially implemented. Each of the parks was to have its own special character.

In Douglas Park, Jensen drained part of a shallow pond in the southern portion of the park to create a large meadow. Apparently the pond had been a constant headache to park authorities because insufficient water circulation led to stagnant conditions in the late summer months. Jensen's plan called for the new meadow to be surrounded by "sufficient foliage or woodland plantations . . . to make it picturesque and beautiful." The

---

Figure 20. Douglas Park, 1912. Courtesy of Special Collections, Chicago Park District.

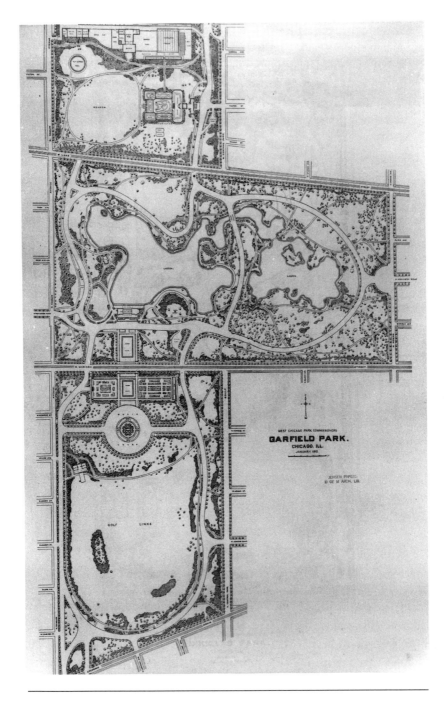

Figure 21. Garfield Park, 1912. Courtesy of Jensen Collection, Art and Architecture Library, University of Michigan, Ann Arbor.

meadow would be used for picnics, ball games, and "for more fully enjoying the flowers, trees, and shrubbery and all of the blessings for which the
parks are created." In addition, a new boat landing and pavilion were
added, as was a music court, with pavilions on either side and views to the
large meadow (Figure 20).[10]

Garfield Park benefited from many similar improvements. In an area
that had once featured bicycle and race tracks, a meadow was created to
make room for newly popular sports such as golf, baseball, and tennis.
New entrances were created at major boulevards, and the general boundaries of the park were planted with shrub and tree masses. A rectilinear
water and music court, with shaded walkways and broad flower gardens,
formed the center of the park (Figure 21).

At this time, each of the parks had its own small conservatory and
greenhouses, and there was interest in consolidating these functions in
one park to reduce what was seen as a needless waste of energy and
manpower. Jensen concurred and proposed a new, central conservatory in
Garfield Park to replace the smaller ones. Although he wanted a building
on a grand scale, he also wanted the conservatory to fit into the midwestern
landscape: "We did not want our greenhouses to look like a palace, a
chateau, or a Renaissance villa, but like a glass house for the cultivation of
plants which everyone might enjoy. In order to fit them into a prairie
landscape I thought they might well take the outlines of the great hay-
stacks which are so eloquent of the richness of prairie soil."[11]

The conservatory, which was designed by Hitchings and Company of
New York City, was completed in 1907. Originally referred to as "Jensen's
folly," the conservatory was the largest of its kind and at times drew
25,000 or more visitors a day. A part of Jensen's intention was to create an
image of the prehistoric prairie landscape; to this end, in creating the
indoor landscape of the conservatory, he adapted principles that he used
outdoors. In many conservatories the center was used for high benches
and the tallest plants, but Jensen kept the centers of the tree fern house and
the palm house open as a "lawn" of *Lycopodium* or as flat bodies of water.
Water was presented as a complete system—spring, cascade, brook, and
lake—and the effect was so "natural" that many people were fooled into
believing the conservatory had been built around existing water courses:

> Thousands of people cross the little brook by stepping stones, gaze into the
> limpid spring, and exclaim, "No wonder the conservatories were placed
> here, so as to take advantage of this lovely spring." They little suspect that
> this is all consummate art, and that a new type of rock work had to be
> invented to replace the absurd grottoes and conventional mountains of
> ordinary greenhouses.[12]

Figure 22. Workers in the fern room at the Garfield Park Conservatory, 1913. Courtesy of Special Collections, Chicago Park District.

Jensen himself liked to tell an anecdote about the construction of the cascade in the fern room in the conservatory (Figure 22):

For the end of the room I designed a prairie rapids and a prairie waterfall. When the workman who was to build the waterfall had finished it, he expected me to praise him, but I shook my head. I said he was thinking of an abrupt mountain cascade, but here on the prairie we must have a fall that tinkled gently as it made its descent. He tried again and again, but every day I said, "No you haven't it yet." Finally he said, "I can't do any better." I made no comment, but asked him if he could play Mendelssohn's Spring Song. He looked at me in a startled way and answered "No." I asked, "Can your wife play it?" "No." "Do you know anyone who can play it for you?" He thought for a moment and then said that they had a friend who was a good pianist. "Well," I said, "you go to her house tonight and ask her to play the Spring Song over and over for you." This is what I heard later. He had gone home that evening and the first thing he said to his wife was "Jensen's gone cracked. He has so much work to do that it has at last affected his head." She asked what made him talk so, and he repeated the conversation. She considered a while, and then she said, "Maybe he meant something by it. Anyway, we'll go over to Minna tonight and ask her to play." So they did, and the friend played the Spring Song for him four times. Then he jumped up exclaiming, "Now I know what Jensen meant." And the next time I came, he stood to one side, smiling proudly. "Ah," I said, "you have heard the Spring Song." And the water tinkled gently from ledge to ledge, as it should in a prairie country.[13]

A number of improvements were also made in Humboldt Park, and it was perhaps here that Jensen most effectively made the design his own. Sixty acres of the western part of the park were still undeveloped, so Jensen had a freer hand (Figure 23). He narrowed the wide lagoon and landscaped its boundaries with appropriate wetland plants resembling the slow-moving streams on the prairie (Figure 24). The source of water for the stream was suggested by a "spring" emanating from a limestone bluff in a wooded grove. In place of the old greenhouses, which were torn down following the construction of the conservatory in Garfield Park, Jensen created a formal rose garden with a simple rectangular pool at its center and elegant concrete pergolas at either end. He found a kindred spirit in the architect Hugh Garden, who designed the graceful refectory, boat landing, and lanterns that adorn the park.[14]

Jensen was quite pleased with the results at Humboldt Park, which he came to think of as a prototypical "American Garden" (Figure 25). As he later remarked to Alfred Caldwell, "The people come out, one man will bring his mother, children will come, families will come, and they walk in the paths of Humboldt Park. That was very beautiful; that was very fine. That was as fine an experience as I have had in my life" (Figure 26). Other designers took note of Jensen's work at Humboldt Park as well. In a 1912 article entitled "Have We Progressed in Gardening?" Wilhelm Miller singled out Jensen's development of the "prairie-river gardens" in Humboldt Park as a major contribution to the rise of a U.S. western tradition in landscape gardening.[15]

While Jensen was working on the large parks, he was also preparing designs for small playgrounds and recreation areas that were to be scattered throughout the West Chicago area. Jensen's schemes for these early playgrounds and recreation sites were similar to facilities being built in other parts of Chicago and throughout the country. Most often these parks took up one or two city blocks and had a field house, separate open-air gymnasiums for men and women, a large central playing field, a children's playground, a swimming pool with associated lockers and showers, and a wading pool. Plantings were limited to trees and shrubs around the border and perennial beds in front of the buildings, but they gave these centers a

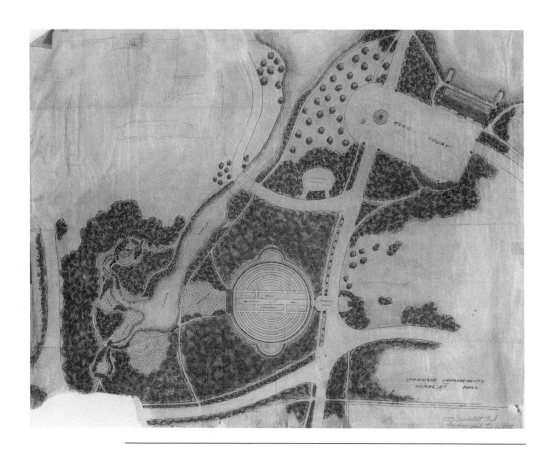

Figure 23. Jensen's "Plan for Proposed Improvements in Humboldt Park" (c. 1907). This plan illustrates Jensen's meshing of formal landscape traditions used in the Music Court and Rose Garden with the Water Garden, or "Prairie River." Courtesy of Special Collections, Chicago Park District.

Figure 24. View of Jensen's "Prairie River" in Humboldt Park. Courtesy of Jensen Collection, Morton Arboretum, Lisle, Illinois.

Figure 25. Entrance to the Rose Garden area of Humboldt Park, showing lanterns as designed by Hugh M. G. Garden. Courtesy of Special Collections, Chicago Park District.

Figure 26. View of Humboldt Park meadow, 1918. Note the irregular grouping of trees, which gives breadth and depth to the meadow view. Courtesy of Special Collections, Chicago Park District.

feeling of home and they softened otherwise hard lines. In Jensen's mind, these small parks were to serve as community centers and as places for active games and physical exercise. As such, their ordered geometry and scale made them fit into the general city fabric.[16]

The large parks, on the other hand, were designed to provide a contrast to the city and to suggest wild nature. For Jensen, the large parks encouraged emotional and spiritual release and served as places in which people could regain contact with the cycles of nature. Emphasis was given to creating large, open spaces that seemed endless; small, intimate spaces in which people could be alone; gathering spaces for conversation and celebration; places where people could watch the sun rise and set; and a general background of plantings that changed dramatically with the seasons. Eventually Jensen found that he could adapt this sense of a "natural park" to smaller park, playground, and school sites. Franklin Park, which Jensen designed in 1916, was a good example of his later thinking, as was Cragin Park, which he developed for the Northwest Park District in 1921.

Jensen also recognized the need for programming to help build an appreciation of the arts and to establish and encourage a sense of community. He noted that the play leaders and directors of these small parks and playgrounds were critical to their success: "He [the play leader or director] must not only be in sympathy with and have full understanding of the work in his care, but should also be closely associated with the community surroundings so as to bring the park and community into harmony. They must provide a home for those who have no real home. They must teach cleanliness and respect for fellow men." With his background in the folk school traditions of Denmark, Jensen was convinced that the outdoor pageants and other celebrations then popular throughout the country were important tools in building a sense of regional heritage and tradition.[17]

The Pageant of the Year and Play Festival, which was held on 5 June 1915 in Garfield Park, is a perfect example of the type of festival that Jensen tried hard to promote (Figure 27). Fourteen hundred children and adults were involved in telling the story of the seasons of the year in costume and dance before an audience of twenty-five to thirty thousand spectators. In their *Annual Report*, Chicago's West Park Commissioners described the pageant vividly:

> First came girls in bright dresses, carrying flowers—they were the garden flowers. Then came other children as butterflies, bees, humming birds and grasshoppers. All danced and skipped merrily about the green, with the light-heartedness of Spring. Liberty and the Thirteen Original States appeared, followed by boys in brown gowns, carrying cherry trees.

Figure 27. Children's pageant in one of Chicago's West Parks. Photograph by Frank A. Waugh, courtesy of Collection of the Department of Landscape Architecture and Regional Planning, University of Massachusetts, Amherst.

Here scarecrows were kept busy driving blackbirds away from the fruit. Birds and insects played among the trees.

The Spirit of Peace ushered in Peace Day, while groups of happy beings followed her. Pretty little girls representing wild flowers added to the scene, all dressed in radiant colors. Late summer flowers were blended into the picture while all the birds, flowers and field insects of summer indulged in a revel. These slowly disappeared and only The Last Rose of Summer remained, to drop her petals over a deserted field.

Autumn was introduced by a flock of small girls, dressed as bluebirds. Apple trees, nut trees, harvesters and ghosts danced about the field in turn. Indian Summer was presented by the wrestling of Hiawatha and Mondamin. A band of Indians followed and danced about fires after having given thanks for the harvest. Winter was next, with snowflakes and snow elves. Winter made way for Father Time and the New Year, attended by little girls representing the twelve months. A confusion of snowbirds, snow men, snowballs, holly and mistletoe romped on.

Snow returned as the dancers departed, only to vanish before the sunshine and wind. Spring came, introduced by Persephone, accompanied by Ceres and her attendants. Arbor Day and St. Patrick's Day entered; April

Figure 28. Fisher Boy Fountain, by Leonard Crunelle, in Humboldt Park.
The sculpture to the left is *Still Hunt,* by Edward Kemeys. Jensen regarded
both of these sculptures as appropriate for a naturalistic setting in a park.
Courtesy of Special Collections, Chicago Park District.

followed, with a thunderstorm and showers. A rainbow led to merrymaking
around a May-pole.

June, with flowers and butterflies, completed the Pageant.[18]

The *Annual Report* went on to comment on the success of the pageant:

This is a remarkable demonstration of the welding together of the distinct
characteristics of the cosmopolitan nature of the West Side population into
a beautiful and harmonious unit, and evidences that America's destiny is,
indeed, to be the Melting Pot of the world, and that opportunity was
afforded for the development and expression of the latent talent of the
children of people gathered from all corners of the globe, shows that these
people enjoy here, as nowhere else, the opportunity of impressing their
lives through works of art and happiness.[19]

Jensen used his connections with members of the art community to
organize art displays in the parks. Because of his concern for what he
considered to be a proliferation of poorly sited and inappropriate sculpture, he sought the help of two of his sculptor friends, Lorado Taft and
Charles Mulligan, as well as the Municipal Art League of Chicago, to
demonstrate how sculpture could be used appropriately in a park setting.

Borrowing pieces of sculpture from the Field Museum of Natural History and from the Columbian Exhibition, he set up the display in Humboldt Park in 1908 and in Garfield Park in 1909. The exhibit consisted of two divisions: a geometrically ordered display arranged in the rose garden of Humboldt Park and later in the Water Court area of Garfield Park, and a loosely arranged display of allegorical sculpture set against the more naturalistic portions of the parks (Figure 28).[20]

Jensen reasoned that "monumental or portrait sculpture fit best in city squares," and he attempted to demonstrate appropriate ways of handling such pieces in the squares and plazas of the parks. Examples used in these formal arrangements included Lorado Taft's monumental statue of George Washington, Daniel C. French's "Statue of the Republic" from the Columbian Exhibition, and Charles J. Mulligan's "Justice and Power" and "Law and Knowledge" from the Illinois state capitol in Springfield. However, Jensen was disturbed by the usual tendency to scatter such monuments throughout the more "sylvan" portions of a park:

> They [the parks] are supposed to be exactly the opposite of what the city represents. Structural work of any kind that has the feeling of intrusion, or disturbing the quiet and peaceful scenic effects, is detrimental to the purpose for which the parks are designed, and, therefore, does not belong to the parks. Sculpture is one of the arts that is used with more or less lavishness for "beautifying" the parks. Indeed, the desire for sculpture in our parks has become so common that pastoral meadows and sylvan dells are intruded upon in the most barbaric manner. No one will doubt that the tender sentiments must be greatly disturbed when one following a pastoral path in a summer night is suddenly presented with the fighting attitude of a war hero.[21]

Jensen believed that pictorial or allegorical sculpture, on the other hand, could fit into the parks at the places where "park and city meet." That kind of sculpture has a "decorative beauty appropriate to its site and surroundings and a meaning in itself that the person of average intelligence can read without the aid of a guide book." According to Lorado Taft, such exhibits were intended to "people our parks, not with long-coated statesmen and restless warriors, but with the figures of airy grace, fit denizens of woods and meadows." Jensen's sculpture exhibition contained numerous examples of how to site such pieces appropriately for the theme of the sculpture and its relationship to the surrounding landscape. These pieces included *Miner and Child*, by Charles Mulligan; *Fisher Boy*, by Leonard Crunelle; *Grief*, by Nellie Walker; and *The Still Hunt*, by Edward Kemeys. Occasionally it was more appropriate to site a piece of portrait sculpture in a naturalistic grouping of trees and shrubs than to position it in a formal court. Such was the case of Charles Mulligan's *Lincoln, the Railsplitter,* which was described as "so natural in his proper environment that one immediately expects to see the historic rails or a cord of wood left by the famous axe."[22]

In 1916, Jensen designed what he regarded as the most successful of his park projects. As he wrote in 1930, "Columbus Park, on the west side of Chicago, is as much an attempt to realize a complete interpretation of the native landscape of Illinois as anything which the author has done." Whereas the other large parks in the West Parks system (Douglas, Garfield, and Humboldt) had originally been designed by Jenney and Dubuis, the 170 acres of Columbus Park provided Jensen with an essentially clean slate, and he relished the opportunity to work with them:

> For years the message of our great prairies had appealed to me. Every leisure moment found me trampling through unspoiled bits of these vast areas. I wanted to understand their force, their enchantment that called on and on. Then came the opportunity to build a large park on the prairies, at the edge of a great metropolis. No one can realize what such an opportunity meant to me at that time in my life.[23]

This square parcel of land, which was known as the "Austin Tract," had been farmed at various times and partially subdivided with trees laid out in gridlike fashion. A portion of the site was already being used informally for golf. The land was flat; its elevation varied by only seven feet across the whole site. The most notable features were a small brook near an old farm site on the north side of the property and a slight depression caused by an ancient beach of prehistoric Lake Chicago running north-south near the eastern edge. To the south were railroads and factories. To the north and east were rapidly expanding Chicago neighborhoods. On the west was the city boundary and the neighboring town of Oak Park.

As happens with many park projects, connecting streets across the park's boundaries became a major issue. West Harrison Street originally bisected the southern part of the Columbus park property, but after two years of negotiation, an agreement was reached that this traffic could be diverted to a route along the park's southern boundary. Jackson Boulevard, a major east-west route near the northern edge of the property, had to transect the park. Jensen curved it gently to the north to serve as a transition between the adjacent neighborhood and the park proper. On the land between Jackson Boulevard and the neighborhood, Jensen sited tennis courts and a quiet lane with a dense planting of native trees and shrubs deliberately chosen to attract wild birds (Figure 29).

The center of the park was kept open to suggest the broad expanse of the prairie. Flatness was regarded as an asset, and hawthorns and other

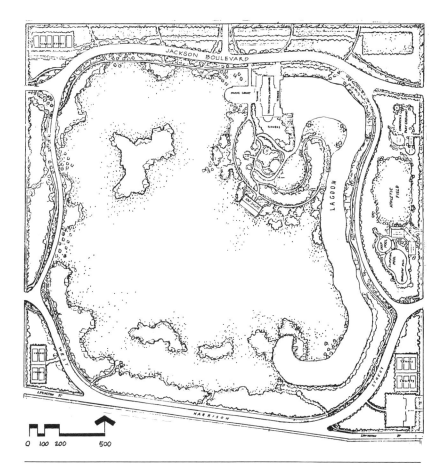

Figure 29. Plan of Columbus Park. Adapted from plan of Columbus Park as published by Jensen in *Siftings* (1939).

horizontally branched trees dotted the wooded perimeter to accentuate the level plain. The large expanse was broken by several irregularly shaped groves of trees so that the boundary would not be completely visible at any point and the space would seem to continue beyond. Although this center space was designed to continue its use as golf course and playing fields, other park users shared in it visually from walkways on the perimeter.

The small brook and ancient-beach depression were shaped and deepened to form a linear lagoon suggestive of a natural "prairie-river." As in the lagoon in Humboldt Park, the shallow borders were planted with "rushes, cat-tails, hibiscus, arrowheads, and water lilies" (Figure 30). In his 1930 article on Columbus Park for *American Landscape Architecture*, Jensen proudly noted that his prairie-river planting had "attracted the great blue heron into the heart of the city." Material excavated from the prairie-river was used to create a slightly elevated area at the river's source, where two springs fed gentle brooks cascading down to the river (Figure 31). Excavated soil was also used to create a slight ridge along the eastern edge of the river to suggest bluffs and to serve as an elevated walkway from which to view the rest of the landscape. From this ridge, Jensen felt that people could watch the drama of the western sky, with its changing patterns over the plain below and its reflection in the waters of the river in the foreground:

> The sky above, with its fleeting clouds and its star-lit heavens, is an indispensable part of the whole. Looking west from the river bluffs at sundown across a quiet bit of meadow, one sees the prairie melt away into the stratified clouds above, touched with gold and purple and reflected in the river below. This gives a feeling of breadth and freedom that only the prairie landscape can give to the human soul. Moonlight nights are equally inspiring and are an important part of the landscape composition. On these occasions, from the prairie and the boat landing may be seen the deep shadows of the river bluffs in contrast with the silvery rays of the poetic moon reflected in the waters.[24]

On the rise between the two brooks that flowed into the lagoon and near the refectory building, Jensen set an outdoor stage, or "players' hill." This, Jensen thought, would be the appropriate setting for outdoor pageants and drama. The audience would sit on the grassy field with the brook between it and the players on the stage area. Performers would use small clearings in the woods as dressing rooms (Figure 32). According to Jensen's plan, the dramas would begin at dusk with the audience facing west. On dark nights, two fires would be lighted at either side of the stage to illuminate the drama. On other nights, the moon rising in the eastern sky would provide adequate lighting (Figure 33).[25]

By the time he designed Columbus Park, Jensen had begun using "council rings" in many of his landscapes. These were low, circular, stone seats set around a council fire, which could be used for storytelling, drama, music, dance, or conversation. Jensen believed that a democratic spirit was created when people came together, all seated on the same level around a central fire pit. For him, this seating arrangement suggested ties with the early pioneers on the wilderness frontiers and with our Amerindian forebears at a council gathering. Two such large rings were planned for Columbus Park, but only one was actually constructed, at the edge of the children's playground, where it was used for storytelling.

The children's playground area in Columbus Park represented a radical shift from the earlier playgrounds developed by Jensen for the West Parks. Gone were the paved courts, rectangular pools, and exercise equipment. Here playground apparatus were provided only for small children; Jensen

Figure 30. Boating scene on lagoon in Columbus Park. Courtesy of David R. Phillips, Chicago Architectural Photographing Company.

Figure 31. Spring in Columbus Park as seen today. The Chicago Park District is currently working on a plan to restore this area of the park. Courtesy of Robert P. Pleva.

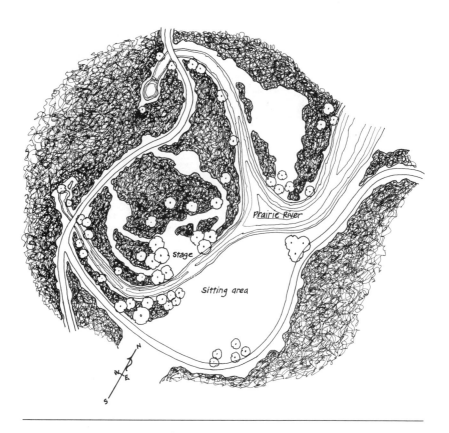

Figure 32. Player's Green area of Columbus Park.

Figure 33. Scene from *A Midsummer Night's Dream*, by William Shake-speare, as performed on the Player's Green of Columbus Park on 30 July 1940. Courtesy of Special Collections, Chicago Park District.

Figure 34. Council ring in children's playground, Columbus Park. Photograph by Frank A. Waugh, courtesy of Collection of the Department of Landscape Architecture and Regional Planning, University of Massachusetts, Amherst.

was more concerned with providing a setting that would stimulate the imagination and provide opportunities for creative play. He was dismayed that so few children in Chicago were able to visit truly wild settings in the countryside, and he was determined to provide at least the image of wild nature for city children to enjoy (Figure 34).[26]

The pool, or "swimming hole," was an attempt to create a rustic swimming pool on a municipal scale similar to those Jensen had created on private estates:

> This is the simple reasoning behind Mr. Jensen's successful attempt to create for the thousands of Chicago children who have never hung their "clothes on a hickory limb," the environment of a real swimming hole. He knows that it is impossible to take many of these children to the country for even a short visit, and that most of them will never know at all the ooze of clean mud between their toes, the splash of a fat bullfrog startled from his shelter under a fern frond, the lazy arms of willow dipping down into the water. "We must bring the country in to them, then," says Mr. Jensen; "instead of a concrete bathtub set in a glare of gravel, we must give them a bit of real woodland—a rocky pool shut in from tall smokestacks and trolley cars by elms and maples; screened around with river alder and dewberry and dogwood; with ferns down to the water's edge, and wild grapevines sprawling over the rocky ledges; and we will make the pool safe

Figure 35. Children's swimming pool in Columbus Park. From Dean 1922.

and sanitary as well, with ladders into the water, a life rail around the edge, easy drainage and a large-volume supply, so that our health cranks may not complain that it is dangerous and unwholesome."[27]

There were two pools in the swimming complex: one, 7–8 feet in depth and 90 feet in diameter, for older children, and a shallow pool 4½ feet deep, 220 feet long, and 60–130 feet wide (Figure 35). Jensen estimated that these two pools could accommodate seven thousand youngsters a day. The pools were set 7–8 feet below the grade of the roadways at the edge of the park and were surrounded by walls of stratified limestone to simulate the river canyons of Illinois. The rock crevices were heavily planted with native shrubs, vines, and ferns; the pools appeared to be fed by a small waterfall that emptied into the larger pool. Another, much smaller wading pool was set at the edge of the playground area and backed by a variety of native plants. Special attention was given to plants that attracted birds, and birdhouses were set at various places around the pools and playground areas. Jensen wanted these plantings and the birds they attracted to provide urban children with an important lesson in natural history.[28]

Columbus Park was the last major park designed by Jensen for the city of Chicago. He did, however, continue to serve as consulting landscape architect to Chicago's West Park Commission until the early 1920s. In 1917, Jensen was asked to prepare a study for the expansion of the park system. The report, known as *A Greater West Park System*, provides perhaps the clearest picture of Jensen's maturing ideas on the relationship of parks, recreation, and the general fabric of the city. For more than a year Jensen conducted field inventory and survey work and prepared a comprehensive set of recommendations illustrated with photographs, drawings, and elaborate plans; he presented the report to the board in December 1918, and it was published in 1920.[29]

For more than two decades, Jensen had been studying the Chicago region and thinking about the need for additional parklands and the preservation of wild areas. In his Special Park Commission work from 1899 to 1904, Jensen had helped survey potential parklands and natural areas for preservation on a regional scale. Then, with Dwight Perkins and other members of the Prairie Club, he had fought vigorously to establish the Forest Preserve System as a network of wild green spaces throughout the metropolitan area. When he began work on the Greater West Park System study, he recognized the crucial need to integrate a more intricate network of gardens and park spaces throughout the city in close relationship to homes, schools, and workplaces.

Jensen's thinking on city-planning issues was undoubtedly influenced by his association with other members of the Chicago City Club. In 1911, as chairman of the club's Committee on City Planning, Jensen published an article entitled "Regulating City Building." He noted that the city of broad promenades and boulevards, as promoted by Burnham and Bennett, was merely a commercial venture and created an illusion of grandeur that was not at all in keeping with the nation's democratic ideals:

> On the face of it, this idea of city planning is a fine thing—broad boulevards, ornate arches, formal promenades, all give one a feeling of excitement, as of being dressed in one's best clothes for some festive occasion. But right here is one of the most salient evils of such a city. It is too often a show city; it is at once the city of palaces and of box-like houses where humanity is packed together like cattle in railroad cars. To build civic centers and magnificent boulevards, leaving the greatest part of the city in filth and squalor, is to tell an untruth, to put on a false front, which vitiates the whole atmosphere of the town. The formal show environment reacts upon the people: the spirit of being on parade, of striving for superficialities, makes of them a city of spendthrifts desirous of a gay life.

Jensen warned against cities' being swept away with grand and glorious plans on paper and the "temporary enthusiasms" for such plans "which sweep the country like prairie winds and leave no permanent effect."

Leonard Eaton, Jensen's biographer, has noted that Burnham and Bennett's plan was much more geometric and arbitrary compared with Jensen's plan, which was fitted to the physical landscape and social fabric of the city. Jensen's aim was "to bring the out-of-doors within reach of the masses of working people on the West Side," while "Burnham wanted to satisfy the affluent membership of the Commercial Club."[30]

The study Jensen prepared for the expansion of the West Park System gave him a chance to demonstrate just how his ideas on city planning could become reality. Noting that Chicago's population, like that of so many other cities, continued to shift westward, Jensen suggested that the West Parks join together with the park boards of Oak Park, Berwyn, and the other small communities west of the city to form a consolidated park board. This metropolitan board could plan in advance for park expansion on a regional scale. At the time of Jensen's study, the heavy use of existing parks made them extremely difficult to maintain; as a result, Jensen called for the creation of a network of parks and open spaces to provide for the growing population's recreational needs. The existing forest preserves could not meet the need for active recreation without destroying their very fabric, and they were also too far removed from people's homes to offer the kind of release from the pressures of city life that Jensen envisioned.

Jensen's plan (Figure 36) called for the creation of a network of pleasure drives and boulevards connecting the parks, a canal for boating to connect the Chicago and Des Plaines rivers, several new large parks, municipal "kitchen" gardens throughout the area (in which people might be able to raise some of their own food), neighborhood cultural centers and playgrounds at school sites, and an agricultural college and art school. The plan contained an in-depth analysis of lands then available and demonstrated how they could best be fitted into an overall system. Jensen suggested that particular attention be given to preserving lands of historical significance, especially around early Indian encampments or travel routes and pioneer settlements. Such lands, he argued, would "add a new sentiment to the parks, and the preservation of memorable spots in our early history will be made secure. The history of the past will be linked up with that of today, and interest in the old history of our region is bound to grow as the distance from those days becomes greater."[31]

Jensen also stressed the importance of considering soil and other ecological conditions when selecting parklands. He noted that most of the prairie land in the Chicago region, such as that found in Douglas and Garfield parks, was characterized by heavy clay soils that made growing trees difficult and park maintenance extremely expensive. In contrast, the gravelly soils of the ancient-beach area were more suitable for tree growth and park forestation. One of Jensen's maps in *A Greater West Park System*

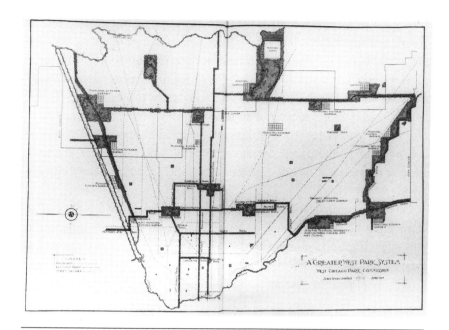

Figure 36. Jensen's plan for a Greater West Park System (1918) as published in Jensen 1920.

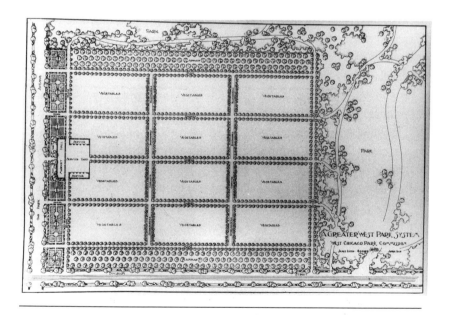

Figure 37. Municipal Kitchen Garden plan (1918), as published in Jensen 1920. These gardens were to be established throughout Chicago's West Side, and produce from them was to be sold to the public in the Market Hall shown on the plan.

shows the relationship of park sites to these geologic formations. Jensen also recommended that first-rate remnant forests or formerly forested areas that could be restored be given priority for preservation and development as parklands. In contrast, areas suggested for his "prairie drives" would preserve native stands of prairie wildflowers such as blazing star (*Liatris pycnostachya*). The sectional plan for one of the proposed prairie drives illustrates some of Jensen's thinking about an ideal integration of homes and parklike open spaces. Stores, apartments, and houses are carefully sited at the edge of meadow spaces along the proposed gently curving drive.

One of the more intriguing aspects of Jensen's plan was his desire that "municipal kitchen gardens" be located throughout the city adjacent to park sites (Figure 37). These gardens were to serve a number of purposes. First of all, they would allow people to grow some of their own food directly or at least to gain an understanding of where food comes from:

> I believe the city should own tracts of land for the growing of vegetables and fruits, where the citizens can see and understand that their real existence comes out of Mother Earth, and that the merchant or peddler is only a means of delivery. They should know that they owe their real livelihood to the man of the soil.[32]

Jensen was a firm agrarian in his belief that direct contact with the soil through gardening promoted better citizenship and provided a diversion to factory work. Gardens helped preserve some of the agricultural heritage of the land as it became woven into the fabric of the city. They would also be developed in conjunction with the establishment of agricultural colleges and would serve as demonstration areas for experimental plantings. As promoted by Jensen, the prototypical agricultural college was a direct outgrowth of his experience with the agricultural schools in Denmark and thus included not only technical training in agriculture but also programs in the arts and humanities. For him, it was natural to combine an art school with an agricultural college. The combination of agriculture and culture was not merely training for a vocation in farming; it was training for life in general.

At the heart of Jensen's plan for an expanded West Park System was his concept of the neighborhood center. As he had urged in his 1911 article "Regulating City Building," such neighborhood centers should be developed around schools. Jensen cited the proposed Lloyd and Logan schools as examples (Figure 38). In both cases, Jensen intended to provide a school building and grounds that would stir a child's imagination and serve as a cultural and recreational center for young and old alike:

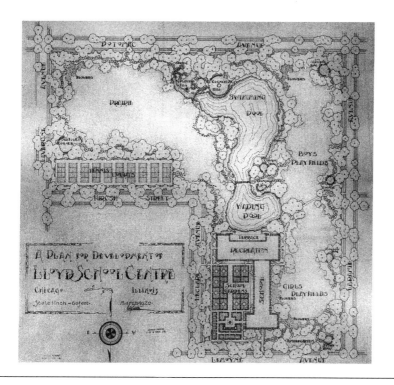

Figure 38. Jensen's plan for the Lloyd School Centre (1920). This plan was the prototype for Jensen's ideas on developing school grounds. Courtesy of Jensen Collection, Art and Architecture Library, University of Michigan, Ann Arbor.

Modern school buildings of factory-like resemblance are cold and barren. They lack soul and create a feeling of indifference in the mind of the child. There is nothing to attract the imagination; nothing to arouse tender feelings. They are factories indeed, and it may be said that stepping from school to most factories is not a startling change. The school must be in accordance with the home or its usefulness will be counteracted. The spirit of the neighborhood center group would be to create a love for the home, to stimulate a desire for beautiful home environs, to discourage tenement and apartment-house living. Gardens create a love for the soil in the minds of the children, that will develop into a desire for better, cleaner, and healthier homes in the mind of an adult. They appeal to the finer feelings of mankind and elevate the depressed in soul and mind to a higher place in the human family and to a greater appreciation of the responsibilities of free-born men and women.[33]

The grounds of these centers were to include school gardens, playing fields, naturalistic swimming pools, tennis courts, council rings, a players' hill area, and, as Jensen called it, an old folks' corner. Plantings of native

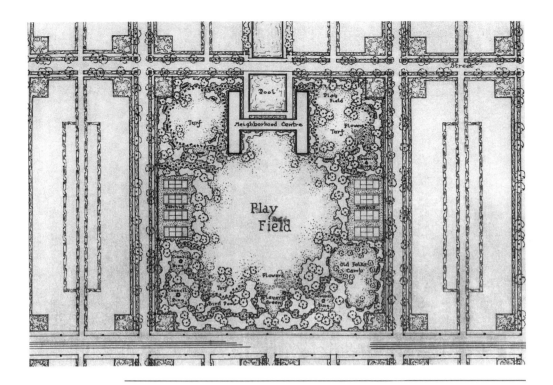

Figure 39. Design for a neighborhood center and playing field from Jensen 1918. This plan illustrates Jensen's thinking on how to fit small parks into the existing grid of the city. Courtesy of Jensen Collection, Art and Architecture Library, University of Michigan, Ann Arbor.

trees and shrubs were to abound, and particular attention was to be given to plants that attract varieties of birds and other wildlife:

> Here [at the Lloyd Center] are found story rings and council rings for outdoor study and pleasure, a players' hill for dramatic art and music, old folks' corner, and a lane through the woodland border; a council hill for gatherings of young and old, where the local poet or dramatist may inspire the community with song and poetry, or the philosopher give his ideas on the philosophy of life. There are bird pools, bird houses, and feeding stations.
>
> The playgrounds consist of a section covered with a sandy loam and parts turfed, especially against the buildings and in such parts of the playgrounds where it adds to the landscape design. There are colonies of flowers, and, as in the Logan Center, the vegetation is native and attractive to our birds.[34]

Jensen's "Plan for a Quarter Section" illustrates how such centers might be integrated into a conventional gridiron section of the city with careful attention to plantings and landscaped squares at every corner (Figure 39). Jensen's ideas on this subject may well have been shaped by the Chicago City Club's competition entitled "City Residential Land Development" (1916), in which he had been a jury member. Several of Jensen's associates from Steinway Hall submitted entries, including Charles A. Tirrell, a landscape architect who had worked in Jensen's office, and architects Irving K. Pond and Walter Burley Griffin. George C. Cone, from O. C. Simonds' office, submitted an entry, and Frank Lloyd Wright prepared a noncompetitive entry. Jensen's own noncompetitive entry in the 1919 City Club competition for the "Design for a Neighborhood Center" was another demonstration of how open spaces, residences, and commercial businesses could be integrated into a city's fabric. Once again he emphasized the school as the neighborhood center and set aside special areas for senior citizens, gardens, swimming, and outdoor theater.[35]

To Jensen, parks were essential to the health and welfare of people in the city, and he was determined that they be preserved as refuges for city residents:

> Parks are a necessity for the cultivating and preserving of a love for nature. They are the seats of learning for the average city-bred being, and their influence is plainly visible in shaded streets and pretty home surroundings. Parks are practical schools of horticulture and the bone and sinew of art out-of-doors. They are necessary for the self-preservation of those who by free will or through forced circumstances have made their homes in a large city.

In Jensen's mind, congested and polluted city conditions were the root failures of American urban society and forced an alienation from the natural environment which would eventually lead to the nation's undoing. His plan for the expansion of Chicago's West Parks was also his suggestion for an alternative urban future:

> Altogether we see in this park plan a more beautiful city; a city whose buildings are interspersed with growing things—trees, shrubs, and flowers—and whose streets are broken by playgrounds and broad stretches of woodlands and meadows; a city that is a fairer world for the city dweller to live in. New interests will be added to his life and his vision will be broadened and extended beyond the narrow confines of his city walls. Sunshine will no longer be at a premium, and sound bodies and happy minds will be a consequence. The cost can never be too great. We have no right to consider ourselves civilized as long as we permit less fortunate residents of our city to live and multiply in unhealthy surroundings that are devoid of beauty and that are a peril to the whole population, and a menace

to the normal development of our civilization. There are those among us for whom the rural influences in the city complex are essential to their very existence. This is well to keep in mind in our future city building, if we desire to prevent from degeneration and eventual extermination some of the sturdiest and noble peoples who have come to our shore.

Unsatisfactory city conditions drive the more fortunate in worldly goods to the building of suburban communities. This is a distinct loss to the city. Usually, men and women of great worth are amongst those who migrate to the suburbs. Those who need to remain in the struggle [of living in the city] . . . are confronted with the needs and wants of the city every day of their life, and thus are [the ones] better fitted to lend their effort and influence to improve the physical and moral life of the city. The average suburban town or village does not present the normal life which is found in a self-sustaining community. Consequently [it] has not the problems of the latter. It is a poor city that drives its people away, and into the suburbs. Both the urbanite and suburbanite suffer by this transaction. To make the modern city livable is the task of our times. If this plan as presented here can help to make life better and more beautiful, it serves its purpose well.[36]

Few of Chicago's West Park Commissioners in 1920 shared Jensen's vision, and consequently few of Jensen's ideas in *A Greater West Park System* were ever implemented. The document does provide, however, the clearest picture of Jensen's theory of urban design and the role of open spaces in a city. Soon after Jensen completed this study, he retired from the Chicago parks, working only on an occasional small park thereafter (Cragin Park, for example, in 1921). He continued to believe that the integrated network of open spaces he had proposed in *A Greater West Park System* was necessary for the continued health and livability of the city, but he was physically tired from the nearly constant political battles he had fought with the park commissioners for almost three decades. His work with the Chicago parks had firmly secured his reputation as a maker of natural parks and gardens, and he now threw his energies into the projects of his design office and his ever-broadening conservation concerns.

Residential Design Work

During the early 1900s, when Jensen was building his reputation as a park designer, he was also becoming one of the most popular designers of estates among the wealthy elite in the Chicago area and the Midwest. He is known primarily for his large commissions, but his practice embraced projects that ranged in size from an acre or less to hundreds of acres. Some of his work was recorded on elaborate plans; in other instances, he gave advice informally, especially to neighbors around his studio in Ravinia or his home in Wilmette. What interested Jensen the most was not the plan scribbled on paper but the composition of the living garden. As in his park work, his design of residential gardens evolved from the tentative gardenesque forms of his early work to the confident spaces and subtle complexities of his mature style. For a recent immigrant without much money and without professional credentials, attracting clients would have been a major problem in building a career as an estate designer. For Jensen, the contacts for these clients came through his ever-broadening network of friends and acquaintances.

The 1890s were an active period in Chicago's social and environmental reform movements, and Jensen was at the heart of many of these groups. For someone with Jensen's idealism, energy, and zeal, these social efforts were more interesting than a career devoted solely to designing gardens for the wealthy. One such group centered on Jane Addams and her work at Hull-House. Like other settlement houses, Hull-House "was a crossroads where social workers, writers, architects, civic-minded citizens, and scientists met to share their interests." Jensen was also a member of the "Committee on the Universe," a group of people who met informally at architect Dwight Perkins' house for Sunday evening dinners. In 1898, the Geographic Society of Chicago was organized to promote inquiries and stimulate interest in the geography of the Chicago region. Again, Jensen became a charter member.[37]

These activities provided Jensen with a variety of intellectual stimuli and an outlet for his energy and inquisitiveness. They also helped him build friendships among the influential and wealthy elite of Chicago, many of whom shared his social and environmental concerns. When, in the midst of heated political squabbles, Jensen found himself out of a job with Chicago's West Park District, these friends gave him contacts for stabler work designing summer homes and country estates. Among the early jobs obtained in this way were the Uihlein property in Lake Geneva, Wisconsin, and the Herman Paepcke property in Glencoe, Illinois, both of which were begun in 1901; the I. B. Grommes property in Lake Geneva, the George W. Maher house in Kenilworth, Illinois, and the Harry Rubens place in Glencoe, Illinois, during 1902 and 1903; and the August Magnus house in Winnetka, Illinois, in 1905.

Working on these projects at his kitchen table, Jensen experimented with a variety of design ideas. Some he would drop in later years; others he would refine and adopt as trademarks. The earlier designs relied more on traditional garden species, while the later plans showed a much greater understanding and use of native plant species as they are found in the wild. As Jensen remembered,

There were two reasons why I turned away from the formal design that employed foreign plants. The first reason was an increasing dissatisfaction with both the plants and the unyielding design—I suppose dissatisfaction with things as they are is always the fundamental cause of revolt—and the second was that I was becoming more and more appreciative of the beauty and decorative quality of the native flora of this country.[38]

Of course, Jensen did not completely abandon formal geometry in his work. He had too many clients who wanted gardens with areas for cut flowers, roses, vegetables, and other features that were best served by a regular geometry. In Jensen's plans, however, these areas increasingly took on a less dominant role in the overall design, and a clear distinction was drawn between the naturalistic landscape and the highly maintained vege-table or rose garden. There were also a few exotic plants that Jensen continued to use throughout his career—most notably, lilacs, hollyhocks, and daylilies. Jensen justified their use because each had such a long association with human settlement, following the "white man like the sparrow and the dog"; in the early years of his career, he placed them in areas close to the house, but occasionally elsewhere as well. In his later designs, such plants were not found in the outlying landscape.[39]

Of particular interest among Jensen's early estate designs is that for the Harry Rubens estate in Glencoe, Illinois, which he included in his 1906 article, "Landscape Art." Jensen published very few of his estate designs himself, but Wilhelm Miller and Frank Waugh frequently used photo-graphs of his work in their publications. Jensen was obviously proud of the Rubens estate, for he used pictures from its gardens and referred to it often in his writing. In his design for the estate, both philosophically and technically, he set in motion themes that would run throughout his career (Figures 40–41). In *Siftings*, although he does not mention the estate by name, it is likely Jensen was referring to the Rubens property when he gave this description of his search for design forms:

> Definite forms were slowly developing, and in the early part of this century they came to fruition on a private estate a little beyond the city. Hawthorns were planted so as to spread over the lawn in their joyous way, as it were. The western crabapple, always colorful and picturesque whether in bloom or bare in winter, was also used to give color to the forest border and to give joyous greeting in May. Here was used, for the first time, the stratified rock underlying our great prairie country, with its quiet and restful picturesque-ness, just like the prairie itself. Other things, which had been given years of thought, as, for instance, the lawn or meadow towards the sunset and the pool with its background of dark cedars in the path of the moon, took actual form. Trees of brilliant colors in the fall landscape were planted in the path of the afterglow so as to receive its full illumination. Plants characteristic of

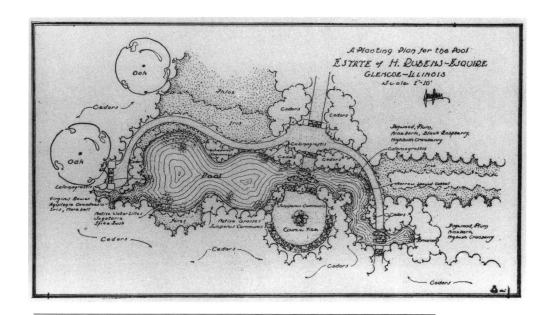

Figure 40. Plan for the pool area of the Harry Rubens estate in Glencoe, Illinois, as published in Dean 1917.

Figure 41. Wetland plantings around the pool area, Harry Rubens estate. Photograph by Frank A. Waugh, courtesy of Collection of the Department of Landscape Architecture and Regional Planning, University of Massachusetts, Amherst.

our lowlands and flowers from the prairies were also included in the plan in the same fitting way. Nor were the birds forgotten. There was another influence that became quite noticeable in the distribution of certain plants in this plan, and that was the "Unfinished Symphony" by Schubert. But with this good beginning, there were still notes of discord which it took years to eliminate.[40]

The illustrations used in Jensen's article "Landscape Art" show quiet gardens of native flowers, pools, beckoning paths, open meadow spaces, shady retreats, and campfires, all of which became Jensen trademarks. Jensen expressed enchantment with sunlight and shadows in a passage describing the emotional effects of moving from the depths of shade into a sunny clearing: "Nothing is so fascinating as the light behind the immedi-ate shade: the lining to the cloud: to some, the hope beyond, which may be the greatest part of life itself; with its allurement of mystery, its enticement for reaching the goal beyond, yet withal, the futility of the effort, the inborn, onward striving of the soul toward the unattainable." He also noted that the "afterglow of the setting sun . . . produces one of the grandest panoramas of our prairie landscape." Later, many of Jensen's designs included a designated "path to the setting sun." At the Rubens estate, Jensen also placed a campfire within a semicircular seat: an early precursor of his council rings.[41]

In 1912, Wilhelm Miller expressed a fascination with the Rubens estate in an article in *Country Life in America*. He was particularly inter-ested in how Jensen created a "prairie-river" out of a "little brook and a mud hole":

> The sheet of water is only 100 feet long and about 30 feet wide at most. But there is a complete water system—spring, brook, cascade, and lake. The rocks are not meaningless piles of brightly colored stones; they are strat-ified, like the St. Peter's sandstone which is the characteristic rock of prairie-rivers. The water lilies are not the kinds that you see in every tub and marble basin the world over; they are the wild white lily of the prairie lakes. And the flowers that fringe the margins of the water are not the bedding plants of every public park, but the flowers that actually grow beside the prairie-rivers.[42]

Gradually, Jensen expanded his private design practice. He developed friendships with many of the Chicago architects who were then experi-menting with the prairie style of design, and he collaborated with many of them on projects (see Chapter 2 and the Appendix). He was particularly drawn to Louis Sullivan, who became something of a mentor. Later, Jensen would describe Sullivan as "the great architect whose forms were inspired by the horizontal lines of the plains and whose decorative art grew out of his love for the native prairie thistle, a plant full of poetry and beauty."[43]

Despite Jensen's close association with these architects, he often battled with them over the relationship between building and garden. At the Harley Clarke property in Evanston, Illinois, Jensen deliberately concealed the house with trees. He told Alfred Caldwell, who was serving as foreman on the project: "It's arrogant. Cover it with trees; it becomes tame. We could live with it." Like many great artists, Jensen was a strong individual with definite ideas, and he found it difficult to conform to the work of another designer.[44]

In general, Jensen strove for a distinct contrast between building forms and the lines of the garden. He used few geometric lines in the landscape except for small, specialized gardens. Wherever possible, he chose to give a completely naturalistic setting to homes rather than blend the two by carrying the lines of the house into the landscape (Figure 42). As landscape design critic Catherine Howett observed of Jensen's design for the Henry Babson estate in Riverside: "The Babson house landscape was deliberately casual and soft edged; the reflection of the house in the pool seemed almost accidental; stepping from the formal porch onto the lawn must have been experienced as a passage into a serene natural landscape."[45]

In 1909, Jensen changed his position with the West Parks from Superintendent and Landscape Architect to Consulting Landscape Architect. While this change may have been precipitated by shifting political power in the parks, the result was that it allowed Jensen to devote more energy to other projects, especially his growing estate work, most of which was done between 1910 and 1930. Shortly after 1910, he designed an estate for Sears and Roebuck founder Julius Rosenwald on the beautiful ravines of Highland Park, Illinois, overlooking Lake Michigan. Jensen's design called for minimal disruption of the ravine, and Rosenwald initially balked at the $1,000 fee for what appeared to be so little work. Jensen responded that lesser men would have charged more to ruin the lovely site. Rosenwald was an important client for Jensen both personally and professionally. Through Rosenwald, Jensen became known among many of the wealthy who were developing estates on the North Shore of Chicago, and his work soon became a measure of status. Many of these patrons cared little about Jensen's philosophy or design ideas; they were mainly interested in his name.[46]

Jensen deeply appreciated those clients who took an honest interest in his work: "Clients are of all sorts. Those with a real understanding of landscaping are the very, very few. Some know too much or have an idea they do, and they are better off left alone. Then there are those who want a

Figure 42. The bird garden designed by Jensen for Julius Rosenwald some-time prior to 1910 in the Hyde Park area of Chicago. Photograph by Henry Fuermann and Son, from W. Miller 1914a.

garden because their neighbor has one, and I am afraid these are in the majority. But there are the few who have a real love for growing things. I have been fortunate in having some of the latter." Rosenwald and his wife seem to have been this last type of client for Jensen. The Rosenwalds never lost touch with their modest beginnings and lent financial support to many of Jensen's endeavors, such as his battle to save the Indiana Dunes (now the site of a state park and national lakeshore). Both Rosenwalds were also charter members of the Friends of Our Native Landscape. Mrs. Rosen-wald served as the group's first vice-president, and after her death, Jensen designed a memorial to her in Highland Park, Illinois.[47]

In 1915, Jensen began one of his stormiest but most important relation-ships with a client, the Ford family. At the time, Henry Ford was building a house on 2,000–3,000 acres in Dearborn, Michigan, along the Rouge River. As the foundation of the house was being roughed in, Ford was concerned that the grades around the house made it look as if it were sliding down the hill. The original architectural firm, von Holst and Fyfe, was from Chicago and knew of Jensen's work, and von Holst recom-mended Jensen to Ford to solve the grading problem around the house. Jensen agreed to examine the site, and upon inspecting it immediately suggested minor grading changes that would make the house appear level.

Figure 43. Dam and associated rockwork along the Rouge River at Fair Lane, the Henry Ford estate in Dearborn, Michigan.

Ford, who was also interested in establishing appropriate gardens to go with the house, then approached Jensen to see if he would be willing to undertake the job. At first Jensen refused, foreseeing that many disagreements would probably arise between Ford and himself. In the end, however, Ford prevailed, and Jensen worked for the Fords to "put the land back to what it was when the American Indians skied down the banks of the River Rouge."[48]

Jensen seemed to share many interests and ideals with Henry Ford, not the least of which was a notion about self-sufficiency and keeping one's roots in the soil. As part of the estate, Ford wanted to establish a hydroelectric generating plant on the Rouge River. Jensen sited the dam so carefully into the river's landscape that it appeared to be a natural rapids. Today, the rockwork along the river is still a spectacular example of creating a wild but accessible river's edge (Figure 43). The estate also contained a working farm, orchards, and a mosaic of open fields and meadows. Apparently both Henry and Clara Ford were avid bird watchers, and the wild shrubs and trees used by Jensen provided excellent food and nesting habitats.[49]

The "Great Meadow" at the Ford house leads out from the terrace with a slight bend in its length. At the far end of the meadow is a small pond with a cluster of white birches on the edge of the woods on the opposite shore. The meadow is set at such an axis that during the summer the early morning sun softly highlights these trees, while the evening sun sets at the end of the meadow. Across the river from the house, another open meadow originally provided a sight line to the setting sun on winter evenings.[50]

Jensen's chief difficulty at Fair Lane was with Clara Ford, Henry's wife, who had conflicting ideas about the type of gardens she wanted. While Jensen tried to accommodate his clients' wants and needs in his designs, he insisted that his creations were works of art that could not be altered in small parts without changing the character of the whole. Clara Ford, on the other hand, wanted a garden in which she could experiment with a variety of garden flowers and garden styles then in vogue. She once commented to Genevieve Gillette that Jensen had not really created the kind of garden she wanted. So, when Jensen would not make certain changes for her, she hired other landscape architects to do the work. The breaking point was a formal rose garden, which she had placed in the middle of one of the meadow spaces. It was not so much that Jensen objected to formal rose gardens; at Fair Lane as well as many other places, he included small formal gardens near the house if that was the client's wish. What Jensen disliked about the particular placement of the rose garden on the Ford property was its lack of continuity with the overall design. He also vehemently objected to another landscape architect's intrusion in what he saw as his personal client relationship, and he quit the American Society of Landscape Architects when that organization refused to reprimand the designer who Jensen felt was acting unethically.[51]

After the conflict over the rose garden, Jensen's work at Fair Lane ceased. He did, however, continue to work for the Fords and the Ford Motor Company over a period of about twenty years in various other capacities. He designed the grounds of the Henry Ford Hospital in Detroit, Michigan, the grounds of numerous Ford office buildings and plants in Ohio and Michigan, and in Dearborn, Michigan, he worked on Greenfield Village, the Dearborn Inn, the Rotunda, and the "Roads of the World" exhibit. Jensen designed the properties of several Ford executives, notably the Dahlinger Farm in Romeo, Michigan, Ernest C. Kanzler's homes in Detroit and Grosse Pointe Shores, Michigan, and A. J. Lepine's home in Dearborn, Michigan. Edsel and Eleanor Ford hired Jensen to design four homes for them between 1922 and 1935—three in Michigan and a summer home in Seal Harbor, Maine. In many ways, Edsel and Eleanor Ford proved to be ideal clients for Jensen. They had no desire for an ostentatious display of wealth, wanting instead the quiet quality that was Jensen's trademark. Ultimately, their Gaukler Pointe home in Grosse Pointe Shores, Michigan, became the most extensive and expensive of any of Jensen's residential designs.[52]

By the time of the Great Depression in the 1930s, most of Jensen's estate work had dried up, as was the case with most other landscape architects. Jensen still had an occasional residential job, but not on the same scale as his earlier work; people could no longer afford the laborers needed to keep up places of such scale. Jensen had always felt a certain ambivalence toward building estates for the wealthy. He justified the work by believing he was adding something beautiful to these people's lives. While these jobs were the mainstay of his private practice, Jensen felt that it was "a great loss or tragedy that I am always doing these estates for these rich. . . . I shouldn't be doing these places. I should be doing great regional parks. That is what I love. That is what I wanted to do. That is the meaning of my life."[53]

Public and Institutional Work

Jensen's public design work was not limited to Chicago parks or to the Illinois area. Much like his residential commissions, his public and institutional projects covered a wide range of project types and were spread across the Midwest and the United States as a whole. The record of these works is rather limited, however. Jensen took many of his office records with him to The Clearing, in Ellison Bay, Wisconsin, when he retired in 1935, and most of these were lost in the fire there in 1937. There is enough of a record, however, to construct an image of the range and types of projects in this category and to gain insights into Jensen's personal interests and values.[54]

The public and institutional projects selected for discussion in this section fall into four distinct categories: hospitals, roads, memorials, and schools. The St. Ann's Hospital project in Chicago, done sometime prior to 1901, is one of the earliest of Jensen's public designs and one of the few he chose to publish. It set the tone for other hospital and sanatorium projects he would design, and it includes features he would eventually refine as part of his mature design style.

Jensen's design for the "ideal section" of the Lincoln Highway is important for several reasons. Although Jensen had serious misgivings about the increasing popularity of and reliance upon the automobile, his involvement with this project demonstrated his interest in finding ways to make "motoring" a force for saving and restoring the nation's roadside landscapes. In this design, he attempted to develop a prototypical approach that could be adapted to other portions of both the Lincoln Highway and other roadways across the United States. The mere fact that he was selected as landscape architect for such a monumental project also demonstrates the respect given him as a designer.

The Shakespeare Garden at Northwestern University in Evanston, Illinois, and Lincoln Memorial Garden in Springfield, Illinois, are examples of the type of memorials designed by Jensen. They are different in scale and style, but both demonstrate Jensen's approach to preserving the memory of an individual for future generations. The Shakespeare Garden, which was built in 1916, at the midpoint of Jensen's career, reflects his views of an appropriate American garden for the great English poet and playwright. In contrast, Lincoln Memorial Garden, which was begun in 1935, represents Jensen's mature thinking about landscape design. It also allowed Jensen to explore his ideas about commemorating an American folk hero who had sprung from the midwestern landscape.

In sum, St. Ann's Hospital, the "ideal section" of Lincoln Highway, the Shakespeare Garden, and Lincoln Memorial Garden represent the full spectrum of Jensen's public design work and illustrate the values that were so important to him as a landscape designer.

ST. ANN'S HOSPITAL, CHICAGO, ILLINOIS

One of the earliest and more interesting examples of Jensen's public design projects was his design for the grounds of St. Ann's Hospital in Chicago (Figure 44). The only record of the project is a short article by Jensen in *Park and Cemetery* in 1901. The building, which was designed by Hugh M. G. Garden, still stands, but a few trees are the only signs of Jensen's landscaping. St. Ann's was a sanatorium for patients with tuberculosis, and Jensen believed that gardens and a parklike landscape should be integral parts of the healing process. The treatment for tuberculosis at this time included generous amounts of outdoor exercise, and in Jensen's view the developed gardens would add to the desirability of the hospital as a treatment center.[55]

Jensen's scheme had three main parts. The southeast corner of the property was planned as "a miniature park, with plenty of walks, pretty scenery, abundance of sunlight and sheltered to the north by [an] evergreen plantation, which in return will have a healthy influence upon the sick, make the garden useful in bright winter weather, and give character to the winter landscape." Curving walks and a central lagoon clearly repeated the pastoral pattern of "scenery" which Olmsted and his associates thought to be "healing" to both mind and body. Rooms in the hospital were situated to receive as much sun as possible and to offer full views of the garden.

The northwest corner of the grounds contained a flower garden, a large lawn for "kindred games," and a spiral maze of walks for exercise. Jensen dotted the lawn with specimen exotic trees, probably intending that the site become somewhat of an arboretum.

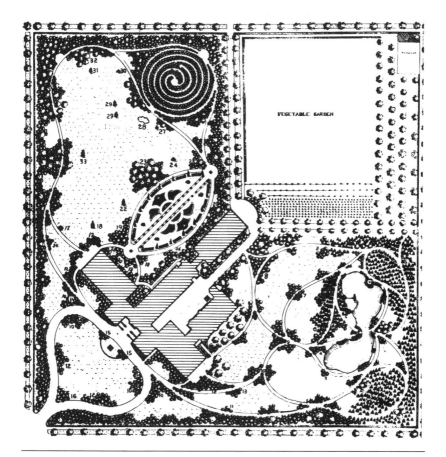

Figure 44. Jensen's plan for St. Ann's Hospital in Chicago as published in Jensen 1901.

The northeast corner was occupied by a vegetable garden bordered by avenues of cherry trees. As at later times in his career, Jensen conceived that a vegetable garden would be utilitarian and would provide a source of pleasure for the patients and visitors to the hospital.

The notion that plants could have a therapeutic affect on the sick and distraught was an often-repeated theme in Jensen's career. He would later design other gardens for the grounds of hospitals. Here, however, Jensen felt it necessary to justify his scheme:

> To prepare plans for the gardens of a hospital designated to the treatment of consumptives is not an every day occurrence. No suggestions were offered by the board of directors or the medical staff. That the patients would receive a large percentage of their treatment from physical exercise became at once apparent and perhaps the gardens would add greatly to the popularity of the hospital as an advertising medium.[56]

Here native plants were quite liberally mixed with non-native varieties, as in some of his early playground designs for Chicago's West Parks. Tree-of-heaven and Russian mulberry, which are often regarded as weeds, were mixed with native trees and shrubs as border plantings. In other projects, Jensen expressed concern over the survivability of many plants under the influence of city pollution, and that concern may have led him to use these plants at St. Ann's. The lagoon area, which featured native plants, was characteristic of Jensen's later work. In the vicinity of the lagoon, Jensen planted alder, arrowhead, cattails, dogwood, grasses, hawthorn, *Iris*, *Potentilla*, *Ribes*, rushes, *Tamarix*, and *Viburnum*. The pond was to be "filled with water lilies and alive with goldfish." As Jensen suggested, "No more interesting and beautiful spot could be created for either sick or healthy." This garden was one of the earliest predecessors of the celebrated "prairie-rivers" that Jensen created in Humboldt and Columbus parks.[57]

Jensen later landscaped the grounds of several other hospitals—notably, the Decatur and Macon County Hospital in Decatur, Illinois, in 1915, and the Henry Ford Hospital in Detroit in 1919. For each of these hospitals, as for St. Ann's, he designed the grounds to provide a restful setting for recuperation. At the Henry Ford Hospital, Jensen created a vegetable garden and an orchard, and included council rings to serve as outdoor gathering areas.[58]

THE "IDEAL SECTION" OF THE LINCOLN HIGHWAY,
LAKE COUNTY, INDIANA

During the early 1920s, Jensen was entrusted with the landscape design for an "ideal section" of the Lincoln Highway between Schererville and Dyer, Indiana, near the Illinois border. A brainchild of Carl Fisher of Indianapolis in 1912, the Lincoln Highway was to provide a completely improved coast-to-coast road. Fisher originally promoted his idea as the "Coast-to-Coast Rock Highway," but changed the name to "Lincoln Highway" at the suggestion of Henry B. Joy, president of the Packard Motor Car Company. Although Fisher was unable to convince Henry Ford to back the project, he did enlist the support of other leaders in the automobile industry. In July 1913 the Lincoln Highway Association was officially organized in Detroit with Joy as president and Fisher as vice-president. By 1921 the organization had selected a one-and-one-third-mile section of the highway on which to demonstrate the use of the most up-to-date technology in lighting, paving, and plantings to create a pleasant route for travel. This stretch of highway became known as the "ideal section."[59]

Henry Ford's refusal to become involved in the project was largely the result of his objection to the precedent of using private capital to build roads; he felt that money should be spent instead on educating the public to support the expenditure of tax dollars on new roads. Jensen also tried to convince the Lincoln Highway Association to seek public funding. He urged the association to prepare propaganda to get legislators to support the project; he believed that the construction of good highways across the country should be fully supported by taxpayers rather than carried out piecemeal by means of private funds. Despite Henry Ford's reluctance to get involved, Edsel Ford contributed both time and money to the project and personally paid Jensen's design fees for the ideal section.[60]

The idea of spending funds to beautify the highway became a volatile issue. The Lincoln Highway Association worried that engineers would consider beautification an "unwarranted and unnecessary expense" that added substantially to the cost of the highway "without increasing its utility." To build support, the association polled highway engineers and landscape architects and found that a majority saw the wisdom of providing tourist camps and general beautification along the route of the highway. O. C. Simonds and Elmer C. Jensen (also a landscape architect from Chicago) encouraged the association to avoid "formal or regular planting" along the highway, arguing instead for "natural grouping[s] of native trees and shrubs to frame roadside views." They also urged the association to name a landscape architect to the technical committee charged with planning the ideal section. Soon thereafter, Jens Jensen was named to the committee.[61]

Jensen planned the ideal section to reflect its prairie setting. At one place, where the road passed through open prairie, native grasses, flowers, and an occasional cluster of hawthorn or crabapple were planted along the roadside. In other places, the road passed through upland prairie and groves of native bur oak and then crossed wooded ravines. A hiking trail wound across the prairie and through groves of trees at the edge of the road. According to the description of the ideal section in *The Lincoln Highway: The Story of a Crusade That Made Transportation History* (1935), Jensen's "artistic ability was especially evident in the laying out of the footpath. This curves through the trees on the south side of the road so that the pedestrian, though only a few feet from the concrete, has constantly in view a delightful vista of timber and shrubbery" (Figure 45).[62]

Jensen looked upon his work on this ideal section as a model for the remainder of the Lincoln Highway and for other roads to be developed across the country. A 1923 press release sent out by the association noted Jensen's exemplary work:

This beautification work, which is under the direction of Jens Jensen, Landscape Architect of Chicago, is expected to set a precedent in the

Figure 45. Pathway along the "ideal section" of the Lincoln Highway. Jensen saw a need to integrate footpaths into the highway systems being developed across the United States. Courtesy of the Lincoln Highway Archives, Department of Rare Books and Special Collections, University Library, University of Michigan, Ann Arbor.

Figure 46. Automobile on the "ideal section" of the Lincoln Highway. Courtesy of the Lincoln Highway Archives, Department of Rare Books and Special Collections, University Library, University of Michigan, Ann Arbor.

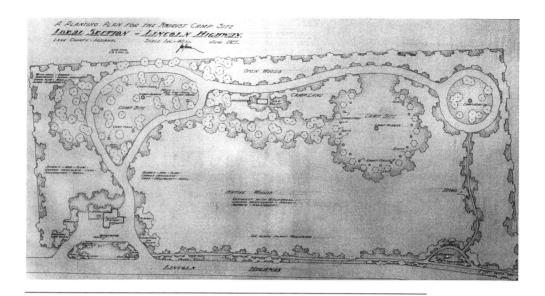

Figure 47. Jensen's plan for a campground area along the "ideal section" of the Lincoln Highway near Merrillville, Indiana. Courtesy of Jensen Collection, Art and Architecture Library, University of Michigan, Ann Arbor.

handling of roadsides in America. Nothing but native plants and shrubs, indigenous to the county in which the section is constructed, will be used but every effort is being made to develop a harmonious plan which with modifications can be adapted along Lincoln Highway and other main roads anywhere between Omaha and New York City.

Jensen urged the association to create a monumental 200–300 foot right-of-way along the highway, except in rural areas, where the right-of-way might be much narrower. While the association pushed for a concrete base to the ideal section, Edsel Ford argued for a crushed stone surface with a Tarvia binder and grassed shoulders without curbs to provide the general appearance of a country road (Figure 46).[63]

Jensen also drew up a plan for a forty-acre campsite and rest area. The association had recognized the need for campsites to be distributed along the highway, and Jensen noted a particular need for outdoor camping areas near major cities. His design provided parking areas for individual campers as well as a council ring where campers could gather around a common fire (Figure 47). A filling station, a store, and rest rooms also were planned for the campground site, and Jensen had his friend John Van Bergen prepare architectural sketches for the buildings. As with his other landscape plans, Jensen hoped that his campsite design would serve as a prototype for rest areas at regular intervals along the highway. Edsel Ford was particularly interested in Jensen's campground ideas and offered to contribute $25,000 toward the construction of such a site. The estimated cost of the campground project soon grew to at least three times that amount, however, so the whole effort was temporarily put on hold. Indeed, by the time the ideal section was completed, motorists seemed to have little interest in open-air camping, and the campground plan was abandoned altogether.[64]

Little remains of Jensen's ideal section of Lincoln Highway. Suburban and strip development along this segment of the highway have combined with road widenings to obliterate all but a few of Jensen's original plantings. Nonetheless, Jensen's design for the ideal section provided an alternative vision of what the nation's highways could have been. His insistence on preserving and restoring native wildflowers, shrubs, and trees along the highway was advanced for his time. Efforts to reestablish wildflowers along highways are considerably more difficult and expensive today than they would have been if such efforts had become a part of the highway-building mentality Jensen advocated.[65]

THE SHAKESPEARE GARDEN, NORTHWESTERN UNIVERSITY, EVANSTON, ILLINOIS

In commemoration of the tercentennial of William Shakespeare's death, Jensen prepared a design for a Shakespeare Garden under the auspices of the Drama League of America, which had been founded in Chicago in 1910. The idea to create the garden was adopted by the Garden Club of Evanston, Illinois, and the garden was built between 1916 and 1930 on what had been a trash dump on the grounds of the Northwestern University campus (Figure 48).[66]

The idea of a "Shakespeare garden" was not original with Jensen. Wilhelm Miller promoted the idea as one of "sixty suggestions for new gardens" in a 1912 article of the same name in *The Garden Magazine*. The Drama League's national quarterly publication in 1915 advocated commemorative gardens as one of many suggestions for celebrating the tercentennial of Shakespeare's death. As a member of the Drama League, Jensen apparently picked up on the idea and used Bacon's essay "On Gardens," as an inspiration for his plan. Alice Houston, who was one of the founding members of the Drama League, learned of Jensen's plan and convinced the Garden Club of Evanston to adopt the garden as its special project. Jensen's Shakespeare Garden was not the only one created for the tercentennial celebration; other gardens were created in Cedar Rapids, Iowa, Rockefeller Park in Cleveland, Ohio, Central Park in New York City, and Vassar College in Poughkeepsie, New York.[67]

Given Jensen's interest in public drama, the Shakespeare Garden was a

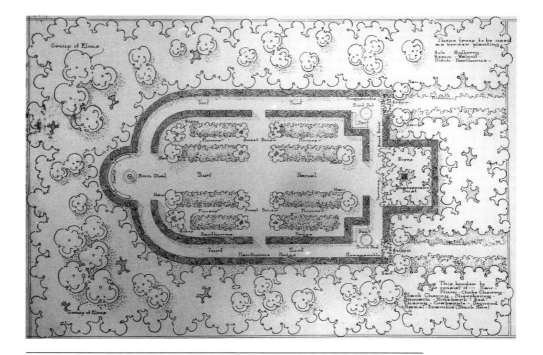

Figure 48. Jensen's plan for the Shakespeare Garden on the campus of Northwestern University, Evanston, Illinois. Courtesy of Bruce Johnson.

logical extension of his work. But Jensen usually avoided the highly geometric forms of the gardens that were typical of Shakespeare's time; thus, this garden presented the personal challenge of adapting historic Tudor garden traditions to the prairie region of Chicago.

Jensen's original idea was to create a garden using plants mentioned by Shakespeare in his writings. As Jensen explored the idea, however, he found that many of the plants listed by Shakespeare either were not hardy in the Chicago area or would become garden pests. His solution was a scheme that would "express a sentiment in honor of the memory of the great poet" and contain plants common to Elizabethan England, even though they were not specific to Shakespeare's writings. Jensen encouraged the members of the Garden Club of Evanston to experiment with many of the plants from Elizabethan England to determine which would be hardy in Evanston.[68]

The design became a simple "hedged-in garden surrounded by a forest border—a sun opening in the woods." A sun dial flanked one end of the garden space; a bust of Shakespeare was intended to mark the other, but a suitable one was never found. In its place, a fountain was donated by Hubert Burnham, son of Daniel H. Burnham, in memory of his mother,

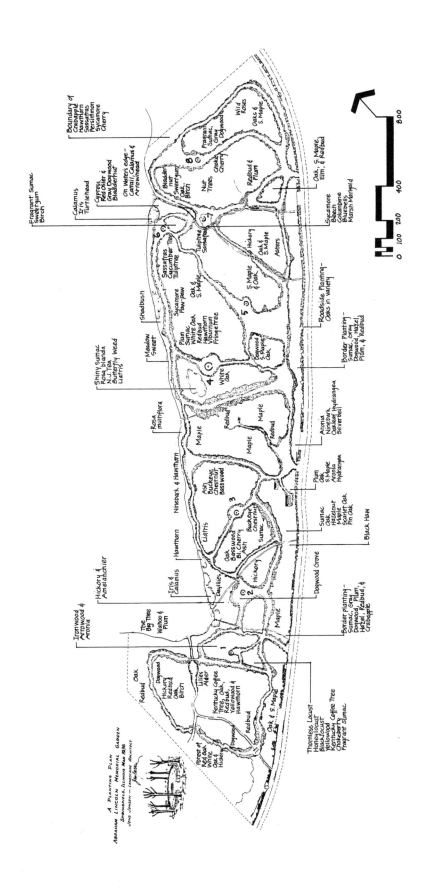

A Planting Plan
Abraham Lincoln Memorial Garden
Springfield, Illinois Mar. 1936
Jens Jensen — Landscape Architect
Jan Jensen

Boundary of
Crabapple
Hawthorn
Sassafras
Persimmon
Sycamore
Cherry

Fragrant Sumac
Sweetgum
Birch

Calamus
Iris
Turtlehead

Cypress
Red Osier
Gray Dogwood
Bladderhut

On Water's edge
Cattail, Calamus &
Arrowhead

Wild
Roses

Oaks &
S. Maple

Fragrant
Sumac,
Gray
Dogwood

Choke
Cherry

Redbud &
Plum

Bladder
nut

Oak,
Sweetgum
Birch

Nut
Trees

Oak, S. Maple,
Elm, & Redbud

Sycamore
Beech
Columbine
Bluebells
Marsh Marigold

Hickory

Oak &
S. Maple

Asters

S. Maple
& Oak

Sassafras
Cucumber Tree
Tuliptree

Tuliptree
Sassafras

Roadside Planting-
Oaks in Variety

Shadbush

Sycamore
Paw-paw

Oak &
S. Maple

Border Planting
Sumac, Gray
Dogwood, Hazel,
Plum, & Redbud

Shiny Sumac
Rosa blanda
N.J. Tea
Butterfly Weed
Liatris

Meadow
Sweet

Plum
Sumac
White Oak
Redbud
Viburnum
Fringetree

White
Oak

Dogwood
S. Maple
Oak

Aronia
Ninebark
Oakleaf
Silverbell

Hydrangea

Rosa
multiflora

Maple

Redbud

Maple

Maple

Redbud

Plum
Oak
S. Maple
Aronia
Hydrangea

Ninebark & Hawthorn

Ash
Buckeye
Chestnut
Basswood

Buckeye
Chestnut
Sumac

Oak
Hazelnut
Maple
Scarlet Oak
Pin Oak

Sumac

Black Haw

Hawthorn

Liatris

Oak
Basswood
Bl. Cherry
Ash

Hickory

Ironwood &
Arrowwood
Aronia

Hickory &
Amelanchier

Iris &
Calamus

Daylilies

Dogwood Grove

Oak

Redbud

Dogwood

Hickory
Redbud
Oak,
Birch

Lilies
Alder

Kentucky Coffee
Tree, Oak,
Redbud,
Yellowwood &
Hawthorn

Dogwood

Redbud

The
Big Tree
Wahoo &
Plum

Maple

Border Planting-
Sumac, Gray
Dogwood, Plum,
Hazel, Redbud, &
Crabapple

Oak & S. Maple

Forest of
Red Oak
Oak &
White
Hickory

Thornless Locust
Honeylocust
Black Locust
Yellowwood
Kentucky Coffee Tree
Aronia
Chokeberry
Fragrant Sumac

0 100 200 400 800

who was an early leader of the Garden Club of Evanston. The fountain was designed by the Burnham Brothers and bears a bronze plaque by the French American sculptor, Leon Hermant, with a likeness of Shakespeare and quotations from *As You Like It, A Midsummer Night's Dream,* and *The Winter's Tale.* In the center of the garden, simple beds of the flowers mentioned by Shakespeare alternate with panels of clipped grass. In Jensen's drawing, arbors and small bird pools mark the corner entrances, but these were never implemented. Hawthorns, so important in Jensen's prairie style, frame the central axis and accent the corners of the garden. The design as a whole reflects Jensen's versatility in effectively adapting a historic garden form to an American setting.[69]

Since its formal dedication in 1930, the Shakespeare Garden has been lovingly maintained by the Garden Club of Evanston. It remains a quiet place for contemplation and romance in the heart of the Northwestern University campus and has always been a popular site for weddings. Since 1988, it has been listed on the National Register of Historic Places.[70]

LINCOLN MEMORIAL GARDEN, SPRINGFIELD, ILLINOIS

Lincoln Memorial Garden began in 1934 as the idea of Harriet Knudson, an active member of the Springfield Civic Garden Association and member of the Board of Directors of the Garden Club of Illinois, for a living memorial to Abraham Lincoln on the shores of Lake Springfield, a reservoir created on Sugar Creek by the City Water, Light, and Power Department of Springfield, Illinois. When Jensen was approached with the commission in 1935, he responded that of all the honors he had received, this was the greatest and that he would charge no fee. Later, he asked for $500 for his plan, saying that he was "too poor to give the plan outright." It is not clear whether he was actually paid, but the story promoted by the garden has always been that Jensen did the design for free. In any case, it is certain that Jensen always regarded his involvement with the garden as a true labor of love. With members of the Garden Club of the State of Illinois, Jensen helped select the site, noting the "gentle slopes and meadows, the little hills and valleys." He spent much time studying the site during the first year, and in 1936 produced what became his working plan for the garden (Figure 49).[71]

Figure 49. Jensen's final plan for Lincoln Memorial Garden in Springfield, Illinois (1936). The names of plants shown on Jensen's plan have been relabeled for clarity. Council rings are labeled by number. Courtesy of Lincoln Memorial Garden Archives, Lincoln Memorial Garden Nature Center, Springfield, Illinois.

Because many of the species suggested by Jensen were unavailable from nurseries, the school children and garden clubs of Illinois were called on to help collect acorns and other seeds and to gather plants from natural areas that were being destroyed across the state. The acorns were planted in a grand ceremony by local Boy Scouts and Girl Scouts (Figure 50); hundreds of young saplings were carefully placed by hand by other helpers. Numerous garden clubs, the Chicago Wild Flower Preservation Society, and the Morton Arboretum took responsibility for planting various parts of the garden. Volunteers brought in wild plants in their automobiles by the trunkful, and as shade developed, understory plants were added.[72]

Jensen noted that the "contours of the land suggested lanes or open grades," and his basic design for the garden consisted of a series of fingerlike open spaces surrounded by woodland. Each lane was to showcase certain plants native to Illinois, particularly the small trees such as redbud (*Cercis canadensis*), flowering dogwood (*Cornus florida*), hawthorn (*Crataegus spp.*), and prairie crabapple (*Malus ioensis*), which would typically be found at the woodland's edge. As Jensen wrote, "The lower levels, along Lake Springfield, [were] filled with sun-loving flowers," and the uplands were covered with "trees native to the states in which Lincoln lived."[73]

Jensen went through several versions of plans for the garden before completing the design, which was drafted and dated March 1936. It is interesting to compare this final plan with one produced just three months earlier, in December 1935, in Jensen's own hand (Figure 51). The earlier plan had fewer linear open spaces throughout the site, and they were organized around several large, circular, open meadow spaces. These meadow spaces were reminiscent of Jensen's design work at Columbus Park and on other projects where the design was focused on a large central meadow, with council rings and smaller spaces tucked into the woodland border. The 1935 plan also had some major lanes, shown as forty to sixty feet wide and edged by tree canopies, and trails, shown as five feet narrower, which were probably intended to be woodland paths. By comparison, the finalized version of 1936 had trails that were fifteen to twenty feet wide, but no distinction was made between open trails and shady woodland paths. Similarly, in the 1935 plan, several wide lanes cut directly through the garden property, offering direct views of the lake. In the final plan, however, the lanes curved ever so slightly, creating a sense of mystery, and one had to walk down the trails before getting even a glimpse of the lake.

The 1935 plan had fourteen council rings as compared to the eight included in the final version. Whereas in the final plan the council rings

Figure 50. The grand procession at acorn-planting ceremonies in Lincoln Memorial Garden, 1936. Courtesy of Lincoln Memorial Garden Archives, Lincoln Memorial Garden Nature Center, Springfield, Illinois.

were placed along major trails with views down the length of the trail, in the 1935 plan they were positioned on short spurs off the main trail, in groves of crabapple and other small trees, or on the edge of a clearing or along the lakeshore (Figure 52). Despite other changes in the plan, several of the council rings were set in the same locations on the final plan as on the earlier plan. This suggests that Jensen was confident of their placement for topographic or other reasons and saw no reason to change them as the rest of the plan developed. The most notable of these similarities was the Lincoln Council Ring (no. 4), which was located in the same place on both plans—in a grove of white oaks (*Quercus alba*)—and provided a dramatic view of Lake Springfield. Jensen had evidently given much thought to this part of the plan; in several places he wrote that this grove of oaks was a particularly appropriate living monument to Abraham Lincoln. He may have thought that these oaks were fitting to Lincoln's image as a rail-splitter, but it is more likely that he chose white oaks because they live for centuries as individuals and for millennia as a grove. Jensen delighted in thinking that this "living" monument to Lincoln would outlast any monuments built of stone:

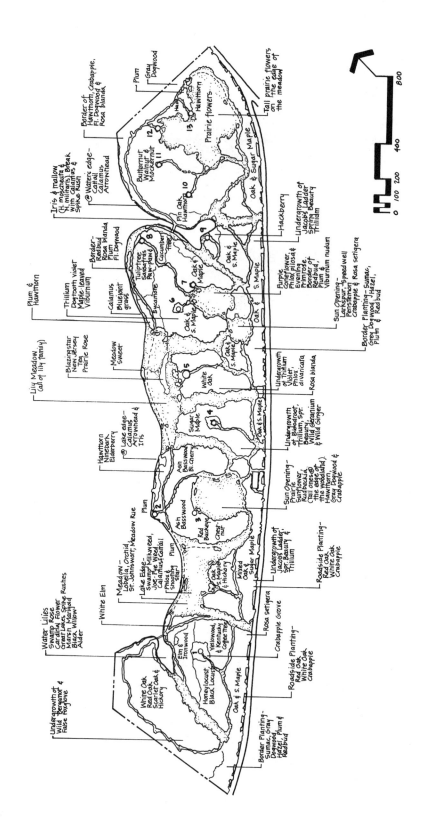

I planted white acorns (plants were not to be had), a noble tree which needed more care than our nurserymen cared to give it. The white oak is the noblest tree in Illinois. It will live to be a thousand years old on soil best fitted for it. The acorns are now small trees, three years old. Someday they will tower over the prairie landscape one foot high. If they are permitted to scatter their acorns and so perpetuate themselves, and the glaciers or other disturbances are not to change the climate of the land, there will be white oaks on this hillock thousands of years hence when every artificial monument erected in his [Lincoln's] honor has long gone into dust—and so the native white oak will sing its song in memory of our great president to unborn generations.

Leonard Eaton has noted that Jensen may have been thinking about using a grove of oaks such as this for some time and that, because in this case the immediate impact of the landscape was not crucial, he was able to plant acorns rather than substitute a faster-growing species.[74]

The several small creeks that drained across the property in the final version were not included on the 1935 plan. Also, the lagoons at either end of the garden were both larger and more prominent on the 1935 plan, and were situated at the end of major lanes. As in Jensen's famous prairie-river designs, these lagoons were to be planted with sweet flag (*Acorus calamus*), marsh marigold (*Caltha palustris*), spike rushes (*Eleocharis spp.*), swamp mallow (*Hibiscus palustris*), iris (*Iris virginica shrevei*), water lilies (*Nymphaea spp.*), swamp rose (*Rosa palustris*), and arrowhead (*Sagittaria latifolia*). Evidently Jensen decided that the creation of a major prairie-river did not fit with the rest of his design. He did, however, plant along the lake's edge many of the species he had commonly used in his prairie-rivers, but the abrupt slopes, wave action, and fluctuating water levels in the reservoir doomed them to failure.

The detailing of species was considerably greater on the 1935 plan than on the later one, but the general arrangement of plant communities was similar on both. The 1935 plan lists many more of the shrub and ground-layer species desired by Jensen, and the lines between community types are much more distinct. Likewise, clusters of trees at the edge of openings or along trails are drawn with much greater care on this earlier plan (for example, individual trees are noted). In addition, the pattern of bays and promontories along trails or at the edge of a woodland on the 1935 plan

---

Figure 51. Jensen's preliminary plan for Lincoln Memorial Garden (1935). Compare this to the 1936 plan, which has much larger openings and includes more herbaceous plants.

clearly show the sequence of spaces Jensen typically used along trails.

Some of these differences, especially those with regard to the level of detail, may be attributable to the fact that the 1935 plan was an intermediate version in which Jensen was still formulating his ideas for the garden, whereas the 1936 plan was a final drawing that was to be used as a general guide for those doing the planting. Since Jensen himself staked out the trails and many of the plantings, he was probably unconcerned with putting more detail into the final plan. Therefore, the 1935 drawing and other earlier plans help us decipher some of Jensen's thoughts as he worked on the design and guide us in determining what elements were most firmly established in his mind.

As one of Jensen's last major public designs, Lincoln Memorial Garden represents a mature level of his thinking and style. The process by which the garden was planted also lends significance to the design. Jensen did not work out the details for the garden in a finely honed plan. Fortunately, Knudson and the others who tended the garden through its early years seemed to share Jensen's vision. In a letter to Knudson on 9 December 1935 (probably enclosing a copy of the earlier plan), Jensen wrote: "As you will note, I have allowed considerable freedom in the execution of the plans, which is essential with a plan of this kind, but this freedom demands a strict adherence to the harmony and principle of the plan." This same philosophy undoubtedly applied to the final plan as well. The garden as it currently exists is a testament to the loving labors of many people, most of them volunteers, both in planting and in managing the garden. From its start, when the first acorns were collected by school children and planted by local scouts, the garden has served as a rich depository of native flora rescued by people from across the state of Illinois who were intent on preserving these small pieces of their natural heritage (Figure 53).[75]

Today, Lincoln Memorial Garden is one of the few remaining Jensen landscapes—especially public landscapes—that has not been consciously changed and that is still used as Jensen originally intended. In the late 1950s, the Lincoln Memorial Garden Foundation was established to oversee the maintenance and running of the garden, and it continues in operation to this day. The few changes that have taken place, such as the construction of the nature center building in the 1960s, do not detract from the integrity of the remaining parts of the garden. In recent years, the staff of the garden has taken a renewed interest in preserving and managing the unique qualities of Jensen's design for the site while using the garden as a regional center for environmental education. Such a program reflects Jensen's own intentions that his parks and gardens serve as places

Figure 52. Pathway leading to Council Ring no. 6 in Lincoln Memorial Garden, Springfield, Illinois.

Figure 53. Bloodroot (*Sanguinaria canadensis*) in Lincoln Memorial Garden. Jensen sought to create natural groupings of ground layer plantings as well as overstory trees and shrubs in the garden. Many of these herbaceous plants were rescued from natural areas that were being destroyed across Illinois and were later added to the garden as shade developed.

where people could discover, study, and enjoy their natural heritage. Every year, hundreds of school children and adults participate in guided walks and other programs at the garden. Many more come to the garden as individuals or in small groups to study the flora and fauna or simply to relax while walking down one of the garden's trails. Lincoln Memorial Garden is currently in the process of being listed on the National Register of Historic Places.[76]

Conservation Efforts

Although designing estates was not Jensen's chief passion, he used that work to prevail upon many of his clients to support his conservation activities. For Jensen, conservation was a logical extension of his design work. Through his design work, he hoped to instill a deeper appreciation for nature that would lead people to protect whatever vestiges of wild nature remained. Jensen belonged to a number of conservation organizations, and he himself organized two groups to support his conservation projects: the Prairie Club and the Friends of Our Native Landscape. A genuine sense of stewardship permeated Jensen's outlook on life, and he sought to translate his convictions into positive action.

During his early days in Chicago, Jensen joined volunteer organizations that supported causes dear to his heart. These included the Cliff Dwellers, the City Club, the Municipal Science Club, the Municipal Art League, the Outdoor Art League, and the Geographic Society, to name a few. Through these groups, Jensen became acquainted with others who shared his interests, and he began to establish a network of resource people—botanists, writers, politicians, artists, social workers, and philanthropists—that he would later use to support specific projects.

Shortly after the turn of the twentieth century, Jensen helped organize Chicago's Playground Association, which sought to provide a variety of play areas for children trapped in the heart of Chicago. At the time, Jensen was deeply involved in the work of the Special Park Commission, whose report advocated creation of a network of small parks and playgrounds throughout the city and a band of larger, wilder parks around the city's perimeter. For years, Jensen had taken his family on weekend outings to many of these special places, and he became convinced that others would enjoy these areas as well. In the spring of 1908, Jensen, together with other members of the Playground Association, arranged a series of "Saturday Afternoon Walking Trips" to acquaint people with the beauty of the land surrounding Chicago. The group became so popular that its members formed an association to manage these walks and, at Jensen's suggestion, named it "The Prairie Club."[77]

Figure 54. Photograph taken by Jensen on a trip to the limestone bluffs of the Rock River in Illinois. Courtesy of Jensen Collection, Morton Arboretum, Lisle, Illinois.

To lead these walks, the club drew upon a diverse group of naturalists, artists, and community leaders, many of whom were members of other organizations to which Jensen belonged. Besides Jensen, leaders of these walks included Henry C. Cowles (professor of plant ecology at the University of Chicago), William M. R. French (former partner of H. W. S. Cleveland and director of the Art Institute), Walter Burley Griffin (architect and landscape architect), Dwight Perkins (architect), Gertrude Simonds (daughter of O. C. Simonds), and Lorado Taft (sculptor) (Figure 54).[78]

Groups met in the city and took the train to the outskirts for day trips or occasionally for overnight camping trips. Sometimes trips were made to parks or other locations in the city, such as the "Sunrise Bird Walk" led by Gertrude Simonds to the Wooded Island in Jackson Park on 14 May 1910. Many of the most popular sites were proposed as forest preserves in the Special Park Commission's report in 1904. Dwight Perkins and Jensen must have seen the value in building a public consensus for setting aside these lands as forest preserves, and the Prairie Club became one of the most ardent supporters of the bill creating the County Forest Preserves, which passed the Illinois legislature in 1913 and was approved by referendum in 1914. Other popular destinations included the Rock River area (from Dixon to Oregon, Illinois), Starved Rock, and the Indiana

Dunes. Jensen remained a core member of the Prairie Club, serving as its director from 1911 to 1914, as its president in 1914, and as chair of the Conservation Committee. The Conservation Committee counted Stephen Mather, future first director of the National Park Service, as one of its members.[79]

The "Saturday Afternoon Walking Trips" and the other outings sponsored by the Prairie Club never became recreational outlets for the poor of Chicago's ghettos and settlement houses, as Jensen and the club's other organizers had hoped. These activities did, however, acquaint a large group of middle-class professionals and intellectuals with the diverse natural areas in the region, and that group served as an important lobbying base, first for the Forest Preserves, and later for other conservation projects, most notably the Indiana Dunes.[80]

The first official "Saturday Afternoon Walking Trip"—to the Indiana Dunes—was held in 1908, and 338 people came to hike in the area near Gary. Thereafter, the dunes were a regular destination for the group, and many of the hikes were led by Jensen (Figure 55). In 1913, the Prairie Club built a permanent cabin at Tremont, Indiana, on land owned by architect Stanford White. Jensen himself selected the spot for the building, and architect Walter H. Kattelle drew up the plans. On 19 October 1913, the cabin was dedicated with a special masque entitled "The Spirit of the Dunes" written by Mrs. Jacob Abt. The masque, which was a moving outdoor presentation celebrating the beauty of the wild and censuring "civilized" man's abuse of wild nature, became a tradition associated with Jensen's conservation activities, especially at the Dunes.[81]

On 13 April 1913, Jensen invited a group of influential friends to meet with him to form a new conservation organization, which he wanted to call the "Friends of Our Native Landscape." Among those invited were Avery Coonley, Harold Ickes, Stephen Mather, Harriet Monroe, Dwight Perkins, and Mrs. Julius Rosenwald. The Friends (as the group came to be known) was described by Ragna Eskil as a group of "doers, of people who got things done." The primary goals of the group were to collect information about areas "of historic and scenic value" in Illinois and to promote legislation to protect such areas. Four meetings were to be held each year: a "fireside" business meeting on the third Tuesday in January, a "Pilgrimage to the Crab-apple Blossom" on a Saturday in May, a "Meeting to the Full Leaf" at sundown on the second Saturday in June, and a "Meeting to the Fallen Leaf" in the Indiana Dunes on an autumn Sunday. Each year, the "Meeting to the Full Leaf" was to be held at a different place worthy of being preserved as a park. The first of these attracted 200 people to the White Pine Forest of Ogle County, near Oregon, Illinois, on 14 June 1913. On that occasion Vachel Lindsay recited his poem "Hawk of

Figure 55. Cookout in the Indiana Dunes. Mrs. Jensen is seated to the left. Photograph is by Jensen. Courtesy of Jensen Collection, Morton Arboretum, Lisle, Illinois.

Figure 56. Indiana Dunes scene labeled by Henry C. Cowles as "Destruction of a forested dune by moving sand." The constantly changing character of the dunes is part of what attracted Jensen and his friends to this small stretch of land along the southern shore of Lake Michigan. Photograph by S. B. Meyers, courtesy of University of Chicago Archives.

the Rock" and a group performed Kenneth Sawyer Goodman's masque "The Beauty of the Wild." Thereafter, the masque became an annual ritual, attracting not only the sixty to a hundred Friends, but often a thousand or more local people. Many of the places where the masque was performed were later designated as preserves. These included the Illinois state parks Apple River Canyon, Governor Lowden's Sinnissippi Farm, Nauvoo, Starved Rock, and White Pines; Funks Grove, Illinois; the Wisconsin Dells and Devil's Lake State Park in Wisconsin; and Ludington State Park in Michigan.[82]

From the beginning, the Friends combined scientific and humanistic approaches to studying and appreciating nature, and promoted the preservation of the nation's heritage as part of an individual's democratic responsibility. Among its members were botanists and educators such as Henry C. Cowles and George D. Fuller from the University of Chicago; politicians such as Harold Ickes; writers such as Vachel Lindsay and Carl Sandburg; O. M. Schantz, president of the Illinois Audubon Society; and Stephen A. Forbes, who later became chief of the Illinois Natural History Survey.[83]

Preservation of the Indiana Dunes became an early battle for the Friends as well as the Prairie Club. For the membership of both groups (which overlapped in many instances), the Dunes served as a sacred center. Jensen tried various approaches to preserving the Dunes. He suggested that the University of Chicago establish an outdoor laboratory there for botanical research. Later, he was almost successful in creating a school of horticulture, forestry, and landscape design jointly run by himself, faculty members from the University of Chicago, and Frank Waugh from the Massachusetts Agricultural College in Amherst. Jensen approached Julius Rosenwald to sponsor the idea, but Rosenwald was not interested. Jensen then approached Henry Ford, suggesting that he buy 3,000–4,000 acres of the Dunes and establish a public arboretum of native plants. Upon learning that Henry Ford might be involved, however, local speculators raised the price of the land so high that Ford backed down.[84]

Throughout these efforts, the Friends and members of the Prairie Club kept up their push for the government to purchase and protect the dunes. On 30 October 1916, Stephen Mather, newly appointed director of the National Park Service, organized a public hearing to examine a proposal to establish a national park in the Indiana Dunes. Members from the Prairie Club, Friends of Our Native Landscape, and other civic organizations provided avid testimony in support of a national park in the Dunes.[85]

Henry Cowles explained the significance of the Dunes as a botanical crossroads and suggested that the area's plant communities presented a drama that was meaningful to botanists and citizens alike (Figure 56):[86]

> The struggle for existence always interests, because our life is such a struggle. Nowhere perhaps in the entire world of plants does the struggle for life take on such dramatic and spectacular phases as in the dunes. A dune in the early days of its career is a moving landscape, a place that is never twice alike; it is a body of sand which under the influence of wind moves indifferently over swamp, town or forest.

For many of the Dunes supporters, this fragile stretch of land along the southern shore of Lake Michigan represented a true wilderness experience for the people of Chicago and northern Indiana. Here, they argued, people would find relief from the pressures of city life. T. W. Allinson of the Prairie Club testified on this aspect of the dunes: "No man can get a complete absence of care, a freedom from harassing worries, so well as the man who leaves the city behind him, with its noise, its dust, its confusion and turmoil, and goes out in the quiet of the dunes." He went on to suggest that camping out on the dunes, sleeping on the sand, and cooking over an open fire provided both physical and spiritual refreshment for city dwellers:

> They walk; they ramble; they botanize; they geologize; they play games. They find health and rest. Nothing is better than that. Getting out in the open air, as I said, is the greatest possible panacea for tired bodies and weary souls. Then they come home in the evening, having had from 24 to 36 hours of real rest, and they come back new men and women. What we need in our country are many such places as this, and no city park, with its artificial surroundings, its conventionalized environments, can meet that need.[87]

Other supporters at the hearing presented additional pleas for saving the Dunes. Representing the American Civic Association, Wilhelm Miller argued for the preservation of the Dunes as an inspiration for America's artists. He noted that throughout history great artists had frequently turned to wild nature for inspiration. If the United States, and the Midwest in particular, was to develop culturally, he contended, a wilderness area such as the Dunes was absolutely necessary:

> The musicians must have it, the painters must have it, the poets, dramatists, sculptors, architects, landscape architects must have it, or this civilization will become conventionalized, like that of Egypt and Syria, and will perish off the face of the earth. We must have those things that will help us create a national style of architecture, landscape gardening, and interior decoration in order to make a perfect home for our people. To accomplish these things

we must have one of the great original sources of nature. In my judgment we have in the dunes an infinite reservoir of primitive force for the making of better men and women. As a landscape architect I have no hesitancy in saying that they [the dunes] are by far the best proposition in the Middle West for a national park.[88]

Jensen, who had helped orchestrate the hearing, offered verbal testimony during the proceedings and later wrote an essay which was included in the final report. For Jensen, who by this time had been nicknamed "apostle of the Dunes" for his tireless efforts to preserve them, the Dunes represented the very best of the Midwest's landscapes:

The dunes [area] of northern Indiana is one of the great expressions of wild beauty in this country. They are the greatest of nature's expressions of this beauty in the Middle West and as a type of landscape they are unequaled anywhere in the world. They are to us what the Adirondacks and the Catskills are to our eastern [friends] and the Rocky Mountains are to our western friends. Their beauty of wildness and romance must be measured by comparison with the level plains of the Middle West. They are less severe and less melancholy perhaps than the dune countries of the Italian coast or the western coasts of France and Denmark. They are more poetic, more free, more joyful, something that appeals more to the average human being and which has greater influence on him than the colder, more severe and overwhelming forms of landscape.[89]

Jensen suggested that the value of the Dunes could be measured in part by how a person visiting the area was reminded of his or her relative insignificance against the forces of nature. Here was a landscape of great power and beauty that was in constant flux but that was also timeless. Visitors would experience it in much the same way as earlier generations:

Along the trail asters stand in a blaze of glory as so many candles lighting up the way of the pilgrim who ventures into the woods on dark and gloomy autumn days, and in the wind rustling through the trees that have seen generations pass below one fancies he can hear the chanting song of the Red Man, or the cradle song of the Indian squaw when listening to the murmuring waves breaking over the sandy beach of this dune country.[90]

For Jensen, the Dunes represented the last great chance to provide the millions of workers and their children in the Chicago area an intimate experience with nature. He likened the Dunes to "the greatest of all books," which had the potential to satisfy our basic need "to know something about mother earth, her great beauty, mysterious life, and neverending change." Jensen noted that the city worker "needs something as a balance, something that will make his work more endurable, more cheerful, something that will broaden his vision and save him or his descendants from the destruction sure to follow the grind of his daily life."[91]

Jensen argued that the "great national reservations of the West" were beyond the reach of most Chicago citizens. The Dunes provided a great opportunity to preserve a truly wild landscape near where people live:

> There is no other place in our country where this wild beauty lies so close to great industrial communities. The dunes of northern Indiana are almost within a stone's throw of perhaps one of the greatest industrial communities of the world. It is the only landscape of its kind within reach of the millions that need its softening influence for the restoration of their souls and the balance of their minds.[92]

Stephen Mather returned to Washington and recommended that Congress purchase a mile-wide and twenty-five-mile-long stretch of undeveloped shoreline between Michigan City and Miller, Indiana. Although Indiana senator Thomas Taggart supported the park, northern Indiana counties objected to creating a park for Chicagoans out of the counties' only stretch of lakeshore, to which they hoped to attract industry. In 1916, Congress was heavily involved in war politics, and a bill creating a new national park, especially one that involved setting the precedent of buying private land, had little chance of being passed. Nevertheless, the Prairie Club did not let the issue die. In an attempt to rally support for the Sand Dunes National Park, the club planned a festive Dunes Pageant for Memorial Day 1917. Thomas Wood Stevens wrote an epic drama telling the history of the dunes from 1675 through 1840. The pageant, which employed a massive cast (estimates range from 200–700 members) and was staged in a natural amphitheater called the Jens Jensen Blowout, began in the afternoon and ended under artificial light later that night. Despite a drenching rain, an estimated ten to twenty thousand people attended the performance on May 30. The pageant was repeated on its rain date, June 3, and at that time was seen by approximately fifty thousand people (Figure 57). Despite these valiant efforts, however, Congress turned a deaf ear to the plea for a Dunes National Park, and when Stephen Mather saw that Congress was unlikely to appropriate money for purchasing private land, he, too, moved on to other battles.[93]

Undaunted, the Prairie Club continued its fight to save the Dunes, turning next to advocating the creation of a state park. In Richard Lieber, the newly appointed director of the Department of Conservation for the state of Indiana and a former art and music critic of the *Indianapolis Journal*, the Prairie Club found a friend. Jensen personally gave Lieber a guided tour of the Dunes, pointing out their "hidden secrets, their rich vegetation, the struggle between moving sand and the dunes' flora." Short-

Figure 57. Dunes Pageant, held on 3 June 1917 and seen by an estimated fifty thousand people in the Jens Jensen Blowout in the Indiana Dunes. The Prairie Club's beach house can be seen in the background of this photograph. Courtesy of O. C. Simonds Collection, Morton Arboretum, Lisle, Illinois.

ly thereafter, Lieber began pushing for a state park. Finally, in 1926, Indiana set aside 2,250 acres along a three-and-three-fourths-mile stretch of lakeshore as Indiana Dunes State Park (Figure 58).[94]

Meanwhile, the Friends of Our Native Landscape investigated scenic and historic lands for inclusion in an Illinois state park system. In 1911, with Jensen as a member, the Geographic Society of Chicago had fought to establish the Illinois Park Commission and to designate Starved Rock Park as Illinois's first state park (Figure 59). The Friends organized a state park committee, appointed Jensen as its chair, and from 1918 to 1921 surveyed lands across the state to recommend areas for preservation as state parks. In 1921 the committee issued its report, *Proposed Park Areas in the State of Illinois: A Report with Recommendations.* So as not to conflict with county forest districts that were actively preserving smaller parcels of land, the committee looked only at tracts that were 1,000 acres in size or larger. The committee reasoned that "it requires large areas to preserve the native flora and fauna in all its wild and mysterious beauty. Overcrowded parks or preserves mean the destruction of all such."[95]

The committee's report highlighted twenty different sites for consideration as state parks (Figure 60). According to Jensen's foreword to the report, these sites represented land "of little or no agricultural value." Thus he urged readers to think less of traditional utilitarian concepts of land and

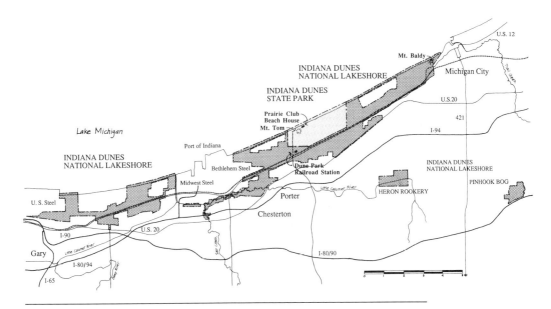

Figure 58. Map showing lands in Indiana Dunes State Park and Indiana Dunes National Lakeshore that are currently protected. Note the location of the Prairie Club beach house next to Mount Tom and close to the Dunes Park railroad station, which provided members easy access to the site. The beach house was torn down when the land was designated a state park. The map is adapted from *Indiana Dunes: Official Map and Guide* (Washington, D.C.: U.S. National Park Service) and *Rand McNally Map of the Indiana Dunes: Wonder Region of the Middle West,* by P. S. Goodman (Chicago, Ill.: Rand McNally and Co.).

"more of the spiritual side": "They [the proposed parklands] represent Illinois as the white man found it—a different world from the man-made one—equally important in developing the cultural life of Illinois. They offer refuge for native wild life and a place of escape for a while, at least, from the grind and cares of daily life." Jensen noted a personal "feeling of insight and intimacy" toward the lands described in the report, and suggested that the whole report was "a work of love and must be accepted as such." Jensen's vision was that the entire state would eventually become "one great park" in which "primitive America will vie in interest and beauty with the rural country, where fields of corn are fringed with our native crabapple and prairie blossoms, and entwined by winding streams and rivers on whose towering bluffs the golden tassels of the oaks are silhouetted against the blue sky of Illinois."[96]

In its emphasis on the acquisition of wild and scenic areas, the Friends of Our Native Landscape advocated a change in the direction of Illinois' development of a state park system. With the exception of Starved Rock,

Figure 59. Scene in Deer Park Canyon photographed on a field trip to the Starved Rock area along the Illinois River in central Illinois. Starved Rock was Illinois' first state park, and both the Prairie Club and the Friends of Our Native Landscape made the saving of lands around Starved Rock a high priority and took numerous field trips to this area. Courtesy of University of Chicago Archives.

all other properties until then had been acquired because of their historical associations. Even in the case of Starved Rock, its historical association with Amerindians and a nearby French fort were as important to its early preservation as its scenic value. In 1925, Illinois passed a park act clearly advocating scenic qualities as criteria for land acquisition.[97]

A majority of the park areas recommended by the Friends were located in southern Illinois in areas of "Ozark uplifts," where the land was better suited for forests than for agriculture. Jensen also recommended that much of the forested land outside the proposed park sites be acquired and managed as state forests. He suggested that buffers of forestland be acquired along river courses and that the state should attempt to purchase the entire system of scenic bluffs along the state's rivers. In the palisades area of the Mississippi River, he advocated establishing an "interstate park" by incorporating all the islands, bluffs, and canyons along the river into a giant park and bird preserve. Finally, he recommended that the state

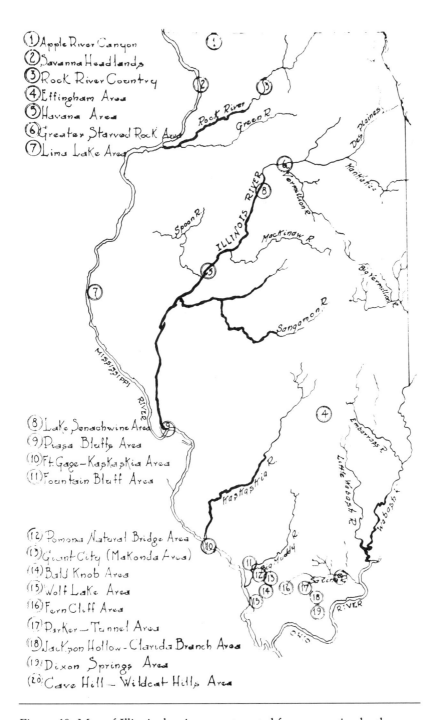

1. Apple River Canyon
2. Savanna Headlands
3. Rock River Country
4. Effingham Area
5. Havana Area
6. Greater Starved Rock Area
7. Lima Lake Area

8. Lake Senachwine Area
9. Piasa Bluffs Area
10. Ft. Gage—Kaskaskia Area
11. Fountain Bluff Area

12. Pomona Natural Bridge Area
13. Giant City (Makonda Area)
14. Bald Knob Area
15. Wolf Lake Area
16. Fern Cliff Area
17. Parker—Tunnel Area
18. Jackson Hollow—Clarida Branch Area
19. Dixon Springs Area
20. Cave Hill—Wildcat Hills Area

Figure 60. Map of Illinois showing areas targeted for preservation by the Friends of Our Native Landscape. From Friends of Our Native Landscape 1921. Courtesy of Jensen Collection, Art and Architecture Library, University of Michigan, Ann Arbor.

develop a network of scenic roads that connected the state parks and followed river courses wherever possible.[98]

In 1926 the Friends published *A Park and Forest Policy for Illinois*, which served as the foundation for a state law passed that same year. The park policy, which was authored by Jensen, advocated a version of the "highest and best use" criterion for determining which lands should be purchased as parks. He noted that many of the scenic areas in the state had little value as agricultural land and were most valuable as state parks. In some cases, as with the White Pines Forest in Ogle County, near Oregon, Illinois, the relic white pines had a "museum" value greater than their value as lumber. In such cases, Jensen argued, the state's policy ought to be to preserve such sites as parkland (Figure 61).[99]

Jensen argued that the purpose of the state's parks and reservations was "to preserve the scenic beauty of Illinois in its primitive form and to hold it as an heritage for generations yet unborn." To perpetuate this primitive quality, park caretakers should protect the natural quality of these lands:

> All replanting should be done with material indigenous to the region; no foreign plants should be introduced. No live material of any kind should be cut or removed, nor should dead trees, except where a section of the reservation has been destroyed by fire or storm. A dead tree may eventually become a world of interest in itself when covered with mosses, fungi, and other plants that soon find a home in the decaying trunk.

In addition, Jensen argued that concessions be kept out of the parks and that the parks be "held as free from man-made reminders as possible." He objected to recreation facilities such as "dance pavilions or merry-go-rounds":

> These things belong in the city and the village; they are out of place in reservations that are dedicated to nature's beauty. There should be sociability in the parks, but it should be the sociability of gathering around the open fire or dancing on a natural meadow. We go to nature to get a different kind of recreation than we can get in built-up areas, and we must not confuse the two.[100]

Jensen took some rather innovative measures to sell these proposals for new state parks directly to politicians and to the general public. On 30 March 1929 he delivered a "radio-logue" describing the various places that had been proposed as park sites. An article in the *Chicago Daily News* included a map showing the locations of each site and noted that Jensen "will discuss the varied scenic elements found in Illinois, commenting upon the practicality of preserving picturesque and rugged natural beauties." People were urged to call in and ask questions.[101]

Figure 61. View of white pine forest area of Ogle County, Illinois, targeted for protection by the Friends of Our Native Landscape. In 1927, the area was named White Pines Forest and was designated a protected park. Illustration is from Friends of Our Native Landscape 1921. Courtesy of Jensen Collection, Art and Architecture Library, University of Michigan, Ann Arbor.

As a result of these efforts by Jensen and the Friends of Our Native Landscape, at least seven of the areas recommended by the Friends were added as state parks in the following decade. These included Apple River Canyon (1932), Buffalo Rock State Park (1929), Fort Kaskaskia (1929), Giant City State Park (1927), Mississippi Palisades State Park or Savanna Headlands (1929), Rock River State Park (acquisition recommended in 1938), and White Pines Forest (1927). The Piasa Bluffs area was added to the Piasa State Parkway, and by 1938, work was under way to develop parkways along several of the rivers Jensen and the Friends had promoted: the Illinois River Parkway, Rock River State Parkway, and Sangamon River State Parkway. Two park areas in the southern part of the state would be added later: Dixon Springs (1946) and Ferne Clyffe (1949). Other southern sites surveyed by the Friends were eventually protected as part of the Shawnee National Forest.[102]

The Friends supported a number of other conservation efforts in the state, among them a crusade to preserve the beauty of the countryside along the state's highways. During the Depression, with Jensen as president, the Friends put together a pamphlet entitled *Roadside Planting and Development* in an effort to build a statewide policy on highways. Although Jensen is not specifically listed as the author of the pamphlet, it is clear that the ideas expressed in it correspond to his own. In the pamphlet, two basic reasons were suggested for preserving beauty along roadsides:

1. Most people have an innate or instinctive desire for beauty. Hence a region or section which creates a favorable impression, constantly increases in value and importance as people consider their environs as well as their immediate surroundings.
2. The touring public is naturally eager to visit or route its trips through the State which it knows maintains fine pavements and attractive scenery and everyone is aware that the money brought into a State by this means goes a long way toward the cost of these features.[103]

The pamphlet suggested that careful attention be given to selecting plants that could be adapted to specific soils and site conditions—especially those indigenous to a particular region of the state—so that they would blend in with the surrounding countryside. Emphasis was placed on deciduous plants, many of which were a source of interest as their character changed with the seasons. Plantings and landforms should be chosen to enhance the natural scenery, making the roadside seem a part of the general countryside. Neighboring woodlots should be extended onto the highway right-of-way by means of new plantings; the open prairie landscape should be enhanced by lower-profile plants such as hawthorn, plum, crabapple, and prairie roses. Finally, the Friends suggested that particular attention be given to encouraging and preserving wildflowers and prairie grasses along roads, as well as to using plantings to provide refuge for birds.[104]

The pamphlet advocated creating footpaths along one side of the road. These would provide routes for walking for enjoyment and exercise, as well as for walking to and from work or school. At regular points along such roads, attractive resting places with spaces for picnics and campfires would further enhance the roadways. The Friends looked forward to the day when power and telephone lines would be placed underground. Until then, they suggested that lines be placed above each other on one side of the road to the outside of the right-of-way.

Jensen also organized chapters of Friends of Our Native Landscape in Wisconsin (1921) and Michigan (1924). Genevieve Gillette, who had worked in Jensen's office in the early 1920s, helped establish a Michigan chapter after she moved back to her home state in 1924, and she worked hard to establish many of Michigan's state parks. In 1927, fifteen to twenty students at the University of Wisconsin formed a junior chapter with the intention of pursuing "purely spontaneous" activities in the out-of-doors. They also admitted to needing "inspiration during exams," and were thrilled at "the possibility of an evening with Jens Jensen." Members of the faculty at the University of Wisconsin were particularly supportive of the Friends' activities; Franz Aust, Alice Drought, and G. William Longenecker in the Landscape Architecture Department all took leadership roles. Aust edited the group's newsletter, *Our Native Landscape*. The first issue contained an essay entitled "A Cry for Beauty," by Glenn Frank, then president of the University of Wisconsin, who claimed to be completely captivated by the dedication of the group to preserving natural beauty. Ultimately, Wisconsin's chapter of the Friends of Our Native Landscape proved to be the most lasting; today it is the only one of these groups still in existence.[105]

In addition to these conservation efforts, Jensen supported a wide range of conservation causes around the country. In 1916, for instance, he prepared a *Report to the Woman's League for the Protection of Riverside Park* in New York City. At the time, the New York Central Railroad had proposed to extend a right-of-way through the park in a covered tunnel. According to the company's plans, the rail lines would hug the bluffs of the Hudson River, and concrete terraces and playgrounds would be built on the roof over the tracks. In his report, Jensen argued against the degradation of the park and pleaded for the protection of the river bluffs.[106]

Other conservation efforts advocated by Jensen included support for a prairie national park, creation of a national park in what is now known as the Boundary Waters Wilderness Area in Minnesota and Ontario, and preservation of the Porcupine Mountains on Michigan's Upper Peninsula. During President Hoover's administration, Jensen was president of the Mississippi River Park Commission, which advocated the creation of a national park in the northern waters of the Mississippi River. During his later years in Wisconsin, Jensen seemed to be a tireless crusader, writing letters and otherwise lending support to preservation efforts. For example, he helped establish the Ridges Sanctuary, a rare boreal forest, in Bailey's Harbor, Wisconsin. In December 1945 he helped prepare *Park Board Report* for the Door County Board of Commissioners; in that report, sweeping proposals were made for setting aside county and township forest reserves, sanctuaries, and school forests. The report also advocated the protection of all headlands and the establishment of a program to reforest tax delinquent land. Jensen and the park board were particularly anxious to preserve reminders of the cultural heritage of the county as well:

"Lands that speak of pioneer and Indian occupation should be set aside as a tribute and a connecting link to the past."[107]

During the 1930s, Jensen thought the Civilian Conservation Corps and the Tennessee Valley Authority were doing great damage by dispersing recreation facilities throughout state parks. He argued for setting aside wild lands that would not be developed:

> There must be a sharp division between the land for physical recreation, which we build, and the lands we do not build. There is no wilderness— we are the wild ones. It is just nature pure and simple. Physical recreation must remain [in] artificial[ly] made centers for that purpose. . . . The C. C. C. camps are, in most instances, doing tremendous injury, and so is the Forest Service, in introducing recreation areas in the woods where the woods, the growth of things, the beauty and mystery of it all, must be the only source for educational and spiritual purposes.

Jensen was also concerned about state hunting policies and wildlife populations in Wisconsin, and he encouraged Aldo Leopold, who was then a professor of wildlife ecology at the University of Wisconsin, Madison, to push for new policies for state lands and for the enforcement of poaching laws. At the national level, Jensen was concerned not only with midwestern landscapes but also with conservation efforts in the Appalachian Mountains, the Everglades in Florida, and the redwoods in California.[108]

The Clearing: Ravinia, Illinois, and Ellison Bay, Wisconsin

For Jensen, the idea of a clearing held special meaning. In many of his designs, clearings provided a welcome contrast to the shade of a forest border and a dramatic interplay of light with the surrounding trees' leaves and tracery of branches. Clearings were places where one watched sunrises and sunsets, cloud patterns, starry nights, and all the other dramas that nature and its cycles provide for the observant eye. On a functional level, clearings became the stage for human theater, pageantry, and song. As habitat, the clearing and its woodland border were suitable settings for the plants Jensen so dearly loved: American plum, crabapple, hawthorn, and prairie rose. As an allegory, the clearing represented all of nature in a microcosm and had therapeutic effects upon the human psyche. In the warm sunlight of a clearing, Jensen felt that one could forget the worries and confusion of human life and come closer to God. It is not surprising that Jensen chose to call two of the very special landscapes in his personal life "The Clearing." The first of these was his studio compound on Dean Avenue in Ravinia, Illinois; the second was his home and school in Ellison

Figure 62. Jensen and his wife, Anne Marie, on the steps of their summer-house in Ravinia (Highlan Park), Illinois. Courtesy of Jensen Collection, Morton Arboretum, Lisle, Illinois.

Bay, Wisconsin, which he described as "both a clearing in the woods and a clearing for the mind."[109]

Jensen acquired the property for The Clearing in Ravinia around 1908. On this heavily wooded site abutting two ravines, Jensen experimented with many design ideas that became standard fare in his work. In the middle of the woods, he cut a sun opening, or clearing, and on its edge he placed the house. The steeply roofed, cathedral-ceilinged house on the property was first used by the Jensens as a summerhouse (Figure 62). Their permanent home was in Wilmette at this time. In 1918, during World War I, Jensen closed his Steinway Hall office in downtown Chicago and set up his studio in the Ravinia summerhouse. At the center of the living room stood an easel with large crayoned drawings and a grand piano. Jensen's daily routine was frequently broken by various visitors, especially during the Ravinia Festival season, and by lunches prepared by Mrs. Jensen or Jensen's secretary. Later, in the early twenties, Jensen winterized the house for his daughter, who had married Marshall Johnson and was starting a family. For his studio, Jensen then built a simple two-

Figure 63. "The Clearing" in Ravinia (Highland Park), Illinois. The house that Jensen built on this property is barely visible through the trees at the center of the picture. Photograph is from Lohmann 1926a.

room structure near the garage, placing it dramatically on the edge of the ravine. One room held two drafting tables; the other room served as Jensen's office.[110]

As he would in so many landscape designs, Jensen used hawthorn trees to soften the edge of the woods of The Clearing in Ravinia (Figure 63):

> Several hawthorns were brought in and placed at prominent points on the edge of the woodland. These trees through their natural spreading characteristics gave the clearing a feeling of breadth; they softened the cold cut I had made and gave the little sun opening a poetic feeling most essential to make it more than a hole in the woods.

For many years this garden provided him with much joy. The simple pleasures of watching the sun set at the end of the day or gazing at the starry heavens through the clearing gave Jensen great peace and helped inspire his work.[111]

Jensen was fascinated by the Amerindian history of the site: "Following the ridge of one of the ravines was an old Indian trail, and at the point where the two ravines met was a chipping station where Indians made arrowheads for hunt and war." Where the trail intersected the ravine, Jensen created one of his first outdoor theaters: "On a little elevation at the intersection of the two was a fitting place for an outdoor stage—we called it 'Player's Hill.' Many plays have been given here, some fitting the moonlight and others the dark and stormy nights."[112]

Here Jensen also developed another of his trademarks, the council ring:

Just below the "Player's Hill," on the slope of the ravine, the first council ring was built—a new adventure. In this friendly circle, around the fire, man becomes himself. Here there is no social caste. All are on the same level, looking each other in the face. A ring speaks of strength and friendship and is one of the great symbols of mankind. The fire in the center portrays the beginnings of civilization, and it was around the fire our forefathers gathered when they first set foot on this continent. This particular council fire is situated where it may be seen from up and down the ravine like a message of greeting to others. The smoke of the fire, illuminated by the moon, forms fantastic shapes which gently float over the deep and penetrating shadows of the ravine. Many of these rings have I built since this first attempt. When they are placed on school grounds or in playfields, I call them story rings. These rings are the beginning of a new social life in the gardens of the America of tomorrow.[113]

Jensen spent as much of his free time as possible at The Clearing in Ravinia, and it was there that he and Mrs. Jensen did much of their outdoor entertaining (Figure 64). Jensen deliberately interspersed his work in the office with walks in the ravine and time taken to enjoy the small pleasures of the changing seasons. His secretary, Mertha Fulkerson, recalled how, during a late winter thaw, a cheery Jensen came into the office urging them all to go for a walk. In the midst of their work, Fulkerson and the others grumbled that they were much too busy for any frivolity. Jensen went out by himself, only to return a short time later with two delicate snowdrop blossoms, the first harbingers of spring. Jensen clearly recognized the human need for life's simpler pleasures, "the clearing in the threatening clouds."[114]

During the late 1920s, Jensen became more and more disillusioned with cities, the automobile, and what he regarded as an increasingly materialistic society. He recognized that private estate work, which had been the mainstay of his office, was dwindling, and that very few commissions for the park work he loved continued to come his way. Gradually, he divorced himself from many of his former civic associations, such as Chicago's City Club, and began to devote an increasing amount of his energies to the Friends and his conservation efforts. When his wife, Anne Marie, died in 1934 after a prolonged and painful illness, he saw little reason to stay in Chicago.

Mrs. Jensen had always been an important force in Jensen's life. From the time he came to America in 1884, she had stood by his side, support-ing his wide-ranging interests and activities. Although she never put herself in the foreground, her warm and genial ways seemed to balance Jensen's impetuous tendencies and helped hold the family together during difficult times. Associates recall that she contributed much to his thinking, and in 1939 Jensen dedicated *Siftings* to her memory.[115]

During the summers, Jensen, his wife, and their children and grand-children vacationed in Door County, Wisconsin, in their cabin on 129 acres of cutover land he had bought on Ellison Bay in 1919 (Figure 65). Mrs. Jensen always enjoyed these visits, but she was not anxious to live there on a year-round basis. She had no desire to trade her Danish friends in Chicago for the isolation of Ellison Bay. When Mrs. Jensen died in 1934, Jensen was at first devastated, but soon saw her death as an oppor-tunity for him to sever his ties to Chicago and to city life in general and move permanently to the Ellison Bay property. He left his office to his son-in-law Marshall Johnson and wrote Genevieve Gillette that he intended "to get a new hold on life" up at Ellison Bay. At seventy-four years of age, Jensen had no plans to retire. Over the next years, he would work on Lincoln Memorial Garden and an occasional estate or park landscape design, but his chief interest was to establish the school that came to be known as "The Clearing."[116]

For the twenty years prior to Jensen's move to Ellison Bay, he had seriously thought about establishing a school based on his experiences with the folk schools and agricultural schools of Denmark. In true folk school tradition, Jensen was interested in educating the whole person, integrating technical training with teaching about life itself. As Jensen noted, "This school shall be where the wilderness and the cultivated meet, so youth can be free to cultivate and nourish its inherent abilities and wisdom, free from the shackles of intellectual decay." He had considered various locations: the Indiana Dunes, the mountains of West Virginia, the western shore of Lake Michigan near Traverse City, Michigan, the shore-line of Lake Superior in Wisconsin and along the Upper Peninsula in Michigan, and the Garrett's Bay area at the tip of the Door Peninsula in Wisconsin.

During the early 1930s, when Jensen was thinking seriously about the school—what form it would take and where it might be located—he depended heavily on the advice of Alice Drought, then an instructor in landscape architecture at the University of Wisconsin. Drought, who was active in the Wisconsin chapter of the Friends of Our Native Landscape, had experience in recreation planning and the design of camps, and Jensen trusted her advice. Their correspondence between 1930 and 1932

Figure 64. Mrs. Jensen (*far right*) leading a circle dance at The Clearing in Ravinia, Illinois. Courtesy of Jensen Collection, Morton Arboretum, Lisle, Illinois.

Figure 65. Cabin at "The Clearing" in Ellison Bay, Wisconsin. This cabin served as the Jensen family's summer home prior to Jensen's founding of his school, after which it became part of the dormitory facilities. Courtesy of E. Genevieve Gillette Collection, Christopher Graham.

hints at the site characteristics that Jensen desired for the school. He wanted a remote piece of land jutting out over open water where "you can see the setting sun, the rising sun, and the northern lights." Varied topography, running water, and at least some large old forest growth also were desirable. Shallow water was needed for swimming. For Jensen, swimming facilities were important: "When man has thrown off his clothes, he has become a child of nature. He then belongs, and from a cultural standpoint, to be able to belong is a point of truth that is essential in a truthful development of mind and body." Jensen clearly wanted students to enjoy attending his school: "If such a school is to be of any import, we must meet all the things in the out-of-doors that both stimulates body and soul. Ruggedness must become a virtue—as the opposite of polish." In June 1932, Drought suggested that the school be located in Door County. Despite the area's lack of running water, it seemed to have all the other qualities Jensen required. It is unclear from Drought's letter, however, whether she meant the Garrett's Bay property near the tip of Door County or the Ellison Bay property that Jensen already owned. The reason for finally selecting the Ellison Bay site probably had as much to do with finances as with anything else.[117]

Jensen also used Drought as a sounding board for many of his evolving ideas about the form the school should take. Two ideas, borrowed from the Danish folk high schools, were definite: teaching was to depend upon the spoken word without the use of textbooks, and accommodations were to be in "the family group plan," whereby everyone would live in dormitories and participate in community meals. Jensen was clear that his school was not to be a copy of the Danish schools; it should be fitting to the United States. He wanted the majority of the classes to be held in the out-of-doors, but he realized the need for a classroom building during inclement weather. Jensen's early suggestions for a program of studies included

> the following interpretations of the out-of-doors—Ecology, including plant harmony in relation to topography; soil studies; landscape construction; drafting; sketching and painting; surveying; floriculture; entomology; sculpture; poetry; drama; music and architecture. There should also be lectures on the flora and the fauna outside of what ecology teaches in the way of plant communities.[118]

Sessions were to run from 1 September through 1 July, with a six-week summer session starting after 4 July. In 1932, Jensen was uncertain whether the program should be a two-, three-, or four-year course of study. He expected to employ three or four teachers, including the director. While there would be no credits, diplomas, or graduations, Jensen did set standards for the students: they would be dismissed "for lack of interest or bad morals." He wanted to ensure that students were genuinely interested in their work: "No one should be permitted to the school that did not have a deep feeling for the art the student wants to study. It should not be a matter of studying something for the sake of making money, but studying something for the love of it, for a life work, for service to his fellow man."[119]

With meager funds but considerable enthusiasm and the help of his trusted secretary, Mertha Fulkerson, "The Clearing" became Jensen's chief endeavor for the remainder of his life. Jensen sought financial support from many of his earlier clients. Henry Babson helped pay for the buildings, and Edsel Ford and the Ford Motor Company provided a tractor and a truck, but the school was never financially secure during Jensen's lifetime. A disastrous fire on Easter Sunday, 1937, destroyed the original house and further set back the school. Shortly thereafter the present lodge and dining hall and the classroom building, all of which reflected Scandinavian building traditions, were constructed of native stone, with Jensen's friends Hugh Garden and John Van Bergen assisting Jensen with the designs (Figures 66–67).[120]

Over the years, Jensen developed several versions of a prospectus for the school, yet his basic theme remained the same: the school was directed to American youth with an emphasis on learning by doing and on building a sense of social responsibility and environmental stewardship. Jensen was deeply concerned about American young people. During his design career, he created numerous school grounds and college campuses for which he advocated homelike settings and an integration of learning with life in the out-of-doors. In a talk at the 1944 annual dinner meeting of the Wisconsin Friends of Our Native Landscape, in Madison, Wisconsin, Jensen expressed his worries about "modern youth who are more interested in taverns and poolrooms than in the simple joys of life." He said that he was "ashamed of the youth of America. They have no interest in their home. Interest in an automobile, yes, but an appreciation of beauty, no." In a letter to Genevieve Gillette following his lecture, he wrote that he was horrified by what he saw of the students in Madison—"the mothers of tomorrow!"[121]

In a subsequent letter to Gillette, he blamed much of the problem with young people on the American system of education, which he said was hopelessly "confused." At his school, The Clearing, he wanted to provide an alternative program that would allow young people to experience a "more profound and simpler life."[122] In a 1944 memo, "Answers to Madison Question," presumably written to the Department of Landscape Architecture at the University of Wisconsin, Jensen described his educational philosophy for The Clearing:

Figure 66. Main lodge under construction at The Clearing in Ellison Bay, Wisconsin. Architect Hugh M. G. Garden assisted Jensen with the design of this building. Courtesy of E. Genevieve Gillette Collection, Christopher Graham.

Figure 67. Classroom building at The Clearing in Ellison Bay, Wisconsin. Architect John S. Van Bergen is reported to have helped with the design of this building. In the foreground is the rock garden created from the pit where rock for the school's buildings was quarried. Courtesy of E. Genevieve Gillette Collection, Christopher Graham.

"The Clearing" is a pioneer name, and this school is pioneering in the field of education. The name signifies the school's real purpose, to clear away all debris of overstuffed learning, steeped in form and tradition, and to get to the source of all wisdom, the soil. It is a school of the philosophy of the soil. . . . I started to [en]vision "The Clearing" when I saw how deep our youth were sinking into the mire of unfounded theories, unprincipled reasoning. It was then I realized that we must first give youth a basic beginning to [their] reasoning that can withstand all the pitfalls that higher learning, so called, has to offer.[123]

Unlike the students at Frank Lloyd Wright's school, Taliesin, in Spring Green, Wisconsin, who were taught to follow their master's directives, Jensen wanted his students at The Clearing to initiate their own studies and projects and to learn as much from each other as from their instructors. In a brochure entitled "This is 'The Clearing' . . . An Assembly of Youth in an Environment Laden with Spiritual Force," Jensen further explained the intent of the programs at The Clearing:

"THE CLEARING" was conceived and designed for the youth who [intend] to study profoundly . . . and believe in themselves . . . and feel that in time they may help advance the life of their people to a higher plane. It is the urge to do things that is found here . . . do things worthwhile . . . not for oneself but for others. In that way only, life has not been wasted. But "THE CLEARING" is not by any means all serious thinking. There is merry making, there is music, there is dancing, there is dramatic expressions in the player's green. The bay has crystal clear water for those that love the water. There are hidden nooks in the cliffs of the bay for the thinker, for those that want to be alone.

Profound in its teaching, this school is a way of life. Here the student receives a penetrating reasoning which follows him in whatever field he chooses for his life work. There are no grades, degrees, or medals nor any other method of ranking the individual. Each student must feel that the joy [of] his own accomplishments is full reward for work well done. . . ."To do your bit well, there lies the honor."[124]

Jensen placed great emphasis on direct study of the landscape. In a letter to Camillo Schneider in 1939, he described the teaching of landscape design at The Clearing (Figure 68):

Here at my school the students do not learn gardening in the class room, but out in the open, amongst the different types of landscapes—the dunes, the bogs, the swamps, the cliffs, the rocks, the forests, the fields. We visit these native gardens on skis in the snow, we visit them in storms, in fogs, in moonlight, at sunrise, at sunsets and when the Northern lights play their mysterious color scheme on the horizon. At each time the landscape, the

Figure 68. Jensen with a visitor at The Clearing in Ellison Bay, Wisconsin. Note the stone wall and open field in the background. Jensen kept these features as a reminder of the pioneer history of the property. Photograph is from a group belonging to G. William Longenecker, from the University of Wisconsin, Madison. Courtesy of Jensen Collection, Morton Arboretum, Lisle, Illinois.

trees, the shrubs, the grasses, have a different message to you. All of the greatest importance to the young student.[125]

The program at The Clearing consisted of field work, lectures by Jensen and others, and courses in a variety of practical skills and arts. The faculty was to consist of "a philosopher, a horticulturalist, a farmer, a painter, and a weaver," as well as visiting teachers, who would "come for a week or two" and "bring fresh air and [a] new spirit to The Clearing." In reality, regular instruction at The Clearing centered mostly on Jensen and on Mertha Fulkerson, who was a proficient weaver. Visiting instructors provided variety and included many of Jensen's personal friends, such as the writer Sherwood Anderson, landscape architect Alfred Caldwell, poet Vachel Lindsay, sculptor Carl Milles, architect Eliel Saarinen, dancer Sybil Shearer, landscape architect Frank Waugh, and architect Frank Lloyd Wright.[126]

The grounds of The Clearing were carefully shaped from the native woods and abandoned fields that Jensen had found when he bought the

Figure 69. View of Green Bay and bluffs of Peninsula State Park as seen from the lodge area of The Clearing in Ellison Bay, Wisconsin. The evening sun sets across this horizon. Jensen carefully thinned the trees here to create this view. Darrel Morrison, Stephen Christy, and others have worked with students at The Clearing, managing the vegetation in this area to preserve the view that Jensen intended.

property. From the main lodge, he cut a path from which one could watch the sun rise across a large, open clearing. In winter, the morning sun flooded the central room of the building with warm light. On the other side of the lodge was a smaller clearing from which one could watch the sun set over the limestone bluffs across Ellison Bay. Here Jensen carefully trimmed around the existing white pines to frame the view (Figure 69). The main school building was set next to a sunken wildflower garden, created from the pit where native rock had been quarried for the buildings. Cabins were moved from other parts of the area and remodeled as dormitories. Each building was carefully sited to preserve the background of untouched forest. Wild roses, daylilies, and other flowers framed the entrances and gave the entire complex a homelike character. Of particular interest to Jensen was a planting of hollyhocks at the front door of the main hall. Hollyhocks had been given to Mrs. Jensen as a token of friendship by a local "pioneer" when the Jensens had first started coming to the Ellison Bay property. Jensen noted that each year the hollyhock blossoms "sing to us who remember the loving hands that both gave and planted the first seeds. And as long as these stone walls remain, the hollyhock will be here to greet the boys and girls who enter this institution, giving them a loving smile as they enter this new field of understanding."[127]

For Jensen, the entire landscape was inextricably woven with the teaching program. Each place held an important message. Jensen listed the characteristics and facilities of The Clearing as follows:

> The rugged shore line and its harmonious landscape of field and forest.
> The placing of buildings to bring out the true character of the land.
> The hardwood forest with its poetic ground covering.
> The Player's Green—An outdoor theater.
> The dancing ring.
> The Council Ring overlooking Green Bay and the northern lights.
> The lofty Hall with its inspiring window.
> The Cliff House on a precipitous ledge facing the setting sun.
> The old orchard, an earmark of past settlers.
> The old Carlson trail to the village, now the students' favorite hike.
> During the winter, the massive ice field of the bay, ice as far as the eye can see when the thermometer reaches thirty below.[128]

For students interested in landscape architecture, the opportunity to study with Jensen at The Clearing was a profoundly moving experience. Because of his association with Franz Aust and G. William Longenecker of the Department of Landscape Architecture at the University of Wisconsin in Madison, Jensen attracted more students from that program than from anywhere else. The education these students received at The Clearing was entirely different from what was being taught at most colleges and universities. One young student wrote back to Jensen to contrast what he had learned at The Clearing with what he saw in the landscape architecture program at Iowa State University in Ames:

> You scolded us at Wisconsin, but we didn't know what a plan was in comparison to the students here. [BUT] we knew what a landscape was. We knew the lakes, the oak woods, the rivers and bluffs, the prairies, the dunes, the rock ledges, and beech-hemlock forests. But out here they don't even know the prairie. They know how to make beautiful, theoretical plans, [how] to make long lists of nursery stock, [and about] the elements of academic design and engineering and botany. Of the arts, music, [and] literature, nothing. Some medieval architectural history. Some see farther, but they walk alone.[129]

Although landscape studies were a central focus of the school, Jensen did not want to limit the enrollment at The Clearing to students in landscape design. Other students also had much to gain from his programs. In

Figure 70. Mertha Fulkerson at The Clearing in Ellison Bay, Wisconsin. After Jensen's death, Fulkerson kept his dream alive and fought to make the current school a reality. Courtesy of Grace Richardson.

one of his brochures, he emphasized that The Clearing was for students from a variety of disciplines and future careers:

> Here the future artist, craftsman, home-maker, scientist, government official, business man, tiller of the soil, and professional man, *find themselves*. And it is just that. With the guidance and encouragement of "THE CLEARING," *they find themselves*.[130]

During Jensen's lifetime, keeping the school going was a never-ending battle. There always was a shortage of students; during World War II there also was a shortage of materials and food. Then, Jensen's health failed in 1946, and near the end he was essentially an invalid. He died quietly at The Clearing on 1 October 1951. Before his death, however, Jensen established for The Clearing a board of directors whose members promised to attend to the continuation of his school.

Immediately after Jensen's death the future of The Clearing seemed doubtful. There were no funds, and Mertha Fulkerson struggled to choose between various potential uses for the property. Finally, in 1953, the Wisconsin Farm Bureau Federation signed a lease for the property and agreed to run a series of summer programs similar to those Jensen had intended. The new programs began in 1954, and Fulkerson invited teachers who had been Jensen's close friends and associates: Alfred Caldwell,

William Deknatel, and Elizabeth Gimmler. Fulkerson managed the programs until her retirement in 1969 (Figure 70). Since that time, a number of capable resident managers have maintained the same types of programs that she initiated in keeping with the spirit of Jensen's original intentions. In 1985, the Farm Bureau notified the Friends of The Clearing—a voluntary group of alumni and other supporters of The Clearing which had been organized in 1952—that it could no longer support the summer programs at the school. Once again, The Clearing faced financial crisis, and only through the dedicated work and monetary help of the Friends of The Clearing and other supporters was the school able to weather the storm.[131]

Today, The Clearing is approaching financial stability and it stands as a fitting tribute to Jensen's life, work, and thinking. As in Jensen's time, the school strives to offer new opportunities for studying nature, the arts, and the humanities, always with a strong sense of being rooted in the landscape. To those who are familiar with Jensen and the programs at The Clearing, it remains a welcome beacon in an often confusing and confused world.

FOUR

Jensen's Design Style

Jensen's career was marked by a consistent philosophy of design, although there was a clear evolution in his style from his early experimental designs for parks and private residences to the more confident work in his retirement years. Throughout his career Jensen demonstrated an unending interest in creating places that soothe the human psyche and celebrate the beauty of nature. While each project had a distinctive character that reflected the nature of the site, the needs of the client, and the process by which the project was undertaken, certain qualities or design features nearly always made the project uniquely Jensen's. Among these qualities or design features were Jensen's adept handling of space and massing, the use of certain "symbolic" plant species, and the inclusion of structures such as his council rings. Despite the change and deterioration that have beset most Jensen landscapes, one can still find something unmistakably characteristic of Jensen in the remnants seen today. In this chapter, Jensen's general philosophy and approach to design are analyzed through a discussion of the trademarks or design principles that were repeated throughout his career and came to characterize his work.

The Use of Native Plants

Jensen's use of native plants in his designs evolved over the course of his career as his knowledge of the plants increased, as his confidence as a designer grew, and as he was given a freer hand in developing landscape designs. Although his design for the American Garden in Chicago's Union Park (1888) was intended to be a showcase for native flowers and shrubs, plans for other early projects, such as St. Ann's Hospital in Chicago (1899), show almost as many horticultural varieties as native trees and shrubs. In fact, in 1900 Jensen wrote several horticultural articles for *Park and Cemetery* in which he promoted the use of plants that clearly were not native to the Midwest. These included *Azalea mollis* and the

"Ghent" varieties, Russian olive (*Elaeagnus angustifolia*), and saucer magnolia (*Magnolia soulangiana*). For the Loeb "bird garden" in the heart of Chicago (1910–11), Jensen substituted tree-of-heaven (*Ailanthus altissima*) for sumac (*Rhus glabra*), fearing that sumac would not survive the air pollution then engulfing the city (Figure 71). Yet even in these early compositions, there is a sense of experimentation with native plants that were not then (and are not now) in common use. In time, Jensen would discontinue using many of the horticultural varieties he selected early in his career and would replace them with natives. He became increasingly concerned with the destruction of the native flora:

> The rich man, when he moves from the city to the suburbs, charmed by the beauty of the surrounding country, goes to work with the axe and removes all of what he calls "scrub oaks," "scrub elms," and "scrub God-knows-what." He thinks he is a great deal wiser than the great Master that built up this beautiful landscape for us, and he puts in a lot of Chinese, and Japanese, and German, and English, and Russian, and French trees which he thinks are better fitted for the American continent. I want to tell you, friends, that there is nothing that fits us better than the beauty that nature has bestowed upon us. The originality, the characteristic beauty of the American landscape we should keep as a sacred treasure.[1]

Still, Jensen never entirely stopped using horticultural varieties, even in his later design work. As Caldwell pointed out, Jensen tried to provide what the client wanted as part of an overall composition. If this included exotic plants, Jensen would group them in a special garden or in an area near the house. The background plantings on the property would invariably be native species. Thus, for example, at the Edsel and Eleanor Ford estate in Grosse Pointe Shores, Michigan, which was designed relatively late in his career, Jensen created a flower lane using a wide variety of both native and horticultural perennials and a mixture of native and exotic shrubs as background. Eleanor Ford also wanted a formal rose garden, so Jensen carefully tucked the garden off to the side of the major meadow, where it would not dominate the estate grounds. With so few trees on the site, Edsel Ford was concerned about saving the existing Norway spruce (*Picea abies*), Scotch pine (*Pinus sylvestris*), and weeping willow (*Salix babylonica*), so Jensen tried to accommodate them in the design wherever he could. In other zones of the estate, however, Jensen was a purist in his plant selection, choosing only plants that would grow together in the wild. Thus, on an island that was created out of dredged material on a sandbar in Lake St. Clair, Jensen planted thickets of wild trees, shrubs, and prairie perennials as a wild bird sanctuary.[2]

Jensen was adamant in objecting to the alterations people tried to make

Figure 71. View of Albert H. Loeb garden, Chicago (Hyde Park area), Illinois. Because Jensen thought that sumac would not survive the city's increasing air pollution, he substituted tree-of-heaven (*Ailanthus altissima*), which serves as the background plant in this photograph. Photograph by Henry Fuermann & Son, from W. Miller 1914a.

in his compositions. On most of his plans he included a note warning people not to make changes. Genevieve Gillette recalled an angry letter that Jensen sent to a client who had asked his opinion about changes she wanted to make in her garden. Presenting himself as an aggrieved artist, Jensen defended the integrity of his creations:

> I racked my brain to give you the choicest things for the particular place you asked me to do and I really spent time going over the things that you particularly liked and placing them where I think they'll be the greatest in your garden and make you a gorgeous picture. Now you come along and have seen some other things that do not combine in color or in texture or in any other way with the thing that I have created for you. And you cannot live with what I gave you. You've asked me what I think about taking care of it. It's your garden, you can do with it what you want. Don't say I ever helped you do anything![3]

When Jensen did have a free hand and a client who seemed to understand his ideas, he concentrated solely on native plants. This was particularly true in his designs for public gardens. Lincoln Memorial Garden is a good example of such a project. Here, the use of native plants in associations that would be found in nature is the strongest unifying element in Jensen's design. Perhaps this garden, more than any of Jensen's other projects, gave him the opportunity to develop a design closely based on natural models. As Stephen Christy pointed out in his studies of Jensen's work, Jensen's design for Lincoln Memorial Garden served not as a detailed plan, but more as a general "framework" that guided the efforts of the volunteers who were involved in the actual planting. By adopting such an approach, Jensen anticipated successional changes in the landscape and allowed "natural processes to take their course." Jensen's plan specified forest trees and a few shrubs; the understory was to be composed of species commonly found in natural association with the trees.[4]

Jensen did, however, take artistic license in establishing the natural framework of his designs. One of the major themes of Lincoln Memorial Garden was to display plants from all the areas of Illinois where Lincoln lived and worked. This concept translated into combining the various habitats found in Illinois on a site located in the tall-grass-prairie/savanna/forest mosaic of central Illinois. This meant planting bald cypress (*Taxodium distichum*) and its associates, from the warmer, swamp habitats at the southern tip of Illinois, as well as white birch (*Betula papyrifera*), which is restricted to a few cooler, sheltered sites in northern Illinois. Some of these regional immigrants have not fared well, and nature has replaced them with other species, both native and exotic.

Jensen carefully analyzed the conditions found on each site and planted species where they would do best. Lincoln Memorial Garden was treated in exactly this way. Here, for example, oaks (*Quercus spp.*) and sugar maples (*Acer saccharum*) were planted on uplands, floodplain trees on lower areas, and woodland-edge trees along open lanes. By comparing the land's contours with Jensen's design and the general species distribution found today in the garden, this relationship becomes obvious. For instance, on the most prominent "hill" overlooking the lake, Jensen set his grove of white oaks (*Quercus alba*) around the Lincoln Council Ring because this is where a grove of white oaks would naturally belong.

There have been problems with many of Jensen's landscapes, however, some of which can be attributed to Jensen's limited understanding of certain ecological processes associated with the plant communities he used. For example, in Lincoln Memorial Garden, Jensen planted none of the prairie grasses in the meadows or "sun openings," although he did include a few of the prairie forbs. While it is clear from his writings that he envisioned broad areas of the prairie's "festive colors," he may not have understood the biological relationships of the grasses and forbs on the native prairie and particularly in prairie restorations. Apparently he did not understand the necessity of fire (or at least mowing) in maintaining the prairie. In all fairness to Jensen, it should be noted that few if any people at this time understood how the prairie and savanna ecosystem functions; in fact, that knowledge remains rudimentary today. Not until 1934, when John Curtis and Henry Greene at the University of Wisconsin, Madison, began experimenting with reestablishing prairie plant communities, was anyone sure it could be done.[5]

A cursory examination of Jensen's planting plans would astound most landscape architects who now prepare working drawings for contractors. Jensen rarely located individual plants on his plans; more often he showed masses of trees or shrubs in an intricate, puzzle-like pattern. The reasons for this are twofold. First, Jensen almost always used plants in masses to attempt to create a sense of harmony and unity in his designs (via repetition of similar plants, textures, forms, and the like), as well as to suggest the natural patterns he observed in the countryside around Chicago. One nurseryman who worked with Jensen was said to have commented that Jensen did not plant trees, he sowed them. Second, Jensen was accustomed to methods of working whereby he had considerable control over the implementation of his design. Either he personally staked out the design, or the planting was done by one of his foremen, who were well trained in his techniques and artistry. In either case, a more detailed plan was unnecessary. Unlike some of his contemporaries, who tried to distance themselves from gardening, Jensen felt that a direct involvement with the soil was necessary for the art of landscaping. He preferred to think of his work as an art and a craft rather than as a profession.[6]

In his plant massings, Jensen deliberately sought arrangements that were similar to the groupings he found in native habitats. Like O. C. Simonds, Jensen knew the difficulties of creating a planting that has the charm of nature. In his book, *Landscape Gardening* (1920), Simonds described the difficulties of creating a truly irregular planting and noted that the directions for arranging plants in a natural composition must be explicit. He also observed that planting in regular arrangements seems to come instinctively to humans, but planting as nature plants requires conscious effort and is sometimes difficult to communicate. Rarely did Jensen write down his directions to clients, but when he did, he tried to provide practical suggestions for achieving the spirit he intended in the garden. Often his advice was general, and in many cases he must have frustrated clients who wanted specific answers. For example, in one letter to a client, Jensen gave instructions for planting a group of hawthorns: "I have shown on the plan hawthorns. You can plant not less than five and not more than fifteen plants, seven to eight feet apart." In a letter to Harriet Knudson describing the plantings at Lincoln Memorial Garden, Jensen was more specific, noting that "young trees and shrubs" should be "planted close to each other so one can protect the other." In another letter, he gave instructions for planting lilies in a low-lying area of the garden: "When I say a foot apart, I do not mean they should all be that far apart. Plant them in groups and leave five or six feet and then another group. Do not plant them circular or in any other form. In time they might cover up the spaces between the different groups, or other flowers will come in between them."[7]

Jensen also insisted that plants should be kept in their natural forms. From the early days of his career, he violently opposed the clipping of plants into topiary forms and hedges, except in vegetable gardens and orchards, where he occasionally used clipped hedges himself. He also objected to floral arrangements that "are full of brutal disregard for the spirit and character of the plants." In a 1902 article for *Park and Cemetery*, Jensen colorfully described topiary gardeners as "men with little intellect and plenty of money who, for the sake of popularity, will turn their gardens into museums of freaks where even the stalwart moonshiner would hesitate to pass through at the midnight hour." His dislike for topiary was one of the reasons he objected to the introduction of Italian gardens into the United States, where clipped evergreens were substituted for the Italian cypress. He wrote: "To create the Italian garden without the stately cypress is impossible. These gardens had their origin in southern countries and only there attain their true character." The art of American gardening, he argued, should rely on the natural forms of American plants.[8]

If Jensen had a favorite plant, it was most likely the hawthorn (*Crataegus spp.*). In fact, Jensen used a hawthorn motif on the letterhead of the stationery from his Ravinia office. No other plant was used as frequently or as masterfully or mentioned as often in his writings. Because of its horizontal branches, Jensen considered the hawthorn particularly expressive of the prairie region (Figure 72). This view was also held by other proponents of the prairie schools of landscape gardening and architecture. Prairie architect Robert Spencer, for example, borrowed the hawthorn motif from Jensen's landscape design for the August Magnus estate when he designed the stained-glass windows for the house. In his discussion of the "prairie style" of landscape gardening, Wilhelm Miller promoted the use of "stratified" plant materials (for example, those with horizontal branching habits or flower clusters) and mentioned hawthorn as a prime example.[9]

Hawthorns survive in many of Jensen's projects; in many places, however, time and insensitive pruning have reduced their visual impact. Nevertheless, on some of the old estates and parks that have benefited from more conscientious care (or benevolent neglect in some cases), the now old and gnarled hawthorns continue to provide much of the effect that

Figure 72. The graceful lines of a hawthorn at the Edsel and Eleanor Ford house in Grosse Pointe Shores, Michigan. For Jensen, the hawthorn, with its low, horizontal branching habit, was a symbol of the prairie, and he used it often in his designs.

Jensen intended. In the large central open spaces included in his designs for parks and estates, hawthorn trees were used as scattered individuals within an otherwise open meadow; they were also used in loose masses along the borders, together with other small trees such as alternate-leaf dogwood (*Cornus alternifolia*), prairie crabapple (*Malus ioensis*), and American plum (*Prunus americana*). Redbud (*Cercis canadensis*) and flowering dogwood (*Cornus florida*) were included in more southern projects. Through repetition, these trees were to guide one's eye down the length of the meadows, enhancing the perspective as they became more distant. Because of their relatively low profile and horizontal branching, they tended to reinforce rather than interrupt the long "prairie" views, and they provided a transition to the larger trees along the woodland borders (oak and maple, for example). Jensen believed that small trees were necessary to "bind together forest and meadow." Quoting Jensen, Miller wrote in *The Prairie Spirit in Landscape Gardening* (1915), "The bold leap that nature often makes from haws and crabs down to the prairie flowers reminds one of some powerful animal, slipping silently from forest shade into a sea of grasses."[10]

Frequently hawthorns, or sometimes prairie crabapple trees, were located at important pivotal points along broad meadows, such as in the designs for the Frank Aldrich estate in Bloomington, Illinois (1918), and the Edsel Ford estate in Grosse Pointe Shores, Michigan (1928). They were also used to mark the peninsulas of shrub vegetation that jut out into the open meadows and "pinch" the space of the meadow, partially concealing the space beyond. Likewise, in a number of plans, Jensen used clusters of hawthorn with other shrub masses to signal important points such as junctions in a trail or road. At Humboldt Park, for instance, one can still find clusters of Jensen's hawthorn trees among the shrubs and other small trees at many of the points where two trails cross. The age of the trees suggests that they were part of the original plantings.

Wilhelm Miller noted that repetition was a leading characteristic of the prairie style of landscaping. For Jensen, the repetition of individual plants—as well as characteristic lines, colors, or forms—around the edges of a space was important in the development of a dominant theme or motif in each design. He chose to emphasize these transitional zones by creating situations of contrast in shade and shadow and by featuring the native trees and shrubs typically found at a forest's edge. A list of the plants most frequently used and mentioned by Jensen—hawthorn, plum, prairie crabapple, and prairie rose, among others—indicates his partiality to plants of the forest border.[11]

A sun opening along the entrance drive at the Henry Babson estate in Riverside, Illinois (1909), illustrates how Jensen repeated plants to give unity to a small space. A cluster of hawthorn trees marks the edge of the woods and the entrance to the opening. Just down the road, in the center of the opening, another hawthorn stands alone, thus unifying the center of the space with the hawthorn trees at the forest's border. While different tree and shrub species were used in this composition, each was repeated at various places around the border of the space to provide an overall unity to the design.

For Jensen, the only meaningful source of inspiration for landscape gardening was the native landscape. As he noted, "Its vegetation, its wild life are due to natural selection for fitness for thousands of years. It is fitting and it belongs. To destroy it is to destroy the real America. To corrupt it is the work of stupidity—it is vandalism." For Jensen, the greatest challenge for the landscape architect was to "fit into a human habitat those plants best suited for this purpose, and in harmony with their surroundings. Every plant has a character of its own, and when it is permitted to develop fully will bring beauty and joy—stunted plants are not an art but a craft."

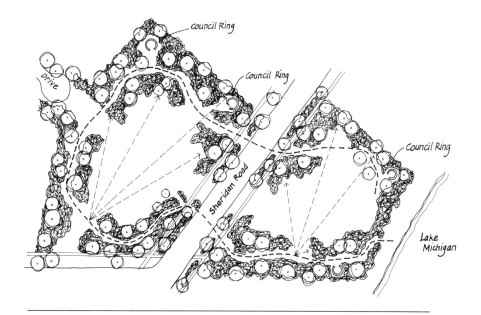

Figure 73. Mahoney Park (Bird Sanctuary and Wildflower Preserve) in Kenilworth, Illinois, designed by Jensen in 1933. Note the path that moves around the central space at the wooded border, providing intermittent views of the meadow between trees and shrub masses. Council rings, which are tucked into the corners of the garden, also provide views out into the central meadow.

He believed that the art of working with native vegetation required much more than casual study; the chapter entitled "Our Native Landscape" in Jensen's *Siftings* (1939) is a testament to his lifetime of studying and testing native plants in his compositions. Perhaps more than any of his contemporaries, Jensen took his love of the native landscape to heart and made it the central theme of his career.[12]

Spaces

One of the most intriguing aspects of Jensen's work was how he handled the open spaces that are found at the core of many, if not most, of his designs. Borrowing extensively from design traditions established in the Midwest by Frederick Law Olmsted, H. W. S. Cleveland, and O. C. Simonds, Jensen created unique, three-dimensional landscapes with flowing spaces and sculptured masses of vegetation. Sometimes these spaces were large, as with the meadows at Chicago's Columbus Park (1917), or at the Henry Ford estate in Dearborn, Michigan (1914). In other designs, such as that for the F. D. Frawley estate in Indianapolis, Indiana (1922), or the Mahoney Bird Sanctuary and Wildflower Preserve (now Mahoney

Park) in Kenilworth, Illinois (1933), the actual extent of the space is limited, but the impression is one of a much larger meadow (Figure 73). Jensen often created this illusion of space (continuing beyond the immediate range of vision) by carefully orchestrating the viewer's position with the shape of a space and its irregular edges. Combined with the generally flat or gently rolling topography of most of Jensen's projects, the illusion evoked the spatial openness of the landscapes that characterize the midwestern prairie and forest-border region. Although these spaces are indeed more limited than natural prairie expanses, the feeling of freedom and openness is much the same.[13]

The axes of many of Jensen's open spaces were often slightly bent so that the end of the space disappeared just around the bend; thus, the space assumed an almost infinite quality. Likewise, the borders of these spaces were frequently made up of a series of irregular coves and promontories of shrub and tree masses that provided a sense of mystery, an illusion that there was space hidden behind the massed plantings. This enticed the viewer to move through a space to see what lay beyond each bend. Similarly, islands of vegetation were frequently set off-center in these meadows—as at the Harry Rubens estate in Glencoe, Illinois (1904) (Figure 74), and at Columbus Park (1917)—with much the same effect. In some of these spaces, the viewer saw the open space through the narrow end of a long, linear space that broadened toward the opposite end. In others, walls of vegetation "pinched" the space one or several times to give the impression of a series of openings (Figure 75).

Jensen frequently employed what came to be known as the "long view." Here one could view a linear or oblong space from one end with masses of trees and shrubs forming the borders on either side. Walking around Douglas and Humboldt parks in Chicago, one still sees signs of these long, linear spaces, despite recent plantings by the parks department that will eventually block the distant prospect and divide the spaces into smaller units. At many large estates designed by Jensen in the Chicago area, the house is prominently situated at the end of a long, open space, and offers a major view along the opening's full length. At the Henry Ford estate, one first gets a glimpse of the long meadow when arriving at the front door, but it is from the terrace on the west end of the house that one can sit and contemplate the large expanse. Similarly, at the Edsel Ford estate, the house is situated at one end overlooking the long space, but the drive cuts across the far end of the meadow, so that the visitor first gets a glimpse of the house through the long, open space. The drive then skirts the edge of the meadow, providing only short glimpses of the open expanse through the bordering trees. Not until one reaches the end of the driveway does one see the entire house and get another view down the

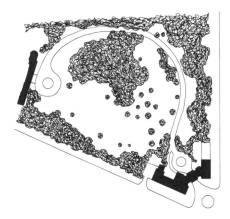

Figure 74. Entrance drive to the Harry Rubens estate, Glencoe, Illinois, designed by Jensen in 1904. Here, as in many other Jensen designs, the entrance road does not lead directly to the house, but circumscribes the meadow. Scattered small trees lead the viewer's eye through the open space, and the large island helps break up the space while partially blocking the view of the house. As a result, the space seems much larger and more dynamic.

Figure 75. View from the porch of the house at the W. E. Simms estate in Spring Station, Kentucky. Notice how the masses of trees and shrubs combine to "pinch" the space of the meadow and frame the old hickory tree in the distance.

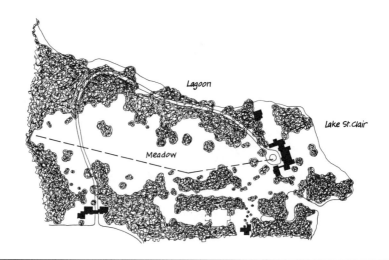

Lagoon

Lake St.Clair

Meadow

Figure 76. Section of the plan for the Edsel and Eleanor Ford house in Grosse Pointe Shores, Michigan. Jensen created a dramatic entrance sequence by providing only a glimpse of the main house through the trees and across the long meadow and then taking the road through a grove of trees. Note the slightly bent axis of the meadow space, which is set to provide views of the setting sun during the summer months. Clusters of hawthorn and other small trees enhance the perspective down the meadow space.

Figure 77. First view of the Edsel and Eleanor Ford house through a cluster of sugar maples and across the meadow as one enters the estate.

long meadow space. The sequence provides a sense of anticipation and ceremony as one proceeds past the end of the meadow, through the woods at the edge of the meadow, and finally to the house. Yet the large Tudor house does not assume extreme prominence as it might have, had it been situated on an axis with a long drive leading through the center of the meadow. Instead, the house is situated to take advantage of the view without ever dominating the landscape (Figures 76–77).[14]

Unlike Jensen's other large public works, Lincoln Memorial Garden (1936) has no large central meadow space. Instead, the design makes use of a narrow band of meadows sloping down to the lakeshore. The views of these meadow spaces are from the uphill side of the slopes looking out to the lake. The two most obvious meadow views are from Council Ring no. 3 and the trail to the west of it, and from Council Ring no. 4 (Lincoln Council Ring). In both places the vistas are framed by trees in the foreground and clusters of hawthorn farther down the slope. These are perhaps the only places in Lincoln Memorial Garden where Jensen was able to emphasize the horizontal expanse of the prairie landscape—what Wilhelm Miller called "the broad view." Although the actual area is modest, the prospect appears to be a boundless combination of earth, water surface, and sky. From these vantage points in the Lincoln Memorial Garden, as on the great prairie expanses that were once so common in Illinois, the open sky with its many moods integrates with the foreground landscape. Here again, hawthorn is used to emphasize the horizontal expanse. The distant view is of the horizontal shoreline on the other side of the lake. In the view from Council Ring no. 4, an island creates another horizontal band, which is repeated by the open landscape in the middle ground and the cluster of hawthorns on the slope. This repetition creates the feeling of a unified landscape and, with the borrowed space of the lake and sky, a landscape that is much larger than the actual confines of Lincoln Memorial Garden.[15]

The other dominant spatial feature at Lincoln Memorial Garden is the pattern of linear, fingerlike spaces that alternate with the wooded portions of the site to create a series of lanes. These linear spaces, combined with the bands of prairie meadow, create a system of openings that penetrate and bring sunlight into the wooded portions of the landscape and extend views down their length. Several of these lanes have an east-west orientation, which allows the low-angled rays of the sun in the late evening or early morning to reach deep into the garden. As in other Jensen designs, sugar maples (*Acer saccharum*), smooth sumac (*Rhus glabra*), and goldenrod (*Solidago spp.*) are positioned to catch the glow of the autumn sun in late afternoon. Other lanes are oriented north-south and catch the low-

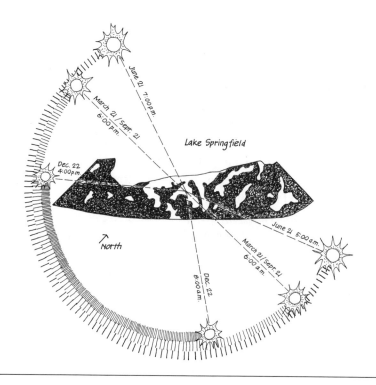

Figure 78. Analysis of seasonal sun angles and openings at Lincoln Memorial Garden, Springfield, Illinois. The various lanes and "sun openings" were consciously designed to create dramatic patterns of sun and shadow that change throughout the day and over the course of the year.

angled afternoon sun "broadside," thereby creating distinctive shadow patterns (Figure 78).

These fingerlike lanes also provide a version of "the long view" that is found in Jensen projects in which one views a linear space bordered by tree and shrub masses from a narrowed end. Where mowed paths run the length of these spaces, the lane often ends with a dramatic view of the lake. Other fingers of open meadow serve primarily to provide visual penetration into the garden landscape. The ends of these spaces are often hidden from view behind some mass of vegetation or around a slight bend in the axis of the space so that the total depth of the lane appears longer than the actual width (600–800 feet at these points) of the garden.

In addition to a large central open space, many of Jensen's designs employ a series of smaller side spaces just off the major meadow. At the Henry Ford estate (1914), interconnected garden rooms are strung together as if on a necklace, with the great meadow serving as the major focal point. Whereas the great meadow is public in its central location, scale, and dramatic effect, the smaller garden rooms provide intimate private

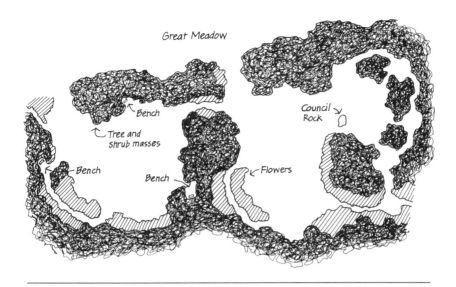

Figure 79. Small garden rooms located just off the main meadow at Fair Lane, the Henry Ford estate in Dearborn, Michigan. Small alcoves with benches in the surrounding trees and shrubs were intended to provide quiet places for retreat and reflection. Narrow openings invite the viewer to walk through a continuing network of these outdoor rooms.

spaces for contemplation and sitting. Even here, however, the spaces are not entirely enclosed, for narrow openings allow glimpses into some other garden room or into the larger space (Figure 79). In Jensen's landscapes, one frequently encounters a series of these rooms along a path or road creating interesting sequences of closed/open/closed canopied spaces.

At Lincoln Memorial Garden, Jensen designed a series of garden rooms under the canopy of sugar maples along the garden trail. By planting a group of five or six maples close together so that their branches intermingled, he created a pocket of dense shade that effectively kept open a garden room similar to the spaces found in maple woods in the wild. On a walk through the garden today, one's awareness of spatial relationships is heightened by the transitions from dense thickets of oak-hickory woods to open garden rooms under the maple trees.

Light and Shadow

The conscious intermingling of light and shadow is characteristic of a Jensen design. Landscape architecture professor Darrel Morrison suggests that in coming from a frequently gray, overcast environment like Denmark, Jensen may have been particularly impressed with the brilliance of the midwestern sun and the dramatic variations in the quality of light at different times of the year. Jensen himself noted that "light and shadow and their distribution during the entire circle of the day and night are important fundamentals in the art of landscaping." The spatial framework for many of Jensen's designs had as much to do with sunlight and shadow as with the physical expression of space.[16]

Long, open spaces were frequently oriented with their major axes in an east-west direction so that the sunrise and sunset could be seen at both ends. At Jensen's school, The Clearing, the open spaces are directed so that in winter the sun rises over the meadow to the east of the main hall, and sets over the cliffs of Green Bay, as seen from the hall's dramatic window facing west.

On several of Jensen's plans—his design for the Aldrich estate in Bloomington, Illinois (1918), for example—these spaces are actually labeled as "path[s] to the rising [or setting] sun." In addition, the directional axes of the spaces permit another of Jensen's effects: the low-angled sun of autumn evenings highlights the bright oranges and reds of the sugar maples and sumac and illuminates the feathery heads of such plants as goldenrod. This technique ensures that the often brief period of brilliant fall color does not go unnoticed.[17]

Smaller clearings, or "sun openings," as Jensen called them, also are central to Jensen's handling of light in many of his designs, and they frequently appear along a road or pathway. The transition from shade to sun to shade is obvious. Traveling along a path or road, a person moves from shadow into full sunlight and into shadow again. In a collection of photographs of the Rubens estate that Jensen published in *Sketchbook* in 1906, one particular image showing this sequence is aptly entitled "the light behind the immediate shade." The pattern also allows a dramatic backlighting of the tree and shrub vegetation, silhouetting the structure of branches and creating memorable windows of the various shades of green. For Jensen, these dramatic openings—with their contrast of shade from the surrounding woods—provided a sense of joy and celebration. In these spaces, he believed that people could be close to the cycles of nature.[18]

It must be noted that Jensen was extremely fond of the paintings of George Inness: "George Inness, whom I consider the greatest landscape painter this country has produced, always has a ray of light in every picture he painted. No matter how storm-tossed the clouds are, there is this ray of hope promising a better day. I am never in the Art Institute of Chicago without making a visit, if only for a few minutes, to the splendid Inness collection there. And every time I come away refreshed. Inness was a great master." In much the same way that Jensen attempted to use sunlight in his designed landscapes, Inness recorded sunlight on his canvases. Thus, the "clearing" and landscapes illuminated by sunlight in the early morning

Figure 80. View through a cluster of sugar maple trees into a "sun opening" at Lincoln Memorial Garden from Council Ring no. 5 (see 1936 plan of the garden).

or late afternoon are recurring themes in the work of both men.[19]

In "Natural Parks and Gardens," which Jensen published with Ragna Eskil in 1930, Jensen commented that "the road should always be in shadow emerging upon the lawn in full sunlight." This is especially true of the paths surrounding many of Jensen's large central openings. Rather than design paths that passed through the center of a space in full sunlight, Jensen made sure that visitors to the garden had to walk around and look into the sunlit areas from a shady path; he believed that sunlight could be better appreciated from such a shade-drenched border. In addition, the view into these open spaces through the branches of trees would give visitors both a glimpse of the shimmering patterns of green from the leaves' transparency and a framed picture of the meadow beyond. Jensen frequently grouped a lot of large trees just outside the buildings in his landscapes to provide a shaded canopy from which to view these larger spaces. The dark silhouettes of the tree trunks provided a human scale and a contrast to the bright expanses of the meadow.[20]

The sun openings at Lincoln Memorial Garden are indicative of the various dimensions used by Jensen. They range from 60 to 70 feet in width—that is, are approximately one and a half times as wide as the height of the surrounding oaks—to spaces only as wide as the canopy of a single tree, 25 to 30 feet across. Only one sun opening was labeled as such on Jensen's final plan, although there are many other small openings on or just off the trail throughout the woodland portions of the garden. These spaces provide pockets of sunlight and create dramatic backlighting effects on the trees and shrubs surrounding the openings (Figure 80). Here, too, are found pockets of sun-loving and forest-edge species such as aster (*Aster spp.*), goldenrod (*Solidago spp.*), sumac (*Rhus spp.*), raspberry (*Rubus spp.*), and wild rose (*Rosa spp.*). Unfortunately, these same conditions also encourage the intrusion of many troublesome plants such as honeysuckle (*Lonicera x-bella* and *L. japonica*), mulberry (*Morus alba*), and multiflora rose (*Rosa multiflora*), which soon become pests and threaten the original landscape design.

Movement

Jensen carefully placed roads to permit visitors to experience a sequence of sun and shade or to walk around the forested edge of a clearing to view the sunny ground from the shaded border. He also laid out his paths in gentle curves rather than in straight lines. He preferred broad, flowing curves, and deliberately avoided creating tight, "snaky" curves (Figures 81–82).

For Jensen, a garden of straight lines and strictly geometric forms was permissible only where absolute order was needed, as in a vegetable garden or a formal rose garden. In other landscape forms, such rigid geometry represented a repression of nature and contradicted the very purpose of a garden as a place of relief. Jensen associated such harsh lines with the autocratic societies he had left behind in Europe: "Straight lines spell autocracy, of which most European gardens are an expression, and their course points to intellectual decay, which soon develops a prison from which the mind can never escape." His forced service in the German army and the time he spent in Berlin no doubt reinforced these beliefs. He regarded gardens similar to those at Versailles and the grand boulevards associated with them as symbols of a despotic government that was more interested in shows of military strength or pompous royalty than in the health and well-being of the people. In the United States, he believed that curves "full of mystery and beauty" were appropriate expressions of democratic ideals.[21]

The curves could not be arbitrary, however; they had to fit the topography, vegetation, or some historical precedent that gave them meaning. For example, at Columbus Park in Chicago (1917), the outline of the lagoon and the road on the ridge above it follow the topography of an ancient

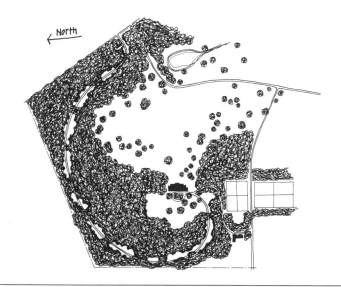

Figure 81. Plan of the W. E. Simms estate in Spring Station, Kentucky. Note the gentle curves of the entrance drive, which leads through a series of openings in the woods to the house. Visitors get only minor glimpses of the meadow until they reach the main house.

Figure 82. Entrance drive at the W. E. Simms estate in Spring Station, Kentucky. Openings in the forest canopy create dancing patterns of sunlight along the road.

Figure 83. Path at Lincoln Memorial Garden, Springfield, Illinois. This view illustrates how Jensen frequently created a sense of mystery by making a curving path disappear behind a dense planting of shrubs or trees. The plantings also created an apparent reason for the bend, so that the curves of the path did not appear to have been placed arbitrarily.

beach. At "The Clearing" in Ravinia, Jensen organized the garden spaces outside his studio around old Indian trails.[22]

In many of his parks and gardens, Jensen planted large trees or groups of hawthorn, prairie crabapple, or other small trees and shrubs on the inside of a curve to provide a visual reason for the bend in the road. Following the path around the trees and shrubs, the visitor is compelled to investigate what lies beyond (Figure 83). While this technique was not new to the art of landscape design, Jensen certainly adopted it as one of his trademarks.[23]

Jensen's gardens also had a hierarchy of trails leading to different parts of the garden. The paths separating gardens or areas around the house were usually wider and were often paved with randomly placed cut stones (Figure 84). Pathways that moved away from the house into a garden either disappeared completely into a mowed lawn or became single stepping stones. Jensen, it seems, wanted people to fully enjoy the garden's

Figure 84. Jensen's hierarchy of garden trails often included wider paths of randomly cut stones leading to major garden features near the house, such as this path in his garden at The Clearing in Ravinia (Highland Park), Illinois. First published in Lohmann 1926a. Photograph courtesy of David R. Phillips, Chicago Architectural Photographing Company.

beauty without distractions; thus, he required movement through the garden spaces not in groups, but individually.

Jensen traveled extensively in the Midwest and across the country during his lifetime, and he thought deeply about roadside (and railroad) landscapes. *Siftings* is full of his observations and comments on places where remnants of a native landscape still remained and provided a sense of regional identity. Jensen published an article on roadside planting in *Landscape Architecture;* put together, with the Friends of Our Native Landscape, a booklet entitled *Roadside Planting and Development;* and wrote several papers on roadside planting for the Lincoln Highway Association. One of the papers written for the Lincoln Highway Association was published as "Roadside Planting" in *Landscape Architecture* and as "Highway Beauty" in *Roycroft.* In it Jensen argued that "roadside planting should be a part of the general character of the landscape so that the roads themselves do not appear as a definite line apart from the rest of the landscape, but a means to an end that is in sympathy with its surroundings." He suggested that on the landscapes of an open prairie, rows of trees are out of place and tend to shut out the views of the surrounding countryside.[24]

Jensen worried about the increasing impact of the automobile on the American landscape and about America's fascination with speed. He thus argued for the preservation and creation of narrower, quieter roads similar to the "pikes" he had found in Kentucky, which came as close to what he considered "a beautiful American highway" as anything he had seen. These were places where "trees seem[ed] to enjoy the roadside and each other's company" and where travelers could enjoy local wildflowers or other native plants as well as the sounds of native songbirds. Jensen's design for the "ideal section" of the Lincoln Highway provided a glimpse of his vision for all the nation's highways.[25]

Water

One of the most recognizable features of a Jensen landscape is a broad, flat body of water. These "prairie rivers," as Jensen called them, were strong elements in his early park work and were representative of the vast prairie wetlands that characterized the Chicago region. Likewise, the stonework with which Jensen backed many of these rivers was an attempt to capture the feeling of "the prairie bluff or stratified rock" of rivers and streams in the Midwest as they cut channels through the horizontal deposits of limestone underlying the ground surface (Figure 85).[26]

It is easy to see that Jensen's inspiration for these features came from the bluffs that border the Illinois, Rock, and Mississippi rivers. Jensen knew Illinois' rivers well, and with the Friends of Our Native Landscape had fought for the protection of a number of particularly scenic river areas as state parks. Many of the sites noted in his 1921 booklet, *Proposed Park Areas in the State of Illinois*—for example, the Savanna headlands on the Mississippi River, the Rock River country, the Greater Starved Rock area on the Illinois River, and the Piasa Bluffs area near St. Louis on the Mississippi—had rugged limestone bluffs similar to those Jensen created in his designs.[27]

Typically, the source of Jensen's water features was in a shady, rocky ledge, much as a natural spring emanates from a limestone aquifer. In some of Jensen's estate designs, these streams then emptied into small pools of water backed by a grove of arborvitae (*Thuja occidentalis*), cedar (*Juniperus virginiana*), or hemlock (*Tsuga canadensis*), with white birch (*Betula papyrifera*) or other light-trunked trees as accents in the foreground. Some of these pools were intended for viewing in the moonlight,

Figure 85. Pool area at the W. E. Simms estate in Spring Station, Kentucky. Jensen carefully integrated quiet pools with artful stonework to capture the feeling of native bluffs. Photograph is from Elwood 1924.

as at the A. G. Becker estate in Highland Park, Illinois (1921), where Jensen created a small pond in a depression and behind it planted "groups of cedars which loomed up with mysterious forms in the evening light, casting deep shadows over the pool. These cedars were placed in the path of the southern moon."[28]

In Jensen's park designs, these streams grew into large, flat prairie rivers bordered by masses of sweet flag (*Acorus calamus*), bluejoint grass (*Calamagrostis canadensis*), iris (*Iris virginica shrevei*), rose mallow (*Hibiscus moscheutos*), arrowhead (*Sagittaria latifolia*), cordgrass (*Stipa spartea*), cattail (*Typha latifolia*), and other wetland species. Perhaps the most effective of these was the "river" Jensen created in Columbus Park. Here, one finds many of Jensen's landscape symbols together in one area. On the small rise where the river begins from a limestone ledge, one can stand and gaze down the slow-moving river, with its borders of wet-meadow vegetation, to a slight rise on the opposite shore, on which sits a small group of hawthorns, with their strong horizontal branches symbolically echoing the broad expanse of the prairie.

Jensen's stonework is a celebrated aspect of his designs. He took great care in selecting and laying the stone around his council rings, pools, ponds, streams, and other structures so that the rockwork would emulate the irregularities of a natural limestone bluff. Much of the stone came out of quarries in Wisconsin, and Jensen depended on the artistic sense of his stonemasons to create the feeling he wanted in these walls. Jensen was particularly concerned with respecting and emphasizing the natural character of the stones he used. In *Siftings* (1939), he noted:

> There is a remarkable nobility in rocks, weatherbeaten and worn by water of past ages. Rocks, like trees, have a character all their own, and this character is emphasized when the rock is rightly placed. Usually only a few plants can be used in connection with these heralds of the past, a little moss and a few clinging plants. One should always keep in mind that the rock has a story to tell, and it should not be vulgarized by a conglomeration of unfitting plants.

To that end, the stones were carefully laid horizontally on each other with the joints brushed out six inches or more and with pockets of soil kept for plantings among the stones.[29]

Jensen used horizontal bands of limestone in a variety of ways: as backdrops to swimming pools and borders along river or lagoon systems, for bird baths, and in constructing park shelters. Some of his most effective stonework was done at the W. E. Simms and K. D. Alexander estates (1911) in Spring Station, Kentucky, where Jensen created dramatic waterfalls complete with a cascade, as well as quiet pools with large outcrops of limestone (Figures 86 and 87). Jensen's work at Henry Ford's Fair Lane (1914) was the most extensive of his river-edge rock creations.

Jensen took great pride in his skill with rockwork. When Edsel and Eleanor Ford negotiated to build their Gaukler Pointe estate in Grosse Pointe Shores, a wealthy suburb near Detroit, Edsel questioned whether Jensen's previous swimming pool at the Ford's Jefferson Avenue home in Detroit could be moved to their new property. Jensen fired off this note in a letter to A. J. Lepine at the Ford Motor Company: "Mr. Ford has intimated that he would like to move his present swimming pool if it is possible to Gaukler's Pointe [Grosse Pointe Shores] because I might not be able to build another one as interesting. . . . I have found some fine rocks now and am in hopes that I can beat the old pool in beauty and practicality."[30]

Where he thought they were appropriate, Jensen also used large granitic boulders. A large granitic rock frequently served as a "council rock" in

Figure 86. Detail of rockwork for the pool and falls area of the W. E. Simms estate in Spring Station, Kentucky (1916). Note the suggestion of a heavily planted grove behind the pool area. Courtesy of Jensen Collection, Art and Architecture Library, University of Michigan, Ann Arbor.

Figure 87. Waterfall in the pool area of the Kenneth D. Alexander estate in Spring Station, Kentucky. Photograph is from Elwood 1924.

his designs. At Lincoln Memorial Garden, great amounts of time and energy were spent in shipping several large boulders from Wisconsin quarries to mark the garden's entrances.[31]

Council Rings

Council rings, simple circular stone benches with fire pits in the center which resembled the kivas of the Pueblo Indians in the American South-west, were perhaps the only architectural element that Jensen repeated again and again in his designs. Viewed by Jensen as a symbol of democra-cy, the council ring was intended as a gathering place where all people would be equal. Jensen developed his idea of the council ring and fire by combining elements of his Danish folk school tradition with "the council fires of the Native American, and with [the] fires of the pioneers." Around the council ring, people gathered to participate in free and honest discus-sions, to read poetry or tell stories, to act out dramas, or simply to meditate, especially on humanity's relationship with nature. Historian J. Ronald Engel describes the purpose of the council ring as intended by Jensen:

> The council ring was believed also to encourage the companionship of humanity and nature. In the circle, one is aware of the stars, the smells and the sounds of the woods and flowers, the wind and the earth. In the flame of the leaping fire, uniting heaven and earth, one sees the heat of many summers' suns. Jensen felt an absolute unity emerging from such gather-ings, which encompassed the whole of being—"the brotherhood of all living things." This unity was symbolized in the figure of the circle, the strongest and most perfect geometric form.

Jensen's council rings varied in size from the large ring in Columbus Park, which was never completed but was intended to seat 150 or more people, to the smaller rings like the one used at Jensen's studio in Ravinia, Illinois, just above the ravine, which was intended to seat no more than 8–10 people.[32]

While council rings are found in different situations in Jensen's gar-dens, their locations are similar. Most are tucked into the edge of a woodland border with a view looking outward (Figure 88). In the estates Jensen designed on the North Shore of Lake Michigan, council rings were placed where they had a commanding view of the lake and where the fire "could symbolize the beacon that guides lost wanderers to a place of security and welcome" (Figure 89). On other sites, the view from the ring opened onto a central meadow. While some of these rings were completely surrounded by woods, those at the woodland edge were characterized by small groups of American plum, hawthorn, and prairie crabapple trees,

Figure 88. Jensen typically placed council rings at the edge of a woodland with a view out to a larger meadow space, or provided a quieter, enclosed space in the heart of a woodland.

Figure 89. Council ring overlooking Green Bay at The Clearing in Ellison Bay, Wisconsin. Courtesy of Robert P. Pleva.

which made the entire composition appear as if it belonged to the forest border.[33]

Jensen used more council rings at Lincoln Memorial Garden than in any other project. The eight rings at the garden are located at prominent topographic points that offer views out over the lake or down one or several of the paths. The largest, the Lincoln Council Ring, is set on a prominent overlook above the lake and was intended by Jensen to be the major activity space in the garden as well as a special tribute to Abraham Lincoln. Jensen was particularly proud of the grove of white oak trees that began as acorns planted around this ring. The path leading up to the ring is a highly processional space, yet the oaks are widely spaced in an irregular pattern, much as groves are found in nature. The repetition of the thick trunks unifies the space in all seasons. The trees open out to frame a view of a prairie meadow, the lake, and an island in the center of the lake.

Players' Greens

Jensen delighted in creating a space for outdoor drama, or "a player's green," as he called such places, whenever he found a willing client. As described by Frank Waugh in *Outdoor Theaters* (1917), these garden spaces were designed not as traditional theaters, with a developed stage and seats, but as natural settings for plays, musical offerings, or recitations. For Jensen, outdoor drama provided an opportunity for people to celebrate the human presence in, and respect for, the pageantry of nature. Like Jane Addams, he saw the theater as an outlet for primitive emotions that could be used not only to teach basic human values but also to unite the participants in a shared democratic experience. The Prairie Club and the Friends of Our Native Landscape included outdoor dramas or masques as part of their meetings, and Jensen often arranged for such performances to mark special occasions (Figure 90). Frank Waugh described one such event:

> Last spring, when the wild crab apple trees were in blossom, my friend Mr. Jens Jensen, artist and landscape gardener, arranged an ideal entertainment for some of his friends. He found a grassy glade beside a brook set beautifully with blossoming crab apples. Having seated the audience on a sloping bank, he introduced a pretty girl in white, who sat beneath the crab apple tree and played Mendelssohn's "Spring Song" on the harp. In response to this music there appeared from the dark recesses of the surrounding wood a group of fairies—children dressed in browns—who danced on the grass.
>
> This picture is complete in itself. It does not require a plot, a dramatic

Figure 90. Photograph by Jensen of a performance on a Player's Green. Courtesy of Jensen Collection, Morton Arboretum, Lisle, Illinois.

climax, or a dénouement. It is an ideal type of performance for the outdoor theater or player's green.[34]

The stage in Jensen's theater was usually designed as a small clearing carved out of the edge of a wood, often with a background of red cedar (*Juniperus virginiana*). A larger open area provided seating for the audience, and the edge of the stage was marked by flanking trees and an occasional "council rock." The latter feature was intended "to suggest to susceptible minds the thought of the American aborigines gathered round their council rock for the recitation of their native epics or the enactment of their many mystic rituals." In other cases, Jensen separated the player's green from the seating area using a stream or other water surface, as in the theater designed for Columbus Park, where dressing rooms were located in small clearings behind the stage area. The water surface also provided the opportunity for incorporating water pageants into the theatrical repertoire. Fire pits provided light if the play was held on a cloudy or moonless night; otherwise, the stage was illuminated only by moonlight. Frequently the audience faced west, and performances, beginning at dusk, featured a sun-blazoned sky.[35]

Formal Gardens

Jensen deliberately downplayed his formal garden designs, choosing instead to emphasize the more naturalistic qualities of his work. In 1900, referring to topiary practices, he declared that he hoped "the man with the sheep shears has vanished for the good of garden art." Years later, he described the formal rose garden at Chicago's Humboldt Park (which he had designed in 1907) as a "folly" of his youth. Yet formal gardens remained an integral part of most of his estate designs throughout his career, no doubt at the request of his clients; he evidently acquiesced in order to please them.[36]

The "natural gardens" on these private estates clearly dominated Jensen's overall design scheme, but he also set aside smaller areas to accommodate formal plantings of cultivated flowers and vegetables. Many of Jensen's drawings suggest that he explored numerous geometric patterns before selecting one. The drawings for the Kenneth Alexander estate at Spring Station, Kentucky (1911), for instance, indicate that a series of circular flower and vegetable beds were devised before a fairly simple scheme was settled upon (Figure 91). Likewise, for the Edsel Ford estate (1926), Jensen originally proposed an intricate pattern of walks that resembled a braided tapestry, but in the end settled on a simple pattern of concentric rings set within a square. Such formal gardens were nearly always developed as separate parts of the design and were clearly delineated by walls or plantings of shrubbery.

The vegetable garden was an important component of a Jensen design, for he believed that only through gardening and direct interaction with the soil could people learn to appreciate nature as a whole. In one of the most frequently quoted passages from Jensen's writings, he advised beginning students in landscape design to follow a practical course of instruction (Figure 92):

> First grow cabbages. After that plant a flower. When you have successfully grown a flower, then you can start to think about growing a tree. After watching a tree grow for several years, observing how its character develops from year to year, then you can begin to think of a composition of living plants—a composition of life itself. Then you will know what landscape architecture is.[37]

Community vegetable gardens were an important part of Jensen's Greater West Park Plan (1920), for he considered them a valuable tool in teaching urban people something about agriculture and in helping them appreciate the source of their food. Children's vegetable gardens were actively promoted by the recreation centers of the West Parks. In 1918

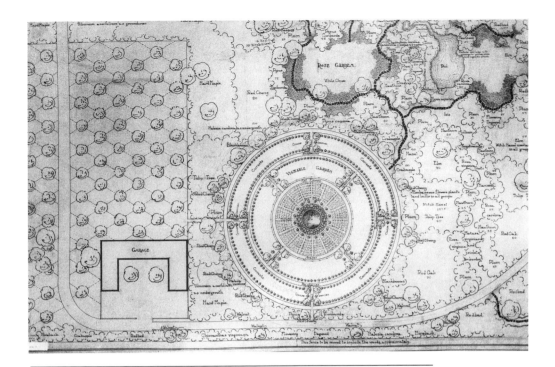

Figure 91. Proposed plan for a vegetable and fruit garden on the Alexander estate in Spring Station, Kentucky. This elaborate circular design was later replaced by a simple rectangular form. Courtesy of Jensen Collection, Art and Architecture Library, University of Michigan, Ann Arbor.

Figure 92. Landscape architecture students from the University of Wisconsin creating a garden at The Clearing in Ellison Bay. Photograph is from a group belonging to G. William Longenecker, from the University of Wisconsin, Madison. Courtesy of Jensen Collection, Morton Arboretum, Lisle, Illinois.

alone, at least a hundred children's vegetable gardens were planted, and so much produce was harvested that the excess was given to local orphanages. In addition, in that same year, large demonstration gardens were planted in Garfield, Humboldt, and Douglas parks.[38]

The form of these vegetable gardens varied from simple rectilinear plots to grand radial beds. Only around these garden spaces did Jensen include clipped hedges. At the Edsel Ford estate, Jensen even planned a clipped honey locust arbor to appear at path intersections in the vegetable gardens. For Jensen, vegetable gardens served to keep alive the traditions of a long heritage of human gardening, and, like the early American pioneer gardens, these plots were surrounded by a semblance of wild nature in the rest of his designs.[39]

Time and Change

The notion of time and change in the landscape is a key theme in Jensen's writings. He was intrigued by the historical continuum of landscapes, and he encouraged respect for both the past and the future. As a factor in his style of design, this emphasis on time and change took three forms. First, he attempted to capture the sense of a moving or changing landscape in a physical form. Second, he delighted in daily and seasonal change. Third, especially in his later designs, he worked with succession, fully expecting the landscape to grow and change as part of the design process.

Examples of designs that are essentially frozen images of a changing scene abound in Jensen's work. At the Edsel Ford estate on Jefferson Avenue in Detroit (1922), he planted a grove of red cedar (*Juniperus virginiana*) on a created rock ledge to suggest a frozen moment in the succession from open field to mature forest. The cedars were carefully selected and arranged according to size to suggest a natural invasion of cedars (Figure 93).

Generally, the plants most commonly used by Jensen were from the forest edge and other transitional plant communities. As he arranged these plants, he created images of the changing landscapes from which he had borrowed them. For instance, in many of his designs he used beds of American plum, gray dogwood (*Cornus foemina*), sumac, or other such plants to suggest a creeping out from the woodlands; or he placed crabapple, hawthorn, and other small trees in such a way as to suggest young trees moving into the meadow in random fashion.

The changing sunlight and seasons were particularly emphasized by Jensen. As he wrote, "The elements one works with are the contours of the earth, the vegetation that covers it, the changing seasons, the rays of

Figure 93. A "frozen" successional planting of red cedar at the Edsel and Eleanor Ford property on Jefferson Avenue in Detroit, Michigan. Courtesy of Jensen Collection, Morton Arboretum, Lisle, Illinois.

the setting sun and the afterglow, and the height of the moon." For Jensen, the landscape was a different place in the morning, noon, and night, and it varied with the weather as well as with the seasons. In contrast to many of his contemporaries, who emphasized unchanging structures or evergreen plantings as the skeleton of their gardens, Jensen often created a path that led to the setting or rising sun. He generally disdained evergreens, except where they provided a special mood or suggested a northern plant community. For Jensen, each season held its particular glory, and it was the landscape designer's job to emphasize such change:

> During winter the winds come in crisp and invigorating from across the prairies. At this season of the year the landscape assumes a dreary look to many who do not see and cannot understand. But to others, when the gray arms of the cottonwood are illuminated by the January sun and silhouetted against the blue sky, when sleeping buds are covered with frost sparkling in the winter sun, when the dormant life of millions of flowers is covered with a blanket of snow, when rich plowed fields await the seed that is to feed the millions, and gray and lavender clouds beckon you on over the prairies, the landscape sings a song of rich tonal beauty, a great prelude to dawn, a reminder before the resurrection of life. Our northern gardens should be as

fitting in winter as in any other season of the year. A garden that cannot stand the rigid winter weather and has to be protected in all sorts of grotesque ways has lost its poetry and charm.

Sugar maple, sumac, and other plants with bright fall colors painted Jensen's landscapes in autumn; American plum, crabapple, and a host of woodland wildflowers welcomed spring. Summer was a mystic time of billowy masses, drifting sunlight and shadow, and various shades of green. Winter brought a delicate tracery of branches highlighted by bright fruits or subtle shades of white, pink, or gray bark and twigs.[40]

Because of Jensen's keen appreciation of time and history, landscape symbols also appealed to him. He was fascinated with Amerindian cultures, and wherever possible he tried to preserve or highlight remnants of their handiwork. At his studio in Ravinia, for instance, an Indian trail became a "fitting path to the garden." His council rocks, fires, and rings were all intended to provide a consciousness of an earlier, Amerindian culture. Moreover, certain plants reminded him of pioneer ways; he called the honey locust "the farmer wife's tree."[41]

The creation of a "prairie river" in Columbus Park at the base of an "ancient beach dating back to the glacial age" is a fine example of how Jensen related the past landscape to the present. His work at the conservatories in Garfield Park, where he sought to create a representation of the prehistoric prairie landscape, is another. In his plan for the "Greater West Parks," Jensen suggested that preserving bits of the historic landscape as part of the parks would "add a new sentiment to the parks" and would link "the history of the past . . . with that of today." Likewise, at the Edsel and Eleanor Ford summer home on the rocky coast of Seal Harbor, Maine (1922), Jensen attempted to create a garden that would fit into "the ruggedness and mystery" of the coast's ancient cliffs.[42]

Jensen deliberately designed for the long-term effect. At the Hugh F. Vandeventer garden in Knoxville, Tennessee (1923), Jensen was naturally cautious about working in an environment with which he was not very familiar. Yet he was determined to create a garden that would have a lasting beauty; he wanted "to make the home livable for man, not just for a month or a year, but for a lifetime." Jensen's cautiousness evidently paid off. He noted that through careful planting he was able to heal construction scars on the landscape and to unify the garden around the house with views of the valley and distant mountains: "The eye that caught this planting also caught the distant hill and saw the continuation of the hill flow gradually up to the porch of the house." Jensen called this one of the "greatest feats" of his career.[43]

In *Siftings*, Jensen relates a talk given to students at the University of

Figure 94. Oak grove near the Lincoln Council Ring in Lincoln Memorial Garden, Springfield, Illinois. These oaks have grown from acorns that were planted at the site by Boy Scouts and Girl Scouts in 1936.

Illinois. He spoke of plants that were so suited to their environment that they would endure through many generations. A native crabapple in bloom gave him his inspiration:

> Sympathetic pioneers had saved it from destruction. They too had loved it. In its early life it perhaps stood on the edge of a forest where woods and prairie met. Since then the forest had been cleared away, but this tree was left in the open field. The storms of spring and fall and icy blasts of many winters had shaken its tender body, even threatened its life. Like a bride in May it greeted us and other wayfarers who passed by. It, too, was a pioneer and was left to tell its story and to give its beauty to the American of today and tomorrow.

Jensen encouraged his students to create gardens that, like this old crab-apple, reflected a "fitness to the soil" that could be enjoyed for many ages. For Jensen, such places provided a sense of continuity and richness to human life.[44]

Particularly late in his career, Jensen apparently chose to work more extensively with long-term change and succession, although it is possible he simply had jobs that provided him with that option. Lincoln Memorial Garden, at which he had a free hand but a limited budget, is probably the best example of this concern: Jensen literally planted acorns in an old meadow, initiating the process of forest succession. The design itself became a passive framework or stage upon which the drama of nature would be played. Jensen consciously strove for a quality of timelessness here, hoping that by working with nature, he would set in motion a process that would continue well beyond anyone's lifetime. His design was merely a beginning (Figure 94).[45]

FIVE

Jensen's Legacy

It has been more than a full century since Jens Jensen created his American Garden in Union Park in 1888 and thereby began his public career as a designer of natural parks and gardens. Yet today, people continue to be fascinated by Jensen's work and ideas, and as Darrel Morrison writes, scholars are rightfully placing Jensen "alongside the other landscape greats—Andrew Jackson Downing, Frederick Law Olmsted, H. W. S. Cleveland, John Nolen, and the like." When he sought a job with Jensen in the mid-1920s, the young Alfred Caldwell noted that Jensen was a man with a keen awareness of environmental problems and a genuine love of people. He confronted issues that had not yet caught on within the scientific community or in society at large. He was also an artist who was capable of creating places that literally stirred one's soul. Jensen's legacy—the places he created and the ideas he promoted—continues to inspire conservationists and ecologically oriented designers today (Figure 95).[1]

Very few of Jensen's designs survive with much integrity. Ironically, of his park work in Chicago, the Garfield Park Conservatory, an indoor garden, comes closest to surviving intact. The Shakespeare Garden at Northwestern University in Evanston, Illinois, is one of the few surviving examples of his small public gardens, and Lincoln Memorial Garden in Springfield, Illinois, is far and away the best example of his large public gardens or parks. Of the more than 350 private residences that were designed by Jensen, fewer than ten percent even retain the basic structure of his original work.

Jensen's landscapes have been altered for a number of reasons and in various ways. Large estates have been subdivided, and meadow spaces have been occupied by houses and parking facilities. Many of Jensen's parks have suffered from neglect as surrounding neighborhoods have changed and park budgets have declined. Structures and stonework have deteriorated, and thousands of shrubs and small trees have been cut down

Figure 95. Jens Jensen at The Clearing, Ellison Bay, Wisconsin. Courtesy of Grace Richardson.

for security reasons or because someone thought they were overgrown. Perhaps the most brutal intrusion was the construction of Interstate 290, the Eisenhower Expressway, through the southern portion of Columbus Park in Chicago. This despite pleas by Jensen that placing freeways through, alongside, or above urban parks would necessarily destroy the qualities they were intended to provide for city people. Where Jensen's landscapes have suffered from benign neglect, they have been invaded by aggressive native and non-native plants that have drastically altered the intent and character of the original design.[2]

One of the great paradoxes of Jensen's landscape designs was that the more successful he was at creating idealized images of nature, the less obvious it was that these were conscious designs and, therefore, the less likely it was that they would be maintained. In his lifetime, Jensen realized the transient nature of landscape design as he saw countless projects destroyed because people did not understand the idea at the heart of his work or because they did not care. He described "the art of landscaping" as "a fleeting thought that must be caught on the wing." Alfred Caldwell compared the art of making landscapes such as those created by Jensen to "making sculptures in the snow. . . . You only have to be foolish an afternoon and it is gone." Late in his career, Jensen seemed to accept the ultimate demise of his work as physical places or "gardens" per se, and fully expected that they would eventually disappear into the background of nature. As he wrote in *Siftings* (1939),

> It matters little if the garden disappears with its maker. Its record is not essential to those who follow because it is for them to solve their own problem, or art will soon decay. Let the garden disappear in the bosom of nature of which it is a part, and although the hand of man is not visible, his spirit remains as long as the plants he planted grow and scatter their seed.[3]

Jensen did, however, live to see several of his landscapes reach maturity, and he recorded some of his observations in *Siftings*. He was particularly pleased when others understood what he had tried to accomplish in Columbus Park:

> It is not always granted that a landscaper can see the fruits of his work near maturity, but such was my good fortune recently when I stood on the bank of the prairie river and enjoyed the peaceful meadow which stretched out before me in the light of the afterglow of the setting sun. My greatest joy, however, was to see that not I alone enjoyed this scene. Others saw the significance of it all, and their silence during nature's great pantomime at the end of the day was the greatest gift I could have received.[4]

Recently, in Chicago, there has been a resurgence of interest in Jensen's park designs and his contributions to the city in general. In 1987, with the Chicago Park District under the direction of architect Walter Netsch, architect Edward Uhlir literally stumbled upon a basement vault containing hundreds of drawings of the parks. Less than two years later, the park district had full-time historic preservation specialists piecing together the history of the Chicago parks and developing preservation and restoration strategies. Suddenly, the landscapes created by Jensen and others came to be regarded as valued resources, as works of art and part of our history, rather than as empty spaces waiting to be filled. In 1989, the Chicago Park District joined with the Special Collections Department of the Chicago Public Library to launch an extensive exhibit on Chicago's neighborhood parks, and in 1991, with the Chicago Historical Society and the Morton Arboretum, it sponsored a follow-up exhibit entitled "Prairie in the City: Naturalism in Chicago Parks, 1870–1940," which focused on the influence of the prairie on both the architecture and landscape architecture of the parks. These efforts, together with other programs, have begun to convince people that such designs have positive value and, as in Jensen's day, are capable of enriching everyday life. Preservation of the actual places created by Jensen is as important as preserving the legacy of his ideas. Now, more than ever, urban as well as suburban and rural people need to feel reconnected to the natural landscape and its cycles. Jensen wanted his designs to provide that link; with proper preservation, the few that survive can yet serve as examples to inspire future designers working with nature.[5]

Compared to the preservation of buildings or engineering structures, landscape designs are prone to a unique set of problems. With vegetation, landforms, water, soil, and sky as raw materials, designed landscapes constantly grow and change, even without human intervention. Add the vagaries of the real estate market, the changing ideas and demographics of landowners and public officials, and the collective impact of recreation, vandalism, and pollution, and it becomes a wonder that designed land-scapes survive at all. Early in his career, Jensen recognized this problem, at least in part, and argued that parks need special care and ongoing manage-ment if they are to become the places envisioned by their designers:

> The development of such vegetation as forms the leading part in the construction of parks is one of years and its nursing needs the best care obtainable. Continual destruction to the park scenery either from natural causes or through such agencies as polluted atmosphere, sewerage, insects, etc., characteristic of city environments needs the watchfulness of the practical and artistic eye, if health and beauty will dominate and the scenery be kept intact. . . . The caretaker must be in thorough sympathy with the plans of the designer and to be so he must be an artist himself.

Jensen relied heavily on foremen such as Alfred Caldwell to interpret and implement his ideas in the field. Recognizing the difficulty of representing many of his design ideas in two-dimensional drawings, he came to regard plans as little more than a general framework for what would actually be developed. This lack of an accurate record of what was implemented makes the restoration of Jensen's landscapes particularly challenging. Like the caretaker, today's restorer must also be an artist, but an artist who approaches the work with modesty, tactfulness, and honesty, trying to understand the patterns of nature that Jensen emulated.[6]

In the spirit of nineteenth-century romanticism, Jensen recognized the basic human need for retreat and quiet as a balancing force in the increas-ingly hectic human-made world. Like Olmsted and other designers before him, he sought to provide people who lived in the city with seemingly natural places in which they could recoup their spirit and be reconnected to the rhythms of nature. These needs, we are told, are as relevant now as they were then, and they are once again being recognized by the scientific and design communities. In *The Experience of Nature* (1989), environ-mental psychologists Rachel and Stephen Kaplan note the restorative value of nearby nature and wilderness settings in overcoming mental fatigue. The qualities they considered characteristic of a restorative environment—the sense of being away, extent (expansiveness), fascination, and compatibility—all were essential to Jensen's design work. His gardens provided a sense of escape and natural scenery in an otherwise urban landscape. In both his large parks and smaller residential gardens, there was always the feeling of expansiveness—a sense of a much larger space than was immediately perceived. Jensen's designs also created a strong sense of being connected to a larger system of nature as well as to the history of a place. Through his emphasis on the subtle beauty of native plants, sunlight, and the changing seasons, Jensen aided what the Kaplans have called "soft fascination," or an attraction to patterns that "readily hold the attention but often in an undramatic fashion," thereby encouraging reflection rather than concentrated thought.[7]

Architectural historian Galen Cranz has noted that in the period following 1930, park designers abandoned social reform ideals and emphasized parks as functional recreational facilities rather than as the natural settings Olmsted and Jensen had envisioned. As Cranz explains, roads were widened, the number of parking areas and paved courts increased, playgrounds were standardized, and Cyclone fences were added to mark boundaries. In contrast, Jensen, like Olmsted, intended that parks be works of art as well as places for play. The careful shaping of spaces, ground forms, and plantings enhanced park activities. Today, many of Jensen's meadows continue to be used as ball fields or golf courses, but they retain their original character because they were deliberately designed as natural settings and because they were intentionally created as spaces for a variety of activities rather than as single-purpose playing surfaces (Figure 96). Many modern parks, on the other hand, are created as a collection of single-use areas (separate areas for swimming, baseball, soccer, driving, bicycle riding, baseball, etc.) rather than as a holistic landscape. Jensen objected to single-purpose sports facilities such as stadiums, which he described as "ugly and unfitting to most towns and cities":

> Here the man with the tee-square has been permitted to play, and how miserably he has failed. I can see future "Bowls" in a setting of the living green, a part of the city because that is where they belong, and yet something of the country which has penetrated into the city complex, opening it up and giving it light and shadow and fresh air.

In Jensen's parks, nature was the pervasive background for all outdoor activities, reinforcing one's view of the land as part of an ecological community.[8]

Jensen believed that people benefit from direct involvement with grow-

Figure 96. Baseball games in the meadows of Douglas Park in Chicago in 1914. Courtesy of Special Collections, Chicago Park District.

ing plants, and he advocated including community gardens in the network of playgrounds and parklands within a city. In a 1901 garden-and-window-box competition sponsored by the *Chicago Tribune,* Jensen helped judge the entries. The remarkable results of the competition were enumerated in the *Bulletin of the American Park and Outdoor Art Association:*

> [Ten thousand] new gardens were started; a number of towns inaugurated similar work; many local improvement associations were formed; half a dozen factories transformed their grounds into gardens; the Chicago and Northwestern Railroad improved their suburban station grounds; leading women's clubs took up the movement; beds were laid out on the grounds of engine houses, schools, police stations, the city hall, etc.; city squares and triangles, and vacant lots were cleared up and improved; the streets were kept in cleaner condition; and in all this movement the boys and girls were among the most interested and untiring of the workers.

In recent years, interest in gardening has grown with the increase in people's leisure time. Interaction with plants has gained respectability as gardening has come to be advocated as a form of physical therapy and as a way of building pride in oneself, the neighborhood, and the local community. Across the country, numerous community gardening organizations attest to hundreds of success stories in which derelict urban lands have been turned into beautiful oases that nurture the human spirit (Figure 97).[9]

Jensen's ideas about schools and playgrounds were precursors of more

Figure 97. Children's vegetable garden in Dvorak Park, Chicago. Courtesy of Special Collections, Chicago Park District.

recent environmental education efforts and movements to incorporate qualities of nature into play spaces. His playgrounds were not limited to the pieces of gymnastic and other play equipment that were then common in most other playgrounds. In his plans for Franklin and Cragin parks (1914 and 1921) and the playground and pool areas of Columbus Park (1917) in Chicago, and in Glenwood Park in Madison, Wisconsin (1945), or at school grounds such as the Logan and Lloyd school centers in Chicago (1918 and 1920), Jensen suggested that play areas emphasize a variety of spaces and settings to stimulate different kinds of creative play and exploration activities, rather than focus only on physical equipment. He was concerned that children, particularly those in urban areas, needed places in which to experience nature firsthand and develop attachments to natural environments at a young age.[10]

Current research in playground design confirms that children respond enthusiastically to diverse environmental settings—including water for splashing and wading, soil and sand for digging, boulders to climb or to use as settings for make-believe, trees for shade and climbing, shrubs that mark places to hide in or explore, and both rough and mowed grass—as well as to more traditional play equipment. Jensen's ideas about play and playgrounds provide a useful model for play areas that emphasize quiet places for reflection and dreams as well as active zones for socialization and physical exercise. Jensen designed sensual spaces that were deliberately open-ended, creating a sense of both enclosure and mystery. In their many layers of vegetation and in the wildlife they attracted, children found great variety and numerous places to explore. Plantings were chosen to recall primitive qualities of the site and to help children sense the rich history of the region. As today's researchers have noted, such qualities are as relevant now as they were in Jensen's time. In *Childhood's Future*, Richard Louv speculates on the connection between our adult relationship with nature and "the fantasies we bring to it as children." He argues for preserving and creating places where children can explore fantasy play in a natural setting. In the United States, perhaps the most successful of the recent attempts to create a natural habitat as part of a play environment is the Washington Environmental Yard in Berkeley, California, which has been documented by Robin Moore (1978, 1989). In 1986, a group of British educators, designers, and other interested people in Berkshire, Hampshire, and Surrey counties organized a three-year study to investigate how school grounds could be designed to enhance environmental education and play. The study, entitled "Learning through Landscapes" (documented in 1989 in *Landscape Design*), stressed many of the themes that Jensen emphasized in his design of school yards and playgrounds. Conservation areas were considered integral parts of the school grounds, both for informal play and as an extension of the classroom. Gardens were created to encourage children to nurture plants and monitor their growth. Like Jensen, the designers of the British program also saw the need to create quiet, sheltered places in which students could gather.[11]

Jensen viewed schools as a potentially strong force for building family and community relationships. In his plan for the expansion of the West Parks in Chicago, schools became neighborhood community centers at which learning would be a lifelong activity for all. The school grounds were designed to appeal to all ages, from the youngest children to senior citizens. Like the settlement houses founded by Jane Addams and the Danish folk schools of Jensen's youth, these neighborhood centers were to promote a balance of arts, crafts, and the direct observation of nature as well as traditional subjects. Ethnic and cultural traditions were to be encouraged and developed as a sense of pride. At The Clearing, Jensen explored his ideas for unfettered learning in a sylvan setting, and this legacy continues in the school's current summer program and in a newly established institute for landscape study.[12]

Certainly one of Jensen's most lasting legacies was his insistence on using native vegetation. In his early designs, he tended to choose native plants because of their individual beauty, much as he might have used exotics in the same design in a horticultural style. Landscape architect Gary Hightshoe has called this "the floristic approach" to using native flora. Later in his career, Jensen demonstrated a clearer understanding of plants and soils and pursued a "community approach," emphasizing the combined aesthetic of the plant community. A careful study of the plants in a landscape such as Columbus Park shows that Jensen grouped and ordered plants as they would be found in nature. He located wetland trees near the lagoon and upland trees on slight topographic rises. Although the original understory of many of Jensen's landscapes has disappeared as a result of public safety concerns or misguided maintenance, his designs demonstrate an understanding of plant growth and regeneration. Grouping trees, shrubs, and ground-layer species as they are found together in the wild creates microconditions that are better suited to the growth of trees than the common urban forests of trees bounded by concrete or mowed lawn. In Jensen's designs, tree plantings were grouped to allow for regeneration, and his lawn areas were clearly open spaces in which the grass could grow best and withstand heavy use. Poorer soils were clothed with dense shrubs or native ground covers. These designs were intended to allow continual growth and natural replacement over time.[13]

Nonetheless, Jensen failed to understand fully the dynamics of these plant communities, especially in an urbanized area. The altered condition of our humanized wilds—degraded soils, changed hydrology, influx of weedy species, and diminished sources for native seeds—creates the need for deliberate, ongoing management programs. Alien species such as Norway maple (*Acer platanoides*), tree-of-heaven (*Ailanthus altissima*), autumn olive (*Eleagnus umbellata*), honeysuckle (*Lonicera x-bella*), purple loosestrife (*Lythrum salicaria*), and buckthorn (*Rhamnus cathartica* and *frangula*) can quickly dominate succession in these wild plantings and completely change the character of a design. As noted by Darrel Morrison, effective restoration of native communities requires management that emulates natural-disturbance regimens such as fires on the prairies and in oak woodlands, or fluctuating water levels in many wetlands. Still, in the long run, these activities cost less in terms of money, human resources, and energy consumed than the routine maintenance required by other types of landscape designs. The types of landscapes advocated by Jensen require an understanding of plant growth and change instead of mindless mowing and clipping.[14]

In landscapes such as Lincoln Memorial Garden, Jensen's attention to developing a long-term landscape serves as a useful model for today's efforts in landscape restoration. The ability to create instantly green landscapes with fertilizer and hybrid plants has created a false sense of environmental health. In contrast, the approach at Lincoln Memorial Garden provides a model of design as a partnership with natural processes and succession to create landscapes with at least some of the function and beauty of natural ecosystems. Within this framework, once-neglected or ignored landscape types such as wetlands and prairies become not only possibilities on one's palette of choices but also integral parts of the overall

Figure 98. The Clearing, Ellison Bay, Wisconsin.

JENSEN'S LEGACY

aesthetic patterns and functional processes of designed landscapes. Such an approach may require a changed aesthetic and an extra measure of patience, but it is a process that invites participation as the landscape changes with time. The work of restoration involves much hand labor and careful nurturing, and the lack of readily available sources of many native plant species requires creative approaches. The work is easily adapted to group efforts and has meaningful rewards in allowing people to be part of the healing process of nature. Like the planting of acorns at Lincoln Memorial Garden, landscape restoration requires a certain amount of faith, but it provides a genuine sense of stewardship and joy in the results.[15]

Jensen's emphasis on landscape ritual and celebration gave his designs and the places he sought to save a richer meaning for those who shared in these experiences. The seasonal pilgrimages by the Prairie Club and the Friends of Our Native Landscape left indelible impressions on those who participated. The Dunes Pageant and the numerous masques, poetry readings, and dances associated with the fight to save the Indiana Dunes forged a marriage of art and landscape that is now a part of the rich heritage of the Dunes. Through his use of council rings and players' greens (or players' hills), Jensen provided settings for such gatherings, and his attention to sunrise, sunset, climate, and seasonal changes in the landscape helped encourage celebration and interaction with nature's cycles (Figure 98).

As a model for designers, Jensen's approach stressed the clear need for careful study of natural landscapes. He objected to design training that was merely academic. He felt that an intimate knowledge of plants and horticulture and a genuine sense of humility were essential for landscape design to reach the level of art. In his case, this meant a lifetime of studying forests, prairies, wetlands, patterns of sunlight, soils, and rock formations, not to mention an understanding of human behavior and cultural traditions.

Perhaps the strongest and most lasting of Jensen's legacies is the clear sense of ethics and idealism that is embodied in his designs. As his work evolved, it reflected a heightened sense of stewardship toward the natural environment and an attempt to awaken in others an appreciation of these same values. Those who debated Jensen's work on mere stylistic grounds understood little of the reasoning behind his choices. His career was a progressive effort to capture the spirit of a natural landscape in a way that could add something strong and powerful to the people who enjoyed his parks and gardens. As a precursor to today's bioregionalists, who are calling for a renewed understanding of local ecosystems, Jensen attempted to help people build a sense of identity with the natural heritage of their region. He believed that if people could learn to appreciate the beauty of his natural gardens—the trees, shrubs, and wildflowers—perhaps they could learn to respect the few remaining wild places in the countryside. Like Liberty Hyde Bailey, who pressed for reverent stewardship of the earth in *The Holy Earth* (1916), and Aldo Leopold, who argued for the development of a land ethic in *Sand County Almanac* (1949), Jensen sought to inspire a conservation ethic through his parks and gardens, his activities with the Friends of Our Native Landscape and the Prairie Club, and his teaching at The Clearing. For him, conservation was not so much a comfortable hobby as it was a sacred responsibility as a human being and particularly as a landscape designer.[16]

Today the potential exists to carry Jensen's vision much further. Although there is much to learn, much more is understood about how natural environments function and how their integrity can be restored. Current efforts at ecological restoration are described as the "flowering of environmentalism," the opportunity for people to interact with their landscape as part of a healing process. At present the world faces the danger of losing not only the natural areas that can serve as models for restoration but also the very raw materials these environments contain. Creative design, management, and planning can help restore natural functions to degraded lands, reconnect fragmented landscapes, and create buffers around fragile wilds. This book has been written in the hope that a knowledge of the ideas and values of Jens Jensen might inspire people to continue where he left off. Rather than lament the legacy of Jensen that has disappeared, it is important to forge ahead with creative efforts in preservation, conservation, and restoration so that, in the spirit of Jensen's work, urban people can be reconnected with their natural environment, and the drama of nature's wild places can be preserved and created for the next generation to experience.[17]

APPENDIX A

Jensen's Projects

This list has been compiled by the author from the plans, photographs, and other documents at various Jensen archives, with additions by the people who kindly reviewed the draft version. No attempt has been made to document the extent of Jensen's involvement in each of these projects, nor is it known whether all of them were implemented. The dates shown are those given on records and plans, and may not accurately reflect Jensen's years of work on a particular project. Where the architects participating in a project are known, their names have been noted. The sources listed are as follows: 1 = Jensen Collection, Morton Arboretum, Lisle, Illinois; 2 = Jensen Collection, Art and Architecture Library, University of Michigan, Ann Arbor; 3 = Special Collections, Chicago Park District. Special note should be made of two references that provided additional information: Highland Park Historic Preservation Commission, "Highland Park, Illinois: Historic Landscape Survey, Final Report" (Highland Park, Ill.: Park District of Highland Park and Illinois Preservation Agency, 1988); and Christopher D. Vernon, "Jens Jensen: Projects in Indiana" (unpublished manuscript prepared for the Committee on Historic Preservation, Indiana Chapter of the American Society of Landscape Architects, 1986).

Name of Project	Date	Place	Architects	Source(s)
Residential Projects				
Adamson	n.d.	Highland Park, Ill.		2
Adler, David J.	1918	Libertyville, Ill.	David J. Adler	2
Albright, F. H.	1908	Benton Harbor, Mich.		2
Aldrich, Frank W.	1918	Bloomington, Ill.		1
Alexander, Kenneth D.	1911– 1917	Spring Station, Ky.		1, 2
Allen, Paul E.	1946	Glenview/Skokie, Ill.		1

Name of Project	Date	Place	Architects	Source(s)
Allison, James A. (Riverdale)	1911	Indianapolis, Ind.	Price & McLanahan	1, 2
Alschuler, A. S.	1920	Winnetka, Ill.		2
Ames, W. V. B.	1916–1917	Libertyville, Ill.		2
Armour, J. Ogden	1906–1916	Lake Forest, Ill.		1, 2
Armstrong, F. H.	1912	Evanston, Ill.		2
Asher, L. E.	1911	Chicago, Ill.		2
Astor, Vincent	n.d.	location unknown		
Austin, H. W.	1912	Oak Park, Ill.		2
Babcock, O. E.	1910–1911	Lake Forest, Ill.		1, 2
Babson, F. K.	1909	Riverside, Ill.		1, 2
Babson, Gustavus	1911	Oak Park, Ill.		2
Babson, Henry B.	1909–1917	Riverside, Ill.	Louis Sullivan	1, 2
Baher, E. E.	1917	Kewanee, Ill.		2
Balhatchet, William	1910	Evanston, Ill.		2
Bangs, William D.	1927	Geneva, Ill.		2
Banks, Mary L.	1914	Delafield, Wis.		2
Barber, O. C.	1922	Akron, Ohio		2
Barber, O. C., and L. D. Brown	1926	Akron, Ohio		2
Barker, Mrs.	1909	Michigan City, Ind.		2
Barnett, O. R.	1912	Glencoe, Ill.		1, 2
Barr	n.d.	location unknown		2
Becker, A. G.	1926	Highland Park, Ill.	Howard Van Doren Shaw	1
Beers, Samuel G.	1939	North Prairie, Wis.		1
Beiger, Martin V. (Trameisus)	1914	Mishawaka, Ind.	Durham & Schneider	1, 2
Bensinger, B. E.	1910	Glencoe, Ill.		1
Berryman, J. B.	1913	Glencoe, Ill.		1, 2
Billesby, H. M. B.	1909	Lake Geneva, Wis.		1, 2
Bishop, D. H.	1909–1910	Dowagiac, Mich.		1
Blumenthal, Oscar	1926	Glencoe, Ill.		2
Bohm (Ye Four Winds)	n.d.	Long Beach, Ind.		
Boles, F. T.	1909	Hinsdale, Ill.		1, 2
Booth, Sherman M.	1911–1912	Glencoe, Ill.	Frank Lloyd Wright	1, 2

Name of Project	Date	Place	Architects	Source(s)
Born, M.	1917	Highland Park, Ill.		2
Boynton, Mrs.	1918	Highland Park, Ill.		2
Braun, E. J.	n.d.	Decatur, Ill.		1
Brooks, Harold C.	1921– 1922	Marshall, Mich.		1, 2
Brown, C. D.	1917	location unknown		2
Brown, Earl C.	1911, 1917	Decatur, Ill.		1, 2
Brown, E. J.	1911– 1915	Decatur, Ill.		2
Brown, F. A.	1930	Libertyville, Ill.		2
Brown, L. D.	1921	Akron, Ohio		2
Brownback, J. M.	1921	Decatur, Ill.		1, 2
Buck, O. J.	1913	Longwood, Ill.		2
Bush, B. H.	1907	Evanston, Ill.		2
Butler, J. F.	1915– 1916	Oak Park, Ill.		2
Calhoun, James K.	1923	Glencoe, Ill.		1
Camp, C. B.	1915	Oak Park, Ill.		2
Cargill, W. W.	1905– 1909	La Crosse, Wis.	Hugh M. G. Garden	1, 2
Carr, Clyde M.	1913– 1916	Lake Forest, Ill.	H. T. Lindeberg	2
Chalmers, W. J.	1904– 1905	Lake Geneva, Wis.		1, 2
Cherry, H. T.	1927	Tama, Iowa		2
Churchill, Arthur	1915	Burlington, Iowa		1, 2
Clark, Jim	1924– 1925	Freeport, Ill.		2
Clark, Kenneth D.	1925– 1927	Glencoe, Ill.	Ralph A. Stoetzel	2
Clarke, Harley L.	1922	Lake Geneva, Wis.		2
Clarke, Harley L.	1926– 1928	Evanston, Ill.	Richard Powers	1, 2
Clow, Harry B.	1910– 1911	Lake Forest, Ill.	Marshall & Fox	1, 2
Cluever, Richard	1913– 1914	Maywood, Ill.		2
Cluten	1929	Highland Park, Ill.		2
Coonley, Avery	1908– 1917	Riverside, Ill.	Frank Lloyd Wright	1, 2
Coonley, Prentiss	1910– 1911,	Lake Forest, Ill.		2

Name of Project	Date	Place	Architects	Source(s)
	1924–1925			
Cooper, Henry S.	1913–1916	Kenosha, Wis.		1, 2
Corbin, Mrs. Dana	1930	Ellison Bay, Wis.		2
Corning, Edwin	1926	N. E. Harbors, Maine		2
Credidio, Vernon J.	1908	Highland Park, Ill.		1
Cresap, Mark W.	n.d.	Kenilworth, Ill.		2
Crilly, Edgar	1922	Winnetka, Ill.	Chatten & Hammond	2
Cudahy, Joseph M.	1912–1914	Lake Forest, Ill.	Marshall & Fox	1, 2
Cudahy, Mrs. Michael	1913	Chicago, Ill.		2
Curtis, F. L.	1911	Highland Park, Ill.	H. R. Wilson & Co.	1, 2
Cushman, Stephen	n.d.	Racine, Wis.		1
Dahlinger Farm (racetrack)	1934	Romeo, Mich.		1
David, Sigmund W.	1925	Glencoe, Ill.		2
DeKieffer, Otto M.	1924	Chicago, Ill.		2
Dell Plain, Morse	1924–1926	Hammond, Ind.	Howard Van Doren Shaw	1, 2
Denkmann, Ruth (see Hauberg, Mrs.)				
Dewey, Charles	1913	Lake Forest, Ill.		1, 2
Dewey, Chauncey P.	1909	Konza Prairie, Manhattan, Kans.		1, 2
Dick, H. E.	1913	Janesville, Wis.		1, 2
Dighton, William	1917	Monticello, Ill.		1, 2
Doering, O. C.	1911–1916	Oak Park, Ill.	Arthur Heun	2
Doering, O. C.	1916–1917	River Forest, Ill.		2
Dryden, George B.	1916	Evanston, Ill.	George W. Maher	2
Dudley, H. C.	1922–1927	Duluth, Minn.		2
Dunham, R. J.	1916–1917	Lake Forest, Ill.		2
Dunlop, Mrs. Jamison	1915	Oak Park, Ill.		1
Durand, Mrs. Scott	1912–1913	Lake Bluff, Ill.	Hugh M. G. Garden	1, 2
Eckhart, B. A.	1906–1907	Lake Forest, Ill.		1, 2

Name of Project	Date	Place	Architects	Source(s)
Eckles, J. H.	n.d.	Oconomowoc, Wis.		1
Eriksen, Jens	1931	Highland Park, Ill.		1
Evans, Frank C.	1917–1919	Crawfordsville, Ind.		1, 2
Everett, David C.	1930	Lake Forest, Ill.		2
Ewing, Mrs. Davis	1923–1924, 1932	Bloomington, Ill.		1, 2
Ewing, Spencer	1911, 1920	Bloomington, Ill.	John S. Van Bergen	1, 2
Fahrney, E. H.	1912–1916	Oak Park, Ill.	White & Christie	2
Fairbanks, Charles Warren	1913	Indianapolis, Ind.	Howard Van Doren Shaw	1
Farson, J.	1905	Oak Park, Ill.		2
Fauntleroy	1925	Lake Geneva, Wis.		2
Fearing, Joseph L.	1916	Highland Park, Ill.		2
Ferris, Edward R.	n.d.	St. Charles, Ill.		1
Fischer, John	1918	Kewanee, Ill.		2
Fish, F. S. (Sunnyside)	1924–1926	South Bend, Ind.		2
Fisher, Carl G. (Blossom Heath)	1910	Indianapolis, Ind.		
Fisher, Charles T.	1929	Oakland County, Mich.		2
Fisher, Charles T. (Dixiana Farm)	n.d.	Lexington, Ky.		2
Fisher, Walter L.	1914–1915	Hubbard Woods, Ill.		2
Florsheim, Harold M.	1925	Highland Park, Ill.	Eugene H. Klaber and Ernest A. Grunsfeld, Jr.	2
Folds, Charles	1923	Lake Forest, Ill.		2
Ford, Edsel B. (Jefferson Avenue)	1922–1926	Detroit, Mich.		1
Ford, Edsel B.	1922–1926	Seal Harbor, Maine	Duncan Chandler	2
Ford, Edsel B.	1926–1932	Grosse Pointe Shores, Mich.	Albert Kahn	2
Ford, Edsel B. (Haven Hill Farm)	1934	Highland, Mich.		1
Ford, Henry (Fair Lane)	1914	Dearborn, Mich.	William H. Van Tine	1

Name of Project	Date	Place	Architects	Source(s)
Ford niece's residence	n.d.	location unknown		1
Foreman, H. E.	1917	Highland Park, Ill.		2
Frank, Jacob	1911	Chicago, Ill.		2
Frawley, F. D.	1922–1924	Indianapolis, Ind.		1, 2
Friedman, I. K.	1911	Winnetka, Ill.		2
Garden, Hugh M. G.	n.d.	Lake Forest, Ill.		2
Gary, John W.	1912–1913	Glencoe, Ill.	Perkins, Fellows & Will	2
Gatzent, August	1916–1930	Glencoe, Ill.		2
Gilchrist, John F.	1927–1931	Frankfort, Ill.	Herman V. von Holst	1
Gill, Wallace	1922	Glencoe, Ill.		1, 2
Gilman, Webster	n.d.	location unknown		1
Glaser, E. L.	1910–1917	Glencoe, Ill.		1, 2
Glasgow, Robert J.	n.d.	Highland Park, Ill.		1
Glavin, Charles F.	1920	Escanaba, Mich.		2
Gourley, Lyle	1929	Highland Park, Ill.		1
Gray, Humphrey S.	1917–1918	Benton Harbor, Mich.		1, 2
Greene, William	1912	Aurora, Ill.	Frank Lloyd Wright	
Greenebaum, Frederick	1926	Highland Park, Ill.	Ernest A. Grunsfeld, Jr.	2
Gregg, Cecil D. (Brentmoor)	1914–1922	Clayton, Mo.		1, 2
Gregory, Mrs. R. B.	1910–1917	Highland Park, Ill.		1, 2
Gridley, Mr.	1927	Geneva, Ill.		2
Grommes, I. B.	1903–1906	Lake Geneva, Wis.	Richard Schmidt	1, 2
Gudeman, Edward	n.d.	location unknown		1
Haight, R. I.	1904	Palos Park, Ill.		2
Hamill, E. A.	1913	Lake Forest, Ill.		2
Hanson, Lucille Evely	1940	location unknown		
Hardin, John H.	1910	Glencoe/Hubbard Woods, Ill.		1, 2
Hart, Harry	1911	Oconomowoc, Wis.		1, 2
Hart, J. M.	1916	Evanston, Ill.		2
Haseltine, W. E.	1915	Ripon, Wis.		2
Hasler, A.	n.d.	Lake Forest, Ill.		1

Name of Project	Date	Place	Architects	Source(s)
Hately, J. C.	1904–1910	Lake Geneva, Wis.		1, 2
Hauberg, Mrs. (same as Denkmann, Ruth)	1909–1910	Rock Island, Ill.		1, 2
Hawkins	1922	Glencoe, Ill.		2
Hellum, P. E.	n.d.	Glencoe, Ill.	Ivar Viehe-Naes	2
Hemingway, G. R.	1916	Wheaton, Ill.		2
Hert, A. T.	1917	Louisville, Ky.		1, 2
Hertz, John	1919–1921	Cary, Ill.		2
Hesler, F. L.	1910	Lake Forest, Ill.		2
Hille, Hermann	1911–1912	Highland Park, Ill.		2
Hitchcock	n.d.	Highland Park, Ill.		1
Holmes, Samuel	1927	Highland Park, Ill.	Robert Seyfarth	1, 2
Howell, Thomas M.	1925	Barrington, Ill.		2
Hubbard, Henry M.	1905	Lake Forest, Ill.		1, 2
Hubbard, I. D.	1909–1927	Lake Forest, Ill.		2
Ickes, Harold	1916	Hubbard Woods, Ill.		2
Insull, Martin	1916	Highland Park, Ill.	Marshall & Fox	2
Insull, Samuel	n.d.	Lake Forest, Ill.		1
Insull, Samuel	1914–1916	Libertyville, Ill.		1
Jackson, Arthur	1927	Lake Forest, Ill.		2
Jensen, Jens ("The Clearing" studio; the Marshall Johnson family lived here)	1908–1934	Highland Park, Ill. (Ravinia)		1
Jensen, Jens (house)	n.d.	Wilmette, Ill.		1
Jerome	n.d.	Lakeside, Mich.		1
Johnson, H. F.	1911	Racine, Wis.		2
Johnson, Halsey	1926	Aurora, Ill.		2
Johnson, Phil	n.d.	Northbrook, Ill.		1
Jones, Clyde W.	1916	Kalamazoo, Mich.		2
Kanzler, Ernest C.	1925–1929	Detroit, Mich. (also Macomb Co.)		2
Kayne, Thomas Y.	1922	Glencoe, Ill.		2
Keehn, Ray D.	1928–1929	Lake Bluff, Ill.		2
Keller, Adelaide (Eagle Point Colony)	1941	Bonaford, Ohio		1
Kelly, Phelps	1926	Lake Bluff, Ill.		2

Name of Project	Date	Place	Architects	Source(s)
Kelly, William V.	1913, 1917, 1922, 1924– 1926	Lake Forest, Ill.	Howard Van Doren Shaw	1, 2
Kensink, E. B.	1916	Decatur, Ill.		2
Kilbourne, L. B.	1905– 1910	Highland Park, Ill.		1, 2
Kilzinger	1925	Glencoe, Ill.		2
King, C. L.	1912	Lake Forest, Ill.		2
Klee, Nathan	1924– 1926	Highland Park, Ill.	Russel S. Wolcott	2
Kniblack, J. W.	n.d.	Lake Forest, Ill.		1
Knudson	n.d.	Chicago, Ill.		1
Kohn, L.	1905	Homewood, Ill.		1, 2
Kuppenheimer, Jonas	1913– 1916	Lake Forest, Ill.		1, 2
Kurth, Herbert	1940	Mequon, Wis.	garage by Thomas Stevens Vail	1
Kurtzen, Morris	1924	Highland Park, Ill.		2
Lackner, F.	1906	Kenilworth, Ill.		2
Lamborn, William H.	1908	Highland Park, Ill.	George W. Maher	2
Lantmann, Herbert M.	1934	Highland Park, Ill.		1
Lasker, A. D.	1913– 1918	Glencoe, Ill.	Henry C. Dangler	2
Lefens, T. J.	1911	Lake Geneva, Wis.		1, 2
Le Forgee, Charles C.	1922– 1923	Decatur, Ill.		1, 2
Lehmann, Augusta	1921	Lake Villa, Ill.		2
Leonard, Clifford M.	1923	Lake Forest, Ill.		2
Lepine, A. J.	1931	Dearborn, Mich.		1
Lichstern, Adolph J.	1915	Highland Park, Ill.	Arthur Heun	1
Link, Goethe	n.d.	Brooklyn, Ind.		
Link, Goethe	1922– 1923	Indianapolis, Ind.		1, 2
Loeb, Albert H.	1910– 1911	Chicago, Ill. (Hyde Park)	Arthur Heun	2
Loeb, Albert H.	1917	Charlevoix, Mich.		1, 2
Loeb, Ernest	1929	Highland Park, Ill.	Arthur Heun	2
Logan, F. G.	1903	Glencoe, Ill.		2
Logan, Frank	1914	Chicago, Ill.		2
Lombard	n.d.	Highland Park, Ill.		1
MacChesney, Nathan W.	1913	Chicago, Ill.		2

Name of Project	Date	Place	Architects	Source(s)
Magnus, A. C.	1904–1905	Winnetka, Ill.	Robert Spencer	1, 2
Maher, George W.	1902–1903	Kenilworth, Ill.		
Martin, Mrs. H. H.	1920	Lake Forest, Ill.		1, 2
Mauran, C. S.	n.d.	Highland Park, Ill.	Lawrence Buck	1
McCarty	1931	Lake Geneva, Wis.		1
McClernon	1909	Highland Park, Ill.		2
McClintock, W. H.	1910	Kenilworth, Ill.		2
McCormick, Mrs. Cyril H.	1917	Lake Forest, Ill.		2
McInnerney, Thomas H.	n.d.	Winnetka, Ill.	Reginald D. Johnson	2
McMaster, A. J.	1941	Lake County, Ill.		1
Meeker, Arthur	1910	Lake Forest, Ill.		1, 2
Meyer, E. A.	1922	Glencoe, Ill.		1
Michaels, Joseph	1924	Highland Park, Ill.		2
Mighell, Lee	1940	Aurora, Ill.		1
Miller, Mrs. Darius	1916	Lake Forest, Ill.	Howard Van Doren Shaw	1, 2
Miner, Marvin E.	1928	Barrington, Ill.		2
Montgomery, R. R.	1916–1918	Decatur, Ill.		1, 2
Moore, Edward S.	1911–1913	Lake Forest, Ill.	Arthur Heun	1, 2
Moore, Dr.	n.d.	Highland Park, Ill.		1, 2
Moore, Robert J.	1921	Niagara Falls, N.Y.		2
Moore, W. D. N.	1924–1927	Wellington County, Ontario		2
Morrison, Helen	1940	Northbrook, Ill.		1
Morton, Joy (Thornhill Farm)	1919	Lisle, Ill.		1, 2
Morton, Misses	1914	Lombard, Ill.		1, 2
Mosser, E. C.	n.d.	Chicago, Ill.	George W. Maher	2
Murray	1916	location unknown		2
Myers, E. Lewis	1924	Lake Geneva, Wis.	Howard Van Doren Shaw	2
Nelson, W. P.	1917	Chicago, Ill.		2
Niblack, William C.	1914–1919	Lake Forest, Ill.		2
Noble, R. A.	1921	Bloomington, Ill.		2
Noel, Joseph R.	1914–1915	Oak Park, Ill.	Howard Van Doren Shaw	2

Name of Project	Date	Place	Architects	Source(s)
Norton, C. D.	1906	Lake Forest, Ill.		2
Oates, J. F.	1915	Evanston, Ill.		2
Oberne, John E.	1917	Knoxville, Tenn.	Spencer & Powers	1, 2
Odell, Benjamin F. J.	1914	Kenilworth, Ill.		1, 2
Oppenheimer, H. D.	1910	Chicago, Ill.		1, 2
Orb, John	1904	Glencoe, Ill.		1, 2
Owen, David Warren	1923	Lake Forest, Ill.	Schmidt, Garden & Martin	1, 2
Pabst, Frederick	1907	Oconomowoc, Wis.		1, 2
Paepcke, Herman (Indianola)	1901– 1914	Glencoe, Ill.	Jebson & Fromann	1, 2
Paxton, Charles E.	1912	Lake Forest, Ill.	Hugh M. G. Garden	1, 2
Pellet, Clarence J.	1916	Oak Park, Ill.		1
Perkins, Dwight	1904	Evanston, Ill.		
Perkins, Frederick W.	1921	location unknown		2
Perry, Norman	1928	Culver, Ind.		2
Pick, Albert	1926	Winnetka, Ill.		2
Pick, George	1915	Highland Park, Ill.	Howard van doren Shaw	2
Platt, Robert S.	1924	Chicago, Ill.		1
Podatz, Jacob	1904	Palos Park, Ill.		2
Pool, M. B.	1911	Chicago, Ill.		2
Potter, Charles F.	1912	Lake Geneva, Wis.		1, 2
Potter, Edwin A.	1912	Lake Geneva, Wis.		2
Pushman, J. T.	1920	Libertyville, Ill.		2
Rackheim, Louis	n.d.	Lakeside, Mich.		1
Rasmussen, G.	1918– 1919	Everett, Ill.		2
Rea	1909	Chicago, Ill.		2
Regnery, W.	n.d.	Hinsdale, Ill.		2
Reimers, J. J.	1910	Davenport, Iowa	Temple & Burrows	1, 2
Reynolds, George M.	1916	Chicago, Ill.		2
Richardson, R. R.	1920	Wheaton, Ill.		2
Roberts, Abby Beecher Longyear	n.d.	Marquette, Mich.	Frank Lloyd Wright	
Roberts, W.	n.d.	Morgan Park, Ill.		1
Roberts, William H.	1913	Chicago, Ill.		2
Robins, Sidney	n.d.	Glencoe, Ill.		1
Rosenbaum, E. S.	1917	Glencoe, Ill.		2
Rosenthal, Benjamin F.	1916	Homewood, Ill.		2

Name of Project	Date	Place	Architects	Source(s)
Rosenwald, Julius	(prior to 1911)	Chicago, Ill. (Hyde Park)		
Rosenwald, Julius	1911–1929	Highland Park, Ill.	Nimmons & Fellows; Lawrence Buck	1, 2
Rosenwald, Morris	1912–1913	Chicago, Ill.	Howard Van Doren Shaw	2
Ross, John D.	1913	Oak Park, Ill.		2
Rubens, Harry	1903–1906	Glencoe, Ill.	George W. Maher	1, 2
Rubovits, Toby	1913	Chicago, Ill.	Arthur Heun	1, 2
Rueckhein, L.	1919	Lakeside, Mich.		2
Rumsey, Henry A.	1912	Lake Forest, Ill.	Shepley, Rutan & Coolidge	2
Ryer, Raymond	n.d.	Highland Park, Ill.		1
Ryerson, E. L.	1913–1920	Lake Forest, Ill.	Howard Van Doren Shaw	1
Ryerson, E. L.	n.d.	Santa Barbara, Calif.		1
Sanders, David T.	n.d.	Highland Park, Ill.		1
Sanford, Hugh W.	1917	Knoxville, Tenn.	Spencer & Powers	2
Saxby, Charles A.	n.d.	Glencoe, Ill.		1
Scarborough, H. C.	1909	Highland Park, Ill.		2
Schlesinger, F.	1917	Milwaukee, Wis.		2
Scott, Donald J.	n.d.	Winnetka, Ill.		1
Scott, Emmett	1922	La Porte, Ind.		1
Scott, F. H.	1914	Hubbard Woods, Ill.		1, 2
Scott, John W.	1914	Hubbard Woods/ Glencoe, Ill.		1, 2
Scott, R. L.	1915	Evanston, Ill.		2
Seabury, C. W.	1912	Oak Park, Ill.	White & Christie	2
Seaman, Col. George G.	1920	Taylorville, Ill.		1, 2
Silberman, S.	1917	Chicago, Ill.		1, 2
Simms, E. F.	1915–1916	Paris, Ky.		1, 2
Simms, W. E.	1911–1917	Spring Station, Ky.		1, 2
Simpson, James	1913	Glencoe, Ill.		2
Sippy, Dr.	n.d.	Lilley, Mich.		1
Skinner, J. F.	1911–1912	Oak Park, Ill.		1, 2

Name of Project	Date	Place	Architects	Source(s)
Smith, Frederick B. (Overbrook)	1909–1910	Terre Haute, Ind.	Spencer & Powers	1, 2
Smith, Frederick H.	1908	Peoria, Ill.		1, 2
Smith, Thomas	1914	St. Joseph, Mo.		1, 2
Smithers, Perry L.	1919–1920	Wilmette, Ill.		2
Snyder, Karl	1924–1925	Freeport, Ill.		2
Sonnenschein, Edward	1926	Glencoe, Ill.		2
Stackler, Sidney	n.d.	location unknown		1
Staley, A. E., Jr.	1930	Decatur, Ill.		1, 2
Stalnaker, F. D. (Qüestover)	1921–1923, 1928	Indianapolis, Ind.		1, 2
Steele, Leo M.	1923	Highland Park, Ill.		1
Stein, B. F.	1923	Lake County, Ill.		2
Stensland, P. O.	1903	Irving Park, Ill.		2
Stern, Alfred	1924	Highland Park, Ill.		2
Stickney, Miss	n.d.	(southern Illinois)		1
Stonehill, C. A.	1910	Glencoe, Ill.		2
Stout, F. D.	1918	Chicago, Ill.		2
Stout, Mr.	n.d.	Cedar Lake, Wis.		1
Straus, Martin	1926–1929	Highland Park, Ill.	Ernest A. Grunsfeld, Jr.	1, 2
Studebaker, J. M., Jr.	1924–1926	South Bend, Ind.		2
Swift, E.	1916	Lake Geneva, Wis.		1, 2
Swift, L. F.	1930	Lake Forest, Ill.	Spencer & Powers	2
Swigart, H. A.	1916	Evanston, Ill.	Howard Van Doren Shaw	2
Tervillian, William	1925	Freeport, Ill.		2
Thompson, Adam G.	1925–1927	Duluth, Minn.	Howard Van Doren Shaw	2
Thompson, John R.	1924	Lake Forest, Ill.		2
Thorne, Charles H.	1910	Winnetka, Ill.		2
Tilt, J. E.	1913	Chicago, Ill.		2
Timson, C. E.	1938	Deerfield, Ill.		1
Tinkoff, Paysoff	1933	Kenilworth, Ill.		2
Trostel, Albert O.	1909–1910	Milwaukee, Wis.	E. R. Liebert	1, 2
Uihlein, Edward G.	1901	Lake Geneva, Wis.		1
Uihlein, Edward G.	1914	Lake Forest, Ill.		2

Name of Project	Date	Place	Architects	Source(s)
Vandeveer, E. A.	1910–1911	Taylorville, Ill.		1, 2
Vandeventer, Hugh F.	1923	Knoxville, Tenn.	A. B. Bowman	2
VanMatre, W. N.	1924	Bluff Lake, Ill.		2
Wacker, Charles	n.d.	Lake Geneva, Wis.		1
Wagner, E. W.	1907	Glencoe, Ill.		2
Waldon, Col.	n.d.	Clarkston, Mich.		1
Waldon, Sidney D.	1930	Detroit, Mich.		2
Wallis, H. M.	1920	Racine, Wis.		2
Warren, E. K.	1909–1910	Lakeside, Mich.		1, 2
Warren, E. K.	1909–1913	Evanston, Ill.	W. Carbys Zimmerman	2
Warren, Fred P.	1922	Evanston, Ill.		2
Wean, Frank L.	1908	Highland Park, Ill.		1, 2
Webster, H. G.	1917	Buchanan, Mich.		2
Weinfield, Gustave	1935	Highland Park		1
Wertheimer, M. A.	1918	Kaukama, Wis.		2
Wheeler, Frank H. (Hawkeye)	1912	Indianapolis, Ind.	Price & McLanahan	
Whitaker, W. E.	1929	Crown Point, Ind.		2
Wieboldt, R. C.	n.d.	Highland Park, Ill.		1
Wieboldt, W. A.	1908	Lake Delavan, Wis.		1, 2
Williams, Albert	n.d.	Lake Forest, Ill.		1
Williams, J. G.	1914	Duluth, Minn.	Perkins, Fellows & Will	1, 2
Williamson, John	1914	Saugatuck, Mich.		2
Willy, C. B.	1918	Lake Bluff, Ill.		2
Wilson, Milton	1912–1913	Lake Forest, Ill.	Chatten & Hammond	2
Wiseberg, Hiram	1928–1929	Syracuse, N.Y.		2
Wizner, Herman	1946	Highland Park, Ill.		1
Wonnell, Kent B.	1929	Highland Park, Ill.		1
Woods, Frank H.	1915	Lincoln, Nebr.	Paul V. Hyland	2
Woods, W. M.	1917	Decatur, Ill.		2
Wortheimer	n.d.	Kaukauna, Wis.		1
Yates, D. M.	1928	Oak Park, Ill.		2
Young, Otto (only reference is in Fulkerson [1941])	n.d.	location unknown		
Younker, A.	1912–1913	Winnetka, Ill.		2

Name of Project	Date	Place	Architects	Source(s)
Zerk, Oscar	1941	Kenosha, Wis.		1
Zimmerman, Herbert Paul	1921–1927	Geneva, Ill.		1, 2

Subdivisions

Name of Project	Date	Place	Architects	Source(s)
Ford subdivision	n.d.	(no location given)		2
Gregg subdivision	1922	Clayton, Mo.		1, 2
Hinsdale subdivision	1908	Hinsdale, Ill.		1
Interstate Land Co. subdivision	1921	MacGregor, Iowa		2
Loomis subdivision (A. R. Loomis)	1922	Fort Dodge, Iowa		2
Macdonald subdivision	1911	Glencoe, Ill.		2
Marquette subdivision	n.d.	Marquette, Iowa		2
Northlake subdivision	n.d.	Lake County, Ill.		2
Owen subdivision	1921	McHenry, Ill.		2
Woods Brothers subdivision	1916	Lincoln, Nebr.		1, 2

Hotels/Resorts/Camps

Name of Project	Date	Place	Architects	Source(s)
Bay View Hotel (Gilbert Wichman)	n.d.	Ellison Bay, Wis.		2
Conference Point (former Chambers estate)	1918	Lake Geneva, Wis.		2
Dearborn Inn	1931	Dearborn, Mich.		1
Edgewater Beach Hotel	1912–1917	Chicago, Ill.	Perkins, Fellows & Hamilton	2
Gad's Hill Encampment	1909	Lake Bluff, Ill.		2
Henry Ford Hotel	1930–1931	Dearborn, Mich.	Albert Kahn	2
North Pigeon (development called "Sky's End" for Roman Brotz)	1947	Sheboygan, Wis.		1
South Bay Hotel grounds	1903	Indiana Harbor, Ind.		2
Willow Run Legion Camp	1929	Ypsilanti, Mich.		1

Name of Project	Date	Place	Architects	Source(s)
Golf Courses				
Grand Beach Co. (subdivision and golf course)	1919	Grand Beach, Mich.		2
Homewood Country Club	1908	Flossmoor, Ill.		2
Lake Shore Country Club	1929	Glencoe, Ill.		1
Milwaukee Country Club	1931	Milwaukee, Wis.	Colt & Allison (golf course architects)	2
Northmoor Country Club	1931	Highland Park, Ill.	Alfred S. Alschuler	2
Racine Country Club	1909	Racine, Wis.		2
Ravisloe Country Club	1910	Homewood, Ill.		2
Parks and Preserves				
Allegheny County Parks (South Park)	1928	Allegheny Co., Pa.		
Camp Algonquin	1911	Algonquin, Ill.		2
Chicago Parks				
Adams Park	1908	Chicago, Ill.		2
Austin Park (became Columbus Park)	1906, 1912, 1916	Chicago, Ill.		2
Buena Park	1908	Chicago, Ill.		2
Campbell Park	n.d.	Chicago, Ill.		2
Columbus Park	1917– 1920	Chicago, Ill.		2, 3
Cragin Park	1921	Chicago, Ill.		1
Crescent Park, Edgebrook	1909	Chicago, Ill.		2
Dauphin Park	n.d.	Chicago, Ill.		2
Douglas Park	1907– 1914	Chicago, Ill.		1, 2, 3
East End Park	1906– 1909	Chicago, Ill.		2
Eckhart Park (B. A. Eckhart)	1907– 1917	Chicago, Ill.		2, 3
Ellis Park	1907	Chicago, Ill.		2
Franklin Park	1914– 1916	Chicago, Ill.		2, 3
Garfield Park	1907	Chicago, Ill.		2, 3

Name of Project	Date	Place	Architects	Source(s)
Grant Park	1903, 1912	Chicago, Ill.		1, 2
Harrison Park	1912– 1918	Chicago, Ill.		2, 3
Holden Annex Playground	1908	Chicago, Ill.		
Holstein Playground	1911	Chicago, Ill.		2
Humboldt Park	1907– 1917	Chicago, Ill.		2, 3
Logan Square	1917	Chicago, Ill.		2
Merrick Park	1906	Chicago, Ill.		2
Midway Plaisance (setting for monument by Lorado Taft)	n.d.	Chicago, Ill.		2
Morgan Park Playground	1915	Chicago, Ill.		2
Norwood Park	1906	Chicago, Ill.		2
Park IV	n.d.	Chicago, Ill.		2
Prospect Garden	1906	Chicago, Ill.		2
Pulaski Park	1911– 1912	Chicago, Ill.		2
Riis Park (Jacob A. Riis)	1910	Chicago, Ill.		1
Sayre and Rutherford Park	1909	Chicago, Ill.		2
Sheridan Park	1913	Chicago, Ill.		2
Stanford Park	1907– 1908	Chicago, Ill.		3
Triangle at 50th and Belle Plaine Avenue	1909	Chicago, Ill.		2
Union Park	1888– 1914	Chicago, Ill.		2, 3
Vernon Park	1917	Chicago, Ill.		2
Chicago Street Improvements				
Barry Avenue	1903	Chicago, Ill.		2
Division Street west of Mozart Street	1909	Chicago, Ill.		2
Humboldt Boulevard	n.d.	Chicago, Ill.		2
Jackson Boulevard	1920	Chicago, Ill.		2
Kedzie between North Avenue and Palmer Square	1905	Chicago, Ill.		2
Northcote Avenue, 143rd Street, and Prentiss Avenue	n.d.	Chicago, Ill.		2
Cook County Forest Preserves (proposed)	n.d.	Cook County, Ill.		1

Name of Project	Date	Place	Architects	Source(s)
Cooper Park	1909	Lincoln, Nebr.		2
De Kalb Public Square	1904	De Kalb, Ill.		2
East Chicago Parks/Streets				
Beacon Street	1903	East Chicago, Ind.		2
Frost Memorial Park	n.d.	Williams Bay, Wis.		1
(Edwin B. Frost)				
Lees Park	1936	East Chicago, Ind.		2
Parks (general)	1903	East Chicago, Ind.		2
Gledden Park	1903	Gledden, Wis.		2
Glencoe Bird Preserve	1919	Glencoe, Ill.		1
Glencoe Streets and Parks				
General Park Plan	1912–1916	Glencoe, Ill.		2
Green Bay Road Park	1915	Glencoe, Ill.		2
Library Park	1912	Glencoe, Ill.		2
Park Avenue	1912	Glencoe, Ill.		2
Parks	1912	Glencoe, Ill.		2
Rail Station Park	1912	Glencoe, Ill.		2
Union Church Park	1912–1913	Glencoe, Ill.	Patten & Miller	2
Vernon Avenue	1912	Glencoe, Ill.		2
Glenwood Children's Park	1945	Madison, Wis.		1
Havana Park	1919	Havana, Ill.		2
Highland Park Parks				
Central Park	1920	Highland Park, Ill.		1, 2
Memorial Garden	n.d.	Highland Park, Ill.		1
Park at Roger Williams, Dean, and St. John streets	1924	Highland Park, Ill.		2
Hot Springs National Park	1916	Hot Springs, Ark.		
Indiana Dunes State Park, Prairie Club Memorial Fountain	1932	Dune Park, Ind.		2
Indiana Harbor Public Park	1903	Indiana Harbor, Ind.		2
Indiana Harbor Waterworks	1903	Indiana Harbor, Ind.		2
Joslyn Conservatory (G. A. Joslyn)	1913	Omaha, Nebr.		2
Kendallville City Park	n.d.	Kendallville, Ind.		2
Kenilworth Park	1909	Kenilworth, Ill.		2
Kenneth Jensen Wheeler Council Ring, University of Wisconsin Arboretum	1938	Madison, Wis.		1, 2

Name of Project	Date	Place	Architects	Source(s)
Klock Park (Jean Klock)	1917–1920	Benton Harbor, Mich.		1
Knickerbocker Boulevard	n.d.	Hammond, Ind.		
La Grange Park	1931–1934	La Grange, Ill.		1, 2
Lake County Forest Preserves (proposed)	1919	Lake County, Ill.		2
Lincoln Highway, Ideal Section (Dyer to Schererville)	1917–1925	Lake County, Ind.		2
Lincoln Memorial Garden	1934–1936	Springfield, Ill.		1
Lombard Parks				
Community Garden and Library	n.d.	Lombard, Ill.		2
Lilacia Park	n.d.	Lombard, Ill.		1
Lombard Rose Garden	1928	Lombard, Ill.		1, 2
Plum Park	1929	Lombard, Ill.		2
Mahoney Park	1933	Kenilworth, Ill.		2
Marquette Park	1921	Miller, Ind.		
Oak Park Parks				
Park no. 2	1913	Oak Park, Ill.		2
Park no. 3	1913	Oak Park, Ill.		2
Scoville Park	1913	Oak Park, Ill.		2
Ottawa Parks (Illinois State Park Commission)	n.d.	Ottawa, Ill.		2
Pasadena Parks				
Central Park	n.d.	Pasadena, Calif.		2
Library Park	1902	Pasadena, Calif.		2
Pawpaw Park	1910	Pawpaw, Ill.		2
Racine Parks				
Bathing Beach	1909	Racine, Wis.		2
Boulevard	1922	Racine, Wis.		2
Cemetery Park	1906	Racine, Wis.		2
Island Park	1906	Racine, Wis.		2
Lewis Field	1909	Racine, Wis.		2
Monument Square	1909	Racine, Wis.		2
Parks (general plan)	1909	Racine, Wis.		2
Riverside Park	1911	Racine, Wis.		2
Washington Park	1910–1914	Racine, Wis.		2
River Forest Parks				
Park no. 1	1917	River Forest, Ill.		2

Name of Project	Date	Place	Architects	Source(s)
Park no. 2	1917	River Forest, Ill.		2
Park no. 3	1917	River Forest, Ill.		2
Shakespeare Garden, Northwestern University	n.d.	Evanston, Ill.		1
Springfield Parks				
Bergen Park	1914	Springfield, Ill.		2
Boathouse	n.d.	Springfield, Ill.		2
Bunn Park	1914	Springfield, Ill.		2
East Side Playground	n.d.	Springfield, Ill.		2
Playground	1914	Springfield, Ill.		2
Pleasure Drives and Parks District	1914	Springfield, Ill.		2
Washington Park (children's playground)	n.d.	Springfield, Ill.		2
Sunset Park	1945	Sturgeon Bay, Wis.		1
Sycamore Courthouse Square	1905	Sycamore, Ill.		2

Schools and Other Educational Facilities

Name of Project	Date	Place	Architects	Source(s)
Allendale Farm	1914	Lake Villa, Ill.	Lawrence Buck	2
Ashland School Grounds	1903	Ashland, Wis.		2
Avery Coonley Kindergarten	1929	Downers Grove, Ill.	Frank Lloyd Wright	1, 2
Bethany Bible School	1915	Chicago, Ill.		2
Cherryland High School	1948	Wisconsin		1
Chicago Junior High School	1934	Elgin, Ill.		2
Chicago Schools				
Austin High School	1908	Chicago, Ill.		2
Chicago Technical University and Agricultural High School	1919	Chicago, Ill.		2
Forestville School	1916	Chicago, Ill.		2
Lloyd School Center	1920	Chicago, Ill.		2
Logan School Center	1918	Chicago, Ill.		2
Helen C. Pierce School	1917	Chicago, Ill.		2
Clearing, The	1935–1951	Ellison Bay, Wis.	Hugh M. G. Garden and John S. Van Bergen, advisory	1
Culver Military Academy	1912, 1929–1932	Culver, Ind.		1, 2
Downers Grove Kindergarten	1912–1913	Downers Grove, Ill.	Perkins, Fellows & Hamilton	1, 2

Name of Project	Date	Place	Architects	Source(s)
Henry Ford Farms (arboretum/school)	n.d.	location unknown		1
Highland Park Schools				
Dean Avenue School	1913	Highland Park, Ill.		2
Green Bay School	1929	Highland Park, Ill.	Holmes & Flinn	2
Lincoln School	1931	Highland Park, Ill.		1
Ravinia School	1921–1926	Highland Park, Ill.	John S. Van Bergen	1
Jennings Seminary	1927	Aurora, Ill.		2
Jewish (Hebrew) Institute	1909–1911	Chicago, Ill.		1, 2
La Porte High School	1924	La Porte, Ind.		1
Lake Forest High School	n.d.	Lake Forest, Ill.		1
Lincoln High School	1925	Plymouth, Ind.	Miller, Fullenwider & Dowling	2
Luther College	1910	Decorah, Iowa		2
Manitowoc Schools				
Lincoln High School	n.d.	Manitowoc, Wis.		1
Manitowoc High School	1920–1925	Manitowoc, Wis.	Perkins, Fellows & Hamilton	2
McKendree College	1910	Lebanon, Ill.		2
National Kindergarten College	1928	Evanston, Ill.		2
North School	1928–1929	Glencoe, Ill.	George W. Maher	2
Oak Park/River Forest High School	1915–1917	Oak Park, Ill.	Robert Spencer (1905); Eben E. Roberts (1912), addition	2
Roosevelt School	1924	Mason City, Iowa		2
St. Patrick's School	1930	Racine, Wis.		1
University of Wisconsin				
Campus theater	1916	Madison, Wis.		2
Entrance plan	n.d.	Madison, Wis.		1
Wisconsin State Normal School	1903	Stevens Point, Wis.		2

Hospitals/Institutional Homes

Chicago House of Correction	1907	Chicago, Ill.		2
Condell Memorial Hospital	1911	Libertyville, Ill.		1
Council Home	1909	Western Springs, Ill.		2

Name of Project	Date	Place	Architects	Source(s)
Danish Old Folks Home	1915	Chicago, Illinois	William Drummond and Louis Guenzel	
Decatur and Macon County Hospital (Decatur Memorial)	1915–1916	Decatur, Ill.	Brooks, Bramhall & Dague	1, 2
Diversey Housing Project	1935	Chicago, Ill.		1
Edward Hines, Jr., Hospital	1915–1930	Maywood, Ill.		2
Ephraim Community House	1926	Door County, Wis.		2
Henry Ford Hospital	1919–1920	Detroit, Mich.		2
Home for Crippled Children	1910–1911	Wheaton, Ill.	Howard Van Doren Shaw	2
Illinois Central Hospital	1915	Chicago, Ill.	Schmidt, Garden & Martin	2
Jewish Home	1909	Western Springs, Ill.		2
Juvenile Home	1924	Aurora, Ill.		2
Milwaukee Convalescent Home	1930	Milwaukee, Wis.		2
Municipal Tuberculosis Sanatorium (children's camp and pool)	1923	Chicago, Ill.	W. A. Otis & E. H. Clark	2
Norwegian Hospital	1910	Chicago, Ill.		2
Oakhaven Old People's Home	1924	Chicago, Ill.		2
Presbyterian Home	1920	Evanston, Ill.		2
Resurrection Fathers' Home	1916	Glenwood, Ill.	Anton Tocha	2
Sacred Heart Convent	n.d.	(no location given)		1
St. Ann's Hospital	1899	Chicago, Ill.	Hugh M. G. Garden	

Companies/Business Offices

Name of Project	Date	Place	Architects	Source(s)
American Coconut Butter Co.	1918	Chicago, Ill.		2
Aurora Sewage Plant	1928	Aurora, Ill.		2
Ford Motor Company*				
Exhibit, Chicago World's Fair	1933	Chicago, Ill.	Marshall Johnson took the leading	1

* Many other projects were done for the Ford Motor Company by Marshall Johnson from 1936 to 1947, after Jensen's retirement from active practice.

Name of Project	Date	Place	Architects	Source(s)
			responsibility for this project	
Greenfield Village	1935	Dearborn, Mich.		1
Rotunda	1935– 1936	Dearborn, Mich.		1
Tractor buildings	1919	Hamilton, Ohio	Frederick G. Mueller	2
Montgomery Ward & Co. Playground	1909– 1910	Chicago, Ill.		2
Northern Indiana Public Service Unit no. 1	1931	Michigan City, Ind.		2
Staley Manufacturing Co.	1928– 1930	Decatur, Ill.	Aschauer & Waggoner	1, 2
O. Torrison Co.	1916– 1922	Manitowoc, Wis.		2
Waukegan Power Station	1924	Waukegan, Ill.		2

Government Centers

Name of Project	Date	Place	Architects	Source(s)
Chenecqua Civic Center	1932	Chenecqua, Wis.		2
Illinois State Capitol	n.d.	Springfield, Ill.		2
Illinois State Supreme Court	1907– 1912	Springfield, Ill.	W. Carbys Zimmerman	2

Miscellaneous

Name of Project	Date	Place	Architects	Source(s)
Alton Hall Farm	n.d.	Guelph, Ontario		2
Bullhatched	n.d.	Evanston, Ill.		1
Cemetery entrance	1904	Mason City, Iowa		2
Fair Oaks (addition to)	1924	Hinsdale, Ill.		2
A garden	1924	location unknown		2
Glen Gables	1921	Glencoe, Ill.		2
St. Elizabeth's Church	1914	Glencoe, Ill.		2
Westbury Apartments	1909	Chicago, Ill.		2
West View Farms Co.	1924– 1925	Everett, Ill.	Howard Van Doren Shaw	2

APPENDIX B

Key Names and Terms

Abt, Mrs. Jacob. Charter member of the Friends of Our Native Landscape and author of the masque "The Spirit of the Dunes," which was performed on 19 October 1913 to dedicate the Prairie Club cabin near Tremont, Indiana. Mrs. Abt and her husband were settlement workers at the Maxwell Street Settlement House.

Addams, Jane (1860–1935). Born in Cedarville, Illinois, Addams helped found Hull-House on Halsted Street in Chicago with Ellen Gate Starr in 1889. A prolific writer and lecturer on social and political reform, Addams was an important catalyst for establishing playgrounds and for efforts to improve the lives of immigrants in Chicago. She was awarded the Nobel Peace Prize in 1931. Through the arts programs at Hull-House, Addams helped foster the arts-and-crafts movement in the Midwest. She recorded her experiences in *Twenty Years at Hull-House* (1910).

Allée. Broad road or promenade lined with trees.

Allinson, T. W. (b. 1862). Born in New York City and educated in Europe, Allinson was head resident of the Henry Booth House Social Settlement in Chicago. He was active in a number of Chicago organizations, including the NAACP, the Chicago Ethical Society, and the Prairie Club.

Alphand, Jean-Charles Adolphe (1817–1891). French engineer and landscape architect, Alphand joined Baron Georges Eugène Haussmann in 1853 to remake the Bois de Boulogne in Paris. Alphand also reshaped the grand boulevards of Paris and designed large suburban cemeteries. His two books, *Les Promenades de Paris* (1867–73) and *L'Art des jardin* (1886), recorded his theory of design and were avidly read by Chicagoans anxious to make their city the Paris of the New World.

American Garden. Originally a collection of American plants created by English gardeners of the last half of the eighteenth century. Through the efforts of John Bartram of Philadelphia and others, seeds of American plants became readily available in Europe, and designers such as Humphry Repton included such gardens in their work. Increasingly, the emphasis was on ericaceous species such as *Rhododendron, Magnolia,* and *Kalmia,* and Olmsted and Vaux followed this pattern in their American Garden in Central Park in New York. In contrast, Jensen's American Garden in Union Park (1888) consisted of the common wildflowers of the countryside around Chicago.

American Park and Outdoor Art Association. An organization founded in Louisville, Kentucky, in 1897 as a general association of persons interested in parks, outdoor sculpture, and landscape art. Warren H. Manning and O. C. Simonds were early leaders in this organization, which was a predecessor to the American Society of Landscape Architects.

American Society of Landscape Architects (ASLA). A professional organization of landscape architects founded in 1899. Its eleven charter members were Nathan F. Barrett, Beatrix C. Jones (later Farrand), Daniel W. Langton, Charles N. Lowrie, Warren H. Manning, Frederick Law Olmsted, Jr., John Charles Olmsted, Samuel Parsons, Jr., George F. Pentecost, Jr., Ossian C. Simonds, and Downing Vaux. Jensen belonged to this organization for only two years.

Anderson, Sherwood (1876–1941). Author, born in Camden, Ohio. Best known for his book *Winesburg, Ohio* (1919). In his later years, he made his home in Marion, Virginia.

Apple River Canyon. State park in Jo Daviess County, Illinois, established through the support and lobbying efforts of the Friends of Our Native Landscape.

Art Institute of Chicago. Incorporated on 24 May 1879 as a museum and school of art. W. M. R. French served as the Art Institute's first director.

Aust, Franz (1885–1968). Born in Defiance, Ohio, Aust grew up on his family's ranch in North Dakota. He studied at Red River Valley University and earned a master's in physics at the University of Minnesota. He then took up landscape design at the University of Michigan, where he earned a second master's degree. Soon thereafter, he joined Wilhelm Miller in the landscape extension program at the University of Illinois. He later became professor at the University of Wisconsin in Madison, where he was active in the Madison Park and Pleasure Drive Association and helped found the University of Wisconsin Arboretum. A leader in the Wisconsin chapter of the Friends of Our Native Landscape, Aust was one of few academics Jensen trusted and counted as a close friend.

Austin Tract. *See* Columbus Park.

Beaux-Arts. A style of design promoted by the École des Beaux-Arts in Paris during the last half of the nineteenth and the early twentieth centuries. Key features included an emphasis on circulation and plan, symmetry, axial organization, and classical orders.

Bennett, Edward H. (1874–1954). English architect, trained at the École des Beaux-Arts in Paris. Bennett worked closely with Daniel H. Burnham to develop plans for San Francisco (1904–5) and Chicago (1906–9). From 1910 to 1930, Bennett served as consultant to the Chicago Plan Commission. In 1915, Bennett's firm—Bennett, Parson, and Forest—prepared plans for Chicago's Grant Park.

Benson, Olaf. Landscape gardener, worked as partner with Swain Nelson and in 1870 prepared plan for extension of Chicago's Lincoln Park from North Avenue to Diversey Parkway. Served as superintendent of Lincoln Park from 1876 to 1881.

Billerica. A series of three magazines created by Warren H. Manning to promote his planning and design interests. The first, which began publication in 1912, focused on Manning's planning efforts for his ancestral town, Billerica, Massachusetts. The second, the *North Shore Illinois Edition,* was financed by Cyrus McCormick and began publication in 1915; edited by Stephen Hamblin, it focused on planning and design issues of the northern suburbs of Chicago along Lake Michigan. The third version, which emphasized Manning's large-scale natural resource planning, was subtitled *A National Plan Magazine.*

Bioregionalism. Philosophy and general approach to life which emphasizes knowing the land and its history and living within its physical and ecological boundaries.

Birkenhead Park. A "country" park begun in 1843 in Liverpool, England, and designed by Joseph Paxton for the Improvement Commissioners of the Borough of Birkenhead. The gently curving paths and broad open spaces of Birkenhead Park left an indelible impression on Frederick Law Olmsted, Sr., when he traveled to England in 1850 and undoubtedly influenced his later work with public parks in the United States.

Bridgeman, Charles (d. 1738). One of the leaders of the English gardening movement of the eighteenth century; served as royal gardener to King George II and Queen Caroline from 1728 to 1738. Bridgeman is credited with inventing the ha-ha, a sunken fence meant to keep cattle and other animals away from lawn areas near the house, related buildings, and their immediate grounds without being visible as a barrier.

Brown, Lancelot "Capability" (1716–1783). A celebrated English landscape designer who was known as "Capability" because of his references to the capabilities of the various places he was charged with improving. Brown reworked many older English estates, obliterating all traces of formalism to create pastoral scenes with rolling lawns, expanses of quiet water, and trees planted by the thousands.

Burnham, Daniel H. (1846–1912). Born in Henderson, New York, Burnham moved to Chicago in 1856. He studied architecture in Massachusetts and Chicago and in 1873 formed a partnership with John Wellborn Root. After Root's death, Burnham formed the firm of D. H. Burnham and Company in 1891. Burnham led the design team for the World's Columbian Exposition in Chicago. Later, with Edward H. Bennett, he co-authored *The Plan of Chicago,* which was presented in 1906 and published in 1909. He designed many commercial buildings and some park structures, and developed city plans for Manila and Baguio, in the Philippines, and San Francisco, California.

Caldwell, Alfred (b. 1903). Born in St. Louis, Caldwell was one of Jensen's ablest foremen, working for Jensen from 1927 until 1932. In this capacity, he served as site supervisor on a number of Jensen's projects. Later he established his own practice and reputation as a designer. Jensen thought highly of Caldwell, writing to P. H. Elwood on 12 July 1934: "He is by far the most able and the most studious young man that has left my employ. He is also very practical, something I find lacking in most landscape graduates." Caldwell's distinguished career in landscape architecture and architecture included his design of Eagle Point Park in Dubuque, Iowa (1933–34), the Lily Pool and Pavilion in Lincoln Park in Chicago (1936–37), and collaborations with architect Ludwig Mies van der Rohe. Caldwell worked for the Chicago Park District from 1936 to 1939. In the mid-1940s he helped establish the architecture program at the Illinois Institute of Technology in Chicago, where he promoted principles of architecture modeled after the order found in nature. From 1959 to 1979 he taught at the University of Southern California, and in 1979 he returned to IIT. He currently divides his time between Chicago and Bristol, Wisconsin.

Caparn, Harold A. (1864–1945). Landscape architect, born in Newark-upon-Trent, Nottinghamshire, Great Britain. Caparn studied in Great Britain, at the École des Beaux-Arts in Paris, and at Columbia University, where he earned a degree in architecture and later taught landscape architecture. From 1894 to 1899, Caparn worked for J. Wilkinson Elliot of Pittsburgh, Pennsylvania. In 1902 he began his own practice, which included extensive park work, school and college grounds, private estates, and considerable work for the Brooklyn Botanical Garden. Caparn wrote widely on design and was a staunch defender of parks and roadside beauty.

Central Park, Chicago. *See* Garfield Park.

Central Park, New York City. The first large landscaped public park in the United States, designed by Frederick Law Olmsted, Sr., and Calvert Vaux after they won the park board's design competition in 1858.

Chicago Architectural Club. An educational club for Chicago architects and draftsmen. Sponsored numerous talks, demonstrations, and design exhibitions, most of which were held at the Art Institute. Jensen frequently submitted works for the exhibitions.

Chicago Arts and Crafts Society. A Chicago group, organized at Hull-House on 22 October 1897 to support the local arts-and-crafts movement. Early membership included many of the Steinway Hall architects.

Chicago Plan (Plan of Chicago). The City Beautiful plan for the Chicago metropolitan area drawn up by Daniel H. Burnham and Edward H. Bennett in 1906 and published in 1909. It included plans for a grand civic center on Chicago's lakefront and a system of parks and boulevards throughout the city.

City Club of Chicago. A Chicago civic organization whose motto was "a social club with a purpose" and whose membership included many local leaders. Jensen was a member from 1904 until the mid-1920s. The City Club provided an important forum for discussions on such civic improvements as a metropolitan park system (1904), the establishment of forest preserves (1905), and the creation of playgrounds (1906 and 1908).

City Residential Land Development Competition. The 1913 competition for designing a prototypical residential development sponsored by the Chicago City Club and recorded in Alfred B. Yeomans, *City Residential Land Development* (1916). Jury members for the competition included George W. Maher and A. W. Woltersdorf (architects), John W. Alvord (engineer), John C. Kennedy (housing expert), Jens Jensen (landscape architect), and Edward H. Barton (director of Roland Park Co., Baltimore, Md.).

The Clearing, Ellison Bay, Wisconsin. The school founded by Jensen after he moved to Ellison Bay.

The Clearing, Ravinia, Illinois. Jensen's design studio in Highland Park, Illinois. The house on this property was first used by the Jensens as a summer home. In the early 1920s it was weatherized for use by Marshall and Edith (Jensen) Johnson and their growing family as a year-round home.

Cleveland, Henry William Shaler (1814–1900). Landscape architect, born in Lancaster, Massachusetts. First in practice with Robert Morris Copeland in 1854, Cleveland later established a partnership with W. M. R. French after moving to Chicago in 1869. In 1886, Cleveland moved to Minneapolis, where he provided the vision for the metropolitan park system of the Twin Cities. His book, *Landscape Architecture as Applied to the Wants of the West*, was a forward-looking discussion of how landscape architects could counter needless destruction of natural beauty and the resulting sameness that was then so prevalent in western towns.

Cliff Dwellers. The men's social organization founded in 1907 by Hamlin Garland as the "Attic Club." Membership included many noted Chicago businessmen and artisans. Jensen was one of the founding members, as were Daniel Burnham, Louis Sullivan, Lorado Taft, and Frank Lloyd Wright. Jensen served as director for a short period in 1914.

Columbian Exposition. The Chicago World's Fair (or World's Columbian Exposition) of 1893. The Chicago firm of Burnham and Root served as consulting architects, and F. L. Olmsted and Company were the consulting landscape architects, in the design of the fair, which was sited in Jackson Park and along the Midway Plaisance.

Columbus Park. The West Chicago park designed by Jensen in 1917–20 for the property known as the Austin Tract, which had been used as a golf course (golf was continued in Jensen's design). Jensen considered Columbus Park his greatest expression of the prairie landscape.

Committee on the Universe. A small, informal group of friends of architect Dwight Perkins who gathered on Sunday evenings to share common interests. Apparently the group, of which Jensen was a member, lasted for only a few years around the turn of the century.

Cone, George Carroll (1862–1942). Born on a farm in Onarga, Illinois, Cone studied architecture at the University of Illinois and was one of the first to study landscape architecture at the Lawrence Scientific School of Harvard University. In 1904 he joined O. C. Simonds and Company in Chicago, where he served as Simonds' chief assistant. Cone began teaching landscape design at the University of Michigan in 1916 and joined the full-time faculty in 1925. He retired from active teaching in 1938.

Cook County Forest Preserve District. The outlying network of connected forest reservations around the city of Chicago created by the Illinois legislature on 27 June 1913. Many of the lands targeted for protection were identified in 1904 by the Special Park Commission, which was then headed by Dwight Perkins and included Jensen as a member. The Regional Planning Association, the Geographic Society of Chicago, and the Prairie Club all fought vigorously for passage of the Forest Preserve legislation. Under its charter, the district was given the authority to "acquire lands containing forests and lands connecting such forests, and to maintain, preserve, restore, and restock such lands together with their flora, fauna, and scenic beauties in their normal condition as nearly as may be for the education, recreation and enjoyment of the people."

Coonley, Avery (1870–1920). Born in Rochester, New York, Coonley founded Coonley Manufacturing Company of Chicago and was active in various social-settlement activities, including the Gads Hill Center. The design of his house in Riverside was an important collaboration for Frank Lloyd Wright and Jensen.

Copeland, Robert Morris. Lexington, Massachusetts, designer who established a "landscape and ornamental gardening" practice with H. W. S. Cleveland in 1854. Copeland and Cleveland submitted an entry in the competition for the design of Central Park. In 1859 Copeland published *Country Life: A Handbook of Agriculture, Horticulture, and Landscape Gardening*.

Coulter, John M. (1851–1928). Botanist, born in Ningpo, China. Coulter worked for the U.S. Geological Survey in the Rocky Mountains in 1872–73 and served as an influential professor of botany at the University of Chicago from 1896 until his retirement in 1925. Among his students was Henry C. Cowles, who later taught at the University of Chicago.

Council ring. The circular stone seat used by Jensen in many of his parks and gardens as a gathering place for storytelling, music, dance, and general discussion. Usually the ring centered on a fire pit, and Jensen likened the gatherings to the council fires of Amerindians.

Council rock. A large rock (usually a glacial boulder) included by Jensen in some of his designs to mark a significant place in the garden. These were intended to serve as gathering places similar to those used by Amerindians in earlier times.

Cowles, Henry Chandler (1869–1939). Born in Kensington, Connecticut, Cowles graduated from Oberlin College in 1893. He began his graduate studies in geology at the University of Chicago in 1896, but under the influence of Professor John M. Coulter, he quickly embraced plant ecology. Cowles received his doctoral degree in 1898, and his dissertation, entitled "The Ecological Relations of the Vegetation on the Sand Dunes of Lake Michigan," became a classic in the emerging science of ecology, with its emphasis on the classification of vegetation as both genetic and dynamic. In 1897, he began a popular and distinguished career of teaching and research at the University of Chicago which lasted until his retirement in 1934. Known for his sense of humor, storytelling, and dedication to his students, Cowles taught many of his classes in the field, encouraging direct study of the regional and geographic aspects of vegetation. Conservation activities became a natural extension of his teaching and research, and Cowles was active in the Prairie Club and served as the first vice-president of the Friends of Our Native Landscape. He helped found the Ecological Society of America in 1914 and became editor of the *Botanical Gazette* in 1926. Other groups that he actively supported included the Association of American Geographers, the Botanical Society of America, the Chicago Academy of Sciences, the Geographic Society of Chicago, and the Illinois State Academy of Science. In 1935, the July issue of *Ecology* was dedicated to Cowles; it was filled with articles by students and colleagues in appreciation of their friend and teacher.

Crunelle, Leonard (1872–1944). Sculptor, born in Leus, Pas-de-Calais, France. Crunelle studied under Lorado Taft at the Art Institute of Chicago and was particularly known for his numerous sculptures of Abraham Lincoln.

Curtis, John T. (1913–1961). Born in Waukesha, Wisconsin, Curtis studied botany at the University of Wisconsin, Madison, where he earned his Ph.D. in 1937 and thereafter became a professor of botany. His pioneering work in ecological restoration began at the University of Wisconsin Arboretum in the 1930s and his influential *Vegetation of Wisconsin* was published in 1959.

Danish folk schools. The system of peasant high schools in Denmark which was intended to preserve and reinforce Danish folk traditions. Teaching was by the spoken word, and many of the classes were held in the out-of-doors. Jensen's experience in the Danish folk schools deeply influenced his thinking on education and his plans for The Clearing in Ellison Bay.

Dean, Ruth (1880–1932). A landscape architect, Dean studied at the University of Chicago and worked for several years in Jensen's office in Steinway Hall. She later established a successful practice of her own in New York.

Dearborn Park. One of the earliest Chicago parks, established in 1839 on the original site of Fort Dearborn, which was ceded to the city by the federal government.

Douglas Park. The West Chicago park named for Illinois senator Stephen A. Douglas.

Downing, Andrew Jackson (1815–1852). One of first great landscape gardeners in America, Downing influenced many later landscape gardeners and landscape architects through his *Treatise on the Theory and Practice of Landscape Gardening, Adapted to North America* (1841) and his editorials in the *Horticulturist*.

Drama League of America. A national organization dedicated to encouraging and educating the public about good drama, the Drama League grew out of the small Drama Club of Evanston, Illinois. Organized at a meeting at the Art Institute of Chicago on 25 April 1910, it was officially launched later that year at the Lyric Theatre in Chicago.

Drought, Alice (b. 1903). With degrees in French and landscape architecture from the University of Wisconsin, Madison, Drought pursued a Ph.D. from 1926 to 1931 while working as a teaching assistant in the landscape architecture program at Wisconsin under Franz Aust and G. William Longenecker. Active in the Wisconsin chapter of the Friends of Our Native Landscape, Drought served as editor of *Our Native Landscape* from 1928 to 1931. Specializing in the design of camps, she advised Jensen on the selection of land and design of The Clearing in Ellison Bay, Wisconsin, became executive camp director of the Girl Scouts U.S.A., and worked as a camp planning consultant from 1935 to 1980. A freelance writer, Drought published many articles and wrote *A Camping Manual* (1943). She currently resides in Arizona.

Dubuis, Oscar F. (1849–1906). Jensen's predecessor as landscape gardener and engineer for Chicago's West Parks. Dubuis began his career as a draftsman for William Le Baron Jenney, was appointed engineer for the West Park Commission in 1877, and served as general superintendent of the West Parks from 1884 to 1888. Dubuis's design work in the West Parks can be seen as a transition from Jenney's work to Jensen's, placing greater emphasis on the plants, landforms, and watercourses typical of the region. Jenney left the West Parks abruptly for political reasons and moved to Peoria, Illinois, where in 1895 he was elected superintendent of parks by the Peoria Board of Park Commissioners.

Dunes Pageant. Drama presented on 30 May 1917 and 3 June 1917 in an effort to build support for the preservation of the Indiana Dunes as a national park. The pageant, written by Thomas Wood Stevens, presented an epic history of the Dunes and involved a cast of hundreds.

Dybbøl. Jensen's birthplace in the Slesvig province of Denmark.

Eckhart, Bernard (1852–1931). Born in Alsace, France, Eckhart immigrated with his family to Milwaukee, Wisconsin, while he was an infant. From 1870 to 1874, Eckhart served as the Chicago representative for Milwaukee's Eagle Milling Company and soon thereafter established the Eckhart and Swan Milling Company, before entering the banking business. In 1905, Eckhart, who was known as one of Chicago's most progressive citizens, was appointed chairman of the West Park Commission. As part of his reforms, he rehired Jensen, making him superintendent of all the West Chicago Parks. Eckhart served as commissioner until 1908.

Eliot, Charles (1859–1897). Landscape architect, born in Cambridge, Massachusetts. Eliot studied with Frederick Law Olmsted, Sr., and later joined the firm of Olmsted, Olmsted, and Eliot. He is remembered most for his work in establishing the Metropolitan Park System in Boston. His writings were published posthumously as *Charles Eliot, Landscape Architect* (1902).

Elmslie, George (1871–1952). One of the prairie architects, Elmslie came to the United States from Scotland in 1884 and went to work for William Le Baron Jenney. Along with George W. Maher and Frank Lloyd Wright, he worked in the office of Joseph Lymon Silsbee before joining the firm of Adler and Sullivan in 1889. In 1909, Elmslie established an architectural practice with William Gray Purcell and George Feick, Jr., in Minneapolis. When Feick left in 1913, the firm became Elmslie and Purcell. This partnership lasted until 1922, and the firm is perhaps best known for its design of a series of bank buildings in towns of the upper Midwest.

Elwood, Philip Homer (1884–1960). Born in Fort Plain, New York, Elwood studied at Michigan State College (now Michigan State University) and earned a master's degree in landscape architecture from Cornell University in 1910. From 1910 to 1913 he worked for the firm of Charles W. Leavitt, Jr., and from 1913 to 1915 he worked with Frank A. Waugh on civic improvement extension projects at Massachusetts State College (now the University of Massachusetts) in Amherst. Elwood organized and led the Department of Landscape Architecture at Ohio State University from 1915 to 1923, leaving there to head the Landscape Architecture Program at Iowa State University from 1923 to 1952.

Emerson, Ralph Waldo (1803–1882). Influential Boston-born naturalist, philosopher, poet, and writer. Emerson studied at the Harvard School of Divinity and thereafter moved to Concord, Massachusetts, where his circle of friends included Henry David Thoreau and Nathaniel Hawthorne. On a trip to Europe in 1832, Emerson came under the influence of the Romantic poets Samuel Taylor Coleridge and William Wordsworth. In 1920, Emerson began recording his thoughts about nature in his "journals," which served as the basis for his writings and teachings, including *Nature*, which was published in 1920. Known largely for his transcendentalist philosophy, Emerson helped organize Brook Farm in 1840.

English style of landscape gardening. Garden style developed in eighteenth-century England emphasizing pastoral and naturalistic scenery instead of the rigid geometry and clipped plants popular in the Tudor period. Writers such as Joseph Addison and Alexander Pope influenced the leading group of designers, which included Stephen Switzer, Charles Bridgeman, William Kent, Lancelot Brown, and Humphry Repton.

Eskil, Ragna Bergliot. A Chicago publicist and writer, Eskil was active in the Friends of Our Native Landscape and directed its masque for nineteen years.

Fair Lane. The Henry Ford Estate in Dearborn, Michigan, which was named for Ford's ancestral home in Ireland. Jensen began designing the grounds of Fair Lane in 1914.

Farm Bureau. The Wisconsin agricultural organization that ran programs at The Clearing from 1954 until recent years.

Field, Marshall (1835–1906). Department store founder, born in Conway, Massachusetts. Field got his early training in a dry goods store in Pittsfield, Massachusetts. He moved to Chicago in 1856, and in 1865 joined with Levi Z. Leiter and Potter Palmer to form the department store known as Field, Palmer, and Leiter. When Leiter and Palmer retired in 1881, Field continued the store as Marshall Field and Company and amassed a considerable fortune. A generous philanthropist, Field founded the Field Museum of Natural History and supported the University of Chicago.

Fisher, Carl G. (1873–1939). An Indianapolis automobile entrepreneur, Fisher was founder of Prest-O-Lite, maker of carbide headlights. He built the Indianapolis Motor Speedway and in 1911 initiated the Indianapolis 500. In 1912, Fisher started promoting his idea for the coast-to-coast Rock Highway, which later became the Lincoln Highway. A shrewd investor, Fisher began developing Miami Beach as a resort area in 1915 and promoted the Dixie Highway as a way of getting people to vacation in Florida. By 1925 he was worth an estimated $100 million, but he lost much of his wealth in the market crash of 1929.

Forbes, Stephen A. (1844–1930). Naturalist, born in Silver Creek, Illinois. Forbes served as curator of the Museum of the Illinois State Natural History Society from 1872 to 1877 and as director of the Illinois State Laboratory of Natural History until his retirement in 1917.

Ford, Edsel Bryant (1893–1943). Son of Henry and Clara Ford, born in Detroit. Ford worked for his father at the Ford Motor Company, where he eventually became treasurer and then president. With his wife, Eleanor Clay, Ford was a generous patron of Jensen, hiring him to design several estates as well as numerous properties for the Ford Motor Company.

Ford, Henry (1863–1947). Born in Dearborn Township, Michigan, the young Ford learned the machinist's trade and became chief engineer for the Edison Illuminating Company. A gifted tinkerer-inventor, he organized the Ford Motor Company in 1903 and served as its president until 1914. Avid lovers of nature, Ford and his wife, Clara Bryant, hired Jensen to design their Dearborn home, Fair Lane, in 1914.

Franklin Park. A large park in Boston designed by Frederick Law Olmsted, Sr., and his stepson John Charles Olmsted as part of Boston's "Emerald Necklace" in 1885. Franklin Park, Central Park (New York), and Prospect Park (Brooklyn) are frequently mentioned as Olmsted's three great park designs.

French, William M. R. (1893–1914). Born in Exeter, New Hampshire, French was the brother of noted sculptor Daniel Chester French. From 1865 until 1877, French worked as a civil engineer and landscape gardener and collaborated with H. W. S. Cleveland on many projects, including the design of the town of Highland Park, Illinois. In 1877 he became associated with the School and Museum of Art in Chicago, and in 1879, when that institution became the Art Institute of Chicago, French was named its first director.

French gardens. Style of design similar to the French gardens of the seventeenth and eighteenth centuries, especially the gardens of Louis XIV at Versailles, designed by Andre Le Notré. These gardens were balanced around a central axis and suggested an infinite expansion in any direction, usually along radial lines. Plants were often trimmed into strict geometric patterns, and water was featured in basins, canals, elaborate fountains, and cascades where topography allowed.

Friends of Our Native Landscape. Conservation organization founded by Jensen in 1913.

Fulkerson, Mertha (1905–1970). Born in rural Indiana, Fulkerson moved with her family to Highland Park in 1917. After taking business courses, she worked for a real estate agent before answering Jensen's classified advertisement for a secretary. When Jensen moved to Ellison Bay in 1935, Fulkerson went along to help him with his school. After Jensen died in 1951, Fulkerson fought to keep Jensen's idea of a school alive and helped maintain The Clearing much as it exists today. An accomplished weaver who had studied at the Cranbrook Academy of Art in Bloomfield Hills, Michigan, for a year and a half, Fulkerson taught weaving at The Clearing until she retired in 1965.

Fuller, George Damon (1869–1961). Born in Adamsville, Quebec, Fuller studied at McGill University and Cornell University before attending the University of Chicago, where he studied under Henry C. Cowles and received his Ph.D. in 1913. He stayed on at the University of Chicago as an instructor and became professor of plant ecology in 1933, the same year he assumed chairmanship of the Department of Botany. Like Cowles, he was active in the Friends of Our Native Landscape. Fuller's *Vegetation of the Chicago Region* was published in 1925.

Garden, Hugh Mackie Gordon (1873–1961). Chicago architect, born in Toronto; moved to Chicago with his family shortly thereafter. Garden worked for various offices—Flanders and Zimmerman, Henry Ives Cobb, and Shepley, Rutan, and Coolidge—before beginning freelance work in 1893. Later he joined the architectural firm of Schmidt, Garden, and Martin, which eventually became Schmidt, Garden, and Erikson. Garden collaborated with Jensen on numerous projects, including work for the West Chicago Parks and St. Ann's Hospital, and took many of his plans to Jensen for consultation.

Garfield Park. Originally called Central Park, Garfield Park was renamed in 1881 in memory of President James Garfield. This West Chicago park was the site of the Garfield Park Conservatory, with its "prehistoric" prairie gardens designed by Jensen.

Geographic Society of Chicago. This group, which counted Jensen and Cowles as active members, was founded in 1898. Among its early activities were efforts to preserve the Starved Rock area on the Illinois River as a state park and the battle to establish the forest preserve system in metropolitan Chicago.

Gillette, Emma Genevieve (1898–1986). Born near Lansing, Michigan, Gillette graduated from Michigan Agricultural College (now Michigan State University) in the first class of landscape architecture students in 1920. She worked for Jensen from 1920 to 1924 and remained a close friend thereafter. After leaving Jensen's office in 1924, Gillette moved back to Michigan, where she helped found a Michigan chapter of the Friends of Our Native Landscape and fought vigorously for Michigan's state parks and many other conservation efforts.

Gilpin, William (1724–1804). An English clergyman and author, Gilpin is chiefly known for his writings on the aesthetic appreciation of the picturesque. His *Remarks on Forest Scenery and Other Woodland Views, Relative Chiefly to Picturesque Beauty, Illustrated for the Scenes of New Forest in Hampshire,* which was published in 1791, influenced Humphry Repton and later Frederick Law Olmsted, Sr., as well as other landscape designers.

Glencoe, Illinois. A North Shore suburb of Chicago, established by Alexander Hammond, a retired physician and farmer from Rockford, Illinois, and incorporated in 1869.

Goodman, Kenneth Sawyer (b. 1883). Born in Chicago, Goodman headed the Goodman Lumber Company in Wisconsin. A fellow member of the Cliff Dwellers, he was persuaded by Jensen to write the masque "The Beauty of the Wild," which was first performed at the inaugural meeting of the Friends of Our Native Landscape in 1913 and became an annual tradition thereafter.

Graceland Cemetery. Noted Chicago cemetery established in 1860 on land purchased by Thomas B. Bryan. The early landscape design history of Graceland is sketchy, with Adolph Strauch, H. W. S. Cleveland, William Saunders, and Swain Nelson all being credited with contributing to the design. As a designed landscape, Graceland is best known for the sensitive naturalistic design work of O. C. Simonds, who became involved with the cemetery in 1878 and was named superintendent in 1881, with Bryan Lathrop (nephew of Thomas B. Bryan) as president.

Greater West Parks. Plan for expanding the West Chicago Parks; developed by Jensen in 1918 and published in 1920.

Greenfield Village. Outdoor historical museum established by Henry Ford in Dearborn, Michigan. Jensen prepared a landscape plan for Greenfield Village in 1935.

Greenleaf, James L. (1857–1933). Born in Kortknight, New York, Greenleaf earned a degree in civil engineering from Columbia University's School of Mines in 1880. From 1882 to 1895 he taught civil engineering at Columbia. In 1894 he began a highly successful landscape design practice, working largely on private estates. In 1918 and 1919 he worked as a camp planner for the U.S. War Department, and from 1923 to 1926 he served as president of the ASLA.

Griffin, Marion Mahony (1871–1962). Prairie architect, Griffin was born in Chicago and became one of the first female graduates of MIT, where she studied architecture. In 1895 she went to work for Frank Lloyd Wright. She was best known for her renderings for Frank Lloyd Wright and later for Walter Burley Griffin, whom she married in 1911.

Griffin, Walter Burley (1876–1937). Prairie architect and landscape architect, Griffin was born in Maywood, Illinois, and raised in Oak Park, Illinois. He studied architecture at the University of Illinois and in 1900 joined the Steinway Hall group as a draftsman for Dwight Perkins. He later went to work for Frank Lloyd Wright in Oak Park. In 1905 he established a private practice and dabbled in a variety of projects, including residences, residential subdivisions, campus and city planning efforts, and a prize-winning plan for Canberra, Australia.

Grundtvig, Bishop Nikolai Frederik Severin (1783–1872). The leading spirit behind Denmark's folk schools, Grundtvig was born a country minister's son and attended "Latin Schools," where he was constantly drilled in the catechism. He later referred to these as "dead schools" because they took away a child's enthusiasm. Shortly after 1801, he began an intense study of the mythology of the North and of traditional Danish folk customs. He determined that for Danes to reach full development, they must hold onto their traditions, and he sought to restore vitality and simplicity to Danish life. Although the realization of his folk school ideas came through others, Grundtvig is credited with providing their philosophical base and with writing many of the songs and hymns that are still celebrated in the schools.

Haussmann, Baron Georges Eugène (1809–1891). The designer who directed the rebuilding of Paris during the 1850s and 1860s. Guided by the classical principles of the École des Beaux-Arts, Haussmann was intent on making Paris a magnificent capital city, on adapting the fabric of the city to its growing population and industrial expansion, and on reducing street violence by creating broad boulevards. Haussmann's work in Paris was emulated by designers all over the world, and his work in Berlin was seen by the young Jensen during the latter's service in the German military.

Highland Park, Illinois. North Shore suburb of Chicago established by Walter Gurnee in 1854 around a train station of the Chicago and Northwestern Railroad (of which Gurnee was president). In 1867, the Highland Park Building Company bought 1,200 acres from Gurnee and hired H. W. S. Cleveland and W. M. R. French to develop plans for a residential community. Highland Park was incorporated in 1869 and became a select area for homes of Chicago's artists and wealthy elite.

Hitchings and Company. Architectural/engineering firm that designed New York's Garfield Park Conservatory (completed in 1908).

Holstein. Originally a Danish province, Holstein, like Slesvig and Lauenburg, was bitterly fought over by the Germans and the Danish during the mid-1800s. Since the Peace of Vienna in 1864, Holstein has been under German rule.

Hotchkiss, Almerin (1816–1903). According to Ebner (1988), Almerin Hotchkiss was the designer of Lake Forest, Illinois, in 1857. Jackson (1972) credits the design of Lake Forest to a Jedediah Hotchkiss (1828–1899), but Ebner makes a stronger case for Almerin Hotchkiss, who is also credited with designing Greenwood Cemetery in Brooklyn, New York, Bellefontaine Cemetery in St. Louis, and Chippianock Cemetery in Rock Island, Illinois.

Hull-House. The pioneering social settlement founded by Jane Addams and Ellen Gates Starr in 1889 on Halsted Street in a large, vacant house originally built by Charles Hull in 1856. The Hull-House compound eventually included thirteen buildings, as well as a playground on the Halsted Street property and a camp near Lake Geneva, Wisconsin. Its facilities included a day nursery, gymnasia, a community kitchen, and a boarding club for working girls. Hull-House offered a variety of programs, including college-level courses, training in arts and crafts, and one of the earliest little theater groups—the Hull-House Players.

Humboldt Park. One of the West Chicago Parks. Named after the great naturalist Alexander von Humboldt, it was popular with the German population in Chicago during its early history. Jensen first developed a full-scale version of a "prairie river" in Humboldt Park.

Hunt, Myron (1868–1952). Chicago architect, born in Sunderland, Massachusetts. Hunt studied at Northwestern University from 1888 to 1890 and at MIT from 1890 to 1892. He was one of the early members of the Steinway Hall group, but in 1903 he formed a partnership with Earl Grey and moved to California, where his most famous design was the Rose Bowl in Pasadena.

Hunt, Richard Morris (1827–1895). Born in Brattleboro, Vermont, Hunt studied at Harvard University and then traveled extensively in Europe, Egypt, and Asia Minor from 1846 to 1854. He was enamored with the Beaux-Arts style in Paris and became famous for his designs of private homes and monuments in the United States. Notable among his designs are the base of the Statue of Liberty and the Biltmore estate (designed for George W. Vanderbilt in 1895 in collaboration with Frederick Law Olmsted, Sr., landscape architect).

Hyde Park, Illinois. The Chicago neighborhood around the University of Chicago campus, originally chartered as a village in 1872.

Ickes, Harold (1874–1952). Born in Holidaysburg, Pennsylvania, Ickes studied law at the University of Chicago. He established a successful law practice in Chicago and served as U.S. secretary of the interior from 1933 to 1946 under Presidents Roosevelt and Truman. Ickes was an early member of the Friends of Our Native Landscape. Jensen designed Ickes's Hubbard Woods, Illinois, home in 1914.

Indiana Dunes. The network of sand dunes at the southern end of Lake Michigan in Indiana. The Indiana Dunes are a rich botanical crossroads where many species typical of northern, southern, eastern, and western plant communities commingle; they were a favored destination of the Prairie Club on its outings. The Indiana Dunes State Park was set aside in 1926, and the Indiana Dunes National Lakeshore was authorized in 1966 and formally established in 1972.

Inness, George (1825–1894). Born in Newburgh, New York, Inness studied painting with Régis Gignoux in Brooklyn and was influenced by the Hudson River School—notably by Thomas Cole and Asher B. Durand. Inness established his own studio in Brooklyn in 1845 and thereafter studied and painted at various times in Rome, Italy; Medford, Massachusetts; and Montclair, New Jersey. Widely respected for his landscape paintings, Inness became the most prosperous painter of his time. Jensen held a particular fondness for Inness's work, which often featured stormy skies and dramatic lighting effects.

Jackson Park. A South Chicago Park, originally designed by Frederick Law Olmsted, Sr., and Calvert Vaux, but only partially improved before the Columbian Exposition, which took place there in 1893. John C. Olmsted is responsible for much of the design that was implemented after the fair.

Jefferson, Thomas (1743–1826). Born in Albemarle County, Virginia, near Charlottesville, Jefferson was a surveyor and lawyer. He was a representative to the Virginia House of Burgesses from 1769 to 1775 and is credited with writing most of the Declaration of Independence in 1776. He served as minister to France from 1785 to 1789 and as the third president of the United States from 1801 to 1809. An avid architect and gardener, Jefferson designed and built his home, Monticello, and the University of Virginia, both of which continue to serve as important models of architectural and landscape design.

Jefferson Park. One of Chicago's earliest parks, established in 1848. Several other parks would also be called "Jefferson Park" in the following years.

Jenney, William Le Baron (1832–1907). Born in Fairhaven, Massachusetts, Jenney studied architecture and engineering at the École Centrale des Arts et Manufactures in Paris in 1856. Jenney came to Chicago in 1868 and in 1870–71 prepared plans for Chicago's West Parks. Jenney is perhaps best known as the father of the skyscraper, for the innovative skeleton construction system first used in his design for the Home Insurance Building in Chicago.

Jensen, Anne Marie Hansen (1881–1934). Wife of Jens Jensen, Anne Marie Hansen also was from the Dybbøl Peninsula in Denmark. A faithful supporter of Jensen's work and various activities, Mrs. Jensen ruled on the home front, providing a stabilizing balance to Jensen's tempestuous personality.

Jensen, Elmer C. (1870–1955). Architect, born in Chicago and educated at the Art Institute of Chicago. In 1885 he went to work for William Le Baron Jenney. In 1907 he organized the firm of Jenney, Mundie, and Jensen, which became Mundie and Jensen upon Jenney's death.

Johnson, Marshall (1892–1967). Born in St. Paul, Minnesota, Johnson moved to

Oak Park, Illinois, during his grade school years and then to Kansas City, Missouri, where he attended high school. In 1915 Johnson graduated from Cornell University with a degree in landscape architecture and afterward went to work in Jensen's Steinway Hall office. In 1919 he married Jensen's daughter Edith, and after living with the Jensens in Wilmette, moved into the house at The Clearing in Ravinia in the early 1920s. Johnson served as office manager for Jensen's Ravinia office and is credited with the beautiful drawings produced by the office. While not well documented, it is known that Johnson took the lead in designing certain projects, such as the Ford Motor Company Exhibit at the 1933 Chicago World's Fair.

Joy, Henry B. (1864–1936). Automobile manufacturer, born in Detroit, Michigan. Joy began his career as an office boy at the Peninsular Car Company and later became manager and director of the Packard Motor Car Company (1901–8). He was one of the founders and moving forces behind the Lincoln Highway Association.

Kattelle, Walter H. Architect for the Prairie Club's cabin at Tremont, Indiana, which was dedicated in 1913.

Kemeys, Edward (1843–1907). Sculptor, born in Savannah, Georgia. Kemeys' varied background included farming in Illinois, active duty in the Civil War, and service in the corps of civil engineers in Central Park. Kemeys became a sculptor in 1870 and studied abroad in 1877. Noted as the pioneer American animal sculptor of his time, Kemeys specialized in depictions of Amerindians and animals, especially wild beasts. He is said to have spent time hunting and camping with various Amerindian groups.

Kent, William (1685–1748). An important English architect and landscape designer, Kent studied painting under Benedetto Luti in Italy. In 1719, the earl of Burlington induced him to return to England, where he embarked on a career of interior decoration, architecture, and landscape gardening. At Chiswick Hall in Middlesex and in other designs, Kent experimented with winding paths, clumps of trees, various architectonic follies, and other garden features that would be refined by Lancelot Brown in the further evolution of the English landscape garden.

Knudson, Harriet (1882–1969). A leading force behind the development of Lincoln Memorial Garden in Springfield, Illinois, designed by Jensen in 1935–36. Knudson originated the idea for the garden in 1934 as an active member of the Springfield Civic Garden Association and member of the board of directors of the Garden Club of Illinois, and she personally directed much of the planting at the garden. She helped establish the Lincoln Memorial Garden Foundation in the 1950s.

Lake Forest, Illinois. Residential community founded in 1857 along the railroad from Chicago to Waukegan, Illinois. Reported by Ebner (1988) to have been designed by Almerin Hotchkiss, designer of the Bellefontaine Cemetery in St.

Louis, Lake Forest was laid out on picturesque principles, with gently curving streets taking advantage of the rolling, ravine-ridden topography.

Lathrop, Bryan (1844–1916). Born in Alexandria, Virginia, Lathrop studied in Germany and France. In 1865 he moved to Chicago, where he practiced real estate. Lathrop served in various public service capacities, including commissioner of Lincoln Park and president of the Chicago Symphony Orchestra Association. He was president of the board of managers of Graceland Cemetery that engaged O. C. Simonds in 1881.

Lauenburg. Originally a Danish province, Lauenburg was alternately under German and Danish rule until the Peace of Vienna of 1864, since which time it has been under continuous German rule.

Leopold, Aldo (1886–1948). Born in Burlington, Iowa, and educated in forestry at Yale University. Leopold went to work as a forestry assistant in the U.S. Forest Service in 1909. From 1925 to 1927 he worked for the Forest Products Laboratory in Madison, Wisconsin, and in 1933 he joined the faculty of the University of Wisconsin as professor of wildlife management. Also in 1933 Leopold published his classic book, *Game Management*. Increasingly concerned about the vanishing wilderness, Leopold helped organize the Wilderness Society. *Sand County Almanac*, with its fervent plea for the development of a land ethic, was published in 1949 after Leopold's death.

Lieber, Richard (1869–1944). Born in St. Johann-Saarbrücken, Germany, Lieber came to the United States in 1891 and worked for the *Indianapolis Journal* and the *Indianapolis Tribune*. From 1917 to 1919, Lieber served on the Indiana State Board of Forestry. In 1919 he became director of conservation for the state of Indiana. Holding that post until 1933, Lieber was a tireless crusader for Indiana state parks and other conservation programs.

Lincoln Highway Association. Formed in 1913 by Detroit and Indianapolis auto executives to promote the development of a coast-to-coast highway, the association contracted with Jensen to design the landscape of the "ideal section" near Merrillville, Indiana.

Lincoln Park. Established in Chicago in 1865, Lincoln Park was originally shaped by nurseryman Swain Nelson and Olaf Benson, who served as superintendent from 1876 to 1881. The original landscape of Lincoln Park was considered to be a barren, sandy waste, and tens of thousands of yards of black soil were imported to create "parklike" scenery. Benson used a series of brush mattresses to stabilize the eroding Lake Michigan shoreline. From its early days, Lincoln Park was filled with numerous memorials and pieces of statuary. O. C. Simonds designed the extension of Lincoln Park north of Diversey Avenue.

Lincoln Park Commission. Together with the South Park Commission and the West Park Commission, one of the three Chicago park districts established by state law in 1869.

Lindsay, Nicholas Vachel (1879–1931). Midwestern poet, born in Springfield, Illinois. Lindsay studied at Hiram College in Ohio, the Art Institute of Chicago, and the New York School of Art. During 1906 Lindsay traveled throughout the southern states, and in 1912 he walked from Illinois to New Mexico, distributing "rhymes" and speaking on behalf of "the gospel of beauty." At the inaugural meeting of the Friends of Our Native Landscape in 1913, Jensen asked Lindsay to recite his poem "Hawk of the Rock."

Longenecker, G. William (1899–1969). Landscape architect, earned undergraduate and master's degrees from the University of Wisconsin, Madison, where he studied under Professor Franz Aust. Longenecker worked briefly for Stark Brothers Nursery in Missouri and for the city of Hannibal, Missouri, before returning to Wisconsin to teach landscape architecture. Longenecker served as executive director of the University of Wisconsin Arboretum and was responsible for much of its design as well as the design of the university's campus as it expanded during his tenure. Longenecker was active in the Friends of Our Native Landscape and frequently took students to visit The Clearing in Ellison Bay, Wisconsin.

Lorraine, Claude (1600–1682). Well-known romantic landscape painter whose work inspired numerous English landscape gardeners, including Lancelot Brown (e.g., his work at Stourhead). Lorraine lived most of his adult life in Rome, visiting the countryside to gain inspiration for the "composed wildness" of his paintings.

Lowden, Frank (1861–1943). Born in Sunrise City, Minnesota, Lowden grew up in Iowa, where he worked as a farmhand and schoolteacher before graduating from Iowa State University. Lowden studied law at Union College in Chicago, opened his own law firm in 1887, and became a prominent corporate lawyer. He was elected to Congress from 1906 to 1911, and from 1917 to 1921 served as governor of Illinois. Lowden never lost his interest in farming, championing farmers' concerns and experimenting with crops and forestry practices on his Sinnissippi Farm near Oregon, Illinois, which O. C. Simonds helped design.

Lowell, Guy (1870–1927). Architect and landscape architect, born in Boston, Massachusetts, and educated at Harvard University, MIT, and the École des Beaux-Arts in Paris. Lowell began his practice in Boston in 1900 and served as lecturer on landscape architecture at MIT from 1900 to 1913. Lowell's influential American Gardens was published in 1902.

Mackaye, Benton (1879–1975). Born in Stamford, Connecticut, Mackaye graduated from Harvard University with a degree in forestry in 1905 and worked for the next thirteen years for the U.S. Forest Service. In 1921 Mackaye published his plan for an Appalachian Trail and joined Lewis Mumford, Clarence Stein, Henry Wright, and others to found the Regional Planning Association of America in 1923. Seeing a conflict between an increasingly urban industrial society and rural community life, Mackaye published many of his planning ideas in The New Exploration: A Philosophy of Regional Planning in 1928. During the 1930s and 1940s, Mackaye served as a regional planner for the Tennessee Valley Authority and the Rural Electrification Administration. A lifelong champion of the environment, he served as president of the Wilderness Society in 1945.

Maher, George Washington (1864–1926). Architect, born in Mill Creek, West Virginia. At the age of thirteen, Maher began working in the Chicago architectural offices of August Bauer and Henry Hill. Maher worked for a short time with George Elmslie and Frank Lloyd Wright at the office of Joseph Lyman Silsbee, and later practiced on his own. Maher specialized in designing residences and suburban towns.

Manning, Warren H. (1860–1938). Landscape architect, born in Reading, Massachusetts. Manning worked for the firm of F. L. Olmsted and Company from 1888 to 1896, first as a horticulturist and later as a design assistant. He opened his own office in 1896 in Boston. Manning later operated his office from the Manning Manse in Billerica, Massachusetts, and from Cambridge, Massachusetts, before his death in 1938. His office was widely active in city planning and the design of private residences, parks, and institutional grounds.

Mather, Stephen Tyng (1867–1930). Born in San Francisco, Mather graduated from the University of California, Berkeley, in 1887. He joined the staff of the *New York Sun* in 1887 and worked there until 1893. In 1894 Mather became the Chicago manager for the Pacific Coast Borax Company, and in 1903 he assumed the presidency of the Sterling Borax Company, also in Chicago. A strong supporter of conservation efforts, Mather was one of the founding members of the Friends of Our Native Landscape. From 1915 to 1917 he served as an assistant to the secretary of the interior, and in 1917 he became the first director of the U.S. National Park Service.

Mawson, Thomas (1861–1933). Born in Lancaster, England, Mawson was perhaps the most prolific English garden designer of the early twentieth century. He was an active supporter of the arts-and-crafts movement, and between 1900 and 1926 he published five editions of *The Art and Craft of Garden-Making*. Mawson was also active in town planning, served for a time as president of the Town Planning Institute, and was the first president of the Institute of Landscape Architects, which was organized in 1928.

McMillan Plan. The highly influential plan for Washington, D.C., prepared in 1901 by a commission made up of architects Daniel H. Burnham and Charles F. McKim, landscape architect Frederick Law Olmsted, Jr., and sculptor Augustus Saint-Gaudens. The plan revived much of Pierre Charles L'Enfant's 1791 plan for the capital and led to the establishment of the National Commission of Fine Arts in 1910.

Memorial Park Cemetery. The cemetery in Skokie, Illinois, where Jensen and his wife are buried.

Midway Plaisance. The strip of parkland joining Jackson and Washington parks in Chicago. Olmsted and Vaux's plan proposed a canal for this area, with an avenue on either side. During the World's Columbian Exposition of 1893, the Midway Plaissance served as an amusement park.

Miller, Wilhelm (1869–1938). Landscape architect, born in King William County, Virginia, but raised in Detroit. Miller graduated from the University of Michigan in 1892 and from Cornell University in 1899. A prolific writer on landscape gardening and related topics, Miller served as associate editor (with Liberty Hyde Bailey) of the *Cyclopedia of American Horticulture* from 1897 to 1901, was on the editorial staff of *Country Life in America* from 1901 to 1912, and edited the *Garden Magazine* from 1905 to 1912. In 1912 Miller became an assistant professor of landscape horticulture at the University of Illinois, Urbana, and in 1914 he was appointed head of the university's Division of Landscape Extension, one of the first of its kind in the United States. Miller promoted the "prairie style" of landscape gardening in his books *The Illinois Way of Beautifying the Farm* (1914) and *The Prairie Spirit in Landscape Gardening* (1915). In 1916 and 1917 Miller worked as a landscape architect in Chicago, in 1918 and 1919 he worked in Detroit, and in 1920 he retired to Beaumont, California. His wife was the noted naturalist-writer Mary Farrand Rogers.

Milles, Carl (1875–1955). Sculptor, born in Uppsala, Sweden. Milles studied at the Technical School in Stockholm from 1895 to 1897, at the École des Beaux-Arts in Paris from 1897 to 1904, and in Munich from 1904 to 1906. Milles came to the United States in 1929 and became a naturalized citizen in 1945. He is known for his figurative sculptures and fountains, which are scattered throughout much of the United States and Sweden. In 1930 Milles began teaching at the Cranbrook Academy of Art in Bloomfield Hills, Michigan, near Detroit.

Monroe, Harriet (1860–1936). A prolific Chicago poet, Monroe studied at the Dearborn Seminary as well as at the Convent of Visitation in Georgetown in the District of Columbia. She received her doctor of letters degree from Baylor University in Waco, Texas. Her first fame came for "Columbian Ode," which was written for the dedication of the World's Columbian Exposition on 21 October 1893. Her sister, Dora Louise Monroe, was married to John Wellborn Root, and in 1896 Harriet Monroe published a biography of her brother-in-law, *John Wellborn Root: A Study of His Life and Work*. In 1912 she founded *Poetry: A Magazine of Verse*, which became an index of major contemporary poets and included works by Vachel Lindsay, Edgar Lee Masters, and Carl Sandburg. Monroe was one of the people invited by Jensen to form the Friends of Our Native Landscape.

Monticello. The home of Thomas Jefferson outside Charlottesville, Virginia.

Mount Royal. Park in Montreal created by Frederick Law Olmsted, Sr., from 1874 to 1881.

Mount Vernon. George Washington's Virginia home outside Washington, D.C.

Muddy River Parkway. A linear park suggested by Frederick Law Olmsted, Sr., in 1876 to connect Boston's Back Bay Fens area with Jamaica Pond. The project, which was not begun until 1890, eventually became known as the Riverway and was part of Boston's "Emerald Necklace" of parks.

Mulligan, Charles (1866–1916). Sculptor, born in Aughnachy, Scotland. Mulligan studied under Lorado Taft at the Art Institute of Chicago as well as at the École des Beaux-Arts in Paris. He sculpted *The Rail Splitter,* a statue of Lincoln which was included in Jensen's sculpture exhibition in Humboldt and Garfield parks.

Mumford, Lewis (1895–1990). Philosopher, social historian, and critic, born in Queens, New York. Mumford studied at Columbia University and the New School for Social Research. Influenced by Patrick Geddes, whom he met in the early 1920s, Mumford was one of the founders of the Regional Planning Association of America and worked for the New York Housing and Regional Planning Commission. He was particularly critical of the dehumanizing aspects of technology, publishing *Brown Decades* in 1924 and *Sticks and Stones* in 1931. From the 1930s to the 1950s he wrote the "Skyline" column for *The New Yorker,* calling for socially responsible architecture and planning.

Municipal Science Club. A small group of Chicagoans who met at Hull-House at the turn of the century to discuss various aspects of urban life. As a result of a Municipal Science Club presentation by Jacob Riis in 1898 on crowded conditions in tenements and the need for children's playgrounds, the Special Park Commission was formed to study parks and playgrounds in and around metropolitan Chicago.

National Playground Association. An organization founded in 1907 to promote playgrounds in American cities. In 1908 a committee of the Chicago chapter established the "Saturday Afternoon Walking Trips," which in turn led to the founding of the Prairie Club.

Neighborhood Center Competition. The competition sponsored by Chicago's City Club and the Illinois chapter of the American Institute of Architects in 1914–15 to design a prototypical neighborhood center that would group neighborhood public and semipublic institutions at a common center to stimulate neighborhood life and reduce the social isolation of families in modern cities. Jensen submitted a noncompetitive entry.

Nelson, Swain (b. 1829). Born in Sweden, Nelson studied landscape gardening there before coming to the United States in 1854. In 1856 he moved to Chicago, where he established a nursery and landscape design practice. Nelson quickly became known for moving large trees to create what he called "landscapes without waiting," and he imported a wide variety of shade trees from England and Scotland to supplement the native trees he found around Chicago. Nelson can be credited with early landscape designs and plantings for Graceland Cemetery, Lincoln Park, and Union Park, and his nursery provided many of the trees and shrubs for the development of the West Parks as well as for many of the prominent estate properties around Chicago, including many designed by Jensen. Jensen is said to have worked for Nelson during periods when he was laid off from the West

Parks in his early years in Chicago. In 1894, Nelson established Glen View Nurseries on 150 acres of land northwest of Chicago.

Nolen, John (1869–1937). Landscape architect and city planner, born in Philadelphia. Nolen studied at the University of Pennsylvania, the University of Munich, and Harvard University. His large and active firm in Cambridge, Massachusetts, designed parks and park systems throughout much of the United States.

Oakwood Cemetery. One of three large "landscape" cemeteries in Chicago, the other two being Rosehill and Graceland. Oakwood was incorporated in 1864 and laid out by Adolph Strauch.

Olmsted, Frederick Law, Sr. (1822–1903). Landscape architect, born in Hartford, Connecticut. Together with Calvert Vaux, Olmsted designed Central Park and Prospect Park in New York City and other parks throughout the United States and Canada. From 1865 to 1872, Olmsted maintained a partnership with Vaux and F. C. Withers; in later years, his practice included his son Frederick Law Olmsted, Jr., and his stepson John Charles Olmsted. His style of naturalistic design featured extensive shrub borders and masses and was widely imitated by his followers. Through his extensive writings and broad practice, Olmsted had a profound and lasting influence on American landscape architecture.

Olmsted, Frederick Law, Jr. (1870–1957). Landscape architect, born on Staten Island, New York. Olmsted graduated from Harvard University in 1894 and thereafter went to work in his father's firm, F. L. Olmsted and Company. He became a partner when the company was renamed the Olmsted Brothers in 1898.

Olmsted, John Charles (1852–1920). Landscape architect, born in Geneva, Switzerland, to John Hull Olmsted (brother of Frederick Law Olmsted, Sr.) and Mary Perkins Olmsted. John Charles became the stepson of Frederick Law Olmsted, Sr., when John Hull Olmsted died and Frederick Law Olmsted married John Charles's mother in 1859. John Charles graduated from Yale University in 1875 and went to work in his stepfather's office in 1878, becoming a partner in the Olmsted office in Brookline, Massachusetts, in 1884.

Parsons, Samuel, Jr. (1844–1923). Landscape architect, born in New Bedford, Massachusetts, to a family of horticulturists. Parsons graduated from Yale University in 1862 and served with the U.S. Sanitary Commission during the remaining years of the Civil War. For a time he was Calvert Vaux's partner, after which he was appointed superintendent of planting in Central Park (1882), superintendent of New York City's parks (1885), and eventually landscape architect to the city of New York and commissioner of parks.

Peets, Elbert (1886–1968). Landscape architect, born in Hudson, Ohio. Peets studied at Western Reserve University and in 1915 he graduated from Harvard University with a master's degree in landscape architecture. He then worked briefly for Pray, Hubbard, and White in Boston before joining Werner Hegemann to develop plans for the company town of Kohler, Wisconsin, in 1916. In

1920 and 1921 Peets studied examples of civic art and garden design in Europe on a Charles Eliot Travelling Fellowship and returned to collaborate with Hegemann on *The American Vitruvius: An Architect's Handbook of Civic Art* (1922). In 1933 he became town planner and landscape architect for the Resettlement Administration at Greendale, Wisconsin. In 1938 Peets was made chief of site planning at the U.S. Housing Authority. During the 1950s he served as consultant to the National Capital Park and Planning Commission and lectured regularly at Yale and Harvard.

Pentecost, George F. (b. 1875). A landscape architect, Pentecost began practice in New York in the 1890s and for a time was a partner of Samuel Parsons, Jr. Pentecost's designs included residences, land developments, parks, and golf courses. He was one of the founding members of the ASLA.

Pepoon, Herman Silas (b. 1860). Born in Warren, Illinois, Pepoon studied at the University of Illinois and received his M.D. from Hahnemann Medical College in 1883. He practiced medicine at Lewistown, Illinois, until 1892. Switching to a teaching career, Pepoon served as head of the Department of Botany at Lakeview High School in Chicago from 1912 until 1930. Active in the Illinois Academy of Science and the Chicago Academy of Science, Pepoon was an expert on the natural history of Chicago's environs. His book, *An Annotated Flora of the Chicago Area*, was published in 1927.

Perkins, Dwight Heald (1867–1941). Chicago architect, born in Memphis, Tennessee. In 1887, Perkins graduated from MIT with a degree in architecture. Moving to Chicago after graduation, he worked in various Chicago architectural offices—most notably that of Burnham and Root from 1888 to 1894—and thereafter on his own. He was a partner in the firm of Perkins and Hamilton from 1905 to 1911; Perkins, Fellows, and Hamilton from 1911 to 1927; and Perkins, Chatten, and Hammond from 1927 until 1935. From 1905 to 1910, Perkins was chief architect for the Chicago Board of Education. He served on numerous park boards with Jensen and was president of the Chicago Regional Planning Association, which fought to pass the enabling legislation to establish forest preserves in Illinois.

Platt, Charles A. (1861–1933). Influential architect and landscape architect, born in New York City. Platt studied in the art schools of New York and Paris. In 1894 he published *Italian Gardens*, which helped stir up interest in Italian Renaissance gardens as a model for American country estates. He is largely known for his designs of houses and gardens.

Player's green. The outdoor theater area included by Jensen in many of his park and garden designs.

Pond, Irving K. (1857–1937). Chicago architect, born in Ann Arbor, Michigan. Pond graduated from the University of Michigan in 1879. He worked with William Le Baron Jenney and S. S. Beman before becoming a partner with his brother Allen in the firm Pond and Pond, which had offices in Steinway Hall from 1886 to 1926. From 1926 until his retirement, Pond was a partner of Edgar

Martin and Alfred Lloyd. He served as president of the American Institute of Architects in 1908.

Pope, Alexander (1688–1744). Influential English poet, essayist, and literary critic. Pope helped publicize the trend toward naturalism in English gardening and argued for gardens that revealed the "genius of the place." His own garden at Twickenham, on the Thames, exemplified his ideas for an "artful wildnes[s]."

Poussin, Nicolas (1594–1665). French painter and promoter of Baroque classicism. Poussin's work was a model for English landscape gardeners. Using classical motifs, Poussin sought to attain an ideal beauty in his work through a study of the laws of reason. His paintings in the late 1640s depicted highly ordered landscape scenes, while those in the mid-1650s portrayed nature in wilder and more luxuriant aspects.

Prairie Club. A group organized by Jensen and his friends in 1908 to sponsor weekend walks and camping trips to scenic places around the Chicago metropolitan area and outlying parts of Illinois, Indiana, and Wisconsin.

Prairie school of architecture. The group of architects in Chicago, centered around Louis Sullivan and Frank Lloyd Wright, who promoted a style of design that drew its strength from the horizontal lines of the great midwestern prairies. Emphasis was on an honest use of building materials, ornamentation that became an organic part of the design, and an open spatial arrangement that seemed to fit the needs of the new suburban middle class. While known primarily for their designs of houses, members also designed schools (Perkins), commercial buildings (Elmslie and Purcell), park pavilions (Garden), and churches (Wright). During the early years of the school in the 1890s, members engaged in spirited discussions at the Chicago Architectural Club and at Steinway Hall, where the majority shared office space for a time. Although many of the architects associated with the prairie school continued to practice long afterward, the Steinway Hall group had disbanded by the early 1920s.

Prairie style of landscape design. The name given by Wilhelm Miller in 1915 to the work of Jensen, O. C. Simonds, and Walter Burley Griffin. Miller characterized the style as capturing the spirit of the prairies through the conservation and restoration of native flora and the repetition of horizontal lines in landforms, stonework, and the natural branching habits of plants.

Price, Uvedale (1747–1849). English writer, best known for his *Essay on the Picturesque* (1794), which influenced the work of many landscape gardeners who followed. Price felt that Lancelot Brown's work impoverished the English countryside by reducing the variety in its landscapes. Although Price occasionally helped design grounds for his friends, his ideas are known primarily from his essays.

Prospect Park. The second of Olmsted and Vaux's major parks in New York, designed for Brooklyn in 1865–66 and largely completed by 1873.

Pückler-Muskau, Prince Herman Ludwig Heinrich von (1785–1871). German prince and landscape gardener, known primarily for his writings and the redesign of his family's landholdings at Muskau. On successive visits to England, Pückler was deeply impressed with the work of Repton, and as a result he helped spread ideas associated with picturesque parklands throughout Europe. A perceptive observer and critic, his writings and accounts of his travels were widely read both in Europe and in the United States.

Purcell, William Gray (1880–1964). Raised in Oak Park, Illinois, Purcell studied architecture at Cornell University and apprenticed with Adler and Sullivan in Chicago and with John Gallen Howard in Berkeley, California, before forming a partnership with his former classmate George Feick, Jr., in Minneapolis. When George Elmslie joined them in 1909, the firm became Purcell, Feick, and Elmslie; when Feick left in 1913, the name became Purcell and Elmslie. The latter partnership continued until 1922 and is perhaps best known for the banks the firm designed for numerous midwestern towns.

Ravinia. A neighborhood in Highland Park, Illinois, annexed in 1889 and so named because of its proximity to Ravinia Park, originally built as an amusement park by the Chicago and Milwaukee Electric Railroad in 1904. After the railroad went into receivership, the Ravinia Park Company was formed and opened its first opera season in 1911. In 1936, the Ravinia Festival was organized, and thereafter Ravinia became the summer home of the Chicago Symphony Orchestra.

Regional Planning Association of America (RPAA). The influential group of architects, planners, and social critics organized in 1923 to develop effective approaches to community and regional planning. Members included Stuart Chase, economist; Benton Mackaye, originator of the Appalachian Trail; Lewis Mumford, social critic; Clarence Stein, chief architect of Radburn, New Jersey, and Sunnyside, New York; Charles Harris Whitaker, editor of the *Journal of the American Institute of Architects;* Edith Elmer Wood, housing expert; Henry Wright, Clarence Stein's co-planner; and Catherine Bauer Wurster, housing expert.

Rehmann, Elsa. Writer and landscape architect, Rehmann was an active proponent of native plantings as found in the wild. As a lecturer in landscape gardening at Vassar College from 1923 to 1927, Rehmann teamed up with Edith Roberts, with whom she wrote a series of articles on plant ecology for *House Beautiful* in 1927–28. That series served as the basis for Roberts and Rehmann's book, *American Plants for American Gardens* (1929).

Repton, Humphry (1752–1818). A leading English landscape architect of the second half of the eighteenth century who continued and expanded the traditions established by Lancelot Brown. Repton became famous for his "Red Books," which showed before-and-after views of his designs. His lasting influence rested largely on his writings, which included *Sketches and Hints on Landscape Gardening* (1795) and *Observations on the Theory and Practice of Landscape Gardening* (1803).

Ridges Sanctuary. A preserve of fragile beach ridges and depressions in Baileys Harbor, Door County, Wisconsin, which is home to a unique array of plant and animal species. Jensen, who is credited with suggesting that it be called a sanctuary, was a key player in the founding of the Ridges Sanctuary in 1937 and served on its board until his death in 1951.

Riis, Jacob (1849–1914). Born in Ribe, Denmark, Riis immigrated to the United States in 1870. Between 1870 and 1890, he earned his way as an itinerant laborer, as a writer for a small Brooklyn paper, and finally as an accomplished police reporter first for the *New York Tribune* and then for the *New York Evening Sun*. Riis's experiences as a reporter made him well aware of life in the tenements of New York City, and he recorded them in *How the Other Half Lives* (1890) and *Children of the Poor* (1892). He became one of the leaders of the small parks and playground movement and was a strong promoter of tenement house and school reform. His talk at Hull-House in the late 1890s helped fuel Chicago's playground movement.

Riis, Paul B. A naturalist and parks promoter who helped develop Yellowstone and other national parks, worked for the park system in Rockford, Illinois, and was hired by Pennsylvania's Allegheny County Department of Parks to develop a system of country parks. Riis was instrumental in hiring Jensen to design the swimming pools for South Park in Allegheny County.

Riverside, Illinois. The Chicago suburb established as a speculative venture by eastern businessmen who founded the Riverside Improvement Company in 1868. Planned as a domestic enclave connected to the city by commuter rail lines, Riverside, with its curving streets and generous open space, was designed by Olmsted and Vaux in 1869 and became a model for many other suburban developments.

Riverside Park. A scenic New York park on the bluffs of the Hudson River which became the subject of a heated dispute when the New York Central Railroad proposed changes to its lines in 1916. Jensen prepared a report for the Woman's League for the Protection of Riverside Park (dated 29 November 1916), urging the preservation of the park.

Roberts, Edith (1881–1977). Born in Rollensford, New Hampshire, Roberts studied at Smith College and the University of Chicago, where she earned a Ph.D. in 1915. From 1919 to 1950 she served as associate professor and then professor in the Department of Botany at Vassar College. In 1927–28, Roberts teamed up with Elsa Rehmann to write a series of articles on plant ecology for *House Beautiful*. In 1929 these articles were collected and published as *American Plants for American Gardens*. At Vassar, Roberts developed a four-acre ecologically oriented outdoor botanical laboratory, one of the first of its kind in the United States. After retiring from Vassar in 1950, Roberts served as a consultant in biology to MIT.

Robinson, William W. (1838–1935). Irish gardener and writer, known as "the father of natural gardening." and a mentor of Gertrude Jekyll. During a period when gardens were as apt to be designed by an architect as by a landscape gardener, Robinson argued that gardens belong in the domain of horticulture rather than architecture. From 1861 to 1866 he worked at the Royal Botanical Garden in Regent's Park in London. Thereafter he served as a special correspondent for *The Gardener's Chronicle* and traveled extensively in Europe and the United States, studying plants and gardens. In 1870 he published *The Wild Garden*, which encouraged a wilder approach to gardening. His other books include *The English Flower Garden* (1883) and *The Garden Beautiful: Home Woods and Home Landscape* (1907). From 1871 until 1899 Robinson published *The Garden*, a weekly journal of horticulture and garden design.

Rockefeller, John D. (1839–1937). Born in Richford, New York. In 1853 Rockefeller and his family moved to Cleveland, Ohio, where he went into the oil refining business. In 1870 he established the Standard Oil Company. Rockefeller was known for his philanthropy, which included generous endowments to the University of Chicago.

Rock River. River of north-central Illinois and southern Wisconsin. The dramatic limestone bluffs along the river near Oregon, Illinois, became a popular destination for the Prairie Club and members of the Friends of Our Native Landscape.

Rond, *or* Roundabout. A circular junction point in garden paths or roads, the rond was characteristic of eighteenth-century French parks and gardens.

Root, John Wellborn (1850–1891). Born in Lumpkin, Georgia, Root moved with his family to New York after the Civil War. In 1869 he earned a degree in science and civil engineering from the University of the City of New York. In 1872 he moved to Chicago as the construction foreman for the architectural firm of Peter B. Wight. There he met Daniel H. Burnham, who had recently joined the firm, and in 1873 the two of them formed a new partnership, Burnham and Root. With the Rookery Building (1885–87) and the Monadnock Building (1889–91), the firm took the lead in the design of high-rise commercial buildings in Chicago. Root was named consulting architect to the World's Columbian Exposition, but in 1891 he died unexpectedly, leaving Burnham to continue as director of works.

Rosa, Salvator (1615–1673). Italian painter, poet, musician, and actor, known for his flamboyant and dramatic style of landscape painting. The dramatic lighting and wild, natural settings of Rosa's paintings influenced eighteenth-century sublime and picturesque ideals.

Rosehill Cemetery. One of the three large "landscape" cemeteries in Chicago, the other two being Oakwood and Graceland. Rosehill was chartered in 1859 and designed by William Saunders.

Rosenwald, Julius (1862–1932). Born in Springfield, Illinois, Rosenwald began his career in retailing with Hammershlough Brothers in New York, where he worked from 1879 to 1885. In 1885 he moved to Chicago and became a partner in Rosenwald and Weil. In 1895 he was named vice-president and treasurer of

Sears, Roebuck and Company, and later president and chairman of the board. Rosenwald was known as a generous philanthropist and supported many of Jensen's conservation activities. Rosenwald's wife, Augusta Nusbaum, served as the first vice-president of the Friends of Our Native Landscape. Jensen designed the Rosenwalds' home in Highland Park, Illinois, which is now the site of Rosewood Park.

Saarinen, Gottlieb Eliel (1873–1950). Finnish architect, educated at the Polytechnic Institute in Helsinki. From 1896 to 1907 Saarinen was associated with architects Herman Gesellius and Armas Lindgren in Finland. In 1925 Saarinen designed the buildings of the Cranbrook Foundation in Bloomfield Hills, Michigan, where he headed the Cranbrook Academy of Art and supervised the Departments of Architecture and City Planning.

Sandburg, Carl (1878–1967). Born in Galesburg, Illinois, to Swedish immigrant parents, Sandburg worked his way through Lombard College in Galesburg, graduating in 1902. For the next few years he gained a deeply personal knowledge of the landscape while wandering as a hobo, working as an itinerant newspaperman, and briefly editing an obscure Chicago magazine. In 1913 he moved to Chicago, and by 1914 several of his poems had been published in Harriet Monroe's *Poetry* magazine. Sandburg's *Chicago Poems*, published in 1916, was instantly successful, and he won a Pulitzer Prize for *Cornhuskers*, which was published in 1918. In 1919 Sandburg began working as a feature editor for the *Chicago Daily News*, and from 1926 to 1939 he published his six-volume biography of Abraham Lincoln, which brought him a second Pulitzer Prize. An avid collector of folklore, he published *American Songbag* in 1927 and *New American Songbag* in 1950. Sandburg's *Complete Poems* (1950) won him a third Pulitzer Prize.

Sargent, Charles Sprague (1841–1927). Influential dendrologist, born in Boston, Massachusetts, and educated at Harvard University, from which he graduated in 1862. Sargent became director of the Arnold Arboretum in 1872, and from 1887 to 1897 he edited *Garden and Forest*. Through his writings, teaching, and friendship with landscape designers like Frederick Law Olmsted, Sr., and Charles Eliot, Sargent contributed much to the early history of landscape architecture.

Saturday Afternoon Walking Trips. Outings arranged by Jensen and other members of the Playground Association to acquaint people with the beauty of the land around Chicago. The first walk was held in April 1908 and proved so successful that shortly thereafter the group formed an association, the Prairie Club, to sponsor such walks on a regular basis.

Saunders, William (1822–1900). Nurseryman and landscape gardener, born in St. Andrews, Scotland. Saunders studied at Kew Gardens and immigrated to the United States in 1848. In 1854 he formed a partnership with Thomas Meehan of Philadelphia. Saunders completed much of Andrew Jackson Downing's unfinished planting work in the national capital's park system and planned many other residences, parks, and cemeteries, including the grounds of Clifton, the home of Johns Hopkins in Baltimore; Rosehill Cemetery in Chicago; Oak Ridge Cemetery in Springfield, Illinois; and the National Cemetery in Gettysburg, Pennsylvania. In 1862 Saunders was appointed botanist and secretary of horticulture at the U.S. Department of Agriculture, and in that capacity he was influential in introducing many important varieties of cultivated fruits to American farms.

Schmidt, Richard E. (1865–1958). Born in Ebern, Germany, Schmidt moved with his family to Chicago when he was quite young. He studied architecture at MIT from 1883 to 1885 and began practicing in Chicago in 1887. In 1906 he organized the firm of Schmidt, Garden, and Martin.

Shakespeare Garden. Garden at Northwestern University in Evanston, Illinois, designed by Jensen in 1916.

Shaw, Howard Van Doren (1869–1926). Born in Chicago, Illinois, Shaw studied at Yale University and MIT. He worked with the firm of Jenney and Mundie before establishing his own private architectural practice in 1897. Described by some as a midwestern equivalent of Sir Edwin Lutyens, Shaw displayed in his designs for many houses an eclectic mixture of English Renaissance architecture and the contemporary arts-and-crafts movement.

Shearer, Sybil. A noted Chicago dancer, Shearer was raised on Long Island and graduated from Skidmore College. She made her debut at Carnegie Hall and was acclaimed by New York dance critics, but soon thereafter she traded the New York art world for Chicago. Through her manager, Helen Morrison, Shearer became good friends with Jensen. The large council ring at The Clearing in Ellison Bay, Wisconsin, was built by Jensen for performances by Shearer and her dance students. Shearer is currently president of the Morrison-Shearer Foundation and Museum in Northbrook, Illinois.

Shelford, Victor (1878–1968). Born in Chemay, New York, Shelford studied at West Virginia University and later at the University of Chicago, where he served as an instructor in the Department of Zoology. From 1914 to 1929 he directed the research laboratories of the Illinois State Natural History Survey, and from 1914 to 1946 he served as professor at the University of Illinois. Shelford was the editor of *Naturalist's Guide to the Americas* (1926), which became an important directory of remnant natural areas at that time. In 1939 he founded the Grassland Research Foundation, and in 1946 he became chair of the scientific advisory board for the Ecologist's Union, the forerunner of the Nature Conservancy.

Simonds, Gertrude. Daughter of O. C. Simonds, active in the Prairie Club.

Simonds, Ossian Cole (1855–1931). Born near Grand Rapids, Michigan, Simonds studied architecture and civil engineering at the University of Michigan. After graduation, he went to work for William Le Baron Jenney in Chicago. In about 1880 he left that firm to form Holabird and Simonds. In 1881 he became superintendent of Graceland Cemetery, where he firmly established his reputation as a landscape designer. Like Jensen, Simonds advocated a design approach that emphasized local landforms and native plantings, and like Jensen and Walter Burley Griffin, he was considered an initiator of the "prairie style" of landscape gardening. Simonds' designs included parks, residences, college campuses, and cemeteries throughout the Midwest and the United States as a whole.

Skokie lagoons. The marsh environment in the bed of a prehistoric lake along the Skokie River in Glencoe, Illinois. The lagoons were a popular destination of the Prairie Club and an early target for conservationists seeking to set aside land as a forest preserve.

Slesvig (Schleswig). Province of Denmark in which Jensen was born and raised. Denmark lost control of the Slesvig province to Germany in the Peace of Vienna in 1864 and regained only a portion of the province in 1920 following World War I.

Smiley, Edythe. Secretary in Jensen's office, birth and death dates unknown.

South Park. Collective name for the Chicago parkland that became Jackson and Washington parks and the Midway Plaisance. Olmsted and Vaux were hired by the South Park Commission in 1869 to design the lands of South Park.

South Park Commission. One of three original Chicago park commissions established by the state legislature in 1869.

Special Park Commission. A nongeographic park commission organized in Chicago in 1899 as a result of a study of parks and playgrounds by the Municipal Science Club. The commission was charged with carrying out a systematic study of parks and recreation grounds to develop a consistent plan for a regional metropolitan park system. Although not a member of the original commission, Jensen was appointed sometime before the commission's 1904 report and served until 1913.

Spencer, Robert C. (1865–1953). Born in Milwaukee, Wisconsin, Spencer graduated from the University of Wisconsin in 1886 and soon thereafter began his studies in architecture at MIT. In 1893 he went to work for Shepley, Rutan, and Coolidge, first in Boston and then in Chicago. In 1895 Spencer began his own practice, and in 1905 he joined with Horace S. Powers to form Spencer and Powers. Spencer was a member of the original Steinway Hall group of prairie architects, one of whom, Dwight Perkins, had been his classmate at MIT. Spencer's work included several collaborations with Jensen, including the Magnus house in Winnetka, Illinois.

Starved Rock. An area of steep bluffs and canyons along the Illinois River near La Salle, Illinois, which in 1911 became Illinois' first state park. The Starved Rock area was frequently the destination of members of the Prairie Club and the Friends of Our Native Landscape on their outings, and in its 1921 report, *Proposed Park Areas in the State of Illinois: A Report with Recommendations*, the FONL called for the protection of an even larger tract of land.

Steinway Hall. Located at 64 East Van Buren Street in downtown Chicago, this eleven-story office and theater building was designed by Dwight H. Perkins in 1894 and completed in 1896. The loft and top floor became offices for a number of the leading prairie architects. The original group in 1896–97 consisted of Myron C. Hunt, Perkins, Robert C. Spencer, and Frank Lloyd Wright. Others who would join the group included Adamo Boari, Walter Burley Griffin, Birch Burdette Long, Allen Bartlit Pond, Irving K. Pond, and Henry Webster Tomlinson. Jensen opened his office there in 1908.

Stevens, Thomas Wood (1880–1942). Author, born in Daysville, Illinois. Stevens studied mechanical engineering at the Armour Institute of Technology in Chicago. In 1902 he founded the Blue Sky Press in Chicago, and in 1903 he took charge of the Department of Illustration at the Art Institute of Chicago. Stevens was active in the pageant movement. In 1913 he moved to Pittsburgh, where he became head of the School of Drama at the Carnegie Institute of Technology. Stevens wrote the Dunes Pageant, which was performed in 1917 as part of the effort to preserve the Indiana Dunes as a national park.

Strauch, Adolph (1822–1883). Landscape gardener, born in Prussia. Strauch traveled extensively in Europe before coming to the United States in 1851. He became famous for his parklike cemetery designs, especially Spring Grove Cemetery in Cincinnati, Ohio, and was responsible for Oakwood Cemetery in Chicago as well as work in Buffalo, New York; Cleveland and Toledo, Ohio; Detroit, Michigan; Indianapolis, Indiana; Nashville, Tennessee; and Hartford, Connecticut. His work was admired by Frederick Law Olmsted, Sr., and provided inspiration for O. C. Simonds, who later created designs for Graceland Cemetery in Chicago.

Sturgis, Russell (1836–1909). Born in Baltimore, Maryland, Sturgis graduated from City College of New York and studied architecture in Europe. The author of many articles on fine and decorative arts, Sturgis is perhaps best known as the editor of the influential *Dictionary of Architecture and Building* (1901–2).

Sullivan, Louis (1856–1924). Born in Boston, Massachusetts, Sullivan studied architecture at MIT and at the École des Beaux-Arts in Paris. From 1883 to 1895 he was involved in a partnership with Dankmar Adler in the firm of Sullivan and Adler in Chicago, and after 1895 practiced alone. Regarded as one of the leaders of modern American architecture, Sullivan sought to create a unity of structure, materials, decoration, and function in his buildings. Frank Lloyd Wright apprenticed with Sullivan and affectionately called him "Lieber master." To Jensen, Sullivan was a close friend, mentor, and, above all, a great artist.

Switzer, Stephen (1682–1745). English writer and garden designer, Switzer published *Iconographica Rustica*, a book on the practical aspects of landscape gardening, in 1718. He argued that the whole estate should be the subject of design rather than just confined garden areas.

Taft, Lorado (1860–1936). Sculptor, born in Elmwood, Illinois, Taft studied at the University of Illinois and at the École des Beaux-Arts in Paris. In 1886 he began teaching sculpture at the Art Institute of Chicago, where he influenced many of the leading sculptors of Chicago and the Midwest. Taft helped develop an extension department in the arts at the University of Chicago from 1892 to 1902. One of the founders of the Cliff Dwellers, Taft was also active in the Prairie Club and joined Jensen in various projects, including sculpture exhibits in Chicago's West Parks in 1908 and 1909.

Taggert, Thomas (1856–1929). Born in Monyhan, Ireland, Taggert moved with his family to Xenia, Ohio, in 1861. In 1877 Taggert became president of the French Lick Springs Hotel. From 1895 to 1901 he served as mayor of Indianapolis, and in 1916 was appointed U.S. senator from Indiana. Taggert served as senator during the period of Jensen's efforts to create a national park in the Indiana Dunes.

Taliesin. The 600-acre home and school of Frank Lloyd Wright in Spring Green, Wisconsin. Here Wright experimented with many of his design ideas and created the Hillside Home School Complex and the Romeo and Juliet Windmill, designed in 1896. The Taliesin Fellowship, a group of architects who trained under Wright, continue his practice and school, living communally at the site during the summer months.

Taylor, Graham (1851–1938). Sociologist, born in Schenectady, New York. Taylor studied at Rutgers College and the Reformed Theological Seminary in Rutgers, New Jersey. An ordained pastor in the Reformed Church, Taylor joined the faculty of the Chicago Theological Seminary in 1892 and founded the Chicago Commons Social Settlement in 1894. He also served as editor of the *Survey* and as a contributing editor to the *Chicago Daily News*. In 1936 he published *Chicago Commons through Forty Years*.

Thoreau, Henry David (1817–1862). Naturalist, philosopher, and author, born in Concord, Massachusetts. After a brief period at Harvard University, Thoreau taught for a time in Concord and then entered his family's pencil-making business. In 1839 he formed a private school with his brother, John, and introduced the idea of trips for nature study, a novel idea at the time. In 1841 he went to work for Ralph Waldo Emerson as a handyman and joined Emerson's Transcendental Club. In 1845 Thoreau moved to Walden Pond and began an experiment in simple, contemplative living, keeping voluminous journals of his experiences and observations which he published in 1854 as *Walden; or, Life in the Woods*. Thoreau's work was not fully appreciated until the twentieth century.

Tirrell, Charles A. Worked in Jensen's Steinway Hall office as a landscape architect and engineer.

Tune Agricultural School. Danish agricultural college located outside Copenhagen. Attended by Jensen.

Union Park. Established in Chicago in 1854, Union Park served as the headquarters for the West Park Commission, which was established in 1869. Union Park was the site of Jensen's earliest known landscape design, the American Garden (1888). Jensen was named superintendent of Union Park in 1895.

Unwin, Raymond (1863–1940). A leading British architect and town planner, Unwin was born in Rotherham, Yorkshire, England, and studied engineering and architecture. In 1896 he began to practice with Richard Barry Parker. Unwin and Parker designed the garden city of Letchworth (1904–5) and the Hampstead Garden suburb north of London (1905–14). In 1909 Unwin published his thoughts about planning in *Town Planning in Practice*, and in 1910 he organized the Town Planning Conference of the Royal Institute of British Architects. He taught town planning at the University of Birmingham, and in 1936 was a visiting professor at Columbia University in New York.

Van Bergen, John S. (1885–1969). Born in Oak Park, Illinois, Van Bergen went to work in Walter Burley Griffin's office in 1907 without any advance training. In 1908 he left Griffin's office to study at the Chicago Technical College, and in 1909 he began working for Frank Lloyd Wright. Later Van Bergen developed his own architectural practice, concentrating largely on residential designs.

Vaux, Calvert (1824–1895). Architect and landscape gardener, born in London. Vaux came to the United States as an associate of Andrew Jackson Downing. In 1858 Vaux convinced Frederick Law Olmsted, Sr., to join with him to enter the design competition for Central Park in New York. Their winning "Greensward" design was followed by other "rural" park designs in Brooklyn, Albany, Chicago, San Francisco, and other towns across the United States. Vaux and Olmsted remained partners until 1872.

Veblen, Thorstein (1857–1929). Social theorist and researcher, Veblen studied at Carleton College and the Johns Hopkins University. In 1892 he began study at the University of Chicago on a fellowship, and later stayed on as a professor. Veblen published his influential *Theory of the Leisure Class* in 1899. He taught at Stanford from 1906 to 1909 and at the University of Missouri from 1911 to 1918. In 1918 he joined the faculty at the New School for Social Research.

Vernon Park. An early Chicago park, established in 1857.

Vinding. Location of the folk high school Jensen attended in Denmark.

von Holst, Herman Valetin (1874–1955). Chicago architect, born in Freiburg, Baden, Germany, von Holst studied at the University of Chicago and MIT. In 1896 he joined the Chicago office of Shepley, Rutan, and Coolidge and later formed the firm of von Holst and Fyfe. The von Holst firm, with Marion Mahoney Griffin, prepared the original design for Henry Ford's house at Fair Lane, but after a disagreement with Ford, von Holst was replaced by Pittsburgh architect William van Tine.

Walker, Nellie (1874–1973). Sculptor, born in Red Oak, Iowa. Walker studied under Lorado Taft at the Art Institute of Chicago and exhibited her work widely throughout the Midwest.

Walpole, Horace (1717–1797). English writer and gardener who acknowledged the work of William Kent in his "Essay on Modern Gardening." He also cited John Milton and Claude Lorraine as the inspiration for his ideas on gardening, which he displayed at Strawberry Hill on the Thames at Twickenham, a project he worked on for fifty years (1747–97).

Washington, George (1732–1799). Born in Westmoreland County, Virginia, Washington grew up on his family's plantation. His irregular schooling ended at the age of fifteen, and he became a surveyor. In 1754 he was named lieutenant colonel of the Virginia Regiment and was sent to the Ohio Territory, where he directed the construction of Fort Necessity. From 1758 to 1774 he served in the Virginia House of Burgesses, and during the Revolutionary War he was commander in chief of the Continental army. In 1789 Washington became the first president of the United States. After his retirement from the presidency in 1797, Washington returned to the life of a country gentleman at Mount Vernon. His various improvements at Mount Vernon and his experimentation with native trees and shrubs in his gardens served as early models for American gardens in the nineteenth century.

Washington Environmental Yard. The schoolyard at Washington Elementary School in Berkeley, California, which was begun in 1971 as a joint effort by students, parents, and teachers at the school as well as by students and faculty from the University of California. The schoolyard, which combines a variety of different scaled places, plantings, water areas, and playground equipment, is a challenging and stimulating play and learning environment.

Washington Park. The westernmost tract of South Park, Chicago, designed in 1871 by Olmsted and Vaux. Washington Park is linked to Jackson Park by the Midway Plaisance.

Washington Square. An early Chicago park created in 1842 by a group of speculators, the American Land Company.

Waugh, Dorothy. Daughter of Frank A. Waugh; visited with the Jensens while studying at the Art Institute of Chicago. She now resides in New York City.

Waugh, Frank A. (1869–1943). Born in Sheboygan Falls, Wisconsin, and educated at the Kansas State Agricultural College (now Kansas State University), Waugh earned degrees in horticulture and botany. He later also studied under Willy Lange at the Gärtnerlehranstalt zu Dahlen in Germany. Waugh taught horticulture at the Oklahoma Agricultural and Mechanical College (now Oklahoma State University) and the University of Vermont. In 1902 he joined the faculty of the Massachusetts Agricultural College (now the University of Massachusetts), where he established the Department of Landscape Gardening. Waugh, a prolific photographer, writer, artist, musician, and teacher, was one of the few academics deeply admired by Jensen.

West Park Commission. One of three original park districts established in Chicago in 1869. In 1870 the firm of Jenney, Schermerhorn and Bogart was hired to develop plans for the West Parks. Jensen spent much of his career with the West Park Commission.

White, Stanford (1853–1906). Born in New York, White received his architectural training under Charles D. Gambrell and Henry H. Richardson. He traveled and studied in Europe from 1878 to 1880, promoting a style that borrowed heavily from classical traditions for public buildings and a colonial style for private dwellings. In 1881 he helped form the firm of McKim, Mead, and White.

White, Stanley Hart (1891–1979). Born in Brooklyn, New York, White studied at Cornell University, where he earned a bachelor of science degree in agriculture in 1912. He graduated from Harvard with a master's degree in landscape architecture in 1915 and in 1916 went to work for the Olmsted Brothers firm in Brookline, Massachusetts. From 1920 to 1922, White practiced on his own, but in 1922 he joined the faculty at the University of Illinois in Urbana, thereby beginning a long and dynamic career as a teacher of landscape architecture.

Withers, Frederick Clarke (1828–1901). Born in England, Withers came to the United States to work as an architect with Andrew Jackson Downing in Newark, New Jersey, just prior to Downing's death in 1852. Thereafter Withers formed a partnership with Calvert Vaux in Newburgh, New York, and continued working on projects for many of Downing's clients. Withers assisted Vaux in publishing *Villas and Cottages* (1857), and when Vaux left the partnership in 1856 to work with Frederick Law Olmsted, Sr., on Central Park, Withers began to work on his own, designing houses and specializing in the design of Gothic churches.

Wooded Island. A naturalistic island park area designed by Frederick Law Olmsted, Sr., at the center of the World's Columbian Exposition in Chicago in 1893.

Wright, Frank Lloyd (1869–1959). Born in Richland Center, Wisconsin, Wright attended the University of Wisconsin for only three terms before going to work for the architectural firm of Joseph Lymon Silsbee in the spring of 1887. Six months later he joined the firm of Adler and Sullivan, staying until 1893, when he established his own practice. His Winslow Homer House, designed in 1893, was the first of more than seven hundred designs. In 1896 Wright opened an office in Steinway Hall; in 1900 he moved to Oak Park, Illinois, where he stayed until 1909. After 1911 he worked out of Taliesin, at Spring Green, Wisconsin. Wright's buildings are known for their characteristic flow of space inside and outside the building, as well as for their low proportions, hanging rooflines, and horizontal band of windows—all of which were intended to reflect the prairie and encourage interaction with nature. Wright founded the Taliesin Fellowship in 1932 as an apprenticeship system that would permit young architects to study with him.

Wright, John S. (1815–1874). Born in Sheffield, Massachusetts, Wright came to Chicago in 1834 to work as an editor and to set up a real estate business. He built the first public school building in Chicago in 1835. In 1839 he published the *Union Agriculturalist*, which was eventually renamed the *Prairie Farmer*. A staunch advocate of railroads, Wright was influential in making Chicago the major railroad center of the Midwest.

Zimmerman, Johann Georg von (1728–1795). Born in Brugg, Switzerland, Zimmerman studied medicine and philosophy at the University of Berne and the University of Göttingen, from which he graduated in 1751. After a year of traveling through Holland and France, Zimmerman returned to Berne as a scholar, philosopher, and physician. In 1768 he became physician to the king of England at Hanover, and in 1771 he moved to Berlin, where he set up a practice in surgery. A strong believer in nature's ability to heal the troubled mind, Zimmerman recorded his ideas in *Ueber Die Einsamkeit*, or *Solitude Considered with Respect to Its Influence on the Mind and the Heart*, as it was translated in 1791 (London: C. Dilly). Zimmerman's writings have been credited with influencing Frederick Law Olmsted Sr.'s theories on landscape design.

Zueblin, Charles S. (1866–1924). Born in Pendleton, Indiana, Zueblin studied at Northwestern University, Yale University, and the University of Leipzig. He founded the Northwestern University Settlement House in 1891, and from 1892 to 1908 was an instructor at the University of Chicago. A strong advocate of playgrounds, Zueblin served as a member of Chicago's Special Park Commission from 1901 until 1905. He was editor of *Twentieth Century Magazine* in Boston from 1910 to 1913.

Notes

There are two major archives of Jensen's papers: the Jensen Collection at the Morton Arboretum in Lisle, Illinois, and the Jensen Collection at the Art and Architecture Library, University of Michigan, Ann Arbor. In these notes, the Morton Arboretum collection is referred to as MA, the Art and Architecture Library collection at the University of Michigan as UM.

Two basic reference styles are used throughout the notes: author-date citations, for sources that appear in the bibliography; and full-title/short-title citations, for those that do not.

CHAPTER ONE: JENSEN'S EARLY BACKGROUND

1. Alfred Caldwell, interview by Malcolm Collier, January 1981, transcript of tape recording, MA, tape no. 2: 4–5.

2. Caldwell interview, January 1981, tape no. 1: 15.

3. Caldwell interview, January 1981, tape no. 1: 16.

4. Jens Jensen 1939, 14. *Siftings* was reprinted in 1956 as *"Siftings," the Major Portion of "The Clearing," and Collected Writings.* In 1990, the Johns Hopkins University Press reissued *Siftings* as part of its American Land Classics series.

5. Jens Jensen 1939, 14–16.

6. Eaton 1964, 5.

7. Foght 1915, 198–202; Oakley 1972, 171; Begtrup, Lund, and Manniche 1936, 108; Rørdam 1980, 45–71; Skovmond 1973, 85–100.

8. Foght 1915, 157; Christianson 1982, 11; Eaton 1964, 6–7; Collier 1977, 50; Rørdam 1980, 48–59, 68.

9. Jones 1986, 61; Jens Jensen 1939, 34–35. In a similar vein, Noah Porter contrasts the "mathematical designs" of Jesuit colleges and their emphasis on "obedience and dependence" with the "English park" landscapes of Protestant colleges, where "the freedom and independence of individual man" was emphasized. Noah Porter, quoted in Stevenson 1986, 120–21.

10. Jensen's wife had come from a farm that had been in her family for more than 300 years. Her father, however, had taken to drink and lost the farm. According to Jensen, his own family "could not forgive the daughter, who certainly was guiltless, for this—that's why I emigrated. I had no great desire to be a farmer." Jens Jensen to Johannes Tholle, 15 October 1950, MA. See also Eaton 1964, 10–12; Christianson 1982, 5–6.

11. After arriving in the United States in 1884, Jensen worked as a gardener for Major Parsons in Bayport, Florida. In 1885, he moved to Iowa, where he tried farming. In 1886,

he went to Chicago, where he first worked for Kirk's Soap Factory and later became a common laborer in the Chicago parks. Fulkerson 1941, 1958; Alfred Caldwell, interview by the author, 17 December 1989; Bluestone 1984, 103–5. Bluestone notes that Nelson and H. W. S. Cleveland worked as supervisors for early plantings at Graceland Cemetery in Chicago. The original design of Graceland was by William Saunders, but was later modified by O. C. Simonds. For further discussion of Graceland Cemetery, see Chapter 2 of the present volume.

12. Jens Jensen 1939, 19–21; Jensen noted that on many of these trips the train conductor was reluctant to let them back on board because they were carrying laundry baskets full of plants they had collected. Jens Jensen to Camillo Schneider, 15 April 1939 (from the personal files of Darrel Morrison).

13. Jensen later published two articles in the *The Garden Magazine* which evidence his experience in working with horticultural flower beds in the parks. See Jensen 1905 and Jensen 1906a. For Jensen's notes on the American Garden, see Jensen and Eskil 1930, 18–19.

14. Jensen and Eskil 1930, 19. Jensen's transition from more "formal" plantings to "natural" gardens was not immediate. He would later design formal rose and perennial gardens in Humboldt and Garfield parks, and throughout his career he continued to create smaller, geometric gardens for vegetables and flowers for clients who wanted them. With time, however, the free-flowing forms of his natural gardens dominated his work, while the formal gardens became more incidental.

15. Olmsted's, Cleveland's, and Simonds' work is discussed in greater detail in Chapter 2. For an overview of Olmsted's ideas, see Beveridge and Schuyler 1983, 1–48; Beveridge 1977; and Ranney 1972. For Cleveland's work, see Tishler 1989; Cleveland [1871] 1965, vii-xxi; and T. Hubbard 1930. For Ossian Cole Simonds, see Grese 1989; and Gelbloom 1975.

16. Chicago, West Park Commission, 1889, 774; Chicago, West Park Commission, 1896, 74.

CHAPTER TWO: A CULTURAL CONTEXT FOR JENSEN'S WORK

1. It should be noted that prior to 1910, the fields of landscape architecture and landscape planning were one and the same. Moreover, while other American landscape architects such as Frederick Law Olmsted became well known in Europe, Jens Jensen is perhaps unique in that his renown was as great or perhaps greater in parts of Europe than in the United States. He was offered knighthood by the king of Denmark, and his work was widely published in Germany. Caldwell interview, January 1981, tape no. 1: 24; tape no. 2: 1. For German publications on Jensen's work, see Koch 1914; Jensen and Fischmann 1923; Jensen and Mappes 1937a, 1937b; and Jensen and Schneider 1937.

2. The "nature" that influenced these designers was not so much true "wilds" as the meadows and open forest groves of the hunting parks that had been carefully husbanded for centuries. For a good discussion of the development of English landscape gardening traditions, see Hunter 1985, 89–125. See also Hunt 1978; Hunt and Willis 1975; Batey 1982; Newton 1971, 207–16.

3. Hunt and Willis 1975, 30–31; Batey 1984.

4. Gilpin 1791; Price 1794; Batey 1984, 44–48.

5. Capability Brown, in particular, had advocated various formulas and rules for achieving pleasing landscape scenes; Repton, on the other hand, suggested a more flexible approach to design, relying on architectural as well as natural features of the setting. See Repton 1795, [1803] 1980, 105.

6. Thomas Jefferson to William Hamilton, July 1806, in Jefferson [1824] 1944, 322–24. For further insights into Jefferson's ideas about landscape design, see C. Miller 1988, 115–16; and McLaughlin 1988, 339–43, 354. See also Chase 1973; and Creese 1985, 11–44. For Jefferson's general views on nature, the garden, and pastoral ideals, see Marx 1964, 116–44. Beiswanger (1984, 170–88) provides insights into Jefferson's ideas about the garden and his ideas for a *ferme ornèe*. O'Malley (1986) provides an overview of early American garden traditions.

7. Downing [1841] 1844, 97–104; Creese 1985, 82–83. See also D. Schuyler 1986, 149–56.

8. Downing [1841] 1844, 49–57, 78–87.

9. Downing 1847, 396; Downing 1851, 491.

10. Prince Pückler's letters were translated into English by Sarah Austin and published in 1833 as *Tour in England, Ireland, and France in the Years 1828, 1929: With Remarks on the Manners and Customs of the Inhabitants, and Anecdotes of Public Characters in a Series of Letters by a German Prince*. See F. Brennan 1987, 9; John Nolen, "Note," in Pückler-Muskau [1834] 1917, i-iv.

11. Pückler-Muskau [1834] 1917, 131; Eliot 1902, 363.

12. Pückler-Muskau [1834] 1917, 65, 80–81.

13. Pückler-Muskau [1834] 1917, i, iii; Eliot 1902, 191; Repton 1907. The American Society of Landscape Architects (ASLA) was officially founded in January 1899 to advertise the young profession. Promoting the literature of the profession was one of the society's early activities. It is interesting to note that in addition to the books by Repton and Pückler-Muskau noted here, several works by Andrew Jackson Downing were collected and reprinted in 1921 as *Landscape Gardening*.

14. William Cullen Bryant, editorial, *New York Evening Post*, 3 July 1844; see also Bryant 1851, 169–70. For a discussion of the ideology leading up to the development of Central Park, see Huth 1957, 54–70; and D. Schuyler 1986, 59–76. Olmsted discussed the health benefits of parks in a talk presented at the 25 February 1870 meeting of the American Social Science Association at the Lowell Institute in Boston, Mass. See Olmsted [1870] 1970, 32–34; Kelly 1981, 6; D. Schuyler 1986, 40; and Beveridge 1977. For a discussion of the thinking of Emerson and Thoreau, see Marx 1964, 227–65; Huth 1957, 87–104; and Worster 1977, 58–111. For a discussion of the toll that the construction of Central Park took on Olmsted's health, see Beveridge and Schuyler 1983, 1–48.

15. Olmsted [1870] 1970, 32–34. See also Frederick Law Olmsted, "Description of the Central Park" (1859), in Beveridge and Schuyler 1983, 212–13; Douglas 1898; Johnston 1896 (response to paper by H. C. Alexander); and Perkins 1904, 52–55.

16. Olmsted [1870] 1970, 18–19.

17. Olmsted [1870] 1970, 19–22, 34.

18. Beveridge 1977; quote is from Olmsted [1852] 1967, 52. For a comparison of Olmsted's ideas of park design with those of Downing, see D. Schuyler 1986, 59–76. For Olmsted's reactions to other European parks, see Frederick Law Olmsted, "Park" (originally published in the *New American Cyclopaedia* in 1861), in Beveridge and Schuyler 1983, 346–67.

19. Olmsted [1870] 1970, 23; Frederick Law Olmsted and Calvert Vaux, "Chicago: Taming the Waterfront" (originally printed in 1871 as "Report Accompanying Plan for Laying Out the South Park" and submitted to Chicago's South Park Commission), in Sutton 1971, 161–63; Beveridge 1983, 16–18. For Olmsted's discussion of his own work, see Frederick Law Olmsted, "Description of a Plan for the Improvement of the Central Park: 'Greensward,' " "Description of the Central Park," and "Park," in Beveridge and Schuyler 1983, 119–87, 204–19, and 346–67. For other analyses of Olmsted's

design work, see Reed 1981; and Kelly 1981. For further discussion of the principles of Olmsted's work, see the chapter on American gardens by Frank Waugh in Gothein [1928] 1966, 427–30.

20. Olmsted 1895, 257; Frederick Law Olmsted, "Montreal: A Mountaintop Park and Some Thoughts on Art and Nature" (originally published in 1881 as *Mount Royal*), in Sutton 1971, 197–220; Olmsted [1870] 1970, 23–24.

21. Olmsted 1895, 258; Beveridge and Schuyler 1983, 215–16.

22. For a discussion of Hunt's challenge to Olmsted and Vaux, see D. Schuyler 1986, 95–100; see also Kowsky 1986.

23. Frederick Law Olmsted to the Board of Commissioners of the Central Park, 16 October 1857, and Olmsted, "Description of a Plan for the Improvement of the Central Park: 'Greensward,' " in Beveridge and Schuyler 1983, 106–11 and 130, 133, 151, 153, 162–63.

24. Beveridge and Schuyler 1983, 130.

25. Beveridge 1977; Reed 1981, 129; Fein 1981, 103–5; Kelly 1981, 39; Frederick Law Olmsted to the Board of Commissioners of Central Park, 16 October 1957, and Olmsted, "Description of the Central Park," in Beveridge and Schuyler 1983, 106–11 and 217; Frederick Law Olmsted to Mr. Ignaz A. Pilat, 26 September 1863, in Olmsted and Kimball [1928] 1973, 343–49; Olmsted 1888.

26. Simutis argues that Olmsted relied on English landscape scenery as well as American rural scenery as models for these early landscape parks. See Simutis 1972; see also Frederick Law Olmsted and Calvert Vaux's discussion of their design approach in Prospect Park, "Preliminary Report to the Commissioners for Laying Out a Park in Brooklyn, New York" (originally published in 1866), in Fein 1967, 104–7. For a discussion of neoclassical challenges to Olmsted and Vaux's art in Central Park, see D. Schuyler 1986, 185–95. Smithson (1973) has suggested that Central Park should be seen as analogous to a large earth sculpture. For another discussion of Central Park as a work of art, see Caparn 1912. Tuan (1989, 88–93) discusses the development of garden art and the "artificiality" of seventeenth- and eighteenth-century "natural" garden designs.

27. Simutis 1972, 279–80; Peets 1927. Jensen also referred to some landscape architects as "high priests" because they refused to get "their nose in the soil." Jens Jensen to Genevieve Gillette, 8 April 1942, MA.

28. Newton 1971, 337–52.

29. M. Schuyler 1895. For further discussion of Hunt's work, see Stein 1986; Baker 1985; Newton 1971, 427–46; and Lynes 1954, 98–102.

30. Platt 1893, 1894. For the response to Platt's writings on Italian gardens, see *Garden and Forest* 6, no. 280 (5 July 1893): 290; Eliot 1893; and Morgan 1985, 42–46. Platt's younger brother William served as an apprentice in Frederick Law Olmsted's office in the early 1890s, when Charles decided to take William along on his trip to study and draw Italy's great Renaissance gardens. Charles evidently felt that William was not learning enough of the "architectural" aspects of design from Olmsted. See Morgan 1985, 36–37.

31. Sturgis 1901; Wharton 1903. Architect Charles F. McKim (of the firm of McKim, Mead, and White) became convinced that young designers should study the classical traditions of Renaissance Italy and helped found the American School of Architecture in Rome in 1894. The American Academy of Rome was formally organized in 1897, and a three-year fellowship in landscape architecture was established at the academy in 1915. See Newton 1971, 393–96.

32. Pentecost 1902, 190–94; Olmsted 1920, 307–8, 314. For a further discussion of small parks and playgrounds in Chicago, see Tippens and Sniderman 1989.

33. "Architects and Landscape Architects," *Architectural Record* 12, no. 7 (December

1902): 762–64; Root 1921a, 13. Frank Lloyd Wright also saw landscape as an extension of the house; see Howett 1982, 36.

34. Lowell 1901; Elwood 1924; American Society of Landscape Architects 1931, 1932, 1933, 1934.

35. Pentecost 1902, 181, 190; Root 1921a, 15; Caparn 1903.

36. Lowell 1901, 8; Root 1921b, 22.

37. Waugh 1921, 67–69; Crody 1904; Sturgis 1901.

38. Lohmann 1926b, 3–4. Later, Jensen was invited to attend the society's 1942 meeting in Chicago as guest of honor, but he refused to go; see Jens Jensen to Genevieve Gillette, 7 February 1942, MA.

39. Duncan 1965, xv-xvii.

40. Bluestone 1984, 29–54; Turak 1986, 78.

41. Quotation is from Pullen 1891, 412. See also Wille 1972, 46–58; Turak 1986, 77–80.

42. Wille 1972, 54–55; Olmsted and Vaux, "Chicago: Taming the Waterfront," 156–80. As Wilhelm Miller (1915, 14–15) noted, in order to plant on the sandy soil of many of Chicago's parks (notably in Lincoln Park and the South Parks), the city's districts bought whole farms, skimmed off the topsoil, and moved it to the parks for lawn establishment. At most this was only a temporary solution. Miller quoted Jensen as saying that the districts should instead create "dune parks," using plants native to Lake Michigan's sand dunes.

43. Newton 1971, 311–12.

44. Hubbard 1930; Haglund 1976.

45. Cleveland [1871] 1965, 3–4, 22; Jackson 1972, 73–78; Haglund 1976, 68; Cleveland 1869, 7.

46. Cleveland 1869, 13; H. W. S. Cleveland to Frederick Law Olmsted, 8 November 1893, excerpted in Haglund 1976, 70.

47. Cleveland 1869, 14–17. For further discussion of H. W. S. Cleveland and his proposed boulevards, see Jackson 1972, 73–79; Burnham and Bennett [1909] 1970, 43–60; and Jens Jensen 1920, 21–44.

48. Andreas 1886, 167–69; Ebner 1988, 36–37; Hubbard 1930; Tishler 1989; Tishler and Luckhardt 1985. William H. Tishler is presently writing a biography of Cleveland.

49. Pullen 1891; Bluestone 1984, 100; Alfred Caldwell, interview by the author, Bristol, Wis., 17 December 1989.

50. Andreas 1886, 182–84; Pullen 1891, 423; Alexander 1896; Bluestone 1984, 105–7; Wille 1972, 58; Chicago Park District 1991, 7–12, 19–21; Simonds 1930, 8; O. C. Simonds to Wilhelm Miller, 20 July 1915, Willhelm Miller Papers, University Archives, University Library, University of Illinois, Urbana.

51. Bluestone 1984, 108; Pullen 1891, 412, 416.

52. For a discussion of Jenney's plans compared with Olmsted and Vaux's work in the South Parks, see D. Schuyler 1986, 136–38; and Newton 1971, 241–45.

53. Sniderman and Tippens 1990, 4–6; Turak 1986, 81–84; Bluestone 1984, 110.

54. Turak 1986, 84–97. Turak notes that Jenney's accomplishment in the parks was largely an amalgam of Olmstedian thought and the French picturesque tradition.

55. Andreas 1886, 182; Chicago, West Park Commission, "Official Proceedings, 1874–1893," Special Collections, Chicago Park District. See also Sniderman 1991, 22–24.

56. Oscar F. Dubuis, "Plan for Humboldt Park," 24 December 1889, Special Collections, Chicago Park District.

57. Commission on Chicago Historical and Architectural Landmarks, "Graceland

Cemetery: Preliminary Summary of Information" (unpublished report, 1982), 3–4; Blue-stone 1984, 103–5. For a general discussion of cemeteries and design, see Sloane 1991.

58. Simonds readily acknowledged the work of Adolph Strauch at Spring Grove Cemetery in Cincinnati, Ohio, as an influence on his own work, and he had an unending admiration for the work of Frederick Law Olmsted, Sr. Simonds felt that plant masses and lawns rather than monuments should dominate views in a cemetery. For a discussion of O. C. Simonds and his work at Graceland, see Simonds 1921, 1932a; Gelbloom 1975; Creese 1985, 209–12. For a discussion of various American cemetery types, see Sloane 1991, 3–6, 55–56, 107–9, 181–84.

59. Jackson 1972, 79; Ebner 1988, 27–30, 36–42. The firm of Cleveland and French, Landscape Architects and Engineers, was formed sometime before 1871, when Cleveland's *A Few Hints on Landscape Gardening in the West* and French's *The Relation of Engineering to Landscape Gardening* were published as a single pamphlet. As partners, the two men worked on projects in Illinois, Indiana, Kansas, Nebraska, Minnesota, Michigan, Ohio, and Wisconsin. See Hubbard 1930, 98–99.

60. Frederick Law Olmsted, "Riverside, Illinois: A Planned Community near Chicago" (originally printed in 1868 as "Preliminary Report upon the Proposed Suburban Village at Riverside, near Chicago"), in Sutton 1971, 295, 299; Jens Jensen 1939, 71–73; Censer 1986.

61. Keating 1988, 73–74. See also the discussion of Riverside in Creese 1985, 219–40; and Turak 1986, 96–112.

62. Mayer and Wade 1969, 196. For a general discussion of the Columbian Exposition, see Appelbaum 1980; Badger 1979; and Burg 1976. Olmsted's description of the Wooded Island is from Burnham and Millett 1894, 41–42.

63. For the relationship of the Columbian Exposition to the City Beautiful movement, see Wilson 1989, 53–74; Burnham and Bennett 1970, 4–6, 18, 61–98, 99–118; Peterson 1976, 415–34. For a further discussion of the Chicago Plan, see Condit 1973, 59–65.

64. Sullivan 1924, 324–25; Jens Jensen 1911b, 1204.

65. Burnham and Bennett 1970, v, 43–60. For an elaboration of greenbelts and their contemporary rendition, greenways, see Little 1990, esp. 1, 4–5, 7–25.

66. Jens Jensen 1911b, 1203–5.

67. Unwin 1911.

68. Jens Jensen 1911a. Hough (1990, 5–58) also notes the beauty of places where cities have developed under the constraints of site and climate and argues for urban design that preserves the natural setting of a place.

69. Mumford 1925, 152. For the history and ideals of the Regional Planning Association of America, see Lubove 1963; Sussman 1976. For a discussion of the RPAA and the Garden City movement, see Buder 1990, 157–80.

70. Duncan 1965, xix, 209–18. Among its many wealthy citizens, Chicago developed a tradition of support for cultural institutions like the University of Chicago. For a discussion of Chicago philanthropy, see Horowitz 1976; McCarthy 1982.

71. Duncan 1965, 105. The Chicago Arts and Crafts Society was founded and met regularly at Hull House; see *House Beautiful* 3, no. 1 (December 1897): 29. For a record of the development of Hull House and its programs, see Addams 1910, 388–93; Farrell 1967, 107. For a discussion of Jensen's promotion of pageants in parks, see Chapter 3 of the present volume. For a discussion of his outdoor theaters and council rings, see Chapter 4.

72. Farrell 1967, 107–18.

73. Halsey 1940, 26–28; Special Park Commission 1901, 22–23; Perkins 1904; Special Park Commission 1905. For Charles Zueblin's role in calling for playgrounds in

Chicago, see Zueblin 1898. For further discussion of the development of Chicago's playgrounds, see McArthur 1989; and Pacyga 1989.

74. Tippens and Sniderman 1989, 22, 25–26; Sniderman 1991, 20; Jens Jensen 1908b.

75. Griffin signed drawings both as a landscape architect and as an architect. See Brooks 1972, 22. For a discussion of Wright's landscape design, see Howett 1982. See also "The Character of the Site Is the Beginning of Architecture," *House Beautiful* 97, no. 11 (November 1955); "Wright as a Landscape Architect," ibid.

76. Brooks 1972, 28. Jensen moved out of his Steinway Hall office during World War I; E. Genevieve Gillette, interview by Patricia M. Frank, 1973, transcript of tape recording, Bentley Historical Library, University of Michigan, Ann Arbor, tape no. 16c: 14. For a discussion of Jensen's relation to the Chicago architects, see Eaton 1960.

77. Descriptions of Chicago's original landscape as bleak abound in the landscape literature. As Sargent (1897a, 231) noted, "Every one knows . . . that the surroundings of the city of Chicago are for the most part flat and featureless, that the soil is poor and the vegetation scant and scrubby." Some, nonetheless, saw a brighter picture; see, for example, Perkins 1905. Hubbard and Kimball ([1917] 1959, 165) suggest that these prairie landscape architects focused on the symbolic suggestion of broad prairie expanse rather than the preservation of large open areas in the rapidly developing midwestern cities.

78. W. Miller 1915, 1–3; W. Miller 1916, 591.

79. W. Miller 1915, 19–21; Howett 1982, 36; "Wright as a Landscape Architect," 342. Brooks (1972, 93–94) noted that, at the Magnus estate, Robert Spencer used the hawthorn that Jensen had introduced in the landscape as a motif in stained glass windows in the house. For a discussion of Griffin's landscape architectural work, see Vernon 1989, 11–12.

80. For a listing of Simonds' collaborations with Holabird and Roche, see Bruegmann 1991; Commission on Chicago Historical and Architectural Landmarks 1982, 7. See also Creese 1985, 205–18. For a discussion of Simonds' and Jensen's collaborations with prairie architects in the Chicago parks, see de Wit and Tippens 1991.

81. This list is compiled from Jensen drawings in the collection at the Art and Architecture Library, University of Michigan, Ann Arbor. While Jensen chose to identify the architect on these drawings, on many other projects he did not. See Yeomans 1916, 6; Kimball 1919.

82. Mertha Fulkerson to Leonard K. Eaton, 9 February 1960, MA; Eaton 1960, 150. Jensen (1939, 28) acknowledged Wright as a pupil of Sullivan's who "has developed an architecture that has penetrated every civilized country in the world." Jensen is the only landscape architect acknowledged by Wright in his writings. Wright (1941, 90) called Jensen "a true interpreter of the peculiar charm of our prairie landscape."

83. Jens Jensen to Michael Mappes, 11 March 1937, UM; Jens Jensen, "Answers to [University of Wisconsin,] Madison Question, 29 November 1944," UM, 3. An interesting comparison can be made between Jensen's viewpoints here and May Thielgaard Watts' comments on the rooflines of buildings in Europe and their relationship to the landscape and climatic conditions (Watts 1961). Also a Dane, Watts lived in Highland Park, Illinois, where Jensen's studio was located.

84. W. Miller 1916, 591. Wright relied on indigenous species whenever possible, but just as readily accepted plants that "grew like natives." See "Wright as a Landscape Architect," 345; Vernon 1989, 8–13.

85. Simonds 1920, 46; Jens Jensen to Mrs. T. J. Knudson, 10 February 1936, Lincoln Memorial Garden Archives, Lincoln Memorial Garden Nature Center, Springfield, Ill.

86. W. Miller 1914b; W. Miller 1915, 33–34.

87. Simonds 1932b, 106; Simonds, 1920, 22–23.

88. Jensen respected Simonds' work at Graceland and visited Simonds' Sinnissippi Farm in Oregon, Illinois, designed for Gov. Frank Lowden. Likewise, Simonds is said to have stopped frequently at Jensen's office in Ravinia, Illinois, to "see how things were going." See Leonard K. Eaton, interview by Marshall Johnson, 9 June 1959, MA; Gelbloom 1975.

89. W. Miller 1914c, 39.

90. Simonds 1920, 50, 59.

91. Simonds 1920, 61, 63–64; Simonds 1932b. It is interesting to note that Olmsted and Harrison (1889) also called for similar landscape management practices.

92. O. C. Simonds to Wilhelm Miller, 15 July 1915, Miller Papers. Jensen made numerous references in his letters and other writings to places he had visited, and nearly always he remarked on how the Midwestern landscape was more friendly, more to his liking, than the others.

93. Robinson 1870, 2–39; Cowles 1899b; Collier 1975; Collier 1977, 51. Cowles, who originally studied geology, was an ardent student of the geography of the landscape of the Chicago area. It is quite possible that Jensen and Cowles became acquainted as members of the Geographic Society of Chicago. Cowles's doctoral thesis, "The Ecological Relations of the Vegetation on the Sand Dunes of Lake Michigan," which was published by the University of Chicago Press in 1899, became a landmark in the budding science of ecology. Cowles prepared an extensive overview of the vegetation of the Chicago area in *The Plant Societies of Chicago and Vicinity*, which was published in 1901 as Bulletin of the Geographic Society of Chicago, no. 2.

94. Sargent 1897a, 231; Sargent 1894a, 261. For other pleas for native plants, see Sargent 1890, 1894b, 1895, and 1897b.

95. "Warren H. Manning, Landscape Designer" (obituary), *Landscape Architecture*, April 1938, 148–49; Hans 1938; Deane 1896, iii-viii; W. Manning 1899, 5–13.

96. McFarland 1899; W. Manning 1908.

97. W. Manning 1915; Clarke 1915; Millard 1915. W. Manning (1930, 19) documents a train trip taken by the American Civic Association from Springfield to Chicago, with stops at various schools promoting arts and crafts or at prominent scenic spots. On that trip, O. C. Simonds provided commentary through the prairie countryside.

98. White 1926, 8–9.

99. Durand 1923, 4; Roberts and Rehmann 1929, 2.

100. Edith Roberts and Elsa Rehmann's work was originally published in *House Beautiful* as a series of articles entitled "Plant Ecology" (see Roberts and Rehmann 1927a–1927g, 1928a–1928e). In 1929 these articles were summarized in Roberts and Rehmann's *American Plants for American Gardens*. For a follow-up article, see Rehmann 1933. For a description of Roberts' plantings at Vassar College, see Roberts 1933.

101. Cunningham 1925.

102. Hamblin 1922; Wheelwright 1919; Lay 1920. This problem still persists. Only recently have retail and wholesale nurseries begun to make native grasses and forbs available.

103. Morse 1902, 63; Engel 1983, 81; Riis 1924. Paul Riis was at this time director of the Rockford, Illinois, Park District. He later moved to Pittsburgh, Pennsylvania, where he headed the Allegheny Park System and involved Jensen in designing South Park. See Riis 1931; Gangeware 1986, 15.

104. Caparn 1929.

105. Caparn 1929, 147, 151.

106. Waugh 1899, 1910, 1917a, 1922.

107. Frank A. Waugh to Jens Jensen, 28 March 1938, MA. For further information on The Clearing, see Chapter 3 of the present volume. According to Waugh's daughter,

Dorothy, the Jensens visited them in Amherst, Massachusetts, and the Waughs in turn visited the Jensens in Ravinia, Illinois, as well as at The Clearing in Ellison Bay, Wisconsin. Dorothy Waugh was the same age as the younger of Jensen's daughters and was invited to go on outings with the Jensen family while she was a student at the Art Institute of Chicago. Dorothy Waugh to the author, 22 September and 8 October 1987; Waugh 1917a, 25.

108. Waugh 1917a, 29; DiCarlo 1973, 14, 20.

109. Waugh n.d., 1931a–1931c, 1932a–1932c, 1934.

110. Quote is from Waugh 1925, 154; see also Waugh 1917c. In 1926 Waugh did a more specific analysis of the national forests in the southern Appalachians: "The Present Status of Recreation Uses in District 7 National Forests" (unpublished report, Waugh Collection, University of Massachusetts Library, Amherst). For additional reports on recreation on national park and forest lands, see Waugh 1918a, 1918b, 1923, and the series of articles published in *Parks and Recreation* (Waugh 1936a–1936e). For the work at Mt. Hood, see Waugh 1930. A typewritten sheet by Waugh (shared with the author by Mr. Harold Mosher of Amherst, Mass.) bears the heading "Check List of Descriptive Data on the Landscape of a Region." Accompanying the checklist is another set of typewritten sheets by Waugh entitled "Recreational Resources Study—Outline."

111. Frank A. Waugh to Jens Jensen, 8 April 1936, MA; Waugh, quoted in Jens Jensen to Genevieve Gillette, 8 April 1942, MA; Jens Jensen to Mr. and Mrs. Boardman, n.d., MA.

112. Frank A. Waugh to Jens Jensen, 5 January 1938, MA.

113. Jens Jensen to Camillo Schneider, 15 April 1939 (personal files of Darrel Morrison).

CHAPTER THREE: JENSEN'S DESIGN CAREER

1. Chicago, West Park Commission, 1894, 7.

2. Apparently, during Jensen's early years with the park district, he felt it expedient to adopt the Anglicized name "James." By the turn of the century, however, he had recognized the advantage of emphasizing his Danish heritage and switched back to "Jens"; see James Jensen 1899. Jensen became known in Europe for a paving compound he developed for park roads and for his part in the engineering and design of the Garfield Park Conservatory in Chicago; see Collier 1975. In 1908 he lectured to a convention of park superintendents on the use of concrete in park benches and other structures; see Jens Jensen 1908a.

3. Jens Jensen 1930, 34.

4. James Jensen 1902a, 12. It is interesting to note the remarkable similarities between Jensen's problems with the park commissioners and those of Frederick Law Olmsted in Central Park. For a discussion of Olmsted's problems, see "Spoils of the Park," in Olmsted and Kimball [1928] 1973, 117–55.

5. Perkins 1904.

6. Jens Jensen 1904.

7. Perkins 1904, 80–105; "Proposed Metropolitan Park System for Chicago," *Park and Cemetery* 15, no. 1 (March 1905): 213–14.

8. Lathrop 1903, 7.

9. "Reforms in the West Park System of Chicago," *Park and Cemetery* 15, no. 6 (August 1905): 329–30.

10. Chicago, West Park Commission, 1907, 22.

11. McAdam 1911, 12.

12. "The Biggest Park Conservatory in America," *Park and Cemetery* 23, no. 4 (June

1913): 74; Jensen and Eskil 1930, 19. Quote is from McAdam 1911, 13. In 1912, the park board appointed August Koch of the Missouri Botanical Garden as chief florist for the conservatory and outdoor plantings in the West Parks. Koch revised many of the original plantings in the conservatory, often using species propagated from seeds and spores found in the soil and packing material shipped with orchids, palms, and other plants. Chicago, West Park Commission, 1924, 3.

13. Jensen and Eskil 1930, 19. In his writings, Jensen frequently compared his work to music; at various places he compared gardens to the music of Sousa, Wagner, Beethoven, and Schubert. See, for example, Jens Jensen 1913; Jens Jensen 1908d, 11. It is interesting to note that Frank Lloyd Wright also compared his designs to music. See Williams 1955; Twombly 1979, 15.

14. Jensen seemed to have a particular fondness for Hugh Garden's architectural designs. Garden, who had worked with Louis Sullivan, would later assist with the design of the buildings for Jensen's school at The Clearing, in Ellison Bay, Wisconsin. According to Mertha Fulkerson, Jensen's longtime secretary, Garden often brought his plans to Jensen "for consultation and advice on the landscape treatment. . . . They saw alike in many things when they would sit and talk about various things going on. They seemed to get much out of their common bond of understanding" (Mertha Fulkerson to Leonard Eaton, 9 February 1960, MA).

15. Alfred Caldwell, interview by Malcolm Collier, January 1981, transcript of tape recording, MA, tape no. 8: 7; W. Miller 1912a. Miller also mentions Jensen's prairie river gardens in Glencoe, which were most likely on the Rubens estate.

16. For further discussion of the development of playgrounds and small parks, see Cranz 1982; and Weyeneth 1983.

17. Jens Jensen 1908b, 11. Shortly after the turn of the century, festivals became a popular way of celebrating local history. See Needham 1912; Davol 1914; Glassberg 1990; and Prevots 1990. For a discussion of the progressives' attitudes toward these pageants, see Horowitz 1976, 218–19.

18. Chicago, West Park Commission, 1915, 18–24.

19. Chicago, West Park Commission, 1915, 24.

20. "Chicago's Park Sculpture Show," *Park and Cemetery* 19, no. 8 (1909): 127–30. The Columbian Exposition in 1893 had provided American sculptors with a dramatic opportunity to demonstrate their work on a broad scale. Following the fair, an ever more confident group of sculptors and architects sought out ways of executing their new-found visions of civic pride. For a discussion of the development of public sculpture in this period, see Bogart 1989.

21. Jens Jensen 1908c, 438. Olmsted and Vaux also vigorously defended their vision of Central Park in New York City from those who would have turned the park into a great gallery of public sculpture. See the discussion of Richard Morris Hunt's designs for monumental gateways to Central Park in D. Schuyler 1986, 95–100.

22. "The Sculpture Show in Humboldt Park, Chicago," *Park and Cemetery* 18, no. 9 (November 1908): 439–40; "Chicago's Park Sculpture Show," 127–28.

23. Jens Jensen 1930, 35; Jens Jensen 1939, 81–82.

24. Jens Jensen 1930, 37; Jens Jensen 1917.

25. E. Genevieve Gillette, interview by Scott Hedberg, 27 March 1978; tapes loaned to the author. See also Jens Jensen 1917.

26. A comparison can be made with Jane Addams' attempt to provide alternative play areas for city children. In *Twenty Years at Hull-House* (16–18), she relates her own early "companionship" with nature and suggests that the crude rituals that she and her playmates enacted provided a "sense of identification with man's primitive past."

27. Dean 1922, 138–39.

28. Jens Jensen 1930, 37. Jensen's swimming pool in Columbus Park was destroyed in 1955 and replaced with a conventional concrete pool.

29. Jens Jensen 1920, 9–10.

30. Jens Jensen 1911b; Eaton 1960, 145. As Collier (1982, 7) has pointed out, it is unclear whether the ideas expressed here are Jensen's or those of his committee. Either way, the article was clearly a response to Daniel Burnham's *Plan of Chicago*, which had been issued in 1909. Given Jensen's clear dislike for the imperialistic cities he had experienced in Germany, the ideas are likely his own. For his discussion of "imperialistic cities," see Jens Jensen 1939, 34–37.

31. Jens Jensen 1920, 15. Jensen prepared a stereopticon lecture and used it to sell his ideas to the public.

32. Jens Jensen 1939, 87.

33. Jens Jensen 1920, 47.

34. Jens Jensen 1918, 20. Sometime around 1910, Jensen also urged the city of Chicago to buy 2,000–3,000 acres of land in northern Michigan or Wisconsin as a summer camp for the poorest of the city's children. The children would be transported to the camp by boat. See Jens Jensen, editorial for the *Chicago Daily News*, 3 December 1940, MA.

35. Yeomans 1916, index, 6; Kimball 1919, 45.

36. James Jensen 1911, 13; Jens Jensen 1920, 58–59.

37. Collier 1975, 228; Collier 1982, 5–8. The list of clubs Jensen joined is lengthy. In addition to those mentioned in the text, Collier also notes the Municipal Science Club, which, like the "Committee on the Universe," appears to have been short-lived. Jensen's 1922 office ledger (MA) indicates that at that time he paid dues to the American Geographic Society, the American Scandinavian Foundation, the Audubon Society, the City Club, the Cliff Dwellers, the Chicago Historical Society, the Chicago Outdoors League, and the Redwood League. He was also a board member of the Art Institute of Chicago.

38. Alfred Caldwell, interview by the author, Chicago, Ill., 12 November 1990; Jensen and Eskil 1930, 18.

39. Jens Jensen to Camillo Schneider, 11 March 1937, MA.

40. Jens Jensen 1930, 34–35.

41. Jens Jensen 1906.

42. W. Miller 1912b, 24.

43. Alfred Caldwell, interview by Malcolm Collier, January 1981, tape no. 2: 17–19; quote is from Jens Jensen 1939, 28. Jensen considered many of these architects students of Louis Sullivan, but lamented that they "would twist Sullivan's words to fit their convenience" (Mertha Fulkerson to Leonard Eaton, 9 February 1960). Jensen was deeply bothered by the proposed destruction of Sullivan's Auditorium Building in Chicago. In a letter to the editor of the *Chicago Daily News* (13 June 1941, MA), he wrote: "The Auditorium is the work of the Master of all Architects, Louis Sullivan, an American who saw the beauty of his native land and imprinted it forever on the pages of architecture. His Auditorium has the dignity and the strength of America, and typifies our Country far nobler and truer than the flimsy skyscrapers which have followed."

44. Alfred Caldwell, interview by Malcolm Collier, January 1981, tape no. 1: 23; Mertha Fulkerson to Leonard Eaton, 9 February 1960.

45. Howett 1983, 36.

46. Sybil Shearer, conversation with the author, 25 January 1991.

47. Jens Jensen 1939, 71; E. Genevieve Gillette, interview by Scott Hedberg, 27 March 1978. In 1913, Jensen brought together a group of prominent and influential Chicagoans to form the organization Friends of Our Native Landscape. Included among these early members were the Julius Rosenwalds, Avery Coonley, Harriet Monroe, Dwight

Perkins, Stephen Mather (first director of the U.S. National Park Service), Harold Ickes (secretary of the interior under Franklin D. Roosevelt), the Edward L. Ryersons, Mrs. Tiffany Blake, and Ernst Freund. See Collier 1982, 9–11.

48. Alfred Caldwell, interview by the author and Julia Sniderman, Chicago, Ill., 31 January 1987. Marion Mahoney Griffin prepared the initial design for the von Holst and Fyfe firm. Shortly after the foundation of the house were laid, a dispute arose between Ford and the architects and Ford hired Pittsburgh architect William H. van Tine to redesign the house using the foundation that had been poured. See Brooks 1972, 163.

49. Joseph H. Dodson, from Kankakee, Illinois, listed Henry Ford as a client in his advertisements for building bird sanctuaries. The setting of Fair Lane along the Rouge River is a prime mosquito habitat, and attracting insect-eating songbirds was a major part of an insect control program. Other clients in Mr. Dodson's advertisments included C. W. Seiberling, John D. Rockefeller, Thomas Edison, Harvey Firestone, and the Drs. Mayo. See Dodson 1931.

50. On Jensen's plans, this meadow was part of a golf fairway, and a series of golf holes were positioned throughout the estate. There is no indication, however, that the other holes were ever built or that golf was played on the estate.

51. E. Genevieve Gillette, interview by Scott Hedberg, 27 March 1978. In 1925, Clara Ford hired landscape architect Herbert J. Kellaway and rose expert Harriet R. Foote to design the rose garden. As the design was implemented, Clara Ford altered it completely, making it more her own. Later, in 1927, Clara Ford hired Ellen Shipman from New York to convert Jensen's rose garden near the house into an "English garden" of perennials. See Clark 1952; "Fair Lane: The House and Garden," *Bulletin*, no. 3 (1955), Ford Motor Company Archives, Dearborn, Mich.; Leonard K. Eaton, interview with Marshall Johnson, 9 June 1959, MA. In recent years, concerted efforts to restore the Fair Lane landscape have been made by numerous volunteers and student interns working under the direction of Donn Werling and assisted by the author. For an overview of the estate's current management needs, see Morris 1989.

52. Alfred Caldwell, interview by the author, Chicago, Ill., 12 November 1990.

53. Alfred Caldwell, interview by Malcolm Collier, January 1981, tape no. 8: 19.

54. As is often the case with collected papers, the Jensen records that exist were assembled by a few caring individuals. Leonard Eaton did much to rescue Jensen from obscurity by beginning his research in the late 1950s, when many of the people who had lived and worked with Jensen were still alive. Eaton also rescued an extensive collection of Jensen's office drawings from Marshall Johnson's garage, and these drawings and some miscellaneous papers are in the Jensen Collection at the Art and Architecture Library, University of Michigan, Ann Arbor. Apparently, other office records were taken by Jensen to The Clearing in Ellison Bay, Wisconsin, and most were destroyed in the fire there in 1937. The collection of papers, drawings, and photographs in the Jensen Collection at the Morton Arboretum in Lisle, Illinois, originally consisted of material given to Mary K. Moulton and found at The Clearing by Steve Christy, Carol Doty, and Orvetta Robinson. The majority of these records date from the mid-1930s, during Jensen's years in Wisconsin, but the collection also contains Jensen's photographs of his earlier projects taken before, during, and after construction. As curator of the archives at the Morton Arboretum, Carol Doty has added to the collection as new materials have continued to surface.

55. James Jensen 1901.

56. James Jensen 1901, 185.

57. Wilhelm Miller (1914a) noted that Jensen substituted tree-of-heaven (*Ailanthus altissima*) for sumac (*Rhus spp.*) in the Loeb garden in Chicago because of problems with air pollution. Jensen also mentioned a concern with polluted air in the selection of plants for cities. See Jens Jensen 1903, 1; James Jensen 1901.

58. At the Henry Ford Hospital in Detroit, building additions now take up much of what once was garden space. The same is true at Decatur Memorial Hospital.

59. Hokanson 1988, 5–11; American Scenic and Historical Preservation Society 1916, 408–9.

60. Hokanson 1988, 5–11; Jens Jensen to Gael S. Hoag, 9 April and 2 May 1928, Lincoln Highway Archives, Department of Rare Books and Special Collections, University of Michigan Library, Ann Arbor (hereafter cited as UM-LH).

61. Lincoln Highway Association, "An 'Ideal Section' on the Lincoln Highway: Remarks on Beautification and Embellishment" (unpublished manuscript, n.d.), UM-LH; Edsel Ford to A. F. Bennett, 26 March 1924, UM-LH.

62. Lincoln Highway Association 1935, 203–11.

63. Lincoln Highway Association, "Ideal Section Nears Completion" (press release), 1 May 1923; Jens Jensen to Gael S. Hoag, 9 April, 2 May, and 1 October 1928; and Edsel Ford to Gael S. Hoag, 25 April 1925; all in UM-LH.

64. Jens Jensen to Gael S. Hoag, 9 April 1928; Edsel Ford to A. F. Bennett, 11 March 1924; A. F. Bennett to J. N. Gunn, n.d., UM-LH; Lincoln Highway Association 1935, 207–8.

65. Current efforts to establish native wildflowers along roadsides vary from state to state and locality to locality. Lady Bird Johnson has been one of the more ardent and effective promoters of roadside beauty and native plantings. In 1982, she established the National Wildflower Research Center on a portion of her property in Austin, Texas. Mrs. Johnson's strong advocacy of wildflower plantings along roadsides helped secure passage of the Wildflower Policy Act (1987), which was introduced in Congress by Senator Lloyd Bentsen of Texas. This law stipulates that one-fourth of one percent of the landscape budgets of all highway projects that use federal funds must be spent on wildflower plantings. Since 1987, all states have developed some type of program to promote wildflowers, but Midwestern states have been the undeniable leaders, particularly in restricting the definition of *wildflower* to indigenous species.

66. Hubbert 1935; Sniderman and Nathan 1988, sec. 7, p. 1.

67. W. Miller 1912c, 200; Chubb 1915; Sniderman and Nathan 1988, sec. 7, p. 2.

68. Jens Jensen 1916b; Sniderman and Nathan 1988, sec. 8, p. 5.

69. Jens Jensen 1916b, 168; Sniderman and Nathan 1988, sec. 7, p. 3.

70. Sniderman and Nathan 1988, sec. 7, p. 4.

71. "The Lincoln Memorial Garden," *Garden Glories*, September 1938, 4–5; Jens Jensen to Mrs. T. J. (Harriet) Knudson, 8 February 1936, UM.

72. Mrs. T. J. Knudson and Mrs. Raymond Knotts, "The Abraham Lincoln Memorial Garden Foundation, Inc.: Early Plantings, 1937–1938" (typed manuscript, n.d.), Lincoln Memorial Garden Archives, Lincoln Memorial Garden Nature Center, Springfield, Ill.

73. Jens Jensen 1939, 86–87.

74. Jens Jensen 1939, 87; quote is from Jens Jensen to Camillo Schneider, 15 April 1939; Eaton 1964, 43–44.

75. Groves and Kweder 1975, 4; Jens Jensen to Mrs. T. J. Knudson, 9 December 1935, Lincoln Memorial Garden Archives, Springfield, Ill. It should be pointed out that on many earlier plans, Jensen noted that close adherence to the details of the drawing was critical.

76. The author prepared a management analysis of the garden's landscape under a grant from the National Endowment for the Arts in 1983–84. See Grese 1984.

77. Collier 1982, 8–9. The Prairie Club still exists today and continues the tradition of outdoor programs for residents of the Chicago region and surrounding states. During its most prosperous years (in the 1950s), the club counted more than 1,000 members. The

archives of the Prairie Club are now located in the Thomas Memorial Library, Chesterton, Indiana (hereafter referred to as TML).

78. In the "Prairie Club Notes" (1909–14, TML), which advertised the early "Saturday Afternoon Walking Trips," the public was "invited to a series of walks with the members of the following organizations": the Geographical Society of Chicago, the Chicago Architectural Club, the Illinois chapter of the Institute of Architects, the teaching staffs of the universities, the Women's Outdoor Art League, the Social Science Club, Art Institute instructors, the Chicago Principals Club, the Little Room, the Illinois Audubon Society, Residents of the Social Settlements, the Pallett and Chisel Club, the Cliff Dwellers, the City Club of Chicago, and the Chicago Library Club.

79. Perkins, 1904, 64–77; Halsey 1940, 26–28.

80. Franklin and Schaeffer 1983, 24–48; Norma Schaeffer and Kay Franklin, "The Prairie Club Seventy-five Years Young at Heart" (unpublished paper), TML.

81. Franklin and Schaeffer 1983, 43–46; Collier 1982, 9–11; Engel 1983, 24–25. For another description of the Friends' early meeting, see Henderson 1985.

82. Doty 1971. For the text of "A Masque" (later called "The Beauty of the Wild" by the Friends), see Goodman 1971.

83. Jensen's approach to organizing the Friends and building a strong base for his conservation projects is remarkably similar to Charles Eliot's dramatic efforts to establish the Metropolitan Parks System in the Boston region in the 1880s and 1890s. Eliot proved to be particularly adept in bringing together knowledgeable and influential people to get the parks established. See Eliot 1902, 318–82; Newton 1971, 318–415, 420–545, 593–612, 646–89, 709–41.

84. Doeserich, Sherburne, and Wey 1941, 96–97. See also Engel 1983, 75; Read 1986.

85. Doeserich, Sherburne, and Wey 1941, 98; "Prairie Club Early Park Supporter," *Singing Sands Almanac* (Chesterton, Ind.: Indiana Dunes National Lakeshore, U.S. National Park Service, 1979); Mather 1917, 1–24.

86. Mather 1917, 45.

87. Mather 1917, 59.

88. Mather 1917, 79.

89. Mather 1917, 98.

90. Mather 1917, 99.

91. Mather 1917, 99.

92. Mather 1917, 100.

93. The Prairie Club had a long tradition of commemorating Memorial Day at the Dunes. Services would be held at the Beach House, followed by a masque or other program. See G. Brennan 1923, 163; Doeserich, Sherburne, and Wey 1941, 98–100; Franklin and Schaeffer 1982. For a detailed account of the Dunes Pageant and its meaning, see Engel 1983, 11–42.

94. Engel 1983, 249; Fulkerson 1941, 98.

95. Friends of Our Native Landscape (hereafter referred to as FONL) 1921, 11.

96. Jens Jensen 1921a, 15–16.

97. Jens Jensen 1921a, 15; Trotter 1962, 97–100.

98. Jens Jensen 1921a, 15; Jens Jensen 1921b, 117–20 (see also map on 13).

99. Jens Jensen 1926, 11–12. The ideas presented in this pamphlet echoed similar ideas espoused earlier by Charles Eliot in arguments for protecting the Waverly Oaks; see Eliot 1890.

100. Jens Jensen 1926, 12–15.

101. "Some Glimpses of Native Beauty and a Survey of the State's Scenic Resources and Public Parks," *Chicago Daily News*, 29 March 1929.

102. White Pines Forest was not included in the Friends' 1921 report on proposed park areas in Illinois (FONL 1921), but it was noted in their 1926 recommendations for a state park and forest policy (FONL 1926). For a history of the acquisition of parkland, see Trotter 1962, 61–96. For land acquisition through the 1930s, see Illinois Board of State Park Advisors 1932; Illinois State Planning Commission n.d.

103. FONL n.d., 8.

104. FONL n.d., 8–11. The use of highway rights-of-way continues to be an important means of preserving indigenous species; see Little 1990, esp. 92–104, 117–20, 143–48.

105. Frank 1927 (loaned to the author by Christopher Graham).

106. Jens Jensen 1916a, 1–10. For another mention of Jensen's report, see American Scenic and Historical Preservation Society 1917, 279.

107. Park Board, Door County, Wisconsin, "Park Board Report," December 1945, UM.

108. Alfred Caldwell, interview by Malcolm Collier, January 1981, tape no. 1: 15. Quote is from Jens Jensen to Malcolm Dill (Tennessee Valley Authority), 2 April 1936, MA; Jens Jensen to Aldo Leopold, 7 June 1944, MA.

109. Jens Jensen n.d., 3.

110. Christy 1976a, 48–49; Eaton 1964, 92; Alfred Caldwell, interview by the author and Julia Sniderman, 31 January 1987; E. Genevieve Gillette, interview by John Blum and Karen Jore, "Genevieve Gillette, an Oral History: Part 1," Winter 1980, videotape, Bentley Historical Library, University of Michigan, Ann Arbor; Bruce Johnson, telephone interview by the author, March 1991.

111. Jens Jensen 1939, 64–65.

112. Jens Jensen 1939, 65–66.

113. Jens Jensen 1939, 66.

114. Fulkerson 1941, 99, 101.

115. Alfred Caldwell, interview by the auther, 12 November 1990; E. Genevieve Gillette, interview by Patricia M. Frank, 1973, transcript of tape recording, Bentley Historical Library, University of Michigan, Ann Arbor, tape no. 16c: 15.

116. Jensen is buried in the family plot in Memorial Park Cemetery in Skokie, Illinois.

117. Jens Jensen, "Answers to [University of Wisconsin,] Madison Question, 29 November 1944," UM; Fulkerson 1941, 100–101; Jens Jensen to Alice Drought, 30 June, 1 July, and 11 September 1930, and 16 June 1932, MA; Alice Drought to Jens Jensen, 26, September 1930, MA.

118. Jens Jensen to Alice Drought, 16 June 1932. For a comparison of The Clearing with Danish folk school traditions, see Takemoto 1987.

119. Jens Jensen to Alice Drought, 16 June 1932. According to Sybil Shearer (conversation with the author, 25 January 1991), Jensen held fast to this rule. After working with ten young men for a year, he surmised that they were not genuinely interested in what he had to teach them and so sent them home, refunding their $1,000 tuition despite the fact that the school was in desperate need of money.

120. Fulkerson and Corson 1972; Christy, Pape, and Tishler 1983, 5, 17.

121. "Must Educate Youth to Love Native Land: Jensen," *Capitol Times* (Madison, Wis.), 28 March 1944; Jens Jensen to Genevieve Gillette, 30 March 1944, MA.

122. Jens Jensen to Genevieve Gillette, 29 January 1944, MA.

123. Jensen, "Answers to [University of Wisconsin,] Madison Question, 29 November 1944."

124. Jensen, "This is 'The Clearing.' "

125. Jens Jensen to Camillo Schneider, 15 April 1939.

126. Fulkerson and Corson 1972, 15.

127. Jens Jensen to Camillo Schneider, 11 March 1937; Jens Jensen, typed manuscript

of untitled article for the *Wisconsin Horticulturalist*, 29 November 1944, 4, MA. In an interview with the author on 12 November 1990, Alfred Caldwell recalled that Jensen had once remarked that the loveliest garden he had ever seen was a cluster of hollyhocks growing next to a fisherman's cottage.

128. Fulkerson and Corson 1972, 15.

129. Alden (last name unknown) to Jens Jensen, 28 February 1939, MA.

130. Jensen, "This is 'The Clearing.'"

131. Fulkerson and Corson 1972, 6, 32–65; [Doty] 1987.

CHAPTER FOUR: JENSEN'S DESIGN STYLE

1. James Jensen 1901, 1900a, 1900b, 1900c; W. Miller 1914a, 47; Christy 1976b, 63; Jens Jensen 1912, 41.

2. Personal correspondence between Jensen and Edsel Ford, November 1926–December 1930, UM. Later at The Clearing in Ellison Bay, Jensen lamented planting a Japanese bittersweet, which grew so rampantly as to take over many of the native plants he was trying to cultivate. He said, "Just think, I, who [plant] nothing but native plants should plant Japanese bittersweet up here in the woods, and what a serious mistake. It is a much quicker growing plant than our native so I presume that is the reason I planted it, but I have learned my lesson" (Jens Jensen to Camillo Schneider, 11 March 1937).

3. Jens Jensen, as quoted by E. Genevieve Gillette, interview by Scott Hedberg, 27 March 1978.

4. Christy 1976b, 66.

5. Jens Jensen 1939, 86–87. An account of the prairie work at the University of Wisconsin, Madison, can be found in Greene and Curtis 1953 and Jordan, Gilpin, and Aber 1987. Aldo Leopold, who was experimenting with replanting prairie plants on his Sand County, Wisconsin, property during this period, describes his struggles with compass plant (*Silphium laciniatum*) (1949, 44–50).

6. Eaton 1964, 93–94. In an interview with the author on 12 November 1990, Alfred Caldwell recalled the comment about Jensen sowing trees from a nurseryman; see also Jens Jensen to Mr. and Mrs. Boardman, n.d., MA.

7. Jens Jensen to William Brandenburg, 12 January 1938, MA; Jens Jensen to Mrs. T. J. Knudson, 9 December 1935; Jens Jensen to Mrs. T. J. Knudson, 7 November 1938, MA.

8. Fulkerson 1958, 8; James Jensen 1902b.

9. Collier 1975, 230–31; W. Miller 1914b, 9–10; W. Miller 1915, 19–21.

10. W. Miller 1915, 17.

11. W. Miller 1915, 19–21; W. Miller 1916.

12. Jens Jensen 1927; Jens Jensen 1939, 39–61.

13. Pentecost (1902, 174–94) was highly critical of the practice of creating "a ficticious impression of spaciousness" with flowing spaces and masses of shrubbery and trees at the border of a property. He particularly objected to such approaches to the handling of space on small sites and suggested that the imposition of the "natural style" on small city parks was "an artistic crime." In a follow-up article ("Architects and Landscape Architects," *Architectural Record* 12, no. 7 [December 1902]: 762–64), the editors of *Architectural Record* suggested that the emphasis on "the informal" or "natural" style of design was costing landscape architects valuable estate jobs. They noted a revived interest in "formal gardens" and suggested that "architects, who are at the same time architects" (such as McKim, Mead, and White, Carrere and Hastings, Charles A. Platt, and Wilson Eyre, Jr.), were better in relating buildings to grounds.

14. W. Miller 1915, 18; Gelbloom 1975.

15. W. Miller 1915, 17–18.

16. Darrel Morrison, conversation with the author, 1983; Jens Jensen 1939, 61.

17. This technique was also used by O. C. Simonds on the grounds of the Julia Larned home designed in 1907 in Hubbard Woods, Illinois, where paths to the sun were labeled and plants such as goldenrod were planted to catch the sun's low-angled rays.

18. Jens Jensen 1906, 24. See also Jensen's description of a small clearing at his studio in Ravinia (Jens Jensen 1939, 60).

19. Jensen and Eskil 1930, 169. The Art Institute of Chicago's collection of paintings by George Inness contains several striking examples of forest clearings or of the sun piercing through a cloudy sky. For a description of some of the Inness paintings in the Art Institute's collections during Jensen's time, see Pattison 1911; Alfred Caldwell, interview by Malcolm Collier, January 1981, tape no. 5: 18.

20. Jensen and Eskil 1930, 169.

21. Jens Jensen 1939, 34–36.

22. Jens Jensen 1939, 67, 81–83.

23. Prince von Pückler-Muskau ([1834] 1917, 80–81) spelled out this very technique.

24. Jens Jensen 1924a, 26; Jensen 1924b, 186. Manuscripts for the following articles by Jensen can be found in the archives of the Lincoln Highway Association at the University of Michigan (UM-LH): "Some Comments on Roadside Planting," 15 March 1924; "Use Thought and Care in Selecting Roadside Trees: Beauty of the Landscape Should Be Enhanced and Emphasized by Planting," 28 April 1924; and "Leading Landscape Architect Impresses Highway Beauty: Kentucky Pikes Cited as Best American Example—Pioneer Roadside Planting Part of Cultural Advancement," 10 June 1924.

25. Jens Jensen 1924b; Jensen, "Leading Landscape Architect Impresses Highway Beauty."

26. Jensen and Eskil 1930, 169.

27. Jensen's article "The Preservation of Our River Courses and Their Natural Setting" was originally published as a chapter in FONL 1921, 115–20. It was later republished under the title "Preserve Water Courses" (Jens Jensen 1923) and was included in "Siftings," the Major Portion of "The Clearing," and Collected Writings (Jens Jensen 1956, 139–45).

28. Jens Jensen 1939, 72–73.

29. Jens Jensen 1939, 67–68.

30. Jens Jensen to A. J. Lepine, Ford Motor Company, 19 November 1926, UM.

31. Franz Aust assisted Jensen in finding the boulders for Lincoln Memorial Garden.

32. Engel 1983, 200–201.

33. Engel 1983, 201.

34. Waugh 1917b, 16–17, 125–30; see also Farrell 1967, 107.

35. Waugh 1917b, 125–30; Jens Jensen 1917, 17; E. Genevieve Gillette, interview by Scott Hedberg, 27 March 1978.

36. James Jensen 1900d; Jensen and Eskil 1930, 18. In an interview with Malcolm Collier in January 1981 (tape no. 4: 14), Alfred Caldwell noted that Jensen wanted to please his clients and would generally include whatever they requested.

37. Norman Blei, article in the *Sunday Chicago Sun Times*, 16 December 1973.

38. Jens Jensen 1920, 39, 51–52; Smergalski 1918.

39. In an article entitled "Landscape Vegetable Gardening" (1917), Ruth Dean, who had earlier worked in Jensen's office, suggested that vegetable gardens should be well ordered. She illustrated her point with photos of grapevines on wire trellises bordering the walks in Jensen's vegetable garden for Harry Rubens in Glencoe, Illinois.

40. Jensen and Eskil 1930, 169; Jens Jensen 1939, 102–3.

41. Jens Jensen 1939, 48, 67; FONL n.d., 22.

42. Jens Jensen 1939, 77, 82; Jensen and Eskil 1930, 19; McAdam 1911; W. Miller 1915, 8–9; Jens Jensen 1920, 15.

43. Jens Jensen 1939, 78–79.

44. Jens Jensen 1939, 51–52.

45. Jens Jensen to Camillo Schneider, 15 April 1939; Jens Jensen 1939, 86–87.

CHAPTER FIVE: JENSEN'S LEGACY

1. Alfred Caldwell, interview by Malcolm Collier, January 1981, tape no. 1: 15–17. Quote is from Jensen [1939] 1990, 117; see also Charles Little's foreword (xi-xv) and Darrel Morrison's afterword (111–18).

2. Jens Jensen, untitled response to a report from the Chicago Plan Commission entitled "Expressways" (n.d., MA). Many of the same problems have beset New York's Central Park. For a description of preservation/restoration efforts there, see Rogers 1987. For the political problems of historic landscapes like Central Park, see Heckscher 1974, 269–76.

3. Jens Jensen 1939, 37, 109–10. According to Mertha Fulkerson, Jensen rarely dwelt on work that he had finished, considering each job a "closed book" once it was done (Mertha Fulkerson to Leonard K. Eaton, 9 February 1960; Alfred Caldwell, interview by Malcolm Collier, January 1981, tape no. 7: 4–5).

4. Jens Jensen 1939, 85.

5. Levinsohn 1987; Sheaffer 1987; Gordon and Hussey-Arntson 1989; Ryckbosch 1991, 7; Chicago Historical Society 1991. An extensive landscape survey in Highland Park, Illinois, marked the beginning of an effort to build public appreciation of Jensen's landscape designs there (Highland Park Historic Preservation Commission 1988).

6. James Jensen 1902a, 13. According to Alfred Caldwell (interview with the author, December 1989), Jensen often remarked that "plans are bunk," referring to their ineffectiveness in communicating the full range of a landscape design. For an overview of the problems of managing historic landscapes, see Fitch 1976, Bratton 1988, Firth 1988, and Meier 1991.

7. Kaplan and Kaplan 1989, 177–200. Michael Laurie (1979) argues that the ideals of the nineteenth-century romanticists are still relevant for modern urban planning. Rachel Kaplan (1983) discusses the human need for nature. See also O. Manning 1979.

8. Cranz 1982, 101–33. Quotation is from Jens Jensen 1939, 99.

9. Quote is from "In the Interest of General Outdoor Improvement," *Bulletin of the American Park and Outdoor Art Association* 5, no. 2 (1901): 46. For a general discussion of the value of gardens in urban areas, see Lewis 1990 and "Comment: Healing in the Urban Environment. A Person/Plant Viewpoint," *American Planning Association Journal* 45, no. 3 (July 1979): 330–38. For a discussion of the relationship of gardening to personal satisfaction, see Kaplan 1973; and Kaplan 1983, 148–53.

10. See, in particular, Jensen's discussion of playgrounds for schools and neighborhood centers (1920, 45–53).

11. The literature relating the importance of natural environment to play is extensive. See Moore and Young 1978; Tuan 1978; Harvey 1988; Moore 1989; Talbot and Frost 1989; Louv 1990, 173–74. An issue of *Children's Environments Quarterly* has been devoted to children and outdoor landscapes; see Moore and Schneekloth (1989). The "Learning through Landscapes" research project was documented in a series of articles in the June 1989 issue of *Landscape Design;* see Denton-Thompson (12–15); Adams (16–19); Butler (22–23); Humphries and Rowe (25–28); Green (29–30); and King and Ball (32–33).

12. The first meeting of the institute was held in September 1990.

13. Hightshoe 1988, 364. Hightshoe makes many references to Jensen, using his work and writings as a model for working with native plants (361–69). For a discussion of urban tree planting, see Urban, Sievert, and Patterson 1989; and Perry and Hennen 1989. For more sustainable approaches to designing urban vegetation, see Hough 1984, 125–60; and Fairbrother 1974, 52–68.

14. Morrison 1987, 160, 167–68.

15. At Lincoln Memorial Garden, Jensen relied heavily on Harriet (Mrs. T. J.) Knudson for implementing his design. He noted that one of the most difficult tasks for a "Landscape Composer" was "to give the client his vision" (Jens Jensen to Mrs. T. J. Knudson, 14 October 1935). For a discussion of management recommendations for Lincoln Memorial Garden, see Grese 1984.

16. Bailey 1916, 10–31; Leopold 1949, 201–26. Nash (1989) records the history of the development of environmental ethics, and Berry (1988) offers an eloquent plea for the future. The current bioregional philosophy has been articulated by Sale (1985). The ideals of bioregionalism are described by Zuckerman (1987); and Hough (1990) presents similar principles for regional design. Hiss (1990, 27–52, 186–220) describes the bioregional attitude as "connectedness."

17. Jordan 1986. Several recent books on landscape design have suggested approaches to developing holistic design strategies. Of particular note are Hough 1984, Hough 1990, and Lyle 1985.

Bibliography

Adams, Eileen. 1989. "Learning through Landscapes." *Landscape Design* 181 (June): 16–19.

Addams, Jane. 1910. *Twenty Years at Hull-House*. New York: Macmillan Co.

Alexander, H. C. 1896. "Parks and Park Roads." *Journal of the Western Society of Engineers* 1, no. 5 (October): 649–59.

American Scenic and Historical Preservation Society. 1916. *Twenty-first Annual Report of the American Scenic and Historical Preservation Society*. Albany, N.Y.: J. B. Lyons Co.

———. 1917. *Twenty-second Annual Report of the American Scenic and Historical Preservation Society*. Albany, N.Y.: J. B. Lyons Co.

American Society of Landscape Architects. 1931, 1932, 1933, 1934. *Illustrations of Work of Members*. New York: House of Hayden Twiss.

Andreas, Alfred Theodore. 1886. *History of Chicago*. Vol. 3, *1871–1885*. Chicago: A. T. Andreas Co.

Appelbaum, Stanley. 1980. *The Chicago World's Fair of 1893: A Photographic Record*. New York: Dover Publications.

"Architects and Landscape Architects." *Architectural Record* 12, no. 7 (December 1902): 762–64.

Badger, Reid. 1979. *The Great American Fair: The World's Columbian Exposition and American Culture*. Chicago: Nelson Hall.

Bailey, Liberty Hyde. 1916. *The Holy Earth*. New York: Charles Scribner's Sons.

Baker, Paul R. 1985. "Richard Morris Hunt." In *Master Builders: A Guide to the Famous American Architects*, edited by Diane Maddex, 88–91. Washington, D.C.: The National Trust for Historic Preservation.

Batey, Mavis. 1982. "The Evolution of the English Landscape Park." *Landscape Research* 7, no. 1 (Spring): 2–8.

———. 1984. "The High Phase of English Landscape Gardening." In *British and American Gardens in the Eighteenth Century*, edited by Robert Maccubbin and Peter Martin, 44–50. Williamsburg, Va.: Colonial Williamsburg Foundation.

Begtrup, Holger, Hans Lund, and Peter Manniche. 1936. *The Folk High Schools of Denmark and the Development of a Farming Community*. London: Oxford University Press.

Beiswanger, William L. 1984. "The Temple in the Garden: Thomas Jefferson's Vision of the Monticello Landscape." In *British and American Gardens in the Eighteenth Century*, edited by Robert Maccubbin and Peter Martin, 170–88. Williamsburg, Va.: Colonial Williamsburg Foundation.

Berry, Thomas. 1988. *The Dream of the Earth*. San Francisco: Sierra Club Books.

Beveridge, Charles E. 1977. "Frederick Law Olmsted's Theory on Landscape Design." *Nineteenth Century* 3, no. 2 (Summer): 38–43.

———. 1983. Introduction to *The Papers of Frederick Law Olmsted*, vol. 3, *Creating Central Park, 1857–1861*, edited by Charles E. Beveridge and David Schuyler, 1–48. Baltimore: Johns Hopkins University Press.

Beveridge, Charles E., and David Schuyler, eds. 1983. *The Papers of Frederick Law Olmsted*, vol. 3, *Creating Central Park, 1857–1861*. Baltimore: Johns Hopkins University Press.

"The Biggest Park Conservatory in America." *Park and Cemetery* 23, no. 4 (June 1913): 74.

Bluestone, Daniel M. 1984. "Landscape and Culture in Nineteenth-Century Chicago." Ph.D. diss., University of Chicago.

Bogart, Michele H. 1989. *Public Sculpture and the Civic Ideal in New York City, 1890–1930*. Chicago: University of Chicago Press.

Bratton, Susan P. 1988. "The Management of Historic Ecosystems and Landscapes in National Parks." In *Proceedings of the Conference on Science in the National Parks*, vol. 4, *Vegetation Change and Historic Landscape Management*, 3–43. Washington, D.C.: George Wright Society and U.S. National Park Service.

Brennan, Flora. 1987. *Pückler's Progress*. London: Collins.

Brennan, George A. 1923. *The Wonders of the Dunes*. Indianapolis, Ind.: Bobbs-Merrill Co.

Brooks, H. Allen. 1972. *The Prairie School: Frank Lloyd Wright and His Midwest Contemporaries*. Toronto: University of Toronto Press.

Bruegmann, Robert. 1991. *Holabird & Roche and Holabird & Root: An Illustrated Catalog of Works, 1880–1945*. Chicago: Garland Publishing Co.

Bryant, William Cullen. 1851. *Letters of a Traveller; or, Notes of Things Seen in Europe and America*. New York.

Buder, Stanley. 1990. *Visionaries and Planners: The Garden City Movement and the Modern Community*. New York: Oxford University Press.

Burg, David F. 1976. *Chicago's White City of 1893*. Lexington: University Press of Kentucky.

Burnham, Daniel H., and Edward H. Bennett. [1909] 1970. *Plan of Chicago*, edited by Charles H. Moore. New York: Da Capo Press.

Burnham, Daniel H., and Francis D. Millett. 1894. *World's Columbian Exposition: The Book of the Builders*. Chicago: Columbian Memorial Publication Society.

Butler, Kirsty. 1989. "Environmental Education at St. Luke's." *Landscape Design* 181 (June): 22–23.

Caparn, Harold A. 1903. "Informal Garden Art." *Architectural Record* 13, no. 3 (March): 265–66.

———. 1912. "Central Park: A Work of Art." *Landscape Architecture* 2, no. 4 (July): 168–69.

———. 1929. "Thoughts on Planting Composition." *Landscape Architecture* 19, no. 3 (April): 140–56.

Censer, Jane Turner, ed. 1986. *The Papers of Frederick Law Olmsted*. Vol. 4, *Defending the Union: The Civil War and the U.S. Sanitary Commission, 1861–1863*. Baltimore: Johns Hopkins University Press.

"The Character of the Site Is the Beginning of Architecture." *House Beautiful* 97, no. 11 (November 1955): 248–49, 292, 299–300, 302.

"Charles Platt." *Garden and Forest* 6 (5 July 1893): 290.

Chase, David B. 1973. "The Beginnings of the Landscape Tradition in America." *Historic Preservation* 25 (January–March): 35–41.

Chicago, Special Park Commission. 1901. *Report of the Special Park Commission*. Chicago: Special Park Commission.

———. 1905. *A Plea for Playgrounds*. Chicago: Special Park Commission.

Chicago, West Park Commission. 1888. *Nineteenth Annual Report of the West Chicago Park Commissioners*. Chicago: West Park Commission.

———. 1895. *Twenty-sixth Annual Report of the West Chicago Park Commissioners*. Chicago: West Park Commission.

———. 1897. *Twenty-eighth Annual Report of the West Chicago Park Commissioners*. Chicago: West Park Commission.

———. 1908. *Thirty-ninth Annual Report of the West Chicago Park Commissioners*. Chicago: West Park Commission.

———. 1916. *Forty-seventh Annual Report of the West Chicago Park Commissioners*. Chicago: West Park Commission.

———. 1918. *Forty-ninth Annual Report of the West Chicago Park Commissioners*. Chicago: West Park Commission.

———. 1919. *Fiftieth Annual Report of the West Chicago Park Commissioners*. Chicago: West Park Commission.

———. 1924. *Catalog Guide to Garfield Park Conservatory*. Chicago: West Park Commission.

Chicago Historical Society. 1991. *Prairie in the City: Naturalism in Chicago's Parks, 1870–1940*. Chicago: Chicago Historical Society.

Chicago Park District, Office of Research and Planning. 1991. "Lincoln Park Restoration and Management Plan." Chicago Park District Offices, Chicago, Ill.

Chicago Park District, Special Collections, Chicago Park District Offices, Chicago, Ill.

"Chicago's Park Sculpture Show." *Park and Cemetery* 19, no. 8 (October 1909): 127–30.

"Children and Vegetation." *Children's Environments Quarterly* 6, no. 1 (Spring 1989).

Christianson, J. R. 1982. "Scandinavia and the Prairie School: Chicago Landscape Artist Jens Jensen." *The Bridge: Journal of the Danish American Heritage Society* 5, no. 2: 5–18.

Christy, Stephen F. 1976a. "The Growth of an Artist: Jens Jensen and Landscape Architecture." Master's thesis, Department of Landscape Architecture, University of Wisconsin.

———. 1976b. "Jens Jensen: The Metamorphosis of an Artist." *Landscape Architecture* 66, no. 1 (January): 60–66.

Christy, Stephen F., Alan Pape, and William H. Tishler. 1983. "Advisory Report on the Management of the Landscape and Buildings." Unpublished report sponsored by the Friends of The Clearing, Ellison Bay, Wis. Copy available at the Morton Arboretum, Lisle, Ill.

Chubb, Percival. 1915. "The Shakespeare Tercentennary." *The Drama: A Quarterly Review of Dramatic Literature* 19 (August): 535.

Clark, Keith. 1952. *The Reminiscences of Mr. Alphons de Caluse*. Dearborn, Mich.: Ford Motor Co. Archives, Oral History Section.

Clarke, Georgia Douglas. 1915. "Wild Flowers of the North Shore." *Billerica: The North Shore Illinois Edition* 4, no. 6, pt. 2 (November): 4–7.

Cleveland, H. W. S. 1869. *The Public Grounds of Chicago: How to Give Them Character and Expression*. Chicago: Charles D. Lakey.

———. [1871] 1965. *Landscape Architecture as Applied to the Wants of the West*, edited by Roy Lubove. Pittsburgh: University of Pittsburgh Press.

Cleveland, H. W. S., and William M. R. French. 1871. *A Few Hints on Landscape Gardening in the West and the Relation of Engineering to Landscape Gardening*. Chicago: Hazlitt and Reed.

Collier, Malcolm. 1975. "Jens Jensen and Columbus Park." *Chicago History* 4, no. 4 (Winter): 225–35.

———. 1977. "Prairie Profile: Jens Jensen and the Midwest Landscape." *Morton Arboretum Quarterly* 13, no. 4: 49–55.

———. 1982. "Organizations and Ideas in the Life of Jens Jensen." Unpublished paper presented at the Annual Meeting of the National Association of Olmsted Parks, Chicago, and on file at the Jensen Collection, Morton Arboretum, Lisle, Ill.

Commission on Chicago Historical and Architectural Landmarks. 1982. "Graceland Cemetery: Preliminary Summary of Information." Unpublished report.

Condit, Carl W. 1973. *Chicago, 1910–1929: Building, Planning, and Urban Technology.* Chicago: University of Chicago Press.

Cowles, Henry C. 1899a. "The Ecological Relations of the Vegetation on the Sand Dunes of Lake Michigan." University of Chicago. Typescript.

———. 1899b. "The Ecological Relations of the Vegetation on the Sand Dunes of Lake Michigan." *Botanical Gazette* 27: 97–117, 167–202, 281–308, 361–91.

———. 1901. *The Plant Societies of Chicago and Vicinity.* Bulletin of the Geographic Society of Chicago, no. 2. Chicago: Geographic Society of Chicago.

Cranz, Galen. 1982. *The Politics of Park Design: A History of Urban Parks in America.* Cambridge, Mass.: MIT Press.

Creese, Walter L. 1985. *The Crowning of the American Landscape: Eight Great Spaces and Their Buildings.* Princeton: Princeton University Press.

Crody, Herbert. 1904. "The Layout of a Large Estate." *Architectural Record* 16, no. 6 (December): 531–35.

Cunningham, Mary. 1925. "New Uses for Native Plants." *Country Life in America* 47, no. 4 (February): 37.

"Das Haus im Garten: Ein Gartenheim in Wisconsin." *Gartenschönheit* 18 (1937): 357–59.

Davol, Ralph. 1914. *A Handbook of American Pageantry.* Taunton, Mass.: Davol Publishing Co.

Dean, Ruth. 1917. "Landscape Vegetable Gardening." *Country Life in America* 31, no. 5 (March): 45–47.

———. 1922. "A 'Swimming Hole' in Chicago." *National Municipal Review* 11, no. 5 (May): 138–40.

Deane, Walter. 1896. *Flora of the Blue Hills, Middlesex Fells, Stony Brook, and Beaver Brook Reservations.* Boston: C. M. Barrows and Co.

Denton-Thompson, Merrick. 1989. "Learning through Landscapes: The Research Project. An Introduction." *Landscape Design* 181 (June): 12.

de Wit, Wim, and William W. Tippens. 1991. "Prairie School in the Parks." In *Prairie in the City: Naturalism in Chicago's Parks, 1870–1940,* 33–41. Chicago: Chicago Historical Society.

DiCarlo, Joseph A. 1973. "Monograph on Dr. Frank A. Waugh and His Influence on the Development of the Department of Landscape Architecture and Regional Planning." University of Massachusetts.

"Die Landschaftsgärtnerei—Eine Kunst." *Gartenschönheit* 4 (1923): 68–69.

Dodson, Joseph H. 1931. "Joseph H. Dodson, Inc." *American Landscape Architect* 1, no. 4 (October): advertisement.

Doeserich, Emma, Mary Sherburne, and Anna B. Wey. 1941. *Outdoors with the Prairie Club.* Chicago: Paqui Publishers.

Doty, Carol. 1971. "About the Masque." *Morton Arboretum Quarterly* 7, nos. 1 and 2 (Spring and Summer): 8, 16–17.

[Doty, Carol]. 1987. *The Clearing: A Unique School—Will It Continue?* Ellison Bay, Wis.: The Clearing in Transition. Informational pamphlet.

Douglas, Orlando B. 1898. "The Relation of Public Parks to Public Health." In *Second Report of the American Park and Outdoor Art Association*, 123–32. Boston: Rockwell and Churchill Press.

Downing, Andrew Jackson. [1841] 1844. *A Treatise on the Theory and Practice of Landscape Gardening, Adapted to North America*. New York: Wiley and Putnam.

———. 1847. "Trees in Towns and Villages." *Horticulturist and Journal of Rural Art and Rural Taste* 1, no. 9 (March): 396.

———. 1851. "A Few Hints in Landscape Gardening." *Horticulturist and Journal of Rural Art and Rural Taste* 6, no. 11 (November): 491.

Duncan, Hugh Dalziel. 1965. *Culture and Democracy: The Struggle for Form in Society and Architecture in Chicago and the Middle West during the Life and Times of Louis Sullivan*. Chicago: Bedminster Press.

Durand, Herbert. 1923. *Taming the Wild Things*. New York: G. P. Putnam's Sons.

Eaton, Leonard K. 1960. "Jens Jensen and the Chicago School." *Progressive Architecture* 41, no. 12 (December): 144–50.

———. 1964. *Landscape Artist in America: The Life and Work of Jens Jensen*. Chicago: University of Chicago Press.

Ebner, Michael H. 1988. *Creating Chicago's North Shore: A Suburban History*. Chicago: University of Chicago Press.

Eliot, Charles. 1890. "The Waverly Oaks: A Plea for Their Preservation by the People." *Garden and Forest*, 22 February, 316–18.

———. 1893. Review of *Italian Gardens*, by Charles A. Platt. *Nation* 57, no. 1487 (28 December): 491.

———. 1902. *Charles Eliot, Landscape Architect*. Boston: Houghton Mifflin, Riverside Publishing.

Elwood, P. H., Jr., ed. 1924. *American Landscape Architecture*. New York: Architecture Book Publishing Co.

Engel, J. Ronald. 1983. *Sacred Sands: The Struggle for Community in the Indiana Dunes*. Middletown, Conn.: Wesleyan University Press.

Fairbrother, Nan. 1974. *The Nature of Landscape Design*. New York: Architectural Press.

Fair Lane: The House and Garden. 1955. Ford Motor Co. Archives. Dearborn, Mich.

Farrell, John C. 1967. *Beloved Lady: A History of Jane Addams' Ideas on Reform and Peace*. Baltimore: Johns Hopkins Press.

Fein, Albert. 1967. *Landscape into Cityscape: Frederick Law Olmsted's Plan for a Greater New York City*. Ithaca, N.Y.: Cornell University Press.

———. 1981. "The Olmsted Renaissance: A Search for National Purpose." In *Art of the Olmsted Landscape*, edited by Bruce Kelly, Gail Travis Guillet, and Mary Ellen W. Hern, 99–111. New York: Landmarks Preservation Committee and Arts Publisher, Inc.

Firth, Ian J. W. 1988. "Management of Biotic Cultural Resources." In *Proceedings of the Conference on Science in the National Parks*, vol. 4, *Vegetation Change and Historic Landscape Management*, 44–71. Washington, D.C.: George Wright Society and U.S. National Park Service.

Fitch, James Marston. 1976. "Preservation Requires Tact, Modesty, and Honesty among Designers." *Landscape Architecture* 66, no. 3 (May): 276–80.

Foght, Harold W. 1915. *Rural Denmark and Its Schools*. New York: Macmillan Co.

Frank, Glenn. 1927. "A Cry for Beauty." *Our Native Landscape* 1, no. 1 (June): 1–8.

Franklin, Kay, and Norma Schaeffer. 1982. "The Dunes Pageant of 1917." *Dunes Country Magazine* 5, no. 5 (Spring): 9–14.

————. 1983. *Duel for the Dunes: Land Use Conflicts on the Shores of Lake Michigan.* Urbana: University of Illinois Press.

Friends of Our Native Landscape (FONL). 1921. *Proposed Park Areas in the State of Illinois: A Report with Recommendations.* Chicago: Friends of Our Native Landscape.

————. 1926. *A Park and Forest Policy for Illinois.* Chicago: Friends of Our Native Landscape.

————. n.d. *Roadside Planting and Development.* Chicago: Friends of Our Native Landscape.

Fulkerson, Mertha. 1941. "Jens Jensen and The Clearing." *Parks and Recreation* 25 (November): 92–102.

————. 1958. "Jens Jensen, Friend of Our Native Landscape." *Peninsula* 3 (June): 7–11.

Fulkerson, Mertha, and Ada Corson. 1972. *The Story of The Clearing.* Chicago: Coach House Press.

Fuller, George D. 1925. *Vegetation of the Chicago Region.* Chicago: University of Chicago Press.

Funnell, Keith. 1989. "Managing Educational Landscapes." *Landscape Design* 181 (June): 13–15.

Gangeware, R. Jay. 1986. "Allegheny County Parks." *Carnegie Magazine* 58, no. 4 (July/August): 12–22.

Gelbloom, Mara. 1975. "Ossian Simonds: Prairie Spirit in Landscape Gardening." *Prairie School Review* 12, no. 2: 5–18.

Gillette, E. Genevieve. Archives. Bentley Historical Library, University of Michigan, Ann Arbor, Mich.

Gilpin, William. 1791. *Remarks on Forest Scenery and Other Woodland Views, Relative Chiefly to Picturesque Beauty, Illustrated for the Scenes of New Forest in Hampshire.* London: R. Blamire.

Glassberg, David. 1990. *American Historical Pageantry: The Uses of Tradition in the Early Twentieth Century.* Chapel Hill: University of North Carolina Press.

Goodman, Kenneth Sawyer. 1971. "A Masque [later called 'The Beauty of the Wild' by the Friends]." *Morton Arboretum Quarterly* 7, nos. 1 and 2 (Spring and Summer): 9–15.

Gordon, Constance, and Kathy Hussey-Arnston, eds. 1989. *A Breath of Fresh Air: Chicago's Neighborhood Parks of the Progressive Reform Era, 1900–1925.* Chicago: Chicago Park District.

Gothein, Marie Luise. [1928] 1966. *History of Garden Art,* vol. 2. Edited by Walter P. Wright, translated by Mrs. Archer-Hind. New York: Hacker Art Books.

Green, John. 1989. "The Norton School Conservation Project." *Landscape Design* 181 (June): 29–30.

Greene, Henry C., and John T. Curtis. 1953. "The Re-establishment of an Artificial Prairie at the University of Wisconsin Arboretum." *Wild Flower* 29: 77–78.

Grese, Robert E. 1984. "A Process for the Interpretation and Management of a Designed Landscape: The Landscape Art of Jens Jensen at Lincoln Memorial Garden, Springfield, Illinois." Master's thesis, Department of Landscape Architecture, University of Wisconsin.

————. 1989. "Ossian Cole Simonds." In *American Landscape Architecture,* edited by William H. Tishler, 74–77. Washington, D.C.: Preservation Press.

Groves, Judith, and Melinda Kweder, eds. 1975. *Abraham Lincoln Memorial Garden: Interviews with Berta Cochran, Margaret Gaule, Mollie Gray, Homer McLaren, Jeanette Sayer, and Milton Thompson.* Springfield, Ill.: Oral History Office, Sangamon State University.

Haglund, Karl. 1976. "Rural Tastes, Rectangular Ideas, and the Skirmishes of H. W. S. Cleveland." *Landscape Architecture* 66, no. 1 (January): 67–70, 78.

Halsey, Elizabeth. 1940. *The Development of Public Recreation in Metropolitan Chicago.* Chicago: Chicago Recreation Commission.

Hamblin, Stephen. 1922. "Increasing Native Perennials." *Landscape Architecture* 13, no. 1 (October): 1–18.

Hans, Egbert. 1938. "Warren H. Manning." *Parks and Recreation* 21, no. 11 (July): 561–63.

Harvard University, Graduate School of Design. Microfilms Collection. Warren H. Frances Loeb Library, Cambridge, Mass.

Harvey, Margaret. 1988. "Children's Experiences with Vegetation, Their General Attitudes to Vegetation, and Their Environmental Dispositions." Master's thesis, Department of Landscape Architecture, University of Wisconsin.

Heckscher, August. 1974. *Alive in the City: Memoirs of an Ex-Commissioner.* New York: Charles Scribner's Sons.

Henderson, Harold. 1985. "To Make the Prairie Speak: The Life and Art of a Forgotten Prophet, Chicago Landscape Architect Jens Jensen." *Reader,* 25 October, 22, 24–25.

Highland Park Historic Preservation Commission. 1988. *Highland Park, Illinois: Historic Landscape Survey, Final Report.* Highland Park, Ill.: Park District of Highland Park and the Illinois Historic Preservation Agency.

Hightshoe, Gary. 1988. *Native Trees, Shrubs, and Vines for Urban and Rural America: A Planting Design Manual for Environmental Designers.* New York: Van Nostrand Reinhold.

Hiss, Tony. 1990. *The Experience of Place.* New York: Alfred A. Knopf.

Hokanson, Drake. 1988. *The Lincoln Highway: Main Street across America.* Iowa City: University of Iowa Press.

Horowitz, Helen Lefkowitz. 1976. *Culture and the City: Cultural Philanthropy in Chicago from the 1880s to 1917.* Lexington: University Press of Kentucky.

Hough, Michael. 1984. *City Form and Natural Process.* New York: Van Nostrand Reinhold.

———. 1990. *Out of Place: Restoring Identity to the Regional Landscape.* New Haven, Conn.: Yale University Press.

House Beautiful 3, no. 1 (December 1897): 29.

Howett, Catherine M. 1982. "Frank Lloyd Wright and American Residential Landscaping." *Landscape* 26, no. 1: 33–40.

———. 1983. "Landscape Research: Keeping the Faith with Today and Tomorrow." In *Yearbook of Landscape Architecture: Historic Preservation,* edited by Richard Austin, Thomas Kane, Robert Z. Melnick, and Suzanne Turner, 3–7. New York: Van Nostrand Reinhold.

Hubbard, Henry Vincent, and Theodora Kimball. [1917] 1959. *Introduction to the Study of Landscape Architecture.* Boston: Cuneo Press.

Hubbard, Theodora Kimball. 1930. "H. W. S. Cleveland: An American Pioneer in Landscape Architecture and City Planning." *Landscape Architecture* 20, no. 2 (January): 92–111.

Hubbert, Edith. 1935. "America's First Shakespeare Garden." Unpublished manuscript, Jensen Collection, Morton Arboretum, Lisle, Ill.

Humphries, Susan, and Susan Rowe. 1989. "A Landscape for Life: The Coombes County Infant School." *Landscape Design* 181 (June): 25–28.

Hunt, John Dixon. 1978. *The Figure in the Landscape: Poetry, Painting, and Gardening during the Eighteenth Century.* Baltimore: Johns Hopkins University Press.

Hunt, John Dixon, and Peter Willis, eds. 1975. *The Genius of the Place: The English Landscape Garden, 1620–1820*. London: Paul Elek.

Hunter, John Michael. 1985. *Land into Landscape*. London: George Godwin.

Huth, Hans. 1957. *Nature and the American*. Lincoln: University of Nebraska Press.

Illinois. Board of State Park Advisers. 1932. *Report of the System of State Parks in Illinois*. Springfield, Ill.: Board of State Park Advisors.

———. State Planning Commission. n.d. *Illinois Park, Parkway, and Recreational Area Plan*. Chicago: Illinois State Planning Commission.

"In the Interest of General Outdoor Improvement." *Bulletin of the American Park and Outdoor Art Association* 5, no. 2 (1901): 46.

Jackson, John Brinkerhoff. 1972. *American Space: The Centennial Years, 1865–1878*. New York: W. W. Norton and Co.

Jefferson, Thomas. 1944. *Thomas Jefferson's Garden Book, 1766–1824, with Relevant Extracts from His Other Writings*. Annotated by Edwin M. Betts. Philadelphia: American Philosophical Society.

Jensen, James. 1899. "Transplanting Trees during Mid-Winter." *Park and Cemetery* 8, no. 12 (February): 238–39.

———. 1900a. "Azalea mollis and Ghent Varieties." *Park and Cemetery* 10, no. 5 (July): 103.

———. 1900b. "Eleagnus angfustifolia (Russian olive)." *Park and Cemetery* 10, no. 4 (June): 66.

———. 1900c. "Magnolia soulangiana." *Park and Cemetery* 10, no. 3 (May): 69.

———. 1900d. "The Symmetrical and the Natural Flower Garden." *Park and Cemetery* 10, no. 7 (September): 160.

———. 1901. "Plan for Hospital Grounds." *Park and Cemetery* 11, no. 10 (December): 185–86.

———. 1902a. "Parks and Politics." *Sixth Volume of the American Park and Outdoor Art Association* 6, no. 4: 11–14.

———. 1902b. "Topiary Gardening." *Park and Cemetery* 12, no. 5 (July): 320.

Jensen, Jens. Collection. Art and Architecture Library, University of Michigan, Ann Arbor.

———. Collection. Morton Arboretum, Lisle, Ill.

———. 1903. "Urban and Suburban Landscape Gardening." *Park and Cemetery* 13, no. 1 (March): 1.

———. 1904. "Soil Conditions and Tree Growth around Lake Michigan." *Park and Cemetery* 14, nos. 2–3 (April–May): 24–25, 42.

———. 1905. "Original Designs for Bulb Beds." *The Garden Magazine* 2, no. 3 (October): 122–24.

———. 1906a. "Ideal Edging Plants for Walks and Flower Beds." *The Garden Magazine* 3, no. 3 (April): 36–38.

———. 1906b. "Landscape Art: An Inspiration from Our Western Plains." *Sketchbook* 6: 21–28.

———. 1908a. "Beauty and Fitness in Park Concrete Work." *Park and Cemetery* 18, no. 9 (November): 435–37.

———. 1908b. "Chicago Playgrounds and Park Centers." *City Club Bulletin* 2, no. 1 (4 March): 10–11.

———. 1908c. "Object Lesson in Placing Park Sculpture." *Park and Cemetery* 18, no. 9 (November): 438.

———. 1908d. "Some Gardens of the Middle West." *Architectural Review* 15, no. 5 (May): 11–13.

————. 1911a. "Introduction to Thomas Mawson." *City Club Bulletin* 4, no. 23 (21 November): 263–64, 269.

————. 1911b. "Regulating City Building." *Survey* (18 November): 1203–5.

————. 1912. "Discussion Following Address by Enos A. Mills, 'Conservation of Natural Scenery.'" *City Club Bulletin* 3 (14 February): 41.

————. 1913. "Landscape Gardening in the Middle West." *Park and Cemetery* 22, no. 12 (February): 303.

————. 1916a. *Report to the Woman's League for the Protection of Riverside Park on the Proposed Changes in the New York Central Railroad along the Hudson.* New York Public Library, IRGC p.v. 46: 5 (29 November).

————. 1916b. "A Shakespeare Garden Plan." *The Garden Magazine* 23 (April): 168.

————. 1917. "Report of Mr. Jens Jensen, Consulting Landscape Architect on the Design of Columbus Park." In *Forty-ninth Annual Report of the West Chicago Park Commissioners*, 16–18. Chicago: West Park Commission.

————. 1918. "Report of Mr. Jens Jensen, Consulting Landscape Architect, on His Plan for the Greater West Park System." In *Fiftieth Annual Report of the West Chicago Park Commissioners*, 13–20. Chicago: West Park Commission.

————. 1920. *A Greater West Park System.* Chicago: West Park Commission.

————. 1921a. Foreword to *Proposed Park Areas in the State of Illinois: A Report with Recommendations*, by Friends of Our Native Landscape. Chicago: FONL.

————. 1921b. "The Preservation of Our River Courses and Their Natural Setting." In *Proposed Park Areas in the State of Illinois: A Report with Recommendations*, by Friends of Our Native Landscape, 115–20. Chicago: FONL.

————. 1923. "Preserve Water Courses." *Parks and Recreation* 6, no. 4 (March–April): 340–42.

————. 1924a. "Highway Beauty." *Roycroft*, March, 26–28.

————. 1924b. "Roadside Planting." *Landscape Architecture* 14, no. 3 (April): 186–87.

————. 1925. "Amerikanische Gartengedanken." *Gartenschönheit* 6, no. 8 (August): 148.

————. 1926. "The Park Policy." In *A Park and Forest Policy for Illinois*, by Friends of Our Native Land, 11–15. Chicago: FONL.

————. 1927. "Nature the Source." *Vista*, Spring, 8–9.

————. 1930. "The Naturalistic Treatment in a Metropolitan Park." *American Landscape Architecture* 2, no. 1 (January): 34–38.

————. 1939. *Siftings.* Chicago: Ralph Fletcher Seymour.

————. [1939] 1990. *Siftings.* Reprint. Baltimore: Johns Hopkins University Press.

————. 1956. *"Siftings," the Major Portion of "The Clearing," and Collected Writings.* Chicago: Ralph Fletcher Seymour.

————. n.d. *The Voice of The Clearing.* Ellison Bay, Wis.: The Clearing.

Jensen, Jens, and Ragna B. Eskil. 1930. "Natural Parks and Gardens." *Saturday Evening Post* 202, no. 36 (March 8): 18–19, 169–70.

Jensen, Jens, and Hedwig Fischmann. 1923. "Die Landschaftsgärtnerei—eine Kunst." *Gartenschönheit* 4, no. 4 (April): 68–69.

Jensen, Jens, and Michael Mappes. 1937a. "Die 'Lichtung.'" *Gartenkunst* 50, no. 9 (September): 177–81.

————. 1937b. "Grundsätzliches meiner Park- und Landschaftsgestaltung." *Gartenkunst* 50, no. 9 (September): 182–87.

Jensen, Jens, and Camillo Schneider. 1937. "Das Haus im Garten ein Gartenheim in Wisconsin." *Gartenschönheit* 18, no. 8 (August): 357–59.

Johnston, T. T. 1896. "Parks and Park Roads." *Journal of the Western Society of Engineers* 1, no. 5 (October): 653–56.

Jones, W. Glyn. 1986. *Denmark: A Modern History.* London: Croom Helm.

Jordan, William R. 1986. "Restoration and the Reentry of Nature." *Orion Nature Quarterly* 5, no. 2 (Spring): 14–25.

Jordan, William R., III, Michael E. Gilpin, and John D. Aber, eds. 1987. *Restoration Ecology: A Synthetic Approach to Ecological Research.* New York: Cambridge University Press.

Kaplan, Rachel. 1973. "Some Psychological Benefits of Gardening." *Environment and Behavior* 5: 145–62.

———. 1983. "The Role of Nature in the Urban Environment." In *Behavior and the Natural Environment,* edited by Irvin Altman and Joachim F. Wohlwill, 127–61. New York: Plenum Press.

Kaplan, Rachel, and Stephen Kaplan. 1989. *The Experience of Nature: A Psychological Perspective.* New York: Oxford University Press.

Keating, Ann Durkin. 1988. *Building Chicago: Suburban Developers and the Creation of a Divided Metropolis.* Columbus: Ohio State University Press.

Kelly, Bruce. 1981. "Art of the Olmsted Landscape." In *Art of the Olmsted Landscape,* edited by Bruce Kelly, Gail Travis Guillet, and Mary Ellen W. Hern, 1–86. New York: Landmarks Preservation Committee and Arts Publisher, Inc.

Kelly, Bruce, Gail Travis Guillet, and Mary Ellen W. Hern. 1981. *Art of the Olmsted Landscape.* New York: Landmarks Preservation Committee and Arts Publisher, Inc.

Kimball, Fiske. 1919. "The Social Center." *Architectural Record* 46, no. 1 (July): 29–46.

King, Karen, and David Ball. 1989. "Playing Safe." *Landscape Design* 181 (June): 32–33.

Koch, Hugo. 1914. *Gartenkunst im Stadtebau.* Berlin: Ernst Wasmuth Verlag.

Kowsky, Francis R. 1986. "The Central Park Gateways: Harbingers of French Urbanism Confront the American Landscape Tradition." In *The Architecture of Richard Morris Hunt,* edited by Susan R. Stein, 79–89. Chicago: University of Chicago Press.

Lathrop, Bryan. 1903. "Parks and Landscape Gardening." *Sixth Volume of the American Park and Outdoor Art Association* 6, no. 4: 7–10.

Laurie, Michael. 1979. "Nature and City Planning in the Nineteenth Century." In *Nature in Cities,* edited by Ian C. Laurie, 58–63. Chichester, England: John Wiley and Sons.

Lay, Charles Downing. 1920. "What the Nurseries Should Grow." *Landscape Architecture* 10, no. 3 (April): 149–52.

Leopold, Aldo. 1949. *Sand County Almanac.* New York: Oxford University Press.

Levinsohn, Florence Hamlish. 1987. "Hidden Treasures: A Cache of Historic Blueprints Could Usher in Another Golden Age for Chicago Parks." *Chicago Tribune,* Sunday Magazine, 22 March, 10–18, 31–39.

Lewis, Charles A. 1972. "Public Housing Gardens: Landscapes for the Soul." In *Landscapes for Living,* edited by Jack Hayes, 277–82. Yearbook of Agriculture. Washington, D.C.: U.S. Department of Agriculture.

———. 1979. "Healing in the Urban Environment: A Person/Plant Viewpoint." *American Planning Association Journal* 45, no. 3 (July): 330–38.

———. 1990. "Gardens as Healing Process." In *The Meaning of Gardens: Idea, Place, and Action,* edited by Mark Francis and Randolph T. Hester, Jr., 244–51. Cambridge, Mass.: MIT Press.

Lincoln Highway Archives. Department of Rare Books and Special Collections, University Library, University of Michigan, Ann Arbor.

Lincoln Highway Association. 1935. *The Lincoln Highway: The Story of a Crusade That Made Transportation History.* New York: Dodd, Mead and Co.

"The Lincoln Memorial Garden." *Garden Glories,* September 1938, 4–5.

Lincoln Memorial Garden Archives. Lincoln Memorial Garden Nature Center, Springfield, Ill.

Little, Charles E. 1990. *Greenways for America.* Baltimore: Johns Hopkins University Press.

Lohmann, Karl B. 1926a. "Landscape Architecture in the Middle West." *Landscape Architecture* 16, no. 3 (April): 157–68.

———. 1926b. *Twenty-seventh Annual Meeting, American Society of Landscape Architects.* Boston: American Society of Landscape Architects.

Louv, Richard. 1990. *Childhood's Future.* Boston: Houghton Mifflin.

Lowell, Guy, ed. 1901. *American Gardens.* Boston: Bates and Guild Co.

Lubove, Roy. 1963. *Community Planning in the 1920s: The Contribution of the Regional Planning Association of America.* Pittsburgh: University of Pittsburgh Press.

Lyle, John Tillman. 1985. *Design for Human Ecosystems.* New York: Van Nostrand Reinhold.

Lynes, Russell. 1954. *The Tastemakers.* New York: Grosset and Dunlap.

Maccubbin, Robert P., and Maccubbin, Peter, eds. 1984. *British and American Gardens in the Eighteenth Century.* Williamsburg, Va.: Colonial Williamsburg Foundation.

Manning, Owen. 1979. "Designing for Nature in Cities." In *Nature in Cities,* edited by Ian C. Laurie, 3–36. Chichester, England: John Wiley and Sons.

Manning, Warren H. 1899. *A Handbook for Planning and Planting Small Home Grounds.* Menomonie, Wis.: Stout Manual Training School.

———. 1908. "The Two Kinds of Bog Garden." *Country Life in America* 14, no. 4 (August): 379–80.

———. 1915. "Wild Flower Preserves." *Billerica, the North Shore Illinois Edition* 4, no. 6, pt. 2 (November): 3.

———. 1930. "The Citizen-Making Crafts of Illinois." Unpublished paper dated 14 February.

Mappes, Michael. 1937a. "Die Lichtung." *Gartenkunst* 50, no. 9 (September): 177–81.

———. 1937b. "Grundsatzliches meiner Park- und Landschaftsgestaltung." *Gartenkunst* 50, no. 9 (September): 182–87.

Marx, Leo. 1964. *The Machine and the Garden.* London: Oxford University Press.

Mather, Stephen K. 1917. *Report on the Proposed Sand Dunes National Park, Indiana.* Washington, D.C.: U.S. National Park Service.

Mayer, Harold M., and Richard C. Wade. 1969. *Chicago: The Growth of a Metropolis.* Chicago: University of Chicago Press.

McAdam, Thomas. 1911. "Landscape Gardening under Glass." *Country Life in America* 21, no. 4 (December): 10–13, 50–51.

McArthur, Benjamin. 1989. "Parks, Playgrounds, and Progressivism." In *A Breath of Fresh Air: Chicago's Neighborhood Parks of the Progressive Reform Era, 1900–1925,* 9–14. Chicago: Chicago Park District.

McCarthy, Kathleen D. 1982. *Noblesse Oblige: Charity and Cultural Philanthropy in Chicago, 1849–1929.* Chicago: University of Chicago Press.

McFarland, J. Horace. 1899. "An American Garden." *Outlook,* 7 October, 327–33.

McLaughlin, Jack. 1988. *Jefferson and Monticello.* New York: Henry Holt and Co.

Meier, Lauren G. 1991. "National Programs in Historic Landscape Preservation." in *Prairie in the City: Naturalism in Chicago's Parks, 1870–1940,* 42–46. Chicago: Chicago Historical Society.

Millard, Everett L. 1915. "A Municipal Wild Flower Preserve." *Billerica: The North Shore Illinois Edition* 4, no. 6, pt. 2 (November): 7–8.

Miller, Charles A. 1988. *Jefferson and Nature: An Interpretation.* Baltimore: Johns Hopkins University Press.

Miller, Wilhelm. Papers. Unversity Archives, University Library, University of Illinois, Urbana.

————. 1912a. "Have We Progressed in Gardening?" *Country Life in America* 21, no. 12 (15 April): 26.

————. 1912b. "What Is the Matter with Our Water Gardens?" *Country Life in America* 22, no. 4 (15 June): 23–26, 54.

————. 1912c. "Sixty Suggestions for New Gardens." *The Garden Magazine* 16, no. 5 (December): 198–99.

————. 1914a. "Bird Gardens in the City." *Country Life in America* 26, no. 4 (August): 46–47.

————. 1914b. *The Illinois Way of Beautifying the Farm.* Circular no. 170, Agricultural Experiment Station, Department of Horticulture, University of Illinois, Urbana.

————. 1914c. "A Series of Outdoor Salons." *Country Life in America* 25, no. 6 (April): 39–40.

————. 1915. *The Prairie Spirit in Landscape Gardening.* Circular no. 184, Agricultural Experiment Station, Department of Horticulture, University of Illinois, Urbana.

————. 1916. "The Prairie Style of Landscape Architecture." *Architectural Record* 40, no. 6 (December): 590–92.

Moore, Robin C. 1989. "Playgrounds at the Crossroads." In *Public Places and Spaces,* edited by Irwin Altman and Ervin H. Zube, 83–120. New York: Plenum Press.

Moore, Robin C., and Donald Young. 1978. "Childhood Outdoors: Toward a Social Ecology of the Landscape." In *Children and the Environment,* edited by Irwin Altman and Joachim F. Wohlwill, 83–130. New York: Plenum Press.

Morgan, Keith N. 1985. *Charles A. Platt: The Artist as Architect.* Cambridge, Mass.: MIT Press.

Morris, John W. 1989. "The Henry Ford Estate, Fair Lane: A Landscape Restoration and Management Plan." Master's thesis, School of Natural Resources, University of Michigan.

Morrison, Darrel G. 1987. "Landscape Restoration in Response to Previous Disturbance." In *Landscape Heterogeneity and Disturbance,* edited by Monica Goigal Turner, 159–72. New York: Springer-Verlag.

Morse, Frances R. 1902. "Society for the Protection of Native Plants." *Sixth Volume of the American Park and Outdoor Art Association* 6, no. 1: 63.

Mumford, Lewis. 1925. "Regions—To Live In." *Survey Graphic* 7 (May): 151–52.

"Must Educate Youth to Love Native Land: Jensen." *Capitol Times* (Madison, Wis.), 28 March 1944.

Nash, Roderick. 1989. *The Rights of Nature.* Madison: University of Wisconsin Press.

Needham, Mary Master. 1912. *Folk Festivals: Their Growth and How to Give Them.* New York: B. W. Huebsch.

Newton, Norman T. 1971. *Design on the Land.* Cambridge, Mass.: Harvard University Press, Belknap Press.

Oakley, Stewart. 1972. *A Short History of Denmark.* New York: Praeger Publishers.

Olmsted, Frederick Law. [1852] 1967. *Walks and Talks of an American Farmer in England.* Ann Arbor: University of Michigan Press.

————. [1870] 1970. *Public Parks and the Enlargement of Towns.* Reprint. New York: Arno Press and New York Times.

————. 1888. "Foreign Plants and American Scenery." *Garden and Forest* 1 (October): 418.

————. 1895. "Parks, Parkways, and Pleasure Grounds." *Engineering Magazine* 9, no. 2 (May): 253–60.

Olmsted, Frederick Law, and J. B. Harrison. 1889. *Observations on the Treatment of*

Public Plantations, More Especially Relating to the Use of the Axe. Boston: T. R. Marvin and Son.

———. 1913. "The Use of the Axe." *Landscape Architecture* 3, no. 4 (July): 145–52.

Olmsted, Frederick Law, Jr. 1920. "Parks and Playgrounds." *American Magazine of Art* 11, no. 9 (July): 307–15.

Olmsted, Frederick Law, Jr., and Theodora Kimball, eds. [1928] 1973. *Frederick Law Olmsted, Landscape Architect, 1822–1903 (Forty Years of Landscape Architecture: Central Park).* Cambridge, Mass.: MIT Press.

O'Malley, Therese. 1986. "Landscape Gardening in the Early Period." In *Views and Visions: American Landscape before 1830*, edited by Edward J. Nygren and Bruce Robertson, 133–59. Washington, D.C.: Corcoran Gallery of Art.

Pacyga, Dominic. 1989. "Parks for People." In *A Breath of Fresh Air: Chicago's Neighborhood Parks of the Progressive Reform Era, 1900–1925*, 15–20. Chicago: Chicago Park District.

"Parks and Park Work: Chicago's Park Sculpture Show." *Park and Cemetery* 19, no. 8 (1909): 127–30.

Pattison, James William. 1911. "Gifts of Eighteen Pictures by George Inness to the Art Institute, Chicago." *Fine Arts Journal* 24, no. 4 (April): 212–22.

Peets, Elbert. 1927. "The Landscape Priesthood." *American Mercury,* January, 94–100.

Pentecost, George. 1902. "The Informal and Natural Style." *Architectural Record* 12, no. 2 (June): 174–94.

Pepoon, Herman Silas. 1927. *An Annotated Flora of the Chicago Area, with Maps and Many Illustrations from Photographs of Topographic and Plan Features.* Chicago: R. R. Donnelley and Sons.

Perkins, Dwight H. 1904. *Report of the Special Park Commission to the City Council of Chicago on the Subject of a Metropolitan Park System.* Chicago: Special Park Commission.

———. 1905. "A Metropolitan Park System for Chicago." *World Today* 8, no. 3: 271–73.

Perry, Thomas O., and Gary Hennen. 1989. "The Forest Underground." In *Shading Our Cities: A Resource Guide for Urban and Community Forests*, edited by Gary Moll and Sara Ebenreck, 80–89. Washington, D.C.: Island Press.

Peterson, Jon. 1976. "The City Beautiful Movement: Forgotten Origins and Lost Meanings." *Journal of Urban History* 12, no. 4 (August): 415–34.

Platt, Charles A. 1893. "Italian Gardens." Parts 1, 2. *Harpers New Monthly Magazine* 87, nos. 518–19 (July–August): 165–80, 393–406.

———. 1894. *Italian Gardens.* New York: Harper and Brothers.

Prairie Club Archives. Thomas Memorial Library, Chesterton, Ind.

"Prairie Club Early Park Supporter." *Singing Sands Almanac.* Chesterton, Ind.: Indiana Dunes National Lakeshore, U.S. National Park Service, 1979.

Prevots, Norma. 1990. *American Pageantry: A Movement for Art and Democracy.* Ann Arbor, Mich.: UMI Research Press.

Price, Uvedale. 1794. *An Essay on the Picturesque*, vols. 1–3. London: J. Robson.

"Proposed Metropolitan Park System for Chicago." *Park and Cemetery* 15, no. 1 (March 1905): 213–14.

Pückler-Muskau, Herman Ludwig Heinrich furst von. 1833. *The Tour in England, Ireland, and France in the Years 1828, 1829: With Remarks on the Manners and Customs of the Inhabitants, and Anecdotes of Public Characters in a Series of Letters by a German Prince.* Translated by Sarah Austin. Philadelphia: Carey and Lear.

———. [1834] 1917. *Hints on Landscape Gardening.* Translated by Bernard Sickert, edited by Samuel Parsons. Cambridge, Mass.: Houghton Mifflin, Riverside Publishing.

Pullen, Clarence. 1891. "The Parks and Parkways of Chicago." *Harper's Weekly* 35 (6 June): 412–16, 423.

Ranney, Victoria Post. 1972. *Olmsted in Chicago*. Chicago: R. R. Donnelley and Sons.

Read, Herbert P. 1986. "The Prairie Club and the Indiana Dunes." *Dunebeat* 11, no. 15 (30 October): 4–6.

Reed, Henry Hope. 1981. "Central Park: The Genius of the Place." In *Art of the Olmsted Landscape*, edited by Bruce Kelly, Gail Travis Guillet, and Mary Ellen W. Hern, 125–39. New York: Landmarks Preservation Committee and Arts Publisher, Inc.

"Reforms in the West Park System of Chicago." *Park and Cemetery* 15, no. 6 (August 1905): 329–30.

Rehmann, Elsa. 1933. "An Ecological Approach." *Landscape Architecture* 23, no. 4 (July): 239–45.

Repton, Humphry. 1795. *Sketches and Hints on Landscape Gardening*. London: W. Bulmer and Co.

———. [1803] 1980. *Observations on the Theory and Practice of Landscape Gardening*. Oxford: Phaidon Press.

———. 1907. *The Art of Landscape Gardening*. Edited by John Nolen. Cambridge, Mass.: Houghton Mifflin, Riverside Publishing.

Riis, Paul B. 1924. "Game Laws for Plants." *Parks and Recreation* 7, no. 4 (March–April): 406–7.

———. 1931. "Poetic Park Trails." *Parks and Recreation* 15, no. 1 (September): 61–72.

Roberts, Edith A. 1933. "The Development of an Ecological Laboratory for Experimental Ecology." *Ecology* 14, 2 (): 163–223.

Roberts, Edith A., and Elsa Rehmann. 1927a. "Plant Ecology: 1. The Contribution to Naturalistic Planting of This Study of Plants in Relation to Their Environment." *House Beautiful* 61, no. 6 (June): 805, 842, 844–45.

———. 1927b. "Plant Ecology: 2. Seaside Planting." *House Beautiful* 62, no. 1 (July): 46, 81, 83–84.

———. 1927c. "Plant Ecology: 3. Natural Water Gardens." *House Beautiful* 62, no. 2 (August): 133, 168–70.

———. 1927d. "Plant Ecology: 4. The Open Field." *House Beautiful* 62, no. 3 (September): 247, 294, 296–98, 300.

———. 1927e. "Plant Ecology: 5. The Juniper Association." *House Beautiful* 62, no. 4 (October): 399, 448, 450, 452, 454.

———. 1927f. "Plant Ecology: 6. Oak Woodlands." *House Beautiful* 62, no. 5 (November): 533, 578–82.

———. 1927g. "Plant Ecology: 7. The Pine Association." *House Beautiful* 62, no. 6 (December): 652.

———. 1928a. "Plant Ecology: 8. The Hemlock Ravine." *House Beautiful* 63, no. 1 (January): 74, 103–4.

———. 1928b. "Plant Ecology: 9. Beech-Maple-Hemlock Association." *House Beautiful* 63, no. 2 (February): 190, 238–40.

———. 1928c. "Plant Ecology: 10. Gray Birches." *House Beautiful* 63, no. 3 (March): 324.

———. 1928d. "Plant Ecology: 11. The Stream-Side Planting." *House Beautiful* 63, no. 4 (April): 464, 500–504.

———. 1928e. "Plant Ecology: 12. The Bog." *House Beautiful* 63, no. 5 (May): 626.

———. 1929. *American Plants for American Gardens*. New York: Macmillan Co.

Robinson, William. 1870. *The Wild Garden*. London: John Murray.

Rogers, Elizabeth Barlow. 1987. *Rebuilding Central Park: A Management and Restoration Plan.* Cambridge, Mass.: MIT Press.

Root, Ralph Rodney. 1921a. *Landscape Garden Series.* Vol. 7, *Garden Design.* Davenport, Iowa: Garden Press.

———. 1921b. *Landscape Garden Series.* Vol. 9, *Country Estates.* Davenport, Iowa: Garden Press.

Rørdam, Thomas. 1980. *The Danish Folk Schools.* Copenhagen: Det Danske Selskab.

Ryckbosch, Bart H. 1991. "Preserving the History of Landscape Design." In *Prairie in the City: Naturalism in Chicago's Parks, 1870–1940,* 6–7. Chicago: Chicago Historical Society.

Sale, Kirkpatrick. 1985. *Dwellers in the Land: The Bioregional Vision.* San Francisco: Sierra Club Books.

Sargent, Charles Sprague. 1890. "Country Roads." *Garden and Forest* 3 (13 August): 389–90.

———. 1893. "Notes." *Garden and Forest* 6 (5 July): 290.

———. 1894a. "Art and Nature." *Garden and Forest* 7 (4 July): 261.

———. 1894b. "Nature and the Rich." *Garden and Forest* 7 (27 June): 251–52.

———. 1895. "Country Roads and Roadsides." *Garden and Forest* 8 (10 July): 271–72.

———. 1897a. "Doing Too Much." *Garden and Forest* 10 (16 June): 231.

———. 1897b. "Native Plants for Ornamental Planting." *Garden and Forest* 10 (8 September): 349–50.

Schuyler, David. 1986. *The New Urban Landscape: The Redefinition of City Form in Nineteenth-Century America.* Baltimore: Johns Hopkins University Press.

Schuyler, Montgomery. 1895. "The Works of the Late Richard M. Hunt." *Architectural Record* 5 (October–December): 97–180.

"The Sculpture Show in Humboldt Park, Chicago." *Park and Cemetery* 18, no. 9 (1908): 439–40.

Sheaffer, Dean. 1987. "A Paradise Lost." *Inland Architect* 31, no. 2 (March/April): 5–6.

Shelford, Victor E., ed. 1926. *Naturalist's Guide to the Americas.* Baltimore: Williams and Wilkins Co.

Simonds, Ossian Cole. 1920. *Landscape Gardening.* New York: Macmillan Co.

———. 1921. "Cemetery Landscape Gardening." In *The Cemetery Handbook,* 66–68. Chicago: Allied Arts Publishers.

———. 1930. "Notes on Graceland." *American Landscape Architect* 2, no. 5 (May): 8–9.

———. 1932a. "Graceland at Chicago." *American Landscape Architect* 4, no. 1 (January): 12–17.

———. 1932b. "Nature as the Great Teacher in Landscape Gardening." *Landscape Architecture* 22, no. 2 (January): 100–108.

Simutis, Leonard. 1972. "Frederick Law Olmsted, Sr.: A Reassessment." *American Institute of Planning Journal* 38, no. 5 (September): 276–84.

Skovmand, Roar. 1973. "The Rise and Growth of the Danish Folk School." In *Grundtvig Studier,* edited by Gustav Albeck and William Michelsen, 85–100. Copenhagen: Danske Boghandleres Kommissionsanstalt.

Sloane, David Charles. 1991. *The Last Great Necessity: Cemeteries in American History.* Baltimore: Johns Hopkins University Press.

Smergalski, T. J. 1918. "Vegetable Gardens in Chicago Parks." *Parks and Recreation* 1, no. 3 (April): 24–27.

Smithson, Robert. 1973. "Frederick Law Olmsted and the Dialectical Landscape." *Artforum* 11 (February): 62–68.

Sniderman, Julia. 1991. "Bringing the Prairie Vision into Focus." In *Prairie in the City:*

Naturalism in Chicago's Parks, 1870–1940, 19–31. Chicago: Chicago Historical Society.

Sniderman, Julia, and Jo Ann Nathan. 1988. "Shakespeare Garden, Evanston, Ill." National Register of Historic Places Registration Form.

Sniderman, Julia, and William W. Tippens. 1990. "The Historic Resources of the Chicago Park District." National Register of Historic Places Multiple Property Documentation Form.

"Some Glimpses of Native Beauty and a Survey of the State's Scenic Resources and Public Parks." *Chicago Daily News,* 29 March 1929.

Soule, Michael. 1985. "What is Conservation Biology?" *Bioscience* 35, no. 11 (December): 727–34.

———, ed. 1986. *Conservation Biology: The Science of Scarcity and Diversity.* Sunderland, Mass.: Sinauer Associates.

Stevenson, Louise L. 1986. *Scholarly Means to Evangelical Ends: The New Haven Scholars and the Transformation of Higher Learning in America, 1830–1890.* Baltimore: Johns Hopkins University Press.

Sturgis, Russell. 1901. "Landscape Architecture." In *A Dictionary of Architecture and Building: Biographical, Historical, and Descriptive,* edited by Russell Sturgis, 696–97. New York: Macmillan Co.

Sullivan, Louis. 1924. *The Autobiography of an Idea.* New York: Press of the American Institute of Architects.

Sussman, Carl, ed. 1976. *Planning the Fourth Migration: The Neglected Vision of the Regional Planning Association of America.* Cambridge, Mass.: MIT Press.

Sutton, S. B., ed. 1971. *Civilizing American Cities: A Selection of Frederick Law Olmsted's Writings on City Landscapes.* Cambridge, Mass.: MIT Press.

Takemoto, Patricia Akiko. 1987. "The Clearing: The Growth and Survival of an American Adult Education Institution in the Danish Folk School Tradition." Ph.D. diss., Northern Illinois University, De Kalb.

Talbot, James, and Joe L. Frost. 1989. "Magical Playscapes." *Childhood Education,* Fall, 11–19.

Tippens, William W., and Julia Sniderman. 1989. "The Planning and Design of Chicago's Neighborhood Parks." In *A Breath of Fresh Air: Chicago's Neighborhood Parks of the Progressive Reform Era, 1900–1925,* 21–28. Chicago: Chicago Park District.

Tishler, William H. 1989. "H. W. S. Cleveland." In *American Landscape Architecture,* edited by William H. Tishler, 24–29. Washington, D.C.: The Preservation Press.

Tishler, William H., and Virginia Luckhardt. 1985. "H. W. S. Cleveland, Pioneer Landscape Architect to the Upper Midwest." *Minnesota History* 49, no. 7 (Fall): 281–91.

Trotter, John E. 1962. *State Park System in Illinois.* Research Paper no. 24. Chicago: University of Chicago, Department of Geography.

Tuan, Yi-Fu. 1978. "Children and the Natural Environment." In *Children and the Environment,* edited by Irwin Altman and Joachim F. Wohlwill, 5–32. New York: Plenum Press.

———. 1989. *Morality and Imagination: Paradoxes of Progress.* Madison: University of Wisconsin Press.

Turak, Theodore. 1986. *William Le Baron Jenney: A Pioneer of Modern Architecture.* Ann Arbor, Mich.: UMI Research Press.

Twombly, Robert C. 1979. *Frank Lloyd Wright: His Life and Architecture.* New York: John Wiley and Sons.

Unwin, Raymond. 1911. "Garden Cities in England." *City Club Bulletin* 4, no. 13 (7 June): 134–35.

Urban, James, Ralph C. Sievert, Jr., and James Patterson. 1989. "A Blueprint for Tomorrow: Getting Trees into Urban Forests." In *Shading Our Cities: A Resource Guide for Urban and Community Forests*, edited by Gary Moll and Sara Ebenreck, 93–101. Washington, D.C.: Island Press.

Vernon, Christopher D. 1986. "Jens Jensen Projects in Indiana." Unpublished paper.

———. 1989. "Walter Burley Griffin, Landscape Architect." Unpublished paper.

Vukelich, George. 1990. "Between Places." *Isthmus*, 21 September, 18, 22.

"Warren H. Manning, Landscape Designer: Tribute to a Pioneer in a New Profession." *Landscape Architecture* 28, no. 3 (April 1938): 148–49.

Watts, May Thielgaard. 1961. "Reading the Roof-lines of Europe." *Landscape* 10, no. 3 (Spring): 9–14.

Waugh, Frank A. Collection. University Archives, University Library, University of Massachusetts, Amherst.

———. 1899. *Landscape Gardening*. New York: Orange Judd Publishing Co.

———. 1910. *The Landscape Beautiful*. New York: Orange Judd Publishing Co.

———. 1917a. *The Natural Style in Landscape Gardening*. Boston: Richard G. Badger.

———. 1917b. *Outdoor Theaters*. Boston: Richard G. Badger.

———. 1917c. *Recreation Uses on the National Forests: A Study of Their Extent and Character, with a Discussion of Public Policies and Recommendations as to Methods of Development and Administration*. Washington, D.C.: U.S. Department of Agriculture, Forest Service.

———. 1918a. *Landscape Engineering in the National Forests*. Washington, D.C.: U.S. Department of Agriculture, Forest Service.

———. 1918b. "Technical Problems in National Park Development." *Scientific Monthly*, June, 560–67.

———. 1922. *Textbook of Landscape Gardening*. New York: John Wiley and Sons.

———. 1923. "Recreation in the National Forests." *National Municipal Review* 12, no. 6 (June): 295–98.

———. 1925. "American Ideals in Landscape Architecture." *Landscape Architecture* 15, no. 3 (April): 154.

———. 1927. *Formal Design in Landscape Architecture*. New York: Orange Judd Publishing Co.

———. 1930. "Large-scale Planning: The Mount Hood National Forest." *American Landscape Architect* 7, no. 6 (June): 20–23.

———. 1931a. "Ecology of the Roadside." *Landscape Architecture* 21, no. 2 (January): 81–92.

———. 1931b. "A Juniper Landscape." *American Landscape Architect* 5, no. 5 (November): 16–20.

———. 1931c. "Natural Plant Groups." *Landscape Architecture* 21, no. 3 (April): 169–78.

———. 1932a. "The Physiography of Lakes and Ponds." *Landscape Architecture* 22, no. 2 (January): 89–99.

———. 1932b. "Pine Woods." *American Landscape Architect* 6, no. 16 (February): 16–20.

———. 1932c. "Running Water." *Landscape Architecture* 22, no. 4 (July): 171–80.

———. 1934. "The Forest Margin." *Journal of Forestry* 32, no. 1 (January): 11–14.

———. 1936a. "Landscape Conservation: Planning the Recreational Use of Our Wild Lands," chap. 1, "Objectives." *Parks and Recreation* 19, no. 6 (February): 177–80.

———. 1936b. "Landscape Conservation: Planning the Recreational Use of Our Wild Lands," chap. 2, "Site Planning." *Parks and Recreation* 19, no. 7 (March): 229–33.

———. 1936c. "Landscape Conservation: Planning the Recreational Use of Our Wild

Lands," chap. 3, "Camps and Camping." *Parks and Recreation* 19, no. 8 (April): 272–76.

———. 1936d. "Landscape Conservation: Planning the Recreational Use of Our Wild Lands," chap. 4, "Sanitation." *Parks and Recreation* 19, no. 9 (May): 328–32.

———. 1936e. "Landscape Conservation: Planning the Recreational Use of Our Wild Lands," chap. 5, "The Forest Stand." *Parks and Recreation* 19, no. 10 (June): 379–81.

———. n.d. "Guide to the Landscape: A Textbook for Motorists, Boy Scouts, and for All Lovers of the Native Landscape, Especially for Painters and Landscape Architects." Unpublished paper, Frank A. Waugh Collection, University Archives, University Library, University of Massachusetts, Amherst.

———, ed. 1921. *Landscape Gardening: Works of Andrew Jackson Downing*. New York: John Wiley and Sons.

Weyeneth, Robert. 1983. "Reforming the Landscape of Leisure in Urban America." Ph.D. diss., University of California.

Wharton, Edith. 1903. *Italian Villas and Their Gardens*. New York: Century Co.

Wheelwright, Robert. 1919. "A Reference Table of the Native Ferns." *Landscape Architecture* 9, no. 3 (April): 128–30.

White, Stanley. 1926. "The Value of Natural Preserves to the Landscape Architect." In *Naturalist's Guide to the Americas*, edited by Victor E. Shelford, 8–9. Baltimore: Williams and Wilkins Co.

Wille, Lois. 1972. *Forever Open, Clear, and Free: The Historic Struggle for Chicago's Lakefront*. Chicago: Henry Regnery Co.

Williams, Richard. 1955. "Music and Frank Lloyd Wright." *House Beautiful* 97, no. 11 (November): 306–9, 351.

Wilson, William H. 1989. *The City Beautiful Movement*. Baltimore: Johns Hopkins University Press.

Windesheim, Susan D. 1975. "Jens Jensen as Planner." Master's thesis, Illinois Institute of Technology, Chicago.

Wisconsin. Door County. *Park Board Report*. December 1945.

Worster, Donald. 1977. *Nature's Economy: The Roots of Ecology*. San Francisco: Sierra Club Books.

Wright, Frank Lloyd. 1941. *Frank Lloyd Wright on Architecture: Selected Writings*. Edited by Frederick Futheim. New York: Duell, Sloan, and Pearl.

"Wright as a Landscape Architect." *House Beautiful* 97, no. 11 (November 1955): 342–47.

Yeomans, Alfred B. 1916. *City Residential Land Development*. Chicago: University of Chicago Press.

Zuckerman, Seth. 1987. "Living There: Call It a Bioregion, a Watershed, or a Life-Place, Your Backyard by Any Other Name Is Just as Sweet." *Sierra* 72, no. 2 (March–April): 61–67.

Zueblin, Charles. 1898. "Municipal Playgrounds in Chicago." *American Journal of Sociology*, September, 146–48.

Index

95; Municipal Art League of Chicago, 120; Municipal Science Club, 43, 120; Outdoor Art League, 120; Prairie Club, 120–22, 124–28, 197
—conservation, 1–2, 135; CCC, 136; Door County, Wis., *Park Board Report*, 135–36; Illinois state parks, 128–33, 172; Indiana Dunes, 121–22, 124–29, 197; Mississippi River Park Commission, 135; relation of design to, 197–98; Ridges Sanctuary, 135; Riverside Park, 135; roadsides, 134; Special Park Commission, 64–67; TVA, 136; use of drama to promote, 122, 124, 127–28, 178, 197; wildlife, 81, 86, 92, 98, 101, 130, 152, 172
—estates and gardens: Aldrich (Bloomington, Ill.), 158, 166; Alexander (Spring Station, Ky.), 25, 174–75, 180–81; Babson (Glencoe, Ill.), 38, 47, 99, 158; Becker (Highland Park, Ill.), 172–73; Booth (Glencoe, Ill.), 47; Clarke (Evanston, Ill.), 99; Dahlinger Farm (Romeo, Mich.), 102; Ford (Edsel) (Detroit, Mich.), 102, 182–83; Ford (Edsel) (Grosse Pointe Shores, Mich.), 102, 152, 157–58, 160, 162–63, 174, 180, 182; Ford (Edsel) (Seal Harbor, Maine), 102, 184; Ford (Henry) (Dearborn, Mich.), 50, 100–102, 159–60, 164–65, 174; Frawley (Bloomington, Ind.), 159–60; Kanzler (Detroit, Mich.), 102; Kanzler (Grosse Pointe Shores, Mich.), 102; Lepine (Dearborn, Mich.), 102; Magnus (Winnetka, Ill.), 47; Maher (Kenilworth, Ill.), 95; Roberts (Marquette, Mich.), 47–48; Rosenwald (Highland Park, Ill.), 99–100; Rubens (Glencoe, Ill.), 47–95, 96–98, 160–61, 166; Simms (Spring Station, Ky.), 25, 161, 169, 173, 174–75; Uihlein (Lake Geneva, Wis.), 95; Vandeventer (Knoxville, Tenn.), 184
—landscape design: as art, 51, 61, 71, 93, 96–98, 102, 152–53, 155, 156, 158–59, 166, 180, 188–89, 191, 197; bioregionalism, 197–98; clearings, 98, 136, 138–39, 166–68, 178–79; council rings, 82, 92, 98, 114–15, 139, 148, 176–78; cultural associations, 48, 71, 88, 126, 128–30, 135–36, 138–39, 170, 176, 179, 182, 184–85, 272n.127; formal gardens, 5–6, 28, 95–96, 99, 156, 168,

180–82, 273n.39; hawthorn trees, 156–58, 163, 173; management as part of, 190, 274n.6; manipulation of space, 160–61; meadow, 161; moonlight, 82, 138–39, 172–73, 179; movement, 168–72; music, 44, 72–73, 98, 178–79, 266n.13; native landscape influences, 2–3, 7–9, 28, 45, 52–53, 64–67, 76, 96–98, 159, 197, 258n.12; native plants, 7–9, 28, 48–49, 52–53, 80, 96–98, 151–59, 272n.2; paths, 107–8, 114–15, 138–39, 148, 166–67, 168–72; player's green, 82, 84, 91–92, 138–39, 148, 178–79, 197; prairie style, 44–51, 73–74, 80–83, 96–98, 106, 117, 156–59, 159–64, 173; relation of, to art, 152–53; repetition, 45–47, 48; restoration, 45–46, 71–73; sculpture, 78–80; seasons, 2–3, 76, 182–84, 197; sky, 76, 82, 96–98; sense of mystery, 170; soil, 88–89, 180, 185, 260n.27; spatial features, 50–51, 80–81, 159–68; stonework, 174–75; sunlight and shadow, 76, 82, 96–98, 147–48, 163–64, 165–68, 179, 182–83; time and change, 182–86, 188–90; water, 73–74, 81–83, 98, 101, 106, 117, 172–73; wildlife, 80–81, 86, 92, 98, 101, 152, 172
—parks: boulevards, 88–90; Columbus Park, 80–86, 159–60, 168, 173, 176, 184, 188–89; Cragin Park, 76; Douglas Park, 68–69, 71, 160, 182; Franklin Park, 44, 76; Garfield Park, 70–73, 78–80, 182, 184, 187, 265–66n.12; *A Greater West Park System*, 87–94, 267n.31; Humboldt Park, 33, 35, 63, 73–75, 78–80, 158, 160, 180, 182; Mahoney Park, 159; playgrounds, 44, 73, 76, 82–86, 93–94, 103, 193; Union Park, 7–9, 50, 63, 187. *See also* Chicago parks
—public and institutional work: Decatur Memorial Hospital (Decatur, Ill.), 106; Ford Motor Company projects (Dearborn, Mich.), 102; Henry Ford Hospital (Detroit, Mich.), 102, 106; Lincoln Highway, "ideal section," 103, 106–10, 171–72; Lincoln Memorial Garden, 50–51, 112–20, 153–56, 163–64, 187, 195–97, 275n.15; Lloyd School Centre, 90–92; Logan School Centre, 90–92; Manitowoc High School (Manitowoc,

Shakespeare Garden, 110; testimony to save the Indiana Dunes, 125

Moonlight: and outdoor performances, 179; players' hill at The Clearing (Ravinia, Ill.), 138–39; relation to landscape design, 82, 172–73

Movement: in Jensen's designs, 168–72. *See also* Paths

Municipal Art League of Chicago, 120; sculpture displayed in the West Parks, 78–79

Municipal kitchen gardens: *A Greater West Park System*, 88–89, 90. *See also* Jensen, urban design (community gardens)

Municipal Science Club, 43, 120

Music: and outdoor performances, 44, 178–79; relation to landscape design, 72–73, 98, 266n.13

Muskau. *See* Pückler-Muskau

National Forest Service: Waugh's efforts for, 60–61. *See also* Recreation

National Park Service: and Waugh, 60; hearing on the Indiana Dunes, 124–27

Native landscape: Downing, 13–14; as inspiration for landscape designers, 44–51, 55–61, 125–26, 155–56, 158–59, 172, 174, 272n.6; Olmsted, 18–21; Pückler-Muskau, 14–15

—Jensen: Columbus Park, 80–86; preservation of, 90; roadsides, 171–72; study of, 2–3, 7, 52–53, 64–67, 159, 197, 258n.12; study of, at The Clearing (Ellison Bay, Wis.), 142, 145–46; use of, in designs, 7–9, 28, 45, 76, 182–86

Native plants: availability problems, 56–57, 264n.102; Downing, 13–14; emphasis on, by landscape designers, 52–59; Olmsted, 21; Pückler-Muskau, 15; Roberts, Edith, and Elsa Rehmann, 56

—Jensen: American Garden, 7–9; botanical studies by, 65; concern about air pollution, 268n.57; and ecological restoration, 194–97; emphasized by, 28, 48–49, 80, 96–98, 151–59, 272n.2; Garfield Park, 9; Lincoln Memorial Garden, 114, 115–17; and need for policy on planting in state parks, 132; prairie design style, 48–49, 173, 182, 185; St. Ann's Hospital, 106

Naturalistic design: arguments against, 23–28, 260n.31, 272n.13; European traditions of, 11–15; native landscape as model for, 55–59, 73, 76; relevance of, today, 190–91, 274n.7

—Jensen, 96–98, 258n.14; playground designs, 44, 82, 85–86, 266n.26; transient nature of landscape designs, 188–89, 274n.2

—Olmsted, 15–22, 260n.26; design for Wooded Island, 38–39

Nature, psychological value of: children's play areas, 42–44, 193–94; gardening, 191–92; Indiana Dunes, 125–27; Jensen's call for a city children's summer camp, 267n.34; restorative and healing role, 16–17, 41, 93–94, 190–91, 274n.7

Neighborhood centers: Jensen's ideas for, 88, 90–94

Nelson, Swain: Jensen's connections with, 7; Lincoln Park, 32

Northwestern University: playgrounds established at settlement houses by, 42; Shakespeare Garden, 104, 110–12

Oakwood Cemetery (Chicago), 35

Olmsted, Frederick Law, Sr., 1, 9, 187; Columbian Exposition of 1893, 38–39; influence of, on other landscape designers, 22, 50; parks, 15–22; Riverside, Ill., 38; South Park, 30; Vanderbilt estate (Biltmore, N.C.), 23

Olmsted, Frederick Law, Jr., 22, 25

Pageants: Dunes Pageant, 127–28; Columbus Park, 82, 84; Hull-House, 42; Jensen's memories of, 3; the West Parks, 76–78, 266n.17. *See also* Drama; Masques

Parks: as works of art, 22; development of, in Chicago, 28–35; Jensen's philosophy, 73, 76, 93–94, 103; Olmsted's philosophy, 16–17; Olmsted and Vaux's design traditions, 18–22; relation to health, 16–17; sculpture displays in, 78–80, 266n.20, 266n.21. *See also* Chicago parks; Jensen, parks

Paths: in Jensen's designs, 168–72; along Lincoln Highway, 107–8; in Lincoln Memorial Garden, 114–15; pattern of sun and shadow along, 166–67; re-use of older trails, 138–39, 148

Perkins, Dwight: collaboration with Jensen, 47; Committee on the Universe, 95; Friends of Our Native Landscape, 122;

BOOKS IN THE SERIES

Robert E. Grese is an assistant professor of landscape architecture in the School of Natural Resources at the University of Michigan, Ann Arbor. Prior to his current appointment he taught landscape architecture at the University of Virginia. He earned his B.L.A. from the School of Environmental Design at the University of Georgia and his M.S. in landscape architecture from the College of Agriculture and Life Sciences, University of Wisconsin, Madison.